FIVE TIMES FASTER

We need to act *five times faster* to avoid dangerous climate change.

As Greenland melts, Australia burns, and greenhouse gas emissions continue to rise, we think we know who the villains are: oil companies, consumerism, weak political leaders. But what if the real blocks to progress are the ideas and institutions that are supposed to be helping us?

Five Times Faster is an inside story from Simon Sharpe, who has spent ten years at the forefront of climate change policy and diplomacy. In our fight to avoid dangerous climate change, science is pulling its punches, diplomacy is picking the wrong battles, and economics has been fighting for the other side. This provocative and engaging book sets out how we should rethink our strategies and reorganise our efforts in the fields of science, economics, and diplomacy, so that we *can* act fast enough to stay safe.

Simon Sharpe is Director of Economics for the Climate Champions Team and a Senior Fellow at the World Resources Institute. He designed and led flagship international campaigns of the UK's Presidency of the UN climate change talks (COP 26) in 2020–2021; worked as the head of private office to a minister of energy and climate change in the UK Government; and has served on diplomatic postings in China and India. He has published influential academic papers and created groundbreaking international initiatives in climate change risk assessment, economics, policy, and diplomacy.

'Pace is truly what matters in the climate fight – and the idea in this book that intrigues me the most is that a certain kind of reductionism has blinded us to the common interests that need to guide our work if it's going to happen in time.'

Bill McKibben, author of *The End of Nature*

'... I strongly support this book, which brings the risks of climate change and potential solutions to a wider audience. There is no-one I can think of in the world who could do this better than Simon Sharpe.'

Sir David King, Founder and Chair, Centre for Climate Repair at Cambridge University; former Chief Scientific Adviser to the British Government; former UK Climate Envoy

'This book needs to be read, and its recommendations embraced, by all those seeking to make rapid progress in the fight to preserve a habitable planet. Simon has witnessed first-hand how progress is being impeded ... [and] his book presents a blueprint for the way climate science should be conducted and presented, how thinking about the economy should change, and international diplomacy be redesigned. It's a much-needed new take on a problem we've been wrestling with for decades.'

Baroness Bryony Worthington, leading creator of the UK's Climate Change Act; former Europe Director, Environmental Defense Fund; member of the UK House of Lords

'In a crowded market, this book promises to stand out head and shoulders above the rest as a seminal, timely, and much needed synthesis of the lessons learned from five decades of effort by scientists, the business community, and politicians on how to address the threat of climate catastrophe. Simon Sharpe has been a thought leader at the core of diplomatic and government activity ... I cannot recommend this book more highly.'

Professor Chris Rapley CBE, former Director of the Science Museum, former Director of the British Antarctic Survey

'Simon Sharpe's informative and accessible book will provide a manual for scientists, CEOs and policy makers to work together to deliver systemic transformation much faster than current efforts.'

Nigel Topping, High-Level Climate Action Champion, UNFCCC COP26

'As the world is suffocating under extreme weather events, widespread food and water scarcity, destruction of ecosystems, and a series of other interrelated climate-linked crises, Simon Sharpe's book is a breath of fresh air ... *Five Times Faster* takes you on a captivating – yet alarming – journey through the complexities of climate change ... Simon's book is an important leap in the right direction.'

Mariana Mazzucato, University College, London, and author of *Mission Economy: A Moonshot Guide to Changing Capitalism*

SIMON SHARPE

FIVE TIMES FASTER

RETHINKING THE SCIENCE, ECONOMICS, AND DIPLOMACY OF CLIMATE CHANGE

CAMBRIDGE
UNIVERSITY PRESS

Shaftesbury Road, Cambridge CB2 8EA, United Kingdom

One Liberty Plaza, 20th Floor, New York, NY 10006, USA

477 Williamstown Road, Port Melbourne, VIC 3207, Australia

314–321, 3rd Floor, Plot 3, Splendor Forum, Jasola District Centre, New Delhi – 110025, India

103 Penang Road, #05–06/07, Visioncrest Commercial, Singapore 238467

Cambridge University Press is part of Cambridge University Press & Assessment, a department of the University of Cambridge.

We share the University's mission to contribute to society through the pursuit of education, learning and research at the highest international levels of excellence.

www.cambridge.org
Information on this title: www.cambridge.org/9781009326490
DOI: 10.1017/9781009326506

First published 2023

Printed in the United Kingdom by TJ Books Limited, Padstow Cornwall

A catalogue record for this publication is available from the British Library.

Library of Congress Cataloging-in-Publication Data
Names: Sharpe, Simon (Researcher on climate change economics), author.
Title: Five times faster : rethinking the science, economics, and diplomacy of climate change / Simon Sharpe.
Description: Cambridge ; New York, NY : Cambridge University Press, 2023. | Includes bibliographic references.
Identifiers: LCCN 2022043186 | ISBN 9781009326490 (hardback) | ISBN 9781009326506 (ebook)
Subjects: LCSH: Climatic changes – Government policy | Climatic changes – Economic aspects. | Climate change mitigation – International cooperation
Classification: LCC QC903 .S532 2023 | DDC 363.738/74561–dc2 3/eng20221121
LC record available at https://lccn.loc.gov/2022043186

ISBN 978-1-009-32649-0 Hardback

For Lily, with love and hope

I am sure that the power of vested interests is vastly exaggerated compared with the gradual encroachment of ideas ... sooner or later, it is ideas, not vested interests, which are dangerous for good or evil.

John Maynard Keynes in *The General Theory of Employment, Interest and Money*

Contents

CONTENTS

Figures

1

INTRODUCTION

Everyone knows that we're not dealing with climate change successfully, but few people understand why. Sure, we all know that politicians are driven by short-term interests, oil companies corrupt politics to maximise their profits, and most of us in the rich world keep driving around burning oil at the same time as we self-consciously buy reusable coffee cups. But we've known all that for a long time.

In the past decade or two, the world has upped its game. Mass protests have put pressure on the politicians. Parliaments have passed laws to limit greenhouse gas emissions, put taxes on carbon, and subsidised solar panels. Oil firms have been sued, coal-burning power plants have been demolished, and global agreements have been reached. Yet still, every year we pump more planet-warming gases into the sky than we did the year before.

By some measures, we are making progress. Last year, eight-tenths of the new power plants built across the world used solar, wind, or other forms of renewable energy. Electric vehicles are visibly proliferating on our streets.

The problem, however, is the pace of change. Over the past two decades, emissions of greenhouse gases for each unit of global gross domestic product (GDP) decreased only by a measly 1.5% per year. To keep the climate just about safe and stable, as it has been for the ten thousand years of human civilisation so far, the countries of the world have agreed to try to limit the increase in global temperatures to below 1.5°C. That requires a reduction in global emissions per unit GDP of around 8% per year over the course of this decade. In other words, we need to rip fossil-burning out of the global economy roughly *five times faster* this decade than we managed over the past two decades.[1]

Almost nobody can tell you how that will be done. Technologically, we can imagine it, but politically, we can't. The common answers are unconvincing. 'The solutions are all available, and action on climate change is a great economic opportunity; all we need is leaders with enough political will, and we can do it.' Or 'Young people care about climate change more than their parents do, and look how fast veganism is spreading. Behaviour change

1

from the bottom up is what will change society for the better.' There is some truth in both of these statements, but also desperation. Do we really expect a new and better crop of political leaders to spring up across the world, or a moral revolution to sweep through society, quickly enough for the global economy to be turned upside down and half the fossil fuels shaken out within the next decade? Hardly. No wonder some of the activists who have immersed themselves most deeply in this problem are telling their children not to have children.

If we want to give ourselves a fighting chance of success, we need to face up to this lack of answers and find some new ones that provide more plausible grounds for hope.

For the past decade, I have hacked away at climate change from various positions within the UK government. The United Kingdom congratulates itself on being a climate change leader, and in some ways it is. Our non-governmental organisation (NGO), business, and academic communities have been at the forefront of global movements in climate science, economics, law, and finance. Our governments, from both the right and the left sides of politics, have been the first in the world to set legally binding limits on emissions and to create a dedicated global network of diplomats to persuade other countries to do the same. We have a strength of social concern and political consensus for acting on climate change that some countries can only dream of. And yet, in many ways we are still failing. Perhaps this makes the UK a good place to think about what is holding the world back, and how we could all do better.

I first got interested in climate change not long after my daughter was born, when I happened to watch a presentation that a scientist had shared online. It was a plain set of graphs with a dry voiceover, but its content was shocking. The problem was far worse than I had realised. I cut short my job on counter-terrorism as soon as my bosses would allow, took an online course on climate change, and moved into the first climate change position I could find. Over the years that followed, I worked on domestic energy, climate, and industrial policy, and international climate change projects, negotiations, and campaigns.

At each stage of this journey, I discovered strange things. The worst potential consequences of climate change seemed to be the least recognised. The most promising policies to do something about it seemed to face the most resistance – even within government itself. As for promoting cooperation between countries, the most effort was going into the approach that seemed least likely to succeed. When I hunted down some of the best experts in the world to help me understand what was going on in each of these areas, what they told me only gave me greater reasons for concern.

One day when I left my office at lunchtime to see the climate change protesters outside Parliament, my heart was lifted by the sight of a small girl, who looked like she was only about seven years old, carrying a sign that said, 'We'll stop protesting when you stop being so shit'.

This book is about why we are still being so shit at dealing with climate change, and how we can stop that without needing to become better people or have better leaders. More specifically, its focus is on the problem of global emissions: how to decarbonise the world's economy five times faster than we have done so far. The problem of how to adapt to the climate change that we cannot avoid is equally important, but it has not been the focus of my work; rather than do it the injustice of a half-treatment, I will leave that book for others to write.

The conclusion I have come to is that there is a great deal we could change, but the targets of the necessary reforms are not as obvious as the oil firms and their pipelines. It's not just the physical plumbing of the global economy that needs to be replaced, but the intellectual plumbing. In the science, economics, and diplomacy of climate change – three fields that are central to how we understand and respond to this civilisation-threatening problem – institutions that should be helping us are holding us back.

In climate science, the most surprising thing is how little world leaders have been told about how bad things could get. You might think they are all given clear assessments of the risk that leave them in no doubt about what is at stake. They are not. While we all assume the scientists have got this covered, the science community is organised for a different purpose. Collectively it assumes, with some justification, that risk assessment is some-one else's job. The result is a lack of serious risk assessment that would be unthinkable in other areas of public policy, such as public health or national security. Unless we fix this, we can hardly be surprised if the actions of leaders fall short. Part I of this book looks into why this situation has arisen, and what we can do about it.

If science has been pulling its punches, economics has been fighting for the other side. Thanks to some strange twists of history, the economics that dominates public debate and policymaking is founded on an assumption that the world is fixed and unchanging. The more we want to change things, the more unhelpful this kind of economics turns out to be. Avoiding dangerous climate change demands the largest and fastest economic changes the world has ever seen. We have to change how we generate electricity, construct buildings, grow food, manufacture materials, and transport ourselves by land, sea, and air – all within a few decades, all over the world. As if this wasn't hard enough already, economics is systematically giving us the wrong advice about how to do it. The result is that policies we know are needed are not put in place; technologies that would work are not deployed; finance that is available is not invested. Part II of this book investigates what has gone wrong and shows how a different approach to economics can be a better guide to fast and effective action.

Diplomacy, for its part, has been picking the wrong battles. For three decades, international talks have focused on countries' long-term economy-wide emissions targets. As we have increasingly accepted the impossibility of agreeing these targets, negotiations have become ever more focused on process, while matters of substance – everything that determines whether emissions go up or down – are left to countries to manage individually. We have all heard rhetoric about climate change being 'a global problem that needs a global solution'. But the reality is we have agreed not to agree; we have become collaborators in non-collaboration. When we go back to first principles, we can readily imagine a way that countries could work together to speed up progress, despite their different interests and competing concerns. Staggeringly, in most respects, serious cooperation of this kind has barely even begun. Part III of this book tells the story of climate diplomacy so far, and sets out how it must be substantially different in its next stage, to effect real – and faster – change.

These criticisms may sound harsh, especially to some of the people working in those fields. In climate change science, economics, and diplomacy there is a great diversity of activity taking place, including movements for change in the directions I am advocating. The target of my criticism is not the frontier of academic knowledge, but the way in which knowledge is being put to use. My concern is less about the best practice and more about the dominant practice. The dominant practice is what decides the pace of change, and in the fight against climate change, speed is everything. Winning slowly is the same as losing.

The good news is that in each of these areas there are structural changes we could make that would give us a better chance of success. Risk assessments that give a clear view of the threat can motivate leaders to do more to address it, without requiring any underlying change in values or preferences. Economics that understands change can enable policies to be dramatically more effective, with the same level of political and financial capital. Diplomacy that is targeted in the right way can help all countries reduce their emissions more quickly, without needing them to take a different view of their national interests.

I wrote this book because I believe this set of problems and solutions is radically under-recognised. The movements for change are growing, but still far too few people recognise the need or even the possibility of doing things differently. Changing institutions from within is difficult – there is great inertia to overcome – so those who are pushing for new approaches need help from outside. But for the most part, the NGOs are not campaigning for the reforms that are needed, and the media is consistently missing the point. Too often, the loudest voices in the climate change community repeat the refrain that everyone needs to 'raise ambition', in other words, 'try harder', as if that were all that is needed.

What I advocate here is certainly not the full set of solutions to climate change, and I do not pretend that it will make all the difference. Avoiding dangerous climate change will be a long and hard battle, and we have made a slow start. I do not know if we can win. But I am sure that if we do not channel our efforts more effectively, we will have absolutely no chance. I believe that in these ways of doing things differently – rethinking our approach to the science, the economics, and the diplomacy – there are plausible grounds for hope. And wherever you stand, whether you are a concerned citizen or a politician, an activist or an investor, there are things you can do to help shake up complacent institutions and promote the spread of new ideas.

PART I

SCIENCE

2

LOOKING UP AT THE DAM

One day in the autumn of 2013, I was eating lunch with some of the top climate change advisers to the government of China. They were visiting London to meet UK government officials and academic experts and talk about climate change and energy policy. At the time, I was a junior official at the Foreign Office.

Over a bowl of Thai chicken curry, I asked one of the Chinese visitors, 'How well do you think your political leaders understand the scale of the risks of climate change? How big a risk do they think it is?' He answered, 'Not well at all. They think it's a small, incremental change, that we'll be able to adapt to it, and we will be OK.' I asked if he thought there was a need for the risks to be better assessed, and better communicated to people at the top of government. 'Definitely,' he said. 'It's only if they think it's a catastrophic risk that they will act on it.'

I had had to argue hard with my colleagues at the UK Department of Energy and Climate Change to be allowed to organise a single meeting in the programme of the Chinese visitors on the subject of the risks of climate change. There was no need, I'd been told; 'the Chinese government accepts the science of climate change'. I found this an oddly binary way of thinking about risk. National security advisers who are responsible for protecting their countries against terrorism and war do not just accept that these risks exist. They do their best to understand how large each risk is, so that they can decide how much effort to put into containing it. The same is true for a doctor treating a patient with a serious disease, or an engineer considering a structure that might be unstable. Why should climate change be any different?

The more I thought about it, the more idiotic it seemed that we could be satisfied with the knowledge that political leaders accepted the reality of climate change, without wondering how thoroughly they understood the risks posed by it. The conversation with the Chinese experts was enough to convince me that not all was as it should be. If the leaders of the world's largest emitter of greenhouse gases thought that everything was going to be fine, then there was a high chance that we were all going to be screwed.

Something clearly needed to be done so that world leaders properly understood how bad things could get if they didn't act in time. I started working up ideas for a project that would expose the shortcomings in climate change risk assessments and show how they could be done better. As I began sharing these ideas, I met a surprising amount of resistance.

The argument that there was no need to work on improving risk assessment because governments already 'accepted the science' came up often, despite being, when you think about it for a second, ridiculous. Perhaps it was a legacy of the well-funded climate denial movement, which had cowed environmental campaigners into an over-cautious way of talking about climate change. In 2009, researchers in the United States and United Kingdom had been accused of manipulating data to exaggerate the risks of climate change. Their email accounts had been hacked, their conversations misrepresented, and their reputations attacked in the media. Investigations eventually showed that the accusations were entirely unfair, there was nothing fundamentally wrong with the scientists' findings, and they had in no way falsely manipulated data. But by that time, a great deal of doubt about climate science had been sown in the minds of the public, and the climate science community had been traumatised and intimidated. The campaign of climate change misinformation has been estimated to receive funding of around a billion dollars a year in the US alone.[1] It is a powerful and frightening force. In the face of such an enemy, perhaps it is not surprising that many people working on climate change became content simply for its reality to be recognised, even while its risks were under-recognised.

The second argument against fully assessing the risks of climate change was that such 'doom-mongering', or even, as one of my colleagues once angrily called it, 'shroud-waving', would be counter-productive. This argument was potent because it seemed to be backed by academic research. Prominent experts in the communication of climate science had written that if people were told how bad climate change could be, it caused them to 'switch off' and give up all hope of doing anything about it. The contrast between the enormity of the problem and the futility of what they might individually do about it – such as switching off lightbulbs – was so great that people's instinctive psychological response was to disengage entirely. The argument went that such communications therefore did more harm than good.

The limitations of this argument, I realised, were that it applied to individuals, but not to governments. Individuals are free to react to unwelcome news of things they can do little about by 'switching off'; that is their right. Governments have no such right. The whole point of having a government is to take difficult decisions on behalf of society. Institutions and processes are created to ensure that these decisions are well informed, taken whenever possible on the basis of hard evidence, dispassionately assessed. Authoritarian populists may decide policy based on their emotional reactions to information. Well-functioning democracies, and professional civil services, do their best not to. Again, a comparison with risk assessment in other fields is helpful. What would become of a national security adviser who stormed out of a briefing on a terrorist threat complaining that it was all too depressing? Or a chief medical officer who decided not to warn political leaders of an approaching pandemic in case the bad news caused them to 'switch off'? Obviously, such negligence is unthinkable.

The irony was that some of those misconceived public communications campaigns – telling people to switch off the lights to solve climate change, and the like – had been carried out by governments themselves. If a government wasn't going to use its enormous regulatory power to push fossil fuels out of the economy, why should anyone take seriously its instructions to fiddle with light switches? Voting for a different government would be a more useful thing to do. It would be rather tragic if civil servants learned the wrong lesson from these mistakes in public communications and then made the even larger mistake of not properly communicating the risks of climate change to their own political leaders.

The final and most difficult argument I needed to overcome was that 'surely someone has already done this – there must be lots of good climate change risk assessments out there'. Proving a negative is always difficult. To confirm that nobody had actually produced a thorough climate change risk assessment, I had to talk to all the people who supposedly had done.

Scientists, naturally, were assumed to have fully assessed the risks of climate change. How could they not have done? It turns out there are several reasons why they have not, which are explored in the coming chapters, but the simplest reason is that not all of the relevant knowledge is what you would call 'science'. How bad climate change could get depends on how many tons of greenhouse gases the world pumps into the sky over the coming decades. That depends on which policies governments put in place, which in turn depends on the battles between activists and vested interests, developments in technology, and international diplomacy. None of those things can be predicted by scientists. Neither can all of the ultimate effects of climate change. For example, will the stresses and strains inspire international unity in the struggle for successful adaptation, or lead to war for control of scarce resources and habitable lands? These are not questions of science; at least, not of the natural sciences. A full risk assessment needs input from a broader range of experts.

Economists, others assumed, had the answer. Nicholas Stern, a former top civil servant at the UK's Treasury, had reviewed the economics of climate change in 2006. His finding that the costs of inaction far outweighed the costs of action quickly became world-famous, and the headline numbers that came out of this giant cost–benefit analysis are still often quoted today. In 2013, however, Stern reflected on his own work and other similar studies. Economic assessments, he wrote, were 'grossly and systematically underestimating the risk', and he concluded that it was 'irresponsible to act as if the economic models currently dominating policy analysis represent a sensible central case'.[2] If this was the view of the world's most famous climate change economist, then it seemed fair to say that economists didn't have the answer either.

Next up in the popular imagination of experts who have got climate change risk all figured out were insurers. I went to meet some, and found several thoughtful people in the City of London, one of the insurance capitals of the world, who were individually interested in climate change and concerned about it. But they explained to me that insurers had no professional interest in assessing the long-term risks of climate change, because insurance policies were only written for one year at a time. Insurers need to know how risks next year will compare to risks this year, but they need not look much further ahead than that.

I saw this for myself when I visited the headquarters of Tokio Marine, the largest property insurer in Japan. Their analysts showed me highly sophisticated computer simulations of typhoons arriving in Tokyo Bay and hitting the city. They had done some work to look at how climate change could affect the intensity of those typhoons. I asked if they had also looked at how the damage done would increase as a result of rising sea levels – an important consideration, since most of the destruction wreaked by typhoons comes from the flooding they cause, not from the wind itself. No, the analysts answered, they had not. This was too long-term and gradual a change to need considering. I crossed another profession off my list: insurers had not got the job done either.[a]

The last resort was the defence community. The Pentagon, I was told, with its enormous budgets and capabilities for analysing every kind of threat, had certainly assessed the risks of climate change. I went to the Pentagon to find out if that was true. The US Department of Defense staff were friendly and welcoming, and told me about the assessments they had

---

[a] Actuaries, I discovered, were interested in longer-term risks, but they too admitted they had no full assessment of the risks of climate change. The Institute and Faculty of Actuaries, the professional body of actuaries in the UK, later became a partner and sponsor of my risk assessment project.

done of the risks posed by climate change to US military assets. They were worried about how rising seas could flood naval bases and other coastal military facilities. They had also thought about how climate change could contribute to instability in other countries, but only within the timeframe of the next twenty-five years. Anything further in the future was out of scope.

For military planning purposes, a twenty-five-year time horizon is enough to make a reasonable assessment of most kinds of risk. Beyond that, nobody knows what weapons technology will look like, how the relations between countries might have changed, or what new threats might have emerged. Climate change is different. All of its risks increase over time. If we only look at the near-term future, we will be ignoring all of the largest risks, and this breaks the first rule of risk assessment: find out what is the worst that could happen. Whether we choose to care about those long-term risks is a different matter; to be able to make that choice, we have to know about them. So, I travelled back from Washington with the defence community crossed off my list.

This tour of the experts had left me feeling somewhat shocked, but also strangely energised. I had cut short a diplomatic posting to India where I had been working on counter-terrorism, after reading about climate change and deciding that it was a much larger threat. I had seen enough of the science to feel a deep fear about what we were letting ourselves in for. When you look at the 800-thousand-year record of the Earth's temperature that has been taken from the ice of Antarctica, you see how unstable the climate can be, and how unusually lucky we have been in these past ten millennia. All that we have become used to, the balance that we depend on, is now at stake. The shocking thing was that nobody had clearly set out the full scale of this threat in a way that the most powerful people in the world could understand and act on. What made me feel energised was that at least I had discovered something we could do better.

Bureaucracies, unfortunately, have a way of sapping people's energy, especially when it's suggested that something should be done differently. Frustratingly, those who opposed the idea of doing a new climate change risk assessment were unmoved by my stories of short-sighted soldiers, unconcerned insurers, and economists who said we'd be irresponsible to take them seriously. The same lazy objections kept being repeated. The leaders of the world might be unaware of the severity of the threat of climate change, but the people whose job it was to inform them didn't seem to think it was worth the bother.

My luck changed when the Foreign Secretary appointed Sir David King as his new Special Representative for Climate Change. Sir David had served as the Government Chief Scientific Adviser, the most senior position at the interface between science and policy. When I pitched to him the idea of a project to assess the full scale of the risks of climate change and communicate this to world leaders, he immediately agreed. He recalled how in that previous role he had assessed the risk of a deadly virus spreading through the UK population. The probability of the outbreak was judged to be less than 1%, but the likely impact was estimated to be a very large number of deaths. Based on this risk assessment, the government of the day had taken swift and decisive action. To Sir David, the need for an equally clear assessment of the risks of climate change was obvious.

Over the following months, Dave (as I came to know him) and I assembled an international coalition of like-minded experts and advisers, committed to working together to assess and communicate the scale of the risks of climate change as fully as we could.

The core members of this coalition were senior advisers to the world's largest-emitting countries. Zhou Dadi is Vice-Chair of the China National Expert Committee on Climate Change, one of the most respected energy policy experts in China, and so dedicated to his work that despite being in his seventies, he could outlast me in staying awake through presentations on tidal energy technologies even after a ten-hour flight. Qi Ye is perhaps the most globally recognised expert on China's emissions. Dan Schrag, Director of the Center for Environment at Harvard University, sat on the President's Advisory Council on Science and Technology and had personally briefed Barack Obama on climate change. Arunabha Ghosh, Director of the Council on Energy, Environment and Water in Delhi, is one of India's most influential climate policy experts.

Around this core, our coalition eventually grew to over sixty experts from eleven countries, including scientists, economists, technologists, health experts, intelligence analysists, and military chiefs. All worked together, most contributing their time without payment, to produce a new model risk assessment. All were driven by the conviction that an important truth needed to be told.

When a year and a half later we started writing up our assessment,[3] we began with the question that had almost prevented the project in the first place: why do we need a risk assessment? We answered it as follows.

> Our starting point is that we have an interest in understanding what the consequences of our decisions might be. When the consequences could be so far-reaching in space and in time, we have an interest in understanding them as fully as possible.

A risk is something bad that might happen. A risk assessment asks the questions: 'What might happen?', 'How bad would that be?' and 'How likely is that?' The answers to these questions can inform decisions about how to respond.

Climate change fits the definition of a risk because it is likely to affect human interests in a negative way, and because many of its consequences are uncertain. We know that adding energy to the Earth system will warm it up, raising temperatures, melting ice, and raising sea levels. But we do not know how fast or how far the climate will warm, and we cannot predict accurately the multitude of associated changes that will take place. The answer to the question 'How bad could it be?' is far from obvious.

Limiting climate change will take some effort. Although many of the policies that would reduce greenhouse gas emissions could also be good for public health, quality of life, and economic growth, they will not necessarily be easy to put in place. They will require the investment of both political and financial capital. Governments and societies will have to decide how much effort they are prepared to make, and how to prioritise this issue in relation to their other objectives. An assessment of the risks will be a necessary basis for judging what would be a proportionate response.

It is sometimes argued that a full assessment of the risks of climate change would be counter-productive, because the risks may be so large and the solutions so difficult that people will be overwhelmed with a feeling of helplessness, and will look the other way. In some cases, this may be true. The geographer Jared Diamond, in addressing the question 'Why do some societies make disastrous decisions?', writes:

... consider a narrow river valley below a high dam, such that if the dam burst, the resulting flood of water would drown people for a considerable distance downstream. When attitude pollsters ask people downstream of the dam how concerned they are about the dam's bursting, it's not surprising that fear of a dam burst is lowest far downstream, and increases among residents increasingly close to the dam. Surprisingly, though, after you get just a few miles below the dam, where fear of the dam's breaking is found to be highest, concern then falls off to zero as you approach closer to the dam! That is, the people living immediately under the dam, the ones most certain to be drowned in a dam burst, profess unconcern. That's because of psychological denial: the only way of preserving one's sanity while looking up every day at the dam is to deny the possibility that it could burst. Although psychological denial is a phenomenon well established in individual psychology, it seems likely to apply to group psychology as well.[4]

Our premise for writing this risk assessment is that we can all choose whether or not to look up at the dam. Governments can choose either to ignore it, or to send their best experts to inspect it closely. We have taken the view that it is better to be well informed than not. As the American nuclear strategist Albert Wohlstetter wrote during the Cold War, '*We must contemplate some extremely unpleasant possibilities, just because we want to avoid them.*'

So how well are we doing, then, at contemplating those extremely unpleasant possibilities?

3

KNOWING THE LEAST ABOUT WHAT MATTERS MOST

My most enduring memory of the first climate science conference I attended is of Emily Shuckburgh, a scientist at the British Antarctic Survey, giving a detailed presentation on climate science to an audience packed full of the UK's most august scientists, in the grandest room of the Royal Society, with her baby daughter hanging off her in one of those special backpack-style baby carriers. I remember the compere saying at the end how well she had behaved ... and that the baby hadn't been bad either.

Emily is only one of the latest in a long line of committed climate scientists that stretches back to John Tyndall, who discovered the green-house effect in 1859 and spent the first decade of his married life living in an upstairs apartment at the Royal Institution. Tyndall's death in 1893 is recorded to have occurred through an accidental overdose of medication, administered by his wife. Part of me cannot help wondering if after eighteen years of marriage, she had simply heard enough about climate science. We owe enormous gratitude to these scientists – for their dedication, skill, generosity in sharing their knowledge, and often, courage in the face of opposition from those who would prefer the facts not to be known.

Thanks to Tyndall and all the others, we know that the Earth's climate has changed dramatically in the past. It has swung in and out of ice ages, at whose peak great swathes of North America, Europe, and northern Asia were covered in sheets of ice three kilometres thick. It has been through periods of extreme heat, where subtropical climates existed in high northern latitudes. Atmospheric temperatures have been as much as 12°C above their present levels, and the height of the oceans has changed by more than 100 metres.

We know that human civilisation has seen few of those changes. Over the ten thousand years or so in which our civilisation emerged, the Earth's climate has been unusually stable (see Figure 3.1). Global temperature and sea levels have hardly varied. We have taken advantage of this period of

17

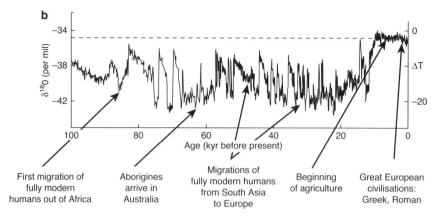

Figure 3.1 Variation in global temperature over the past 100 thousand years, as measured in Greenland. (Note: polar temperatures change by significantly more than the global average.) ΔT, temperature difference; $\delta^{18}O$, a measure of oxygen isotope ratio, in parts per thousand. Reprinted by permission from Springer Science + Business Media, LLC 2009; Young, O. and Steffen, W., 2009. The Earth System: Sustaining Planetary Life-Support Systems. *Principles of Ecosystem Stewardship*, pp. 295–315.[1]

stability: growing crops finely attuned to our climate's patterns of rainfall and temperature; building cities on coastlines set by the level of our seas; and developing a global economy embedded in all the ecosystems that give us clean air, fresh water, and productive land.

We know that the large changes in climate of the past were started by extremely small initial inputs: for example by slight tilts in the axis of the Earth's rotation, which subtly altered the intensity of solar radiation. These small changes were amplified by feedbacks – such as melting of ice leading to greater heat absorption by exposed sea water, leading to more melting; or changes in vegetation giving off more carbon dioxide to the atmosphere, leading to more warming and more changes. The result was swings of 5°C or more in global average air temperature – the difference between today's climate and an ice age.

We know that through our burning of fossil fuels and cutting down of trees, we are now blanketing the atmosphere with an excess of greenhouse gases, trapping heat and adding energy to the Earth system. This flow of additional energy is roughly equivalent to that of four nuclear bombs of the size dropped on Hiroshima, every second. We have discovered how sensitive the climate was to the gentle nudges it was given in the past. Now that we are giving it a giant whack with a sledgehammer, what do we know about how it will behave?

THE INTERGOVERNMENTAL PANEL ON CLIMATE CHANGE

I spent the Christmas holiday of 2013 at my parents' house, reading through the draft chapters of *Climate Change 2014: Impacts, Adaptation, and Vulnerability*, part of the Fifth Assessment Report from the Intergovernmental Panel on Climate Change (IPCC).[2] This was no small task. The IPCC was created in 1988 to give the world's governments an authoritative assessment of climate science, and as the field has grown, each of its reports has been longer than the last. This particular tome came in at thirty chapters, and nearly two thousand pages.

What I was looking for was information that would help me understand the scale of the risks of climate change. Naturally, I wanted to know what was the worst that could happen. Each IPCC report always has a 'Summary for Policymakers', containing information that the scientists consider most worthy of communication. The final versions of these summaries are agreed in special 'approval sessions' attended by the leading scientists, and by representatives of the governments of all interested countries. This arrangement is designed to ensure that all governments have a chance to challenge the conclusions of the scientists, so building their confidence in the robustness of the science. I was going to participate in the approval session for this report, and I wanted to ensure that the Summary for Policymakers included the pieces of information that would most help us understand the risks. I was also on the lookout for changes in the scientists' estimates compared to their previous report, published seven years earlier. I was curious: had the scientists generally been overestimating risks, or underestimating them?

As I read through the draft report, I noticed a pattern. Many of its chapters contained similar statements about our limited understanding of the effects of higher degrees of climate change:

On crops: '*Relatively few studies have considered impacts on cropping systems for scenarios where global mean temperatures increase by 4°C or more.*'

On ecosystems: '*There are few field-scale experiments on ecosystems at the highest CO_2 concentrations projected by RCP8.5 [the highest emissions scenario] for late in the century, and none of these include the effects of other potential confounding factors.*'

On human health: '*Most attempts to quantify health burdens associated with future climate change consider modest increases in global temperature, typically less than 2°C.*'

On poverty: '*Although there is high agreement about the heterogeneity of future impacts on poverty, few studies consider more diverse climate change scenarios, or the potential of four degrees and beyond.*'

On human security: '*Much of the current literature on human security and climate change is informed by <u>contemporary relationships and observation</u> and hence is limited in analyzing the human security implications of rapid or severe climate change.*'

On economics: '<u>*Little is known*</u> *about aggregate economic impacts above 3°C. Impact estimates are incomplete and depend on a large number of assumptions, many of which are disputable.*'

The underlining added is mine. What I found striking about these statements was not that we did not know everything there was to be known; it was the use of words like 'considered' and 'few experiments'. Was it the case that finding out about the impacts of high-end climate change, so far outside the range of human experience, was simply too difficult? Or could it be that for some reason, we were not asking the right questions – not considering what could happen, in the worst-case scenarios?

An experience at the approval session for the IPCC report, held in Yokohama, Japan, in March 2014, confirmed that something was wrong with the questions we were asking. In my pre-reading, I had discovered a section of text in the chapter on human health that appeared deeply alarming. It read:

> In standard (or typical) conditions, core body temperatures will reach lethal levels under sustained periods of wet-bulb temperatures above about 35°C (Sherwood and Huber, 2010). Sherwood and Huber (2010) conclude that a global mean warming of roughly 7°C above current temperatures would create small land areas where metabolic heat dissipation would become impossible. An increase of 11°C to 12°C would enlarge these zones to encompass most of the areas occupied by today's human population. This analysis is likely a conservative estimate of an absolute limit to human heat tolerance because working conditions are hazardous at lower thresholds.[3]

I had looked up the research paper referred to in this text, by Steven Sherwood and Matthew Huber, and found that the threshold of human tolerance for heat stress that it described was indeed an extreme one. It meant that even a person 'out of the sun, in gale-force winds, doused with water, wearing no clothing, and not working' would die of heat stress when exposed to these conditions of heat and humidity. The authors noted that air conditioning could offer some protection, so one could not be sure that regions experiencing these climatic conditions would be uninhabitable. But, they warned,

> the power requirements of air conditioning would soar; it would surely remain unaffordable for billions in the third world and for protection of

most livestock; it would not help the biosphere or protect outside workers; it would regularly imprison people in their homes; and power failures would become life-threatening. Thus it seems improbable that such protections would be satisfying, affordable, and effective for most of humanity.[4]

It seemed to me that few findings could possibly be more important for governments to know about than this, so in Yokohama I asked if it could be mentioned in the Summary for Policymakers. Alistair Woodward, an expert in human health from New Zealand, helped me bring this suggestion to a group of several of the most senior scientists working on the report. They conferred for a while, and then Alistair relayed to me their answer. No, this finding could not be mentioned in the Summary for Policymakers. There was an informal rule to uphold the robustness of the Summary: information could only be included if it was supported by the findings of at least two independent pieces of research.

I asked the scientists if any of them disagreed with Sherwood and Huber's conclusions. Was this a controversial piece of research? 'Well,' they said, 'we do not doubt its conclusions. In fact, we think the limits of human tolerance for heat stress are likely to be experienced at much lower degrees of climate change. This paper almost certainly understates the risk.'

I was left to contemplate the underlying reason for one of the most powerful pieces of information on the scale of the risk posed by climate change, which the experts thought nevertheless to be an understatement, being excluded from the only part of the IPCC's report that most government officials would ever read. Among the twelve thousand peer-reviewed scientific research papers that provided the body of evidence surveyed by the report, only one had asked the question, 'If the world warms up, will it get too hot for humans?' In contrast, I found the report referenced nine research papers that had considered the impacts of climate change on skiing resorts, and thirteen research papers that had investigated the important topic of climate change risks to grape-growing in Europe. Even as someone who enjoys a good drink and a skiing holiday, I found this a bizarre choice of priorities, to say the least. What the hell was going on?

Back in London, I had a similar surprise during the visit of the Chinese Expert Committee on Climate Change. As part of the meeting I had organised for them on the risks of climate change, we listened together to a presentation from a professor of crop science. The professor showed that even at low degrees of climate change, the risks to crop production could be significant. I asked him why it was that, according to the IPCC report, relatively few studies had considered the impact on crops of global temperature increases of 4°C or more. The professor said it was difficult to model such conditions on computers, and perhaps it was also difficult to conduct practical experiments, because if these climate conditions were simulated, the crops might not grow. The Chinese experts, the professor, and I looked at each other and laughed in shock as we realised what had just been said. Was it possible that the very severity of this risk was what was preventing its full assessment?

A rough and ready analysis by the Global Challenges Foundation showed that these were not the only examples of high-end risks escaping attention.[5] The largest number of climate change impacts described in the Summary for Policymakers were those estimated to occur at 2°C – the level of climate change that governments were aiming not to exceed, which could reasonably be described as a best-case scenario. A good number of impacts were assessed at 4°C, only one at 5°C, and none at higher levels than that. It is fair to say that 2–4°C is widely considered the likely range for global temperature rise this century, and for many purposes, it is important to understand the conditions we are most likely to experience. However, the extracts from the IPCC report quoted above suggest that even within this likely range, the upper end is relatively less studied. When this is compared to the much wider possible range of global temperature rise, with an upper end of over 10°C over the next few centuries, we see a whole realm of worst-case climate change that is either unexplored or unreported.

Our host for that meeting with the Chinese experts, held in the old Library Room of the Royal Society, was Professor Sir Brian Hoskins, Chair of the Grantham Institute for Climate Change and the Environment, and as a former President of the International Association of Meteorology and Atmospheric Sciences, one of the UK's most distinguished climate scientists. I put it to him that from a risk assessment perspective, we seemed to know the least about the things that mattered most. He acknowledged that this could perhaps be said, and that it was a curious observation.

How could this be? In the following months, I asked this question of scientists, research funders, and those in government who received climate science research outputs intended for policymakers. What could explain the apparent fact that we were not asking the right questions to understand the most dangerous degrees of climate change? Three contributing reasons emerged: wilful ignorance, a prioritisation of scientific confidence over policy relevance, and a preference for novelty over usefulness.

WILFUL IGNORANCE

The wilful ignorance was displayed by policymakers and research funders, and was actually intended to help. European governments wanted to strengthen the global consensus for the target of keeping global warming below 2°C and were focused on achieving this through negotiations at the United Nations (of which more will be said in Part III of this book). They thought that if they commissioned research into the impacts of higher degrees of climate change, they would be seen by other countries – especially developing countries, and large emerging economies such as China and India – as having given up on the 2°C target. Those other countries might then be less likely to commit to such a target themselves. Because of this, the overwhelming majority of research on the impacts of climate change was focused on the best-case scenario of 2°C or less, at least within Europe.

Research programmes that did focus on the impacts of higher degrees of change were the exceptions that proved the rule. In the UK, the first such programme was set up in 2009.[6] In the European Union's portfolio of climate research, the ground was eventually broken by two programmes that started in 2013[7] and 2014.[8] One of these states on the front page of its website that 'Despite the increasing plausibility of these high-end scenarios [with temperature increases of 4°C or more], there are few studies that assess their potential impacts . . .'.[9] Governments had known enough about the seriousness of climate change to launch the IPCC back in 1988. It is striking that the EU, the world's largest funder of scientific research, only launched research programmes to investigate the impacts of high degrees of warming a full quarter of a century later.

The logic of not researching high-end impacts was obviously perverse. If governments did not know what risks would arise from high degrees of climate change, then what would make them committed to limiting it to low degrees? It was founded on a mistaken assumption: that the aim of discovering more about the impacts of climate change was always to inform the planning of adaption to those impacts. This ignored another, equally important purpose: that of understanding what we might wish to avoid, so that we could decide how much effort to put into avoiding it.

MORE CONFIDENCE THAN RELEVANCE

The second reason lay in the difference between what policymakers most need to know, and what scientists are most confidently able to say. Obviously, these are not always the same. Where the values of confidence and relevance are in conflict, there is a choice to be made about which to prioritise.

The story of our lesson in climate risks to crop production in the library of the Royal Society shows how this choice can affect the direction of scientific research. Apparently, scientists had chosen to look mostly at the effect of low levels of climate change on crops because the findings could be presented with greater confidence. An investigation of high-end impacts would have produced findings that were much less certain, but arguably more relevant to policy – at least for the purposes of risk assessment.

The story of the heat stress study shows how the same trade-off can affect the communication of research findings. When the scientists chose to leave the information about the world getting too hot for humans out of the Summary for Policymakers because it was the finding of only one research study, they made a clear choice to prioritise confidence over policy relevance.

A much more high-profile example was contained in the IPCC's report on the *Physical Science Basis* of climate change in 2013. This was the fifth such report produced by the IPCC, and since the second report in 1995 that described a 'discernible' impact of human activities on climate change, each one had contained a stronger statement about the human-made nature of the problem, reflecting the scientists' growing confidence in their knowledge. The statement on attribution of climate change that the scientists chose to give the greatest prominence in the 2013 report, in the media communications to publicise it, and in their lectures presenting its findings, was that '*It is extremely likely that human influence has been the dominant cause of the observed warming since the mid-20th century.*' By 'extremely likely', they meant a probability in the range of 95–100%, and by 'dominant cause' they meant the cause of more than half of the warming.[10]

The leading authors of the report were visibly proud of the confidence with which this finding was expressed. But as a policymaker and a concerned citizen, I was more interested to know how much of the observed warming was thought to be due to human influence. The answer contained in the report, though given much less fanfare, was simple: '*The best estimate of the human-induced contribution to warming is similar to the observed warming over this period.*' In other words, our best estimate is that we caused all of it! This is surely more relevant to policy than the statement that we were extremely likely to have caused more than half of it, but the scientists had again made a clear choice to prioritise confidence over relevance.

Governments may bear some responsibility for this situation, through having urged scientists over the years to provide findings with ever greater certainty. The intimidation of the science community by the fossil-fuel-funded misinformation campaign, as described in the previous chapter, also surely played its part. Few scientists enjoyed being pitted against highly media-trained lobbyists in head-to-head interviews, where the lines between fact and opinion were deliberately blurred. It was safer to stick to what could be said with greatest confidence than to risk becoming the subject of a smear campaign. But beyond these factors, there are reasons to believe the problem is more deeply rooted in the professional culture of science, which, for good reasons of its own, greatly prizes confidence. We return to this question in Chapter 6.

NOVELTY VERSUS USEFULNESS

The third reason why we may not be asking all the right questions about climate change arises from a fundamental ambiguity about what science is for. That scientists and policymakers are not always interested in the same things was once made clear to me by a conversation with Professor Dan Schrag, the Director of Environment at Harvard University.

We were at Tsinghua University in Beijing, on a cold day in January. We had spent all morning discussing the risks of climate change, in one of the meetings of our risk assessment project. As we sat down for lunch, Dan expressed frustration at how some of the presentations had lacked originality, notably one from a German researcher that had shown how climate change could push some already water-stressed societies below an extreme threshold of water scarcity. On the other hand, Dan told me the presentation he had liked the most was from a young Chinese researcher who had looked at how changing temperatures could alter the migration habits of birds, which could affect the way in which avian viruses could spread between countries. Dan appreciated this piece of research because it was clever, and original: no-one had thought of looking at that before. Dan's comments on the morning surprised me because I had had the opposite reaction to those two presentations. I had found the water stress study useful, because the scale of the risk it described was shockingly large. I had been frustrated by the bird-migration presentation, because it seemed of tangential relevance compared to the much higher-likelihood, higher-impact risks that urgently needed assessing and communicating.

I later discovered that Jane Lubchenco, a former President of the American Association of the Advancement of Science, had written about this difference in interests in 1998, as a contribution to a debate on the relationship between science and society.[11] She wrote, 'Society currently expects two outcomes from its investment in science. The first is the production of the best possible science regardless of area; the second is the production of something useful.' She described the tension between the need for curiosity-driven science, which could expand the frontier of knowledge in any direction at all, and the need for research efforts to address the most pressing interests of society. She argued that when society faces a grave crisis, the scientific community should give high priority to 'producing something useful'. In the past, it had mobilised its resources in times of war, and changed the course of its efforts to respond to shifts in social priorities between national defence, public health, and economic competitiveness. The threats of climate change, biodiversity loss, and all forms of environmental degradation were, she wrote, so extreme that they should be the focus of a new mobilisation. A 'new social contract for science' was needed, which 'would reflect the commitment of individuals and groups of scientists to focus their own efforts to be maximally helpful'.

Twenty years after this bold call to arms from the President of one of the world's leading science associations, a workshop organised by two scientists who shared my interest in climate change risk assessment gave some clues as to how much progress remained to be made. Professor Chris Rapley, a former Director of the Science Museum and of the British Antarctic Survey, and Dr Kris De Meyer, a neuroscientist, brought together a group of thirty policymakers, climate scientists, and research funders, to discuss how better risk assessments could be produced. The group concluded that an important barrier was the culture and practice of prioritising 'novelty' over 'policy relevance' in academic research. This was compounded by academic incentive structures that tended to reward publication of papers as the main measure of academic success, instead of impact on public policy.[12] A comment from one participant summed up the situation this created. Professor Nigel Arnell, the lead scientist on the UK's Climate Change Risk Assessment completed the previous year, said that none of the research papers he had reviewed in the course of this work had been produced for the purpose of informing a risk assessment. The new social contract for science advocated by Lubchenco was, it seemed, far from being fully implemented.

Nobody disputes the need for curiosity-driven scientific research that follows its own path. Equally, there is no doubt that the phenomenal amount of research on climate change and its potential impacts that has been produced, going back decades, has had enormous 'usefulness' value to society.

Everything we know about climate change, we owe to the scientists who have invested their time, effort, and skill in this research – from John Tyndall and his long-suffering wife to Emily Shuckburgh and her well-behaved daughter. Many of the scientists I have met have indeed been focusing their efforts to be 'maximally helpful', in the spirit of Lubchenco's new contract.

The question is: what could be done to produce climate science that is even more useful for society? The group convened by Rapley and De Meyer concluded that structural changes were needed. Academic incentives should shift towards rewarding policy relevance, and funding should be allocated to conduct research for the express purpose of informing climate change risk assessments.

How, we may ask, would such research differ from what is already being done? A simple conclusion of this chapter is that we need more research into the impacts of high degrees of climate change, so that we no longer know the least about what matters most. But this does not go far enough. To produce research expressly for the purpose of informing risk assessments, we also need a change of perspective; a change in the order of the questions we ask. This is the subject of the next chapter.

4

TELLING THE BOILING FROG WHAT HE NEEDS TO KNOW

People sometimes compare our situation with respect to climate change with that of a frog in a slowly boiling pot of water. The frog, supposedly, fails to notice that the water is warming up, or to appreciate the danger. As a result, he does not act in time, and is eventually cooked.

Whether frogs actually behave this way is perhaps known only to French chefs, but there are reasons why the analogy to climate change could be apt. Climate change is a slow-moving process: the world is warming by about 0.2°C each decade.[b] What's more, there is a time-lag between our actions and their consequences. The greenhouse gases we emit today will cause temperature increases for at least the next ten to fifteen years, and much of them will stay in the atmosphere, contributing to further climate change, for centuries. It is hard for us to see the effects of our actions, to appreciate the future dangers, and to motivate ourselves to act, before it is too late.

I like to imagine that the frog in the pot has a chief science adviser. When the frog first notices that the water seems to be getting warmer, he asks his chief science adviser to investigate. The scientist does some tests, analyses the results, and comes back to the frog with his findings. 'The water is getting warmer,' he says. 'I predict that in five minutes' time, the water will be two degrees warmer, plus or minus one degree.' 'Thank you,' says the frog, and he thinks to himself, 'Well, that sounds all right.' He stays where he is. But then the frog thinks again, and wonders if there is more that he should know. He turns to his chief science adviser and says, 'Actually, I didn't want a prediction; I wanted a risk assessment.' 'What do you mean?' asks the scientist. 'Well,' says the frog, 'what's the worst that could happen?' 'Oh,' says the scientist, 'that's easy. You could boil to death.' 'How likely is that?' asks the frog, now looking a lot more worried. The scientist does some more calculations, and tells him, 'In five minutes' time, it's very unlikely; in ten

---

[b]   Specifically, global average near-surface air temperature is warming by roughly this much. Warming is faster over land than over the seas, and it is faster at the poles than in the tropics.

minutes, it will be more likely than not; and after fifteen minutes, it's a certainty.' 'Oh shit!' says the frog, and he jumps out of the pot.

I have had several conversations with climate scientists that went along these lines. The difference between prediction and risk assessment that this story highlights is, I think, critical to giving society the information it needs to understand the threat of climate change, and the motivation to act before it is too late.

In fields where risk assessment is a well-established practice, the normal approach is to first identify a plausible 'worst-case' impact, and then to assess how likely it is to happen. This is the approach taken in the UK's National Risk Register of Civil Emergencies, a systematic assessment of things that could go spectacularly wrong, from coastal flooding and pandemic flu to industrial accidents and adverse space weather.[1]

Typically, a priority for risk management is to reduce the likelihood of these worst-case impacts. For example, the worst thing that could happen to an insurance firm is insolvency, so regulations in the EU require insurance firms to limit this likelihood to below 0.5% in a given year. The worst thing that could happen to a building is its collapse, so building regulations in Japan require the probability of collapse due to an earthquake to be kept at less than 1 in 500. The worst thing that could happen to anyone at work would be their own death, so the guidance of the UK's Health and Safety Executive suggests that the probability of a death in the workplace should be limited to below 1 in 1,000, in any given year.

The principle in each of these cases is clear. Risks are defined in relation to society's objectives, or interests, such as staying alive, safe, healthy, or financially solvent. The 'worst-case' impacts are those that society most wishes to avoid. Risk assessment is focused on identifying those worst-case impacts and understanding how likely they are. Risk management is focused on reducing that probability to a tolerable level.

One characteristic of climate change makes this normal approach to risk assessment less easy to apply. Most risks of concern to society can be thought of as unchanging over time. The probability of a particularly bad earthquake or bout of adverse space weather is roughly the same in any given year. The likelihood of a calamitous industrial accident or terrorist attack might change depending on our own actions, but is not pre-determined to increase or decrease by any laws of nature. Climate change is different. Its risks are sure to keep on increasing until we completely stop emitting greenhouse gases, and even far beyond that, owing to inertia in the system. This means that simply assessing the probability of a worst-case impact at any one moment in time is not enough. For a full picture of the risk, we need to look at how that probability increases over time. Just like the frog, we need to know if nasty outcomes such as boiling to death, which may be unlikely in the present, could become much more likely in future.

NOT TELLING THE BOILING FROG WHAT HE NEEDS TO KNOW

As I worked to understand what climate scientists were doing, I found that they often applied a risk assessment approach to individual extreme weather events. For example, they would identify a worst case for a high-impact typhoon, and assess its likelihood of striking a given place in a given year. These assessments were usually intended to support society in adapting to the climate change that is inevitable in the near future.

In contrast, it seemed to me that the risk assessment approach was much less often applied to understanding climate change over the long term, when not only individual weather events but prevailing climate conditions could themselves become extreme. This sort of understanding is crucial to informing decisions about cutting emissions, because those long-term risks are the ones that lowering emissions can help us reduce or avoid. Instead of fully assessing these risks, scientists seemed more often to be giving us predictions: looking first at what was most likely to happen, and then what the consequences of that would be. If we were the frog, the scientists were telling us that the water would be two degrees warmer in five minutes' time.

I had a chance to test this hypothesis when I found myself stuck for a night in a Moscow airport. Having concentrated too much on the science papers I was reading and not enough on logistics, I had booked myself a hotel at a different Moscow airport from the one I was transiting through, on my journey back from a climate risks workshop in Kazakhstan. The departure lounge was empty of anything except a somewhat threatening ambience and a coffee shop that was about to close. With no prospect of either sleep or travel until the morning, and limited options for entertainment, I bought myself the largest coffee available and settled down to count and categorise all the graphs and charts in the IPCC's latest report on *Climate Change 2014: Impacts, Adaptation, and Vulnerability.*[2]

What I found confirmed my suspicions. The report contained around sixty figures that took the form of predictions: graphs, charts, or sequences of maps that showed the most likely outcomes over a given period of time. It had only six figures that took the form of risk assessment, showing how the probability of some worst-case (or at least undesirable) outcome would increase over time.[3]

One of those exceptions was a figure showing the risks of climate change to corals.[4] The scientists had defined two thresholds that represented 'bad' and 'worst-case' outcomes for the corals. The bad outcome was mass bleaching; the worst-case outcome was mass mortality. These outcomes were defined physically in terms of periods in which ocean temperatures rise above the corals' tolerance limits. The figure showed that as global temperatures increased, the crossing of these thresholds would become ever more likely. In fact, in many regions, it showed that on a high-emissions pathway, mass mortality of corals was a certainty. This did an excellent job of communicating the risk. It left the viewer in no doubt that if we allow global temperatures to keep rising, the corals really don't stand a chance. It will be only a matter of time until they are extinguished. This clear communication of risk was possible because in this case, the scientists had started by asking what it was that we wished to avoid.

Five years later, I repeated this experiment by counting and categorising the graphs and charts in the IPCC's *Special Report on Global Warming of 1.5°C.* I found that the pattern had changed little. Prediction-style figures still predominated. In almost no cases had the scientists started by asking what we wished to avoid, and then investigated how likely it was to happen. On this measure, we are still not telling the boiling frog what he needs to know.

THRESHOLDS OF IMPACT

In the risk assessment project that Sir David King and I kicked off in 2013 with our friends from the US, China, and India, we set out to show how the long-term risks of climate change could be more fully understood and communicated.[5] Our focus was on identifying the worst-case impacts: what it was that society would most want to avoid; and how likely that might become.

Our growing band of collaborators was international and interdisciplinary, and included leading authors of IPCC science assessments. In a demonstration of the public spiritedness of the science community, many of them contributed their time and expertise for very little in return, or entirely pro bono.

I will give just a few examples of their findings here, to show what risks we can uncover, if we go looking for them.

TOO HOT FOR HUMANS

The human body works to keep its core temperature at about 37°C. If its internal temperature rises above this level, the result can be serious injury or death.

31

Many parts of the world have already been hit by heat waves that led to loss of life. Europe's 2003 heat wave is thought to have caused 70,000 early deaths. Pakistan suffered a heat wave in 2014 with temperatures of up to 49°C, in which 2,000 people died. As the world gets warmer, these events will happen more often, and they will become more extreme.

I have always found this one of the most worrying risks of climate change. Since the IPCC had found only one study that had asked if the world might become too hot for humans, we decided to add at least one more.

The scientists leading our study, Alistair Woodward, Tord Kjellström, and Jason Lowe, identified thresholds of heat stress that we all have a strong interest in not crossing. These included limits on people's ability to work outdoors, sleep, and survive. They asked how likely these thresholds were to be crossed in three regions of the world that are already hot, and that are each home to tens or hundreds of millions of people: northern India, southeastern China, and southeastern USA.

Working outdoors is important for many people to make a living, especially in developing countries where many are dependent on agriculture. People doing physical work are at particular risk of heat stress because muscle activity produces heat within the body. The body needs to shed this heat to its surroundings, but that becomes difficult if the surroundings themselves are too hot.

We found that with 4°C of global warming above the present, the ability to work outdoors in these regions would be limited. In northern India, there would be a 30% chance of a whole month of days too hot to work outdoors, in any given year. The probability would rise to 80–100% for all three regions with global warming of 7–8°C. These numbers almost certainty understate the risk, as they were based on working in the shade. Being in afternoon sunlight would increase the measure of heat stress by an extra 3–4°C – a considerable amount.

Our threshold for survivability was defined as climatic conditions so extreme that if a person is exposed to them, core body temperature rises to potentially fatal levels even while sleeping or carrying out low-energy daily tasks. This is an extreme threshold that is seldom, if ever, crossed in the current climate. We looked at how likely it was to be crossed for at least three days in the hottest month of the year.

We found that this probability, effectively zero at present, would begin to rise rapidly after around 4°C of additional global warming. At 6°C of warming, it would reach around 50% in southeastern China, 60% in southeastern USA, and 80% in northern India. In other words, in such a climate, most of the hundreds of millions of people in those regions would

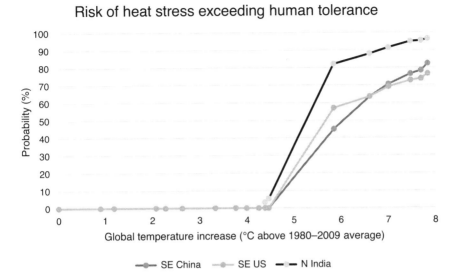

Figure 4.1 Probability of climate conditions exceeding the human body's limit of tolerance for heat stress, in northern India, southeastern China, and southeastern United States. Source: Tord Kjellström

experience climate conditions beyond human tolerance for heat stress, in a typical year. Figure 4.1 shows these results. Later research, done in more detail by some of the same scientists and others, found that these risks could be upon us even earlier than we had estimated: over ten million people each year could be exposed to heat stress exceeding the survivability threshold as early as the 2030s.[6]

As Steven Sherwood and Matthew Huber discussed in their paper quoted above, air conditioning could offer some protection, but not for those who had to work outside for a living. Any failure in the power supply could threaten human life on a barely imaginable scale. Also, as those scientists pointed out, further increases in global temperature would lead to an ever larger proportion of the world's land area experiencing these conditions.

TOO HOT FOR CROPS

The effect of climate change on crop production is harder to predict. Whereas these days there is only one species of human, there are many different crops, grown in different parts of the world. Each of them will be affected by a whole host of climate and environmental variables – including temperature, rainfall, soil quality, and the prevalence of pests, weeds, and diseases. How each of those variables will respond to climate change is far from certain. On top of all that, we cannot entirely predict our own ability to adapt our crops so that they survive and thrive in the new climatic conditions.

Experts generally agree that on the whole, climate change is bad news for crops. But because of these many uncertainties, their predictions vary widely. For example, two studies cited by the IPCC consider the impact of a 3°C temperature rise on wheat production in Pakistan. One estimates a 23% increase in yield, and the other a 24% reduction. Similarly, another study estimates the impact of a 3°C temperature increase on rice production in China to be anywhere between an increase of 0.2% and a reduction of 40%. If the experts' predictions vary that widely, it is hard for any of us to judge the scale of the risk.

In our study, led by Professor John Porter, Dr Manuel Montesino, and Dr Mikhail Semenov, we took a different approach: instead of prediction, we tried risk assessment.

We thought that the most important thing societies would wish to avoid, in relation to crop production, would be crop failure. We defined that as a *'reduction in crop yield to a level that there is no marketable surplus, or the nutritional needs of the community cannot be met'*.

John Porter knew from his research that crops could be badly damaged by short and extreme heat events. If temperatures exceed critical thresholds during sensitive periods of the crop's development, drastic drops in yield can result. Beyond this, there are also lethal temperature limits, above which the plant simply dies. For the world's most important food crops – wheat, rice, and maize – these are in the range of 45–47°C. While some scientists' models of crops' response to climate change incorporate these non-linear effects of high temperatures, the majority do not.

We looked at how likely it was that a threshold for drastic drops in yield would be crossed, for three major crops in three important growing areas: wheat in the Punjab, India; rice in Jiangsu, China; and maize in Illinois, USA. The study considered several varieties of each crop, as well as different planting and sowing dates.

The most shocking result we saw was for rice production in Jiangsu. The probability of exceeding the threshold temperature at least once during the critical period of development was close to zero in the present climate. With a global temperature increase of 4–5°C, the probability would rise to above 25% for two varieties of rice, and 80% for another. Put another way, this

34

meant that a crop failure event that we would currently expect to see only once in 100 years would happen once every 4 years for two varieties, and 4 in every 5 years for the other.

By focusing on a plausible worst case, our study shed some new light on the scale of the risk. It showed that some crop varieties, currently of great importance to food production, could become effectively unviable in the regions where they are currently produced. (If factors beyond temperature increase were considered, such as the effects on crop production of pests, diseases, and changing weather patterns, the risk would be even greater.) To avoid this outcome, we would have to either limit global warming or make great changes in the kind of crops that we produce. Neither of these is an easy option.

HOW HOT WILL IT GET?

The rise in global average temperatures is not a risk in itself, but a contributing factor to many risks, such as those discussed above. Having seen the danger of the world becoming too hot for people and crops, the obvious question is: how likely are these high temperatures to be reached?

Climate change reports for policymakers and the public usually show projections of how global temperatures might increase over the course of this century. These show us what scientists consider the 'likely range' of temperature increase, for high- and low-emissions scenarios. In the IPCC's 2013 report, this range was estimated as an increase of 0.9–5.4°C by the year 2100, compared with pre-industrial times. This is a prediction, not a risk assessment.

We can get a better sense of the risks by looking outside the likely range, at any given moment in time. For example, as Jason Lowe and his colleague Dan Bernie showed in our report, in a low-emissions scenario, an increase of 2°C by 2100 may be most likely, but an increase of 3°C cannot be excluded. In a high-emissions scenario, a rise of 5°C by 2100 is the central estimate, but a rise of over 7°C is possible.

The probabilities of these bad outcomes are far from negligible. Remember that in the examples we considered above, societies have decided the maximum probabilities they will tolerate for the insolvency of an insurance firm, the collapse of a building in an earthquake, and the death of a labourer at work, are 0.5%, 0.2%, and 0.1% respectively. In a medium-emissions scenario such as the world currently appears to be following, the probability of exceeding 4°C by 2100 – a level of climate change often described as catastrophic – may be in the range of 5% to 20%. Apparently we are ten times more tolerant of the risk of catastrophic climate change than we are of an insurance firm going bust.[7] This should certainly make us stop and think.

As we saw in the story of the boiling frog, however, it is not enough to look at the probability of a bad outcome at just one moment in time. We also need to see how that probability may increase over time.

There is no single threshold for global temperature rise that corresponds to 'dangerous' climate change, but we can pick a few levels that society might want to avoid. Countries all over the world have signed international agreements with the aim of keeping warming below 2°C. Warming of 4°C has often been described as extremely dangerous, and the examples of heat stress and risks to crop production given above provide some evidence for this. Warming of 7°C could be considered as a level at which heat stress threatens our ability to survive in some (perhaps many) parts of the world.

Jason Lowe and Dan Bernie looked at how likely these thresholds were to be crossed, in different global emissions scenarios. They found that in a medium-emissions scenario, the probability of exceeding 4°C could rise from 5–20% in 2100 to around 20–50% by 2150. On that timescale, an outcome routinely described as catastrophic is no longer an outlying possibility; it is becoming more or less what we expect to happen. Most strikingly, they found that in a high-emissions scenario the probability of exceeding 7°C was only a few per cent by 2100 but appeared to exceed 50% during the following century.

These studies did not expand the frontier of science, but they helped us see more clearly the likelihood of experiencing degrees of climate change that we would very much prefer to avoid.

Some might argue that high-emissions scenarios are implausible: surely humanity will not be that stupid? To that I can only say: look how many fossil fuels are still in the ground, remember Donald Trump, and count how many US Presidential elections there are from now until 2100. Are you feeling lucky?

Others may hope these high-end temperature rises are merely speculative outputs of untested models. But geological history shows what can happen: in the early Eocene period, around 50 million years ago, global temperatures were around 9–14°C higher than our pre-industrial reference point. Atmospheric CO_2 concentrations were then around 1,000 parts per million, which is slightly higher than is assumed for the year 2100 in the high-emissions scenario used above.[c]

---

[c] This does not mean we could reach such temperatures by the year 2100. The world takes a while to warm up. But a small subset of the climate models used by the IPCC reach global average temperature increases in excess of 10°C above pre-industrial by the year 2300.

Finally, I have often been told that to look beyond the year 2100 is pointless. 'Surely that is too far in the future to worry about!' Personally, I think not. If my daughter lives as long as any of my grandparents did, which I hope she does, then she will see in the twenty-second century. If she has any children, so will they.

TOO MUCH SEA FOR CITIES

Apart from the world warming up, sea level rise is perhaps the most certain outcome of climate change. As temperatures rise, ice melts. The ice that sits on land – in the form of great ice sheets in Antarctica and Greenland, as well as in smaller quantities in glaciers – will increasingly melt, and flow into the seas and oceans. At the same time, thermal expansion will make the water in the oceans take up more space. The result of all this will be rising sea levels.

Scientists are less sure how far sea levels will rise, or how quickly. Their reports for policymakers usually give a 'likely range'. At the time of our project, the latest IPCC report estimated that an increase of 40 cm to 1 m above the pre-industrial level was likely by the end of this century. But this was a prediction, not a risk assessment.

Just as with temperature rise, looking outside the likely range of sea level rise can reveal a larger scale of risk. In a survey of experts carried out in 2014, most thought that the highest that sea levels could rise by the year 2100 was around 1–2 m, but a handful thought that increases of 3–5 m by that time were possible.[8] Experts disagree because they are not sure how quickly ice sheets will break up and melt or slide into the sea.

Looking out over a longer time horizon shows us even more. One of the most shocking figures in the whole of the IPCC's 2013 report is buried deep in its chapter 13, more than a thousand pages away from the Summary for Policymakers and into the territory where only the most curious will ever tread.[9] This graph shows the committed sea level rise that results from sustained global temperature increases. 'Committed' means it will happen, but at some later time. We noted above that it takes a while for global temperature to respond to increases in atmospheric greenhouse gas concentrations. It takes even longer for global sea levels to respond to increases in temperature. (Think of how long it takes an ice cube to melt in a glass of water, and imagine what happens to an ice sheet three kilometres thick and a thousand kilometres across.) When it comes to sea level rise, the consequences of our actions now will not fully manifest themselves for a really long time.

Strikingly, this shows that if we hold global temperatures steady at 2°C above pre-industrial – the level governments all across the world have agreed to aim for as something that might be just about safe – the likely long-term committed sea level rise is about 12 m. Twelve times as much as the upper end of the 'likely range' projected for this century!

Even this is just a fraction of the sea level rise that is possible. The Greenland ice sheet alone holds enough water to raise global sea levels by 7 m. The West Antarctic ice sheet has enough for another 6 m, and the East Antarctic ice sheet is a monster that could add another 50 m. Ice-free worlds, with sea levels over 50 m higher than now, have existed in the Earth's past and could exist again.

What is far less certain is how long any of this will take. Palaeoclimate data suggest that the Greenland ice sheet probably cannot survive in a world where atmospheric carbon concentrations are above 400 parts per million (lower than the 418 ppm already reached), and almost certainly not in a 550 ppm world – the level assumed in the lowest emissions scenarios referred to above. The same is probably true for the West Antarctic ice sheet, and for small parts of the East Antarctic ice sheet. This implies that we may already be committed to some 10–15 m of sea level rise in the long-term future. Whether this will take hundreds of years, or thousands of years, is really not known.

One of the most significant steps forward in risk assessment taken by the IPCC's Sixth Assessment Report, in 2021, was to include an estimate of a plausible worst case for global sea level rise in its Summary for Policymakers. This stated that with high emissions, an increase of 5 m by the year 2150 could not be ruled out, and neither could an increase greater than 15 m by the year 2300.

This is unlikely to be good news for our coastal cities. Our human civilisation emerged and developed during a period of several thousand years in which sea levels were unusually stable. By 2005, there were 136 coastal cities with populations of more than one million people. All of these are threatened by flooding from the sea to varying degrees. Now, at the same time as sea levels are rising, some cities are sinking because of coastal subsidence (often the result of drainage and groundwater extraction). Many coastal cities are growing in size, putting more people and property at risk. How concerned should we be?

Studies of the impact of climate change on coastal cities often try to estimate the economic damage that might be done by more frequent and severe flooding. For our risk assessment, we wanted to know something else. Were there thresholds of sea level rise against which cities could not be defended?

One person who had thought about this was Tim Reeder, a senior climate change adviser to the UK's Environment Agency. Tim was responsible for the science input to planning the flood defences of the Thames Estuary, helping to protect London from sea level rise. He was the scientist leading the development of the Thames Estuary 2100 plan, which had become world-famous as an example of best practice in planning adaption to climate change in a context of uncertainty. The plan set out an array of options: improving the current Thames Barrier; raising upstream or downstream flood defences at the sides of the river; creating flood storage facilities; replacing the Barrier with a larger one; or building a new barrage further out in the estuary. A pathway could be plotted that kept various options in play, protecting the city while deferring some decisions until future needs became clearer.[10]

As part of this work, Tim had asked himself the obvious question: where is the upper limit? At what height of sea level rise will protecting London no longer be possible? Tim conducted a study to come up with an estimate and concluded that the limit lay somewhere around 5 m of global sea level rise.[11] Beyond this, the only remaining solution would be to build a wall around London and pump the River Thames over the top. By that point, moving the capital city to somewhere else would probably be easier.

We searched for other assessments similar to Tim's, identifying limits to adaptation for other major coastal cities. We found none. Tim asked contacts in his professional network of flood protection planners, and we asked climate scientists who specialised in this area. We found that the Netherlands and New York City both had adaptive pathway planning similar to Tim's plan for the Thames Estuary, but for no major city apart from London could we find a study that had taken a long hard look at limits to adaptation.

Was it that no such limits could be expected to be encountered? Our team of experts thought not.[d] At least three kinds of limit were likely to exist. Socio-political limits could set in, if poor governance and failure to protect a city from flooding led its citizens, businesses, and investors to lose confidence in its future, and move out. Economic or financial limits could arise at the point where defending the city becomes more expensive than relocating to higher ground. In the most extreme case, physical or engineering limits could make flood protection practically impossible.

Since we could find no academic estimates of these thresholds, apart from Tim Reeder's study of London, we settled for a simpler method of

---

[d] Our team of experts included Robert Nicholls, a professor of coastal engineering and leading contributor to the IPCC reports on this subject; Tim Reeder, a senior climate change adviser to the UK's Environment Agency; and the scientists Sally Brown and Ivan Haigh.

assessing the risk to three major coastal cities. We took a one-in-a-hundred-year flood as our starting point and asked how much more likely this could become. We found that with 1 m of global sea level rise, the probability of experiencing such a flood would increase by about 40 times in Shanghai, about 200 times in New York, and about 1,000 times in Kolkata. This comparison makes no assumptions about how much adaptation will happen, how much it might cost, or what the damage done by future floods will be. But it does give us some idea of the scale of the risk that we are up against.

I would have liked to find out the likelihood of crossing the one limit to adaptation that we did have an estimate for – London's threshold of 5 m of global sea level rise. I asked one scientist if it would be possible to assess the probability of this amount of sea level rise being reached, if not in relation to time (since time in this case is so uncertain), then at least in relation to global temperature increase. He said yes, easily. It could be done using the data underlying the IPCC's graph of long-term committed sea level rise mentioned above. Would he be interested in doing this for us, I asked hopefully, now that my budget for new science studies had run out? No, he said, this would be too trivial a task, and not at all scientifically interesting. Anyway, he was busy with a large and well-funded research project. This was one of those times when I found myself on the wrong side of the novelty versus usefulness divide, and Jane Lubchenco was not there to rescue me.

With our current knowledge, we can say that the expected long-term committed sea level rise, at the supposedly 'safe' degree of temperature rise that we are aiming to keep to, is more than twice as much as the upper limit that London can take. The Roman city of Londinium was established and thriving on the banks of the Thames nearly 2,000 years ago. We now know that in the worst case, London's 5-m limit could be hit within 150 years, and even in the best case, it is quite possible that, as a result of actions we have already taken, London's future will be shorter than its past.

KNOWING WHAT WE WANT TO AVOID

Across the complex landscape of the impacts of climate change, there are many thresholds that matter to humanity. Some are biophysical, such as the human body's limit of tolerance for heat stress, or a crop's limit of tolerance for high temperatures. Some are socio-economic, such as the minimum water resources required to meet basic human needs, the daylight hours below dangerous levels of heat stress needed for a subsistence agriculture lifestyle to remain viable, or the height of sea level at which it becomes less costly to relocate a coastal city than to continue to protect it against flooding. Others are political, such as the internationally agreed aim of limiting global warming to below 2°C. Still more could be physical, such as the height of sea level that puts an island under water; biochemical, such as the degree of ocean acidity that prevents a shellfish from forming a shell; or even experiential, such as the impact of a past event whose damage is well understood.

Often when a threshold is passed, the consequences become suddenly more severe. A crop fails, instead of suffering a reduction in yield; a person dies, instead of suffering non-fatal heat stress; a coastal city is abandoned, instead of suffering increased costs of flooding.

Some of these thresholds are more objective than others, and some are more permanent than others. But what they all have in common is that they are defined in terms of what we wish to avoid. They are directly relevant to our interests. This is why they help us understand the scale of the risks.

The examples discussed above showed that in a high-emissions scenario, situations we would greatly wish to avoid may become highly likely. This understanding can help inform the most important decision on climate change that societies have to take: how much effort to put into reducing emissions.

I am not saying that all research should be done this way. Many kinds of research are needed to expand our knowledge, and there are many useful ways of presenting information. I do argue that we need risk assessment, informed by a sufficient amount of risk-focused research; otherwise, we have no right to expect our leaders to respond in a manner proportionate to the threat.

Decarbonising the world economy will not be as easy as jumping out of a pot. That makes it all the more important that no opportunity is missed to communicate the severity of the risks to those in charge. The water is already getting warm.

WHY IS IT SO DIFFICULT?

In 2019, a climate scientist who had read our risk assessment report wrote a paper called 'Climate science needs to take risk assessment much more seriously'.[12] Professor Rowan Sutton is Director of Climate Science at the UK's National Centre for Atmospheric Science, and a lead author for the IPCC. In the paper, he argues that there is an 'urgent need' for climate science to take the needs of risk assessment much more seriously. Referring to our report, he asks the question, 'Why did the IPCC not long ago produce a risk assessment like that of King et al. (2015)?'

Sutton's analysis is helpful in explaining why the science community is still not telling the boiling frog what he needs to know. He points out that risk assessment is interdisciplinary: knowledge needs to be drawn from different fields, as in our heat stress study which required expertise in human health as well as climate science. This is something that academics, who specialise in their own fields, always find hard. He cites intimidation from vested interests, leading to a fear of being accused of scaremongering, as a reason why scientists might hold back from talking about worst-case scenarios. He suggests that the historical roots of climate science in meteorology, where weather forecasting is the aim of the game, have led to a widespread view in the community that their primary job is to provide predictions. Finally, he observes that climate science assessments are put together in a 'bottom-up' process: they start from what the scientists know, rather than from what the policymakers need to know.

In my experience, the last of these reasons has felt like the greatest obstacle. The need to start with the interests of society in mind is important not only when compiling a wide-ranging assessment report, but also when conducting a single study. Each of the examples discussed above had to start – before any science was done – with a subjective question: 'What is it that we wish to avoid?' This may seem unnatural to many scientists, since the dominant philosophy of science since the Enlightenment has been one of objectivity: to understand the natural world, we consider ourselves separate from it; we stand back and observe with dispassionate neutrality.

Starting with this question also presents practical difficulties. It is not always easy for scientists to identify what society cares about. Who should they ask? I have seen how difficult this can be. I was once in a meeting to agree the priorities for a multi-year, multi-million-pound research programme. I had been invited to be one of a group of policymakers to give a view on which of the many research areas of interest to the scientists would be relevant to policy. The scientists received as many opinions as there were policymakers. I doubt they left the room much the wiser, but in the absence of consensus for any alternative, support for their proposals was confirmed, and they happily continued with their research.

CO-PRODUCTION

I have also seen more successful attempts. On one memorable occasion, I sat in a draughty office overlooking the Thames Barrier, with Tim Reeder, one of the people responsible for planning the protection of London from flooding; Professor John Church, a lead author of IPCC chapters on sea level rise who has been described as the world's leading expert in this area; and Dr Jason Lowe, a friendly climate scientist who led the 'knowledge integration team' at the Met Office Hadley Centre and had somehow got me invited.

Tim had clear interests. He wanted to know how much sea levels would rise, how quickly, and with what likelihood. He was far more interested in the worst case than in the most likely case. After all, the Thames Barrier had been designed to protect London against a once-in-a-thousand-years storm surge. If that level of tolerance for undesirable outcomes had been deemed appropriate when the Barrier was built in the 1970s, it would be natural to think in similar terms when planning for the 2070s. The answers were far from straightforward. Not all the experts agreed. Not all the uncertainties could be quantified. But through an hour or two of in-depth conversation, Tim found out from John what he knew, what he didn't know, and what he thought. Using this information, and with Jason's help, he could define what he called a 'high plus plus' scenario for global sea level rise that constituted a plausible worst-case scenario for the Thames Estuary. He could then use that as the basis for his plans.

If we are to fully understand the risks of climate change to society, then we need more conversations such as these. Scientists who study the process of science itself have come up with a name for this process: 'co-production'. One of the main conclusions from the workshop on climate change risk assessment organised by Chris Rapley and Kris De Meyer, mentioned in the previous chapter, was that we needed to improve and strengthen processes of co-production. This would need to involve not one-off, ad hoc consultations, but ongoing, iterative dialogue between decision-makers, researchers, and funders of research.[13]

Since this co-production is easier said than done, we also recommended the creation of more dedicated 'knowledge broker' roles, to bridge the gaps in understanding between scientists and policymakers and facilitate useful conversations. These roles exist in other fields. For example, intelligence analysts translate primary information into decision-relevant risk assessments. In public health, facilitators support dialogue between patient groups, medical staff, and the managers of health services. Despite some notable exceptions such as Jason Lowe's role mentioned above, the experts we consulted felt that the roles of risk analyst and 'knowledge broker' were both largely absent from the climate change community.

As a message of hope, I will end this chapter with one more successful example of co-production. When I set out to people the argument for a risk assessment approach to climate science, I am sometimes met with the question, 'Yes, but does it work?' What they mean is, 'Does it motivate people to act?' I hope the logic set out in this chapter is clear enough. For information to motivate us to act, it must relate either to a goal we wish to achieve, or to something that we wish to avoid. If we start by identifying what it is that we most wish to achieve or avoid, we will have more chance of generating relevant information than if we do not. In my view, no more justification than this is needed. But still, empirical confirmation can be satisfying, and there is one example that it gives me pleasure to recall.

Several months after finishing the risk assessment project, I sat having a beer with Professor Donald Wuebbles, a senior climate scientist from the USA who was then the Assistant Director of the White House Office of Science and Technology Policy. I told him the story of the boiling frog and explained why I thought we needed more risk assessments that looked at the probability of crossing a 'worst-case' threshold as a function of time. He sipped his pint of real ale thoughtfully, and then leaned in with a twinkle in his eye. 'You know what?' he said. 'That reminds me of a study our team did once for the government of a large city in our part of the US. We were looking at how climate change could lead to more extreme rainfall, but we didn't know how much rainfall would cause the city a problem. So we asked them. The city government people told us, "What really causes us a problem is when we get more than X inches of rainfall in forty-eight hours. When that happens, our drainage systems can't take it, and we get shit floating in the streets." We took that threshold as the basis of our study, and we came back and gave the city government a graph that showed the increasing likelihood of shit floating in the streets as a function of time. In all our many years of giving science advice to that city government, that was the one time when they really acted on it.'

I have since learned from my neuroscientist friend, Kris De Meyer, that there is a particular circuit in the brain that is colloquially called the 'oh shit' circuit by members of his profession. I assume that this was an instance of that circuit being activated.

5

RUNAWAY TIPPING POINTS OF NO RETURN

Like most people who have decided to spend their working lives trying to do something about climate change, I didn't get into this because of reports that said temperature or rainfall would change by a few per cent here or there. I got into it because I was worried about the big stuff: the things that could go really wrong.

This chapter is about the big stuff. Its title comes from a blog by Gavin Schmidt, a climate modeller at NASA who was poking fun at media coverage of climate science that sometimes confuses concepts, occasionally exaggerating their significance.[1] The concepts it describes, though, are deadly serious. If anything, the scientific community has understated their importance.

Schmidt describes three phenomena that are distinct, but interrelated: feedbacks, tipping points, and irreversibility. These are different from the climate risks we discussed in the previous chapter. They are not risks themselves, directly affecting things we care about. They are ways that parts of the Earth system can behave, which can magnify the effects of climate change and so, indirectly, affect many things we care about. Clearly, that makes them important to know about. How well do we understand them? Before answering that question, let's disentangle the concepts.

FEEDBACKS

Feedbacks are circular loops of cause and effect. They come in two kinds: reinforcing feedbacks, whose effect is to amplify or accelerate change; and balancing feedbacks, whose effect is the reverse. When you put a microphone too close to a speaker and a barely audible sound is amplified into a deafening screech, that is a reinforcing feedback. When your thermostat keeps your house at a steady temperature, warming it every time it gets cold, or cooling it when it gets hot, that is a balancing feedback. In complex systems like ecosystems, the climate, and the Earth itself, the interaction of feedbacks is what determines whether things change (and if so, how rapidly) or stay the same.

Schmidt gives two examples of reinforcing feedbacks in the climate system. When air temperature rises, the amount of water vapour in the atmosphere increases; the water vapour acts as a greenhouse gas and traps heat, leading to further warming. When rising temperatures cause ice floating on the sea to melt, the uncovered water reflects less sunlight and absorbs more, leading to further warming. We instinctively know that these are dangerous, because they involve something that is already bad becoming worse as it gathers its own momentum. In common language, they are 'vicious circles'.

The sea-ice feedback can be thought of as leading to 'runaway' change, because it is making sea-ice disappear at an accelerating rate. This seems likely to continue until all the sea-ice is gone.

The climate contains many feedbacks, both reinforcing and balancing. Over tens of millions of years, its behaviour is dominated by balancing feedbacks. Looked at from this zoomed-out perspective, before we started burning fossils on a grand scale, the Earth had been on a cooling trend for the past fifty million years, after previously having got a bit hot. As Schmidt puts it, the dominance of balancing feedbacks has 'kept Earth's climate somewhere between boiling and freezing for about 4.5 billion years and counting'. On shorter timescales of tens of thousands of years or less, reinforcing feedbacks seem to dominate the climate's behaviour. That is why small tilts in the Earth's axis of rotation have led to dramatic swings in and out of ice ages, with changes of 5°C up and down in global average temperatures. Given the timescale of human civilisation, we have good reason to be concerned about these feedbacks.

TIPPING POINTS

Tipping points are thresholds that when crossed, cause a system to significantly change its behaviour. We learn of their dangers as children: 'Humpty Dumpty sat on a wall; Humpty Dumpty had a great fall . . .'. Lean back past the tipping point when you are sitting on a wall, and you will find yourself falling, instead of sitting comfortably. You don't have to be a climate scientist to guess that tipping points in the climate system are likely to be bad news.

Schmidt says the most common examples of tipping points are in ecosystems, whose healthy functioning relies on a complex web of interdependencies within which there may be many unseen thresholds. He gives the example of a rise in winter temperatures being just enough to allow an insect species to gain a foothold in a new ecosystem, as happened with the pine bark beetles in Alaska. A small step across such a threshold can lead to large-scale effects. Between 2016 and 2018, the bark beetles in Alaska were estimated to have affected more than 900,000 acres of forest.

Some scientists believe the Amazon rainforest may have a tipping point: a minimum area it needs to maintain in order to generate enough water vapour to keep itself watered. If its area falls below this threshold, local rainfall could decrease, depriving the forest of the water it needs, leading to further shrinkage – and perhaps to the end of the forest. The threshold has been estimated at a 20–25% reduction in area compared with its original size; not far off the 17% reduction that has already occurred.[2]

Tipping points like this are highly relevant to our understanding of risks, because they can lead to changes that are faster and larger than we may otherwise expect.

IRREVERSIBILITY

Irreversibility concerns the impossibility of returning something to its previous state, once change has happened. 'All the King's horses and all the King's men, couldn't put Humpty together again.' If change is in an undesirable direction, irreversibility is bad news too.

Schmidt points out that while this is a clear concept when we are thinking about biological changes, such as the extinction of a species, it is less clear when applied to physical changes. There, its definition depends on the timescale we are interested in. He gives the example of the Greenland and West Antarctic ice sheets. At present, the huge bulk of these ice sheets is what keeps them as they are: they are large enough to be high enough to be cold enough to carry on being ice sheets. As they melt, their surfaces will gradually come into contact with warmer air at lower altitudes, leading to more melting. In the current climate, it is unlikely they could grow back. On a geological timescale, these ice sheets have come and gone. But on a human timescale, if we lose them, we might as well consider them gone forever. Irreversibility matters a lot when it concerns anything we might want to keep.

SHAKING UP THE EARTH SYSTEM

What happens when these three phenomena all come together? Feedbacks do not necessarily lead to tipping points, and tipping points do not necessarily lead to irreversible change. But the three can interact in this way, as in the Greenland example: ice-sheet melting and reduction in height creates a reinforcing feedback; at some threshold level of ice-sheet height there is a tipping point, beyond which it can only shrink further; and its eventual loss is irreversible on human timescales. Not good news for London, or other coastal cities.

The presence of feedbacks and tipping points in the Earth system means that the effects of climate change do not have to be gradual and incremental. They can also be abrupt and large-scale. What do we know about these possibilities? Think about them in terms of three parts of the Earth system: large chunks of ice, large stores of carbon, and large flows of air and water.

We have already discussed the large chunks of ice, up to 3 km high, that sit on top of Greenland and Antarctica and hold enough water to raise global sea levels by over 50 m. There are several reinforcing feedbacks that could accelerate their melting. There are also constraints on how fast they can discharge ice to the sea, such as the friction that limits the rate of flow of glaciers. We cannot be sure exactly what rate of change will result from the interaction of these effects. What we can do is use satellites to measure how quickly the ice sheets are losing mass. In 2021, the IPCC reported that the rate of mass loss over the period 2010–2019 was around four times faster than over 1992–1999.[3] Scientists are still unsure how much of this acceleration may be part of some decades-long oscillation, and how much is part of the long-term trend. Research suggests that tipping points for the irreversible loss of the Greenland and West Antarctic ice sheets could exist anywhere between 1–3°C and 1–6°C respectively.[4]

The large stores of carbon include those held in soil, vegetation, forests, permafrost, and frozen methane under the sea. Rising temperatures increase the likelihood of all of these stores of carbon leaking into the atmosphere, where they will strengthen the greenhouse effect and further increase warming. These are vicious circles on a global scale. The amounts of carbon held in these stores are enormous. The permafrost – frozen ground, much of which is in Siberia – holds more than twice as much carbon as is already in the atmosphere.[5] Methane hydrates – ice-like frozen methane buried under sediment beneath the ocean floor – are thought to hold more than ten times as much carbon as is currently in the atmosphere.[6]

When I learned about these huge carbon stores and feedbacks, the obvious question in my mind was how much they might add to the increase in global temperatures. I think anyone would want to know the same. One of the experts I asked was Jason Lowe at the UK's Meteorological Office Hadley Centre, one of the world's top centres of climate science. Jason confirmed what I thought I had understood from the IPCC reports: that most climate models do not include all of these feedbacks, because their effects are so difficult to predict. So when we began our risk assessment project with China, India, and the US, I asked Jason to help us find out more.

In a small study for our project, Jason and Dan Bernie made a first estimate of how the permafrost feedback could affect the probability of exceeding the temperature rise thresholds we had considered of interest. They found that the effect, though highly uncertain, could be significant. If the most extreme estimates were correct, then in a low-emissions scenario of the kind we are all hoping the world will follow, our chances of keeping temperature rise below 2°C this century could be halved.[7] At the time, my colleagues in government who were working towards an international agreement on climate change intended to limit warming to 2°C had no idea that these feedbacks were not included in the models, and none of us knew they could pose such a threat to our goals.

When Jason presented these findings at a conference in Beijing, I was sitting next to a director of one of the US's well-funded national laboratories. He turned to me and said 'This is just what we needed! How much did it cost?' When I told him – a small amount, plus a bit of borrowed time from another research programme, and a hefty dose of public-spirited goodwill from Jason – he looked at me in amazement. In the programmes he directed, he said, nobody would get out of bed for that sort of money. To me, this was one example of a general truth: it does not have to be scientifically difficult or expensive to find out more about the risks, but you do have to ask the right questions, and you do have to find scientists who are willing to take those questions as the starting point.

As far as I know, no-one has yet produced a similar assessment for the methane hydrates. Expert views vary widely. Peter Wadhams, a Cambridge professor who has travelled underneath the Arctic sea-ice in Russian submarines to see what's going on, is convinced that a substantial release of carbon from methane hydrates is likely, and perhaps even beginning. His seems to be an outlying opinion, and most experts think the risk is nowhere near this close to materialising. It may take a lot more research before we know who is right.

The large flows of air and water that we may have to worry about include patterns of atmospheric circulation that influence important seasonal weather conditions such as the monsoons, and the oceanic currents that transport water of varying heat and salt content around the globe and between the shallows and the depths. The importance of these flows may not be immediately obvious, especially to those of us who live in cities. But as Brian

Hoskins wrote in our risk assessment report, 'The amazing thing about the Indian summer monsoon is the large effect of a small variation from year to year: 10% more rainfall and there are floods, 10% less and there are huge problems for farmers.' This is just one indication of the sensitivity of our ecology and economy to changes in these large-scale flows.

Every few years or so an 'El Niño' event occurs, when the temperature of the eastern tropical Pacific Ocean rises half a degree above the long-term average. This usually causes extreme weather events in many parts of the world. Climate change could bring about much larger changes in flows. We have very little understanding so far of how large those changes could be, or how likely they are. One possibility is a weakening or even collapse of the circulatory system of Atlantic currents that bring warm salty water north near the surface, and send colder and fresher water back down south, deep underneath. A large change in this flow would affect temperatures, rainfall, and extreme weather events over large parts of the northern hemisphere.

TIPPING CASCADES

As if all this wasn't already bad enough, these large-scale changes in ice, carbon, air, and water can all influence each other. One change can increase the chances of another, and then another, creating a cascade of change throughout the climate and Earth system.

For example, carbon leaking from permafrost can accelerate warming, speeding up the melting of ice sheets. Faster melting of the Greenland ice sheet could not only raise sea level, but also slow the Atlantic circulatory currents. Changes in ocean flows and sea surface temperatures could lead in turn to a shift in atmospheric circulation, which could damage the health of the Amazon forest and its ability to take up atmospheric carbon. This weakening of an important carbon sink would lead to higher greenhouse gas concentrations in the atmosphere, and further warming.[8]

The activation of Earth system tipping points, such as those described above, could increase the chances of crossing ecosystem tipping points, such as the death of forests or the extinction of species.[9] Ecosystems are linked to each other through flows of water and nutrients and the movement of insects and animals, so the crossing of a tipping point in one can set off a new cascade of changes in another. Presumably, the combination of pressures that humanity has exerted on our environment in the past century has already caused a cascade of this kind, given we are now seeing an accelerating rate of species loss which is widely described as the Earth's sixth mass extinction. Climate change threatens to take that to a whole new level.

In other words, there seems to be a real risk of everything going wrong at once.

A POINT OF NO RETURN?

Thinking about climate change risks can be emotionally draining. You might feel you've heard enough by this point. There are increasing reports of climate change scientists and activists needing psychological support to cope with the strains of constantly staring into the abyss, trying to tell people about it, and witnessing the utter inadequacy of our collective response.[10] I certainly felt like I ran my mental batteries pretty low when I worked on this project. What kept me going was the conviction that we have to understand this stuff if we want to avoid it. We have to look up at the dam. So, if you can, stick with me a little longer.

An obvious question to ask, given all that has been said, is whether the Earth system has some point of no return – a point beyond which climate change will become self-sustaining and run away with itself. In climate policy circles, this question is very rarely discussed. My impression is that people feel embarrassed to raise it, for fear that they would either be accused of 'scaremongering' or seen as gullible consumers of exaggerated media stories. But it is, in fact, a serious question.

Most climate scientists, if you ask them, will be quick to say that they don't think 'runaway climate change', or the existence of a threshold for the Earth system as a whole, is likely. But if you ask whether they can be *sure* no such threshold exists, their response is usually much more hesitant. Quite often they will say no, this possibility cannot be excluded.

Gavin Schmidt concludes his blog on 'runaway tipping points of no return' by saying:

> Much of the discussion about 'dangerous interference' with climate often implicitly assumes that there is just 'a' point at which things tip and become 'dangerous'.... However, it seems more appropriate to view the system as having multiple tipping points and thresholds that range in importance and scale from the smallest ecosystem to the size of the planet. As the system is forced into new configurations more and more of those points are likely to be passed, but some of those points are more globally serious than others.

I believe this statement reflects the mainstream scientific view; I have no doubt it is well informed; and I find it helpful as a guide to how I should think about this aspect of climate change. And yet … he hasn't actually answered the question. Will the increasing passing of these tipping points and thresholds eventually result in change at the global level becoming self-sustaining? We are left to wonder.

In 2018, a group of scientists published a paper that tackled this question head-on. 'Trajectories of the Earth system in the Anthropocene' was authored by many of the most well-known experts in the fields of Earth system feedbacks, tipping points, and thresholds.[11] With typical scientific precision, they broke the 'point of no return' question into three parts. First: is there a planetary threshold that, if crossed, could prevent us stabilising global warming at an intermediate level? Second: if there is such a threshold, where might it be? Third: if such a threshold is crossed, how would that affect the wellbeing of human societies?

The scientists' conclusions were not reassuring. They wrote that the Earth may be approaching a planetary threshold beyond which we would find ourselves stuck on a pathway to much hotter conditions. We would be pushed down that pathway by strong feedbacks that we would be unable to reverse, steer, or substantially slow. They were not sure where such a threshold might be, but thought that it could be around 2°C of warming above the pre-industrial baseline, and so only decades away from being crossed. (We are already more than one degree up.) They described the consequences for humanity as 'massive, sometimes abrupt, and undoubtedly disruptive'. This pathway would eventually take us into a climate 'likely to be uncontrollable and dangerous to many, particularly if we transition into it in only a century or two, and it poses severe risks for health, economies, political stability (especially for the most climate vulnerable), and ultimately, the habitability of the planet for humans'.

My aim in quoting this paper is not to say that its authors are right, and we should all share their assessment of the risk. The paper was controversial in the climate science community, and I believe not all experts agree with its conclusions. My aim is to highlight the importance of the question. If some of the world's most respected climate scientists think that even in a situation where we meet our internationally agreed goals for limiting global temperature rise, we might still push the world onto a pathway that leads irreversibly towards states that threaten the habitability of the planet for humans, then this is surely a question we should take seriously. Could any question be more relevant to policy?

I believe this question is not getting the attention it deserves. In general, the possible large-scale changes in the Earth system that we have discussed above appear to be under-researched, under-reported, and underestimated.

UNDER-RESEARCHED

The field of climate research is so vast, and the published papers so many, that it is hard for anyone to judge which areas are receiving more research attention than they might deserve, and which areas less. However, some scientists well placed to observe the work of their community have suggested that large-scale climate changes of the kind described above are relatively under-studied.

Professor Richard Betts is the Director of the EU's High-End Climate Impacts and Extremes ('HELIX') project, and so probably has a better overview than most people of the research in this field. He has said he is struck by the way the scientific literature on tipping points seems to include a lot of review papers that end up citing the same studies and each other. He says that while there is plenty of interesting theoretical work being done, we have yet to see a similar level of research using climate models that could give more detailed information.[12]

Rowan Sutton, the climate scientist quoted in the previous chapter, says the physical climate science community – the experts best able to expand our understanding of Earth system feedbacks, tipping points, and large-scale changes – has seen risk assessment as 'a job for others'. He believes that their lack of focus on the needs of risk assessment has led to insufficient attention being paid to low-likelihood, high-impact events.[13] Other scientists have suggested that because climate change research has often focused on the next few decades, less attention has been paid to feedbacks that act more slowly, even though their effects over the long term may be larger.[14]

The scientists who want to do more research in this area are probably not helped by general perceptions of what is 'policy-relevant'. People tend to believe 'policy-relevant' climate science is that which can directly inform specific decisions, such as which kinds of crops to plant, or how high to build sea-defences. Earth system feedbacks seem very rarely to be considered policy-relevant, despite their enormous importance for risk assessment, because their impact on things we make decisions about is so indirect. I doubt this helps them win research funding.

UNDER-REPORTED

Tipping points, feedbacks, and irreversibility are popular subjects for the media when writing about climate change, for the good reason that they are highly relevant to understanding the scale of the risks that we face. We instinctively want to read about these things because we guess that they might be important. But media reports do not always provide clarity or reliability. They are not an ideal basis for government decision-making.

If you want to know what information on climate change is being communicated to governments, in a way that they might take seriously, the best place to look is the reports of the IPCC. In particular, you should look at the Summaries for Policymakers, since these are already long, and few policymakers ever read any further. I have referred to these reports frequently because they are authoritative, comprehensive, and referred to by almost all governments. These are great strengths. It is because the IPCC reports are so well established and respected that they serve as a useful benchmark for comparison, and occasionally, criticism.

The Summary for Policymakers of the IPCC's 2021 report on physical climate science mentions several potential large-scale changes: the collapse of ice sheets, abrupt changes in ocean currents, and forest dieback. However, the discussion is critically limited in that there is minimal information on the likelihood of these changes taking place. We are told that they 'cannot be ruled out', and that their probability increases at higher levels of warming, but we are not given any estimates of the levels of warming at which they may occur. Such estimates exist,[15] but presumably their uncertainty was the reason for their exclusion – once again, confidence was prioritised over relevance.

What of the possible 'point of no return'? The Summary does highlight the irreversibility of many aspects of climate change, but it does not discuss the possibility that change could become self-sustaining, leading to ever worse conditions, even if short-term temperature targets are met. This question, arguably the most policy-relevant of all, is not even raised.

National climate change risk assessments seem unlikely to do a better job than the IPCC in plainly communicating the risks of large-scale changes. They are usually narrower in scope, and do not consider it their job to assess the full range of changes that could happen at a global level. The UK's climate change risk assessment is relatively well established and detailed, but gives less information on large-scale changes than can be found in the IPCC's Summary. Tellingly, its list of recommended research priorities is heavily dominated by local concerns, such as 'risks to passengers from high temperatures on public transport'; 'risks to bridges and pipelines from high river flows and erosion'; and 'risks to viability of coastal communities from sea level rise'.[16] While a few concern change at the global level, none relate to Earth system feedbacks, tipping points, or irreversibility. Should it be a priority for the UK to research the risk of passing a threshold of self-sustaining change that leads irreversibly towards a climate that threatens the habitability of the planet for humans? Nope, apparently not. That must be somebody else's job.

UNDERESTIMATED

In several of the examples described above, I have mentioned the uncertainty and disagreement that exists between experts. In these cases, our assessment of the risk depends on which scientists we think are more likely to be right. How do we know?

One option is to go with the majority. According to one survey, 97% of climate scientists think climate change is the result of human activities. It feels safe to trust a majority that size. But what about when the numbers are less clear? If most scientists think sea level rise will be no more than 1 m this century, but one thinks that 7 m is possible, should we discount that opinion or take it seriously?[e] Science is not a vote. Sometimes the one dissenting voice turns out to be right.

Another approach is to read the science for ourselves, as Greta Thunberg has told us we should. I am a fan of this approach, but as a non-expert, I know I might draw unduly strong conclusions from whatever I happen to have read, and fail to appreciate the implications of the much larger body of research findings of which I am unaware. Anyway, if I read enough to discover that the experts disagree, how can I judge between them when their expertise is so much greater than mine?

We could decide to trust authority. If we rely on institutions like the IPCC or the Royal Society, we are trusting the scientists to adjudicate between each other, to communicate the findings of those that are most reliable while keeping the dodgy ones in a quiet corner of the library. But institutions can be cautious, and consensus is not always correct.

In this chapter, we have already come up against the limitations of all these approaches. I believe a fourth option holds more promise. This is to watch how expert judgement changes over time. If the experts change their minds, this tells us something about the reliability or bias of their past

---

[e] In the previous chapter, I cited a 2014 study that asked experts in global sea level rise their opinion on the highest level that we could experience this century. I mentioned that most put the upper bound at 1–2 m, while a handful thought that 3–5 m was possible. I didn't mention that one expert thought 7 m was possible. I discounted that opinion because it seemed to be an outlier, and I didn't want to do the reader the disservice of overstating the risk. But is this omission defensible? It implicitly assumes that all the experts' opinions are equally likely to be valid. Why should they be?

judgements. Tracking how expert judgement changes over time is a technique used in intelligence analysis, another area of high uncertainty and high stakes for society.

A trend over time is visible in the IPCC's analyses of 'Reasons for Concern'. These represent a summary of expert judgement about climate change risks in five categories: risks to unique and threatened systems; extreme weather events; distribution of impacts (meaning the risk of some people being particularly badly affected); global aggregate impacts; and large-scale singular events (also known as tipping points, or critical thresholds). In each of these categories, the risk is rated on a scale from 'undetectable' to 'very high' along an axis of global temperature rise from 0 to 5°C. These are a rough measure of risk, but since the same exercise has been repeated several times, they provide a window into how expert judgement has changed over the years.

In the IPCC's Sixth Assessment Report (published in 2022), the assessments of risk in all five of the Reasons for Concern were revised upward compared to its Fifth Assessment Report (from 2014). The changes in assessment were not small. Very high risks to unique and threatened systems were judged to occur at around 1.5°C of warming, instead of at 2.6°C. High risks in terms of global aggregate impacts were estimated to arise at around 2°C, instead of at 3.6°C. High risks of large-scale singular events were thought likely at around 2°C, instead of at 2.6°C.[17]

Taken together, this shows a dramatic reassessment of risk. Countries spent years debating a half-degree difference in the target for limiting warming, with the Paris Agreement eventually reaching the awkward compromise of aiming to keep global temperature increase 'well below' 2°C, while 'pursuing efforts' to keep it below 1.5°C. Meanwhile, the scientists had just dropped their 'high risk' threshold for 'global aggregate impacts' by three times as much.

This was not the first time the scientists had revised their risk estimates upwards. The Reasons for Concern in the Fifth Assessment Report (2014) revised the risks upwards compared to the Fourth (2007). The Fourth was itself an upward revision of the Third (2001). The estimated threshold for high risk of large-scale singular events (or tipping points) fell all the way from 4–5°C in 2001 to around 2°C in 2019. Professor Timothy Lenton, one of the world's leading experts in tipping points in the Earth system, has put together a chart to show how significant and sustained has been this change over time in expert judgement (see Figure 5.1).

Any student of science knows that if you are wrong in all directions equally often, there's a good chance your error is random; but if you are

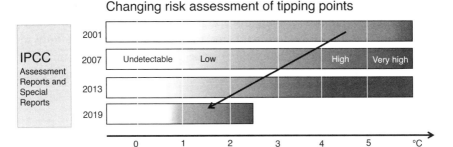

Figure 5.1 Change over time in expert judgement regarding the risk of crossing tipping points in the Earth system. Source: Timothy Lenton

always wrong in the same direction, you may have a systematic error. Although not all climate scientists participate in compiling the Reasons for Concern, and not all would necessarily agree with them, the upward revision of risk judgements over time is so consistent that it is hard not to conclude that these risks have been systematically underestimated. Why might this be?

I once attended a presentation of the findings of the IPCC's 2018 report, where one of its lead authors was asked by a member of the audience whether scientists' views on climate change had changed much over time. He responded that the main physical science projections, such as those regarding the rate of global temperature increase this century, had not changed very much. Early thinking had largely been supported by later findings. But in relation to the more complex interactions between the physical climate and biological systems, the thinking had changed substantially: increasing knowledge was causing estimates of risk to be revised upwards.

My best guess at what is going on is that we are persistently underestimating climate risks because of the Earth system's sheer complexity. The IPCC itself has reported that when risks in different sectors of the human economy are integrated into models, scientists have discovered new risks that had not previously been recognised.[18] If it is difficult to see all the interactions between climate change impacts in different sectors of the human economy, it must be far more difficult to understand all the interactions between biological, chemical, and physical systems at scales from the microbial to the global. We are unlikely ever to know or predict the full range and depth of these interactions. Most of these systems have settled down into a relatively stable state over the past ten thousand years – this period of unusual climatic stability in which human civilisation has grown up. Now that the climate is being disrupted, so are they. In a situation where reinforcing feedbacks are dominant, and where most of the interactions we are aware of tend to accelerate change, it seems reasonable to assume that most of the interactions we are unaware of will tend to do the same.

WHAT CAN BE DONE?

In this chapter, we have seen that large-scale feedbacks, tipping points, and irreversible changes in the Earth system could hugely amplify the risks of climate change. We have also seen reason to believe that these phenomena may be under-researched, under-reported, and underestimated. This cannot be allowed to continue. We can draw some rough conclusions about what should be done, to improve our understanding of the scale of the risks.

First, find out as much as we can. These large-scale changes have enormous implications for the risks that we face. They should be a high priority for climate change research. This must include not only the individual large-scale changes, but also the interactions between them, and the question of whether there exists a general threshold for self-sustaining change. Nobody should think that these questions are not policy-relevant. At the same time as researching potential future changes, we should watch closely what is happening in the present. The behaviour of complex systems can sometimes give clues as to when a tipping point may be approaching.[19]

Second, communicate the best available knowledge and expert judgement as fully as possible. We need to look beyond the 'likely range', and consider low probabilities and long timescales. Risk assessments need to consider the worst case, not just the most likely case. Large-scale changes in the climate system can be assessed using the same boiling frog principle that we discussed in the previous chapter: first identify what we wish to avoid, and then see how likely it may become over the course of time.

Third, systematically monitor changes in expert judgement over time. The IPCC's Reasons for Concern have provided a useful basis for comparison, but this has been somewhat ad hoc. They were not explicitly designed for this purpose, and, by aggregating risks into broad and rough categories, do not necessarily give the clearest possible view of how expert judgement has changed in relation to each of the major risks. A more systematic effort could provide a clearer picture to the public, to governments, and to the experts themselves, helping us all anticipate the direction we are being taken in by the development of new knowledge.

6

THE MEANING OF CONSERVATIVE

If you spend much time around climate scientists, you will probably notice that the things they are willing to tell you in conversation are not the same as the things they are willing to write down. The things they will tell you in conversation are, in general, stronger.

We already saw one example of this in Chapter 3. The scientists at the IPCC meeting in Yokohama were happy to tell me that they agreed with the findings of the paper on heat stress exceeding the limits of human tolerance, and that if anything, they thought it understated the risk; but they were not willing to write its conclusions into their Summary for Policymakers. However important to society this finding might be, for the scientists it was more important that they only wrote down the things they were absolutely sure of.

In Chapter 3 we saw how this preference – prioritising confidence over relevance – could be related to a tendency to focus on prediction rather than risk assessment. I proposed the 'boiling frog' approach as a way to redress the balance: if scientists ask first what we wish to avoid, before considering how likely it is, then their research will be highly relevant to our interests and useful for informing risk assessments.

But will this be enough to give us a clear picture of the risks? There are reasons to believe it will not. There is something deeper that we have to grapple with: a difference in professional ethics between the culture of science, and the culture of risk management.

The person who first explained this to me was Trevor Maynard, a risk modelling expert then at Lloyds of London, one of the world's largest reinsurers. Writing about the principle that risk assessments should always use the best available information, he said the following:

> The best available information can take many forms; sometimes, all we have to rely on is expert judgement. In these cases, it is essential for the expert to communicate without bias. It has always concerned me that our use of the word 'conservative' has the opposite meaning in insurance to its

meaning in science. Scientists are 'conservative' if they constrain their worst fears, and wait for more evidence before communicating them; therefore, 'conservative' predictions tend to understate risk – they are less than best estimates. In insurance, 'conservative' reserves are higher than would be required by best estimates. In matters of risk assessment, I feel the insurance point of view is more appropriate.[1]

The same cultural difference has been noticed by scientists. Dr Jay Gulledge, when I met him, was Director of the Environmental Sciences Division at the Oak Ridge National Laboratory, one of the most important centres of scientific research and technology development sponsored by the US government. In its early days, the Lab had been central to the US government's effort to develop nuclear weapons. Since the Lab operated close to the interface between science and policy, Jay had given considerable thought to the way in which information was communicated between these different communities.

In our risk assessment report, Gulledge dug deeper into the culture of science to find the origin of the issue that Trevor Maynard had identified.[2] He wrote that the scientists who strive to provide useful information about climate change and the decision-makers who seek that information are 'linked by a thin thread of climate information that is relevant to their respective endeavours, but they are separated by different needs, priorities, processes and cultures'. An important difference between these two communities is the way they deal with uncertainty. Scientists, he wrote, 'are conservative about drawing incorrect conclusions – so much so that they would rather draw no conclusion than an incorrect one. Consequently, they have developed standard practices and cultural norms to protect the scientific knowledge pool from being contaminated by falsehoods.' For example, results that appear to confirm a hypothesis may be discarded if there is a more than 5% probability of the predicted outcome having occurred purely by chance. Put another way, the results could be thrown out even if there was a 94% probability that they were *not* by chance.

This attitude shows a strong preference, or bias, between two different ways of being wrong. One way of being wrong is to believe that your hypothesis is correct, when in fact it is not. This is a 'false positive', or what statisticians call a 'type I error'. The other way of being wrong is to believe your hypothesis is incorrect, when in fact it is true. This is a 'false negative', or 'type II error'. Scientists have a strong aversion to false positives but are relatively tolerant of false negatives. In contrast to the careful rooting out of results that appear to confirm hypotheses but might have occurred by chance, in most scientific fields there is no standard practice for checking how likely you are to have thrown out a finding that was actually true.

Gulledge, like Trevor Maynard, observed that professional risk managers usually had the opposite attitude: they were more concerned with false negatives that could lead them to overlook risks, with potentially severe consequences. This meant that when scientists tolerated false negatives, their work might 'lack rigour from the standpoint of the decision-makers they seek to inform'.

In practice, Gulledge writes that this cultural bias has meant that climate scientists have often erred towards underestimating risk when faced with deep uncertainty. He cites the changing assessments of the IPCC's Reasons for Concern, which we discussed in the last chapter, as an example. He suggests that this could interact in a dangerous way with our natural tendency to discount the likelihood of low-probability, high-impact outcomes, leading to 'a serious under-appreciation of the potential severity of climate change impacts among the public and decision-makers'.

I find Gulledge's explanation persuasive. It fits with my own experience: when I was a physics student at university, I knew I would be in trouble with my lab supervisors if I overstated the confidence I had in the findings of my experiments. When I worked for an auditing firm in my first real job, I knew I would be in trouble with my bosses if I understated any findings that might imply risks to the ability of a company we were auditing to continue operating as a legal and profitable 'going concern'. It also explains the speaking and writing difference that I mentioned above. When a scientist speaks to you individually, assuming you are not a journalist, they know that what they say is unrecorded, and there is a good chance that if you show interest and ask intelligent questions, they will tell you what they think. But when they write something down, they know it will be read by other members of their profession and judged according to the professional ethics of that community. Consequently, the bias against false positives compared to false negatives is much stronger in writing than in conversation.

One such conversation I had was with Professor Brian Hoskins, a senior and respected climate scientist and a world-leading expert in atmospheric circulation, who you may remember had hosted the visiting Chinese experts at the Royal Society. Chatting one-to-one during a coffee break at a science conference, Brian told me something that worried him. The Sahara desert, he said, had been green with vegetation some seven thousand years ago. Rainfall patterns then must have been very different from how they are now. Climate models did not seem able to simulate changes this large in the behaviour of the world's monsoon systems, even though they had happened in the past. In conversation, we confirmed a few things that helped me understand why this was so worrying. A small change in monsoon rainfall (of, say, 10%) can have a large and damaging effect on India's agriculture and its economy. A green Sahara implied that large rainfalls must have been occurring hundreds, if not thousands, of kilometres from where they typically occur at present. This change happened during the relatively stable Holocene period, during which global average temperatures had not changed by more than about half a degree.

It was not hard to join the dots. If this could happen at a time when the global climate had differed from the present by half a degree at most, then the risk of similar or even larger changes taking place must surely be considerable in a world four degrees warmer or more, as it could be by the end of this century.

Brian was one of those scientists who kindly contributed to my risk assessment report, giving his time and asking nothing in return, because he saw the value in the exercise. In the process of agreeing a short section on the risk of changes to monsoons, I encouraged him to state the risk as clearly as he had done in our conversation. I believe he went as far as he could, within the boundaries set by the ethics of his profession. But I always felt I had gained a deeper appreciation of the risk from our conversation than anyone would by reading his written summary.

THE DANGERS OF AVERAGING

The science community's preference for prediction and its bias against false positives can come together in a dangerous way through the use of averaging.

If different experts, or different models, each give different answers to the same question, one way of communicating the result is to take the average. An analogy given by risk experts in the finance sector provides a pithy summary of the dangers of this approach:

> Avoiding the dangers of averaging is important in identifying the largest risks.... Imagine three policymakers who like river walking; none of whom can swim. They ask their scientific adviser whether the depth of water ever exceeds head height. The adviser asks three universities to develop models: the first notes that the water exceeds head height near to the west shore, the second believes this is not the case but water exceeds head height in the centre of the river and the third, being very fond of their model, believes the others are both wrong and the water only exceeds head height near the east shore. The adviser, noting the uncertainty in the modelling, believes

the best approach is to average the three results. The outcome is regrettable! The fact is that each of the models predict certain death – but the precise location is not known. By averaging, this crucial information is lost.[3]

I came across a situation similar to this at that IPCC meeting in Yokohama. The scientists needed to decide how to summarise the last half-dozen years of research on the impact of climate change on crop production within a single short paragraph and a single figure, for inclusion in the Summary for Policymakers of their report. In the draft under discussion at the beginning of the meeting, the findings were summarised in the prediction that on average, climate change was expected to reduce crop yields by around 2% per decade over the course of the century. This was an average of projections relating to different crops, in different countries, at different degrees of warming, carried out by different experts, using different assumptions and different models. It masked a world of variation – and risk.

Along with a few other interested policymakers, I worked with the scientists to agree a different choice of information to communicate. We agreed to focus on the ends of the spectrum of possibilities – the best and worst cases – instead of on the centre. The final text read, '*Projected impacts vary across crops and regions and adaptation scenarios, with about 10% of projections for the period 2030–2049 showing yield gains of more than 10%, and about 10% of projections showing yield losses of more than 25%, compared to the late 20th century. After 2050 the risk of more severe yield impacts increases and depends on the level of warming.*'[4] This conveyed more information about the risk than the 2% 'average of averages' would have done, but it still aggregated the data in a way that failed to make visible the wide range of different estimates and possible outcomes. A more detailed figure, included in the report but not in the Summary for Policymakers, gave a much clearer picture. It was from this that one could see, for example, that for wheat yields in temperate regions with 3°C of local warming, projections ranged from a 40% increase to a 40% decrease.[5]

The uncertainty in this projection is itself a valuable piece of information. It is more useful to the policymaker to know that some experts project a 40% increase while others project a 40% decrease, than to know that their average projection is zero. By analogy, if you are walking on a mountain in a fog, and you don't know if you are near or far from a cliff-edge, you are likely to take this ignorance into account when you decide whether to run or walk.

BRIDGING THE CULTURAL DIVIDE

In summary, we have a combination of two problems: from the perspective of the needs of risk assessment, scientists are often choosing the wrong information to communicate, and then communicating it with the wrong kind of error bias.

We should not assume these issues are impossible to resolve. The US National Academy of Sciences has advised that 'Scientific priorities and practices need to change so that the scientific community can provide better support to decision-makers in managing emerging climate risks.'[6] In earlier chapters we discussed how scientists can do this by shifting the focus of their research and communications from the average 'most likely' to the extreme 'worst case', and by starting with the identification of what it is that we might wish to avoid.

To address the error bias problem, an approach we attempted in our risk assessment was to follow the instruction of an old military chief, who is said to have demanded of his subordinates, 'Tell me what you know; tell me what you don't know; and tell me what you think.' It is standard scientific practice to follow the first two parts of this instruction. Following the third part takes more effort but can be crucial to communicating the risk.

Jay Gulledge concluded that to adopt a more risk-sensitive approach, scientists would need in some cases to allow more tolerance of false positives, and less tolerance of false negatives. I believe this is true, and I hope it can happen. In principle, the cultures of science and risk assessment should not be impossible to reconcile: they ought to be able to meet in the middle, resulting in an equal aversion to either kind of error. There are many fields in which the use of science to support risk assessment has become highly developed, such as medicine.

However, it may be unrealistic and unfair of us to expect scientists to do this on their own. No self-respecting professional wants to violate the cultural norms of their field. For the cultures of science and risk assessment to meet in the middle, they each need to be represented by their own experts.

This implies separating out the tasks of information gathering and risk assessment. Those involved in information-gathering activities, such as primary scientific research, should be free to collect whatever is useful or interesting. Those involved in risk assessment should interrogate that evidence in relation to defined objectives, and according to a specific set of principles. Such a separation of tasks is often made within intelligence agencies, as it allows both tasks to be carried out more effectively. The need is surely even greater in relation to climate change, because, unlike in intelligence, the 'information gatherers' do not come from a culture of risk management.

If scientists provide the raw information for climate change risk assessments, then the processing of that information should also involve those for whom risk assessment is a core part of their professional expertise. Qualified individuals could be drawn from fields such as defence, intelligence, insurance, and public health.

All of this could contribute to producing and communicating the science of climate change in a way that, as Jane Lubchenco recommended, would be 'maximally helpful' for society. But for a full assessment of the risks of climate change, we will still need to go further. We will need to go beyond science.

7

MORE THAN SCIENCE

Up until this point, we have focused on the role of science in understanding the risks of climate change. I have argued that in many ways, science could be doing a better job of informing risk assessment. But while science is at the centre, it is not the whole story. The risk of climate change depends to a great extent on factors that are not for science to judge.

For a full picture, there at least two more questions that need to be addressed. First: what will we, humanity, do to the climate? And second: what, in the new climate of the future, might we do to each other?

GLOBAL EMISSIONS: WHAT WILL HUMANITY DO TO THE CLIMATE?

The risks of climate change depend overwhelmingly on the future pathway of global emissions. The more greenhouse gases we emit, the more the world will warm, and the more severe will be all the consequences discussed in earlier chapters.

Global emissions in future could go up, down, or stay the same. A wide range of pathways are possible. There are plenty of fossil fuels still in the ground: a good deal more oil and gas, vast unexploited coal deposits under Russia and Alaska, and even frozen methane under the ocean floor. If we keep on burning our way through whatever fossils we get our hands on, annual global emissions by the end of the century could be double or even triple what they are now. Alternatively, if we take every opportunity to cut emissions, capture carbon and stuff it underground, we could plausibly reach net zero global emissions by around the middle of this century, and even venture into net negative global emissions sometime after that.

Which pathway becomes the reality depends on how fast our population and our global economy grow, and how quickly we develop and deploy zero-emission technologies. Crucially, this last variable is a matter of choice. Not the choice of any one country, but the choices of many people in many countries.

These choices are fundamentally unpredictable. Consider the swinging pendulum of US politics on climate change. President Clinton's Democrats negotiated the Kyoto Protocol, but the Republicans in the Senate chose not to ratify it, and President Bush made no effort to implement it. President Obama did as much as he could to cut emissions by executive decree, avoiding the obstructionists in Congress. President Trump then came along and reversed all of Obama's policies. Now President Biden is in charge and has committed the US to achieving net zero emissions. Who knows what will happen next? How long will it take for the US political system to be reformed so that Republican party politicians can be honest with their voters and responsible towards their children, instead of living in fear of the vested interests that fund their election campaigns?

The US is an extreme example, but in all countries the politics of climate change moves forwards and backwards. If anyone is able to guess where things are going, it is not climate scientists. Financial analysts can see how much money is being poured into finding more fossils to burn, and how much is being reallocated to clean technologies. Technology analysts can track how fast those clean technologies are being developed and deployed in markets across the world. Political analysts can track opinion polls, governments' targets, policies, and political trends, and form some view of whether these are likely to push emissions up or down in the near future.

Taken together, these financial, technological, and political assessments can tell us something about the likely future pathway of global emissions. But only up to a point. The sheer unpredictability of future choices means that we have to recognise a high degree of uncertainty.

Unfortunately, this uncertainty is typically not well handled in the reports given to governments. Science assessments, such as those of the IPCC, usually include a range of high and low scenarios for global emissions, without saying anything about their relative likelihood. This is fair enough, given the likelihood is not a question of science, but it is not very helpful for a risk assessment. Policy assessments often go to the opposite extreme, giving a single central projection for global emissions, along with a corresponding estimate for global temperature rise.

After countries set national emissions targets around the Paris Agreement in 2015, one analysis estimated that the most likely aggregate effect of these targets was an increase in global temperatures of $2.7°C$ by the end of the century.[1] This number was so widely repeated that it became accepted in the policy community as a truth: the Paris Agreement had put the world on course for $2.7°C$ of temperature rise. But how was this number arrived at? Most countries' targets only went as far as the year 2030. To predict a pathway for global emissions all the way to the end of the century, the analysts had to come up with a way of extrapolating 'current policies' for another seventy years. It should be obvious that there is no such thing as a 'current policy' for the year 2083 when most of the people who will be making policy at that time have not yet been born. The number was not much more than a random guess, but few people in government had the time to think about it or the interest to challenge it. However many times I tried to kill it, striking it out of briefing papers for ministers, the bloody thing kept coming back.

The risk is that communication of such central estimates for global emissions and consequent temperature rise, based as they must be on guesses about the future, leads to complacency. It is dangerous to assume that the long-term emissions targets that countries have announced will be met, or that progress in the coming years will be continued in future decades. Everyone involved in climate change knows that the world is 'off track' for meeting the internationally agreed targets for limiting global temperature rise. But far fewer people seem to have a good sense either of how low the chances are becoming of us meeting those goals, or how substantial the chances may still be of us running into much higher degrees of climate change.

With the appropriate analysis and communication, the risk of the world following a high-emissions pathway can be made clear. Science can then be used to explain how the climate may respond. From this, we will be able to identify some direct risks to our interests, as discussed in earlier chapters. We will also be able to contemplate the outlines of a significantly changed future environment.

SYSTEMIC RISKS: IN A FUTURE CLIMATE, WHAT WILL WE DO TO EACH OTHER?

After the catastrophic terrorist attacks that felled the Twin Towers of the World Trade Center in New York on 11 September 2001, the US President and Congress created a National Commission on Terrorist Attacks Upon the United States, to understand how this event had happened, and how such a tragedy could be prevented from happening again.

When this '9/11 Commission', as it became known, published its findings, it concluded, '*We did not grasp the magnitude of a threat that had been gathering over time.*'[2] While there had been many failures – of policy, of management, and of capability, '*the most important failure was one of imagination'.*[3] Security analysts had simply not imagined that a group of extremists from one of the world's poorest countries, using relatively trivial financial resources, might hijack a large aeroplane and fly it into a building. This finding was brought to my attention by the Military Advisory Board of the Center for Naval Analyses (CNA), a group of retired generals and admirals who study issues relevant to US national security and provide analysis to inform policymakers and the public. They warned that with climate change, we must guard against a similar failure of imagination. They urged governments to consider not only the simple, direct impacts of climate change, but also the risks that are more complex and systemic.[4]

These systemic risks exist because climate change affects almost everything. Its impacts on all elements of natural and human systems interact with each other, and from those interactions, new risks emerge. The outcome, in the worst case, can be the failure of those systems.

Already, we can see these systemic risks appearing. In the Arctic, where temperatures are rising twice as fast as the global average, the shrinking area of sea-ice, decline of animal populations, and unpredictable weather patterns are threatening the viability of Indigenous peoples' way of life, while the thawing permafrost threatens to destabilise buildings, roads, pipelines, and airports.[5] In megacities, climate and resource stresses can ripple out through infrastructure systems and across the economy. Sao Paulo's low rainfall and high temperatures in 2014 led to shortages of water affecting the functioning of schools, hospitals, and businesses; the impacts on agriculture and hydroelectric power led to higher prices for food and electricity; these contributed to social unrest in parts of the city; and all this led to economic losses of over $5bn.[6]

In Syria, the extreme drought that hit the country between 2007 and 2011 is thought to have been made two to three times more likely by climate change.[7] The drought caused widespread crop failure and loss of livestock, contributing to the displacement of around two million farmers and herders, many of whom fled to cities already crowded with Iraqi and Palestinian refugees. By 2009, more than 800 thousand Syrians had lost their livelihoods as a result of the drought; by 2011, around a million were extremely food insecure, and two to three million had been driven into extreme poverty.[8] While many other factors were important in driving the political unrest and conflict that followed, it is difficult to imagine that this widespread impoverishment and large-scale displacement did not play a role.

Climate change is also estimated to have made the extreme heat wave suffered by Russia in the summer of 2010 around three times more likely.[9] The heat wave contributed to drought and fire, and reduced Russia's wheat production that year by 30%. At the same time, droughts affected wheat production in China and Ukraine. Reduced production, protectionist measures, commodity speculation, and large-scale purchases on the global market all contributed to a more than doubling of the global wheat price in the second half of 2010. The top nine wheat-importing countries in the world, on a per capita basis, are all in the Middle East and North Africa. Seven of those are developing countries and spend over a third of their average household income on food. All seven experienced political protests resulting in civilian deaths in 2011, with food price rises recognised in many of these countries as one of the contributing factors.[10]

The point is not to attribute all ills in the world to climate change. The point is that many of our systems are fragile, dysfunctional, or unstable already. Climate change puts them under greater stress, increasing the risk of system failure. So, how well are we doing at understanding these risks?

The UK's first national climate change risk assessment commissioned a study, almost as an afterthought, to look into the 'indirect' risks of climate change to the UK: those that arose not within our own borders but elsewhere in the world with the potential to affect our interests. Security risks, and disruption of global food systems, came within this category. The study reached a striking conclusion: the threats to the UK due to climate change impacts around the world could be an order of magnitude greater than those that affected us directly.[11] It reached this finding despite only considering a global temperature increase of 2°C – effectively a best-case scenario.

Understanding what the security risks of climate change might look like in a worst-case, or even a 'most likely' scenario, is difficult. The IPCC makes clear the limitations of academic study. At the very end of its chapter on 'human security', it writes:

> At high levels of warming, the rate of changes in environmental conditions in most places will be without any precedent in human history. Hence analysis concerning human security, in those circumstances of very high impacts, is uncertain. Much of the current literature on human security and climate change is informed by contemporary relationships and observation and hence is limited in analyzing the human security implications of rapid or severe climate change.[12]

In other words: we mostly study the past and present; the future will be completely different, so we have no idea.

The 9/11 Commission found that the US intelligence community had failed to recognise the risk posed by Al-Qaeda because it was a radically new kind of terrorism, posing a threat beyond any the US had previously experienced. The Commission observed that 'Imagination is not a gift usually associated with bureaucracies' and concluded, 'It is therefore crucial to find a way of routinizing, even bureaucratizing, the exercise of imagination.'[13]

Ever since Japan's surprise attack on the US navy in Pearl Harbor in 1941, the US defence and intelligence community has devoted considerable effort to developing processes to exercise imagination in a structured way. These include scenario exercises, where possible future situations are imagined in detail so as to identify risks and test strategies; red teaming, where you put yourself in the shoes of your enemy and imagine what they might think and do; and war gaming, where a simulated encounter between adversaries provides insights into possible actions and outcomes.

One of the institutions that led these efforts was the Center for Naval Analyses (CNA). Founded in 1942 as the 'Antisubmarine Warfare Operations Research Group', it evolved through the decades, analysing the risks of nuclear weapons and guided missiles, guerrilla warfare in Vietnam, and strategic competition with the Soviet Union. In the post-Cold War era, it increasingly considered a wider range of risks including terrorism, humanitarian disasters, and environmental instability.[14]

I was introduced to the experts at the CNA by philanthropists at the Skoll Global Threats Fund, who were interested in whether these techniques could support a better understanding of the security risks of climate change. Together, we decided to see if we could address the gap left by the IPCC: to assess the security risks in a future that might be radically different from the present.

One way we did this was through a scenarios exercise. Climate scientists set out some parameters: what could happen to temperature, sea level, crop production, water resources, etc., in a high-end climate change scenario, based on the academic literature. A diverse group of security experts – former intelligence bosses, army generals, navy admirals, diplomats, and analysts, from the US, Europe, China, and India – then talked to each other about what the security implications might be.

It is fair to say that the experts in the room were not full of optimism. Some of the basic parameters were worrying enough. Many countries in the Middle East are already highly water-stressed, and are expecting population increases of 50–100% over the next few decades, at the same time as climate change could cut renewable freshwater resources by anything from 10% to 50%. In Sub-Saharan Africa, more than a quarter of the population was undernourished in 2010–2012; many countries are expected to double their populations by mid-century, reducing arable land per capita to below the threshold of extreme stress, while climate change is expected to negatively affect the production of crops.[15]

The experts considered how countries would do their best to adapt to climate change, but also how many were struggling to adapt to the low level of change already experienced. They did not find it hard to imagine how things could get worse. At high degrees of climate change, the risks of food and water insecurity, social stresses caused by inequality and large-scale migration, the increasing expense and difficulty of protecting coastal cities, and the breakdown of infrastructure systems subject to multiple stresses, would all intermingle. There would be a growing risk of state failure, even in countries that are currently considered developed and stable.

As a second approach to structured use of the imagination, we organised what was later reported as 'probably the first global climate war game'.[16] The same group of international security experts played the roles of leaders of major countries and regions, taking decisions to advance their national economic and security interests in the context of a changing climate. One of the participants was Major General A. N. M. Muniruzzaman, from Bangladesh. He recounted his experience to a journalist afterwards: 'As climate scenarios became more and more difficult and complex, I would have expected people to be reaching out and being more inclusive. The countries' reactions were just the opposite: they became more inward-looking and insular.'[17] Competition for land, food, and water drove inequality, conflict, and migration. Some developed countries cut back international aid to concentrate on solving their own problems, while those that persisted with an internationalist approach suffered an increasingly insupportable burden.

I will not describe the findings of these exercises at length, because my aim is not to convince you that they are correct. A scenarios exercise or a war game does not prove anything. Its value lies mainly in the insights it generates among its participants. You can form your own view by reading the science and thinking for yourself about the security implications. Any government can make its own assessment by putting its climate scientists and security chiefs in a room together and asking them the right kind of questions. The point is that without some attempt at structured use of the imagination, some of the largest risks of climate change are likely to remain unexplored. And to do this properly, we need experts in the systems whose failure would cause us the greatest concern. We cannot rely solely on the scientists.

8

TELL THE TRUTH

When a pink boat parked in the centre of Oxford Circus by the climate change activists of Extinction Rebellion brought the traffic of London to a standstill in April 2019, the slogan emblazoned on its side was 'TELL THE TRUTH'. Crowds of people turned out to show their support, and many waved flags with the same message. People, it seemed, were worried that someone was not being honest about the gravity of the threat. But who was the guilty party? And was it a sin of commission, or of omission?

Sir David King had seen it as his responsibility, as Government Chief Science Adviser, to make sure that the risks of climate change were fully understood. The project that he and I began with our friends from the US, China, and India ended by publishing its own climate change risk assessment, and by making some recommendations about how this could be done more effectively in future.

Our first recommendation was that the principles of risk assessment should be applied to the greatest extent possible. Above all, that meant telling people what was the worst that could happen. Breaking that down into stages, it meant starting from an understanding of our interests; identifying the biggest risks to those interests; and using the best available information to consider the full range of probabilities, including worst-case scenarios. To provide a full picture of the scale of the threat, the assessment would have to be holistic, considering where global emissions might be heading, how the climate might respond, and how that could affect us both directly and indirectly.

Our second recommendation was to broaden participation in the risk assessment process. To fully understand the risks, we need to bring climate scientists together with decision-makers in a process of co-production, as described in Chapter 4. We also need to involve experts from other fields, for all the reasons discussed in Chapters 6 and 7.

Finally, we recommended that climate change risk assessments should be communicated to heads of government, because only they have the power and authority to direct a response that is proportionate to the scale of the risk.

This last point deserves emphasis. In any country, at any time, a government has multiple competing priorities. Even if addressing climate change is essential for a country's long-term prosperity and security, the actions it involves are bound to conflict with other aims in the short term. An environment minister might argue for strong actions to reduce emissions, but other ministers around the table may be more worried about energy security, industrial competitiveness, or the price of food. Political and financial capital are always limited; the finance minister will always be worried about the budget, and most of the ministers will be worried about their popularity. No matter what the political system, it is only the person at the top who has the authority to balance these interests, and to decide how much effort to put into countering climate change compared to all those other priorities.

The UK prides itself on having some of the world's most developed institutions for climate change governance. We were the first country to introduce legally binding 'carbon budgets', to guide the reduction of emissions in five-year steps along a trajectory consistent with our international climate change goals. The same Act of Parliament that created the carbon budgets had also mandated a five-yearly national climate change risk assessment – one of the world's first. I have seen how this assessment plays a useful role in prompting government departments to plan for adaptation and resilience in the areas of the economy and society for which they are responsible. But I have not seen any evidence of this being used at the top level of government to decide how seriously to take climate change compared to other priorities. In the one instance I am aware of in which the risk of climate change was discussed by the Cabinet during the first five years that I was working on the issue, the information was presented on a set of four slides. These communicated the facts that climate change was happening, that it was caused by human activity, and that the more we continued to emit greenhouse gases, the more the world would warm. If this was the closest that the UK had come to presenting a climate change risk assessment to the head of government, then it gave some cause for concern about the general state of the art.

In 2015, having produced our own risk assessment in our ad hoc international coalition of experts, we did our best to bring it to the attention of political leaders in each of our countries. In the months leading up to the international climate change conference in Paris, our report was presented to the US President's Council of Advisors on Science and Technology, the

Indian Parliament, and a group of Chinese ministers. Whether it influenced their decisions at that time, we will never know. In the UK, it was used as evidence by the Bank of England in its first report on the risks of climate change to the insurance sector, which helped to bring the idea of climate change as a threat to financial stability into the mainstream.[1] In China, it did in later years lead to a new section on risk in the national climate change science assessment, and according to one senior official, informed later discussions on long-term emissions targets.

A few years later, I discovered that our recommendations had been almost entirely reproduced in a 2016 policy brief on 'Assessing the risks of climate change' by the Scientific Advisory Board of the United Nations Secretary-General. *'The risks of climate change should be assessed in the same way as risks to public health or national security,'* it read. *'Start from an understanding of what we wish to avoid, and focus on the best available information to identify worst case scenarios in relation to long-term changes and short-term events, and consider low probability, catastrophic impact events.'* Risk assessments should be repeated regularly and consistently, it advised, allowing changes in expert judgement to be tracked over time, and they should be reported to the highest decision-making authorities.[2]

Despite that unexpected endorsement, when I found myself in charge of science engagement as part of the UK's Presidency of the United Nations climate change talks in 2020–2021, it seemed that little had changed. The recommendations of our 2015 report were still far from being implemented. Experts at the foreign affairs think-tank Chatham House had conducted a careful survey of the various climate change science assessments, risk assessments, and reports produced by governments, think-tanks, and scientific institutions, to see whether any met the criteria we had described for setting out clearly the full scale of the risk to heads of government. They found none that came close.

2021: A TIME FOR TAKING EXTREMES MORE SERIOUSLY

The year of 2021 brought signs of change: a growing awareness in the scientific community that climate change risk assessment needed to be taken more seriously.

A contributing factor was the appearance of extreme weather events that lay outside the boundaries of anything the climate models had predicted. One such was the heat wave that struck Canada in July. The town of Lytton in British Columbia set a new national temperature record of 49.6°C, and then promptly burned to the ground in a giant forest fire the very next day. Jim Abraham, President of the Canadian Meteorological and Oceanographic Society, described this as 'frankly unbelievable'. The new temperature record was about 10°C hotter than the highest daily temperatures normally seen in that location at that time of the year, and was a level of heat that across the whole of North America was normally only reached in the southwestern deserts.[3] The cause was described as a 'heat dome': a large mass of hot air being pushed down over the land by high pressure in the atmosphere, leading to further heating. The weakening of the jet stream due to climate change may have contributed to this current of air holding the high pressure system in place instead of blowing it away.[4] This kind of event would have been hard for a model to predict because it arose not just from the straightforward thermodynamics of climate change – the world gets warmer, and we have more hot days – but also from the messy and complicated physical dynamics of winds and weather.

Only weeks later, experts were shocked by the extent of flooding in Germany and neighbouring areas of Belgium and the Netherlands. Rainfall had broken previous records by large margins. Deaths resulted from evacuation orders not being applied to large enough areas, because planning authorities had not considered flooding on this scale to be possible.[5] Scientists had always expected climate change to increase the frequency and intensity of such events, but the changes being seen were beyond what any of the models had predicted.[6] As Dieter Gerten, professor of climatology and hydrology at the Potsdam Institute for Climate Impact Research, put it, 'We seem to be not just above normal but in domains we didn't expect in terms of spatial extent and the speed it developed. . . . We need to better model nonlinear events.'[7]

Along with the appearance of unexpected extremes in the present, scientists' projections of the future also continued to change. In 2013, the IPCC had predicted sea level rise of 1–3 m by the year 2300, in a high-emissions scenario.[8] In 2021, the IPCC brought out the first part of its Sixth Assessment Report, and updated this projection to a likely range of 2–7 m by the year 2300.[9] Just like the change over time in experts' assessments of the 'Reasons for Concern' that we discussed in Chapter 5, this was not a minor adjustment to the forecast. In less than a decade, our best estimate for global sea level rise in 2300 had more than doubled.

Moreover, in a welcome step towards risk assessment, the IPCC had given policymakers not only the likely range, but also the unlikely range. In its 'low likelihood, high impact storyline, including ice-sheet instability processes' in a high-emissions scenario, sea level rise could be approaching 2 m by 2100, and increases of 5 m by 2150 and over 15 m by 2300 could not be ruled out. Recalling our best estimate of London's limit to adaptation, this update in expert judgement was equivalent to shortening the city's future lifetime (in a world where we are stupid with emissions and unlucky with the climate) from one or two millennia to one or two centuries.

At this point, scientists and non-scientists alike must be wondering how expert judgement will change in the next ten years. After so many upward revisions of our estimates of risk, who would bet on the next revision being downward? Would you like your sea level rise projection with ice-sheet instability processes, or without?

Further advances in the research of tipping points followed the same trend. Tim Lenton (whose work we discussed in Chapter 5) and other scientists were making progress in detecting early warning signals that could show a system was approaching a tipping point. These included an increase in volatility of the system's behaviour, and a slowing down of its recovery from perturbations. Measurements discovered that there was already strong evidence of these early warning signals in relation to several of the Earth system's major potential tipping points: loss of Arctic sea-ice, disintegration of the central western part of the Greenland ice sheet, slowing of the Atlantic Meridional Overturning Circulation, and loss of the Amazon rainforest.[10] Yet again, it seemed that predictions would have to be revised: tipping points could be upon us sooner than we thought.

With concern about tipping points rising, Thomas Stocker, a Swiss professor who had co-chaired the IPCC's 2013 assessment, launched a campaign for the IPCC to produce a Special Report devoted to this subject. If agreed, this would have the effect of encouraging many more scientists to research tipping points, more institutions to fund that research, and more governments to notice the findings. That this call came from as established a figure in the IPCC hierarchy as Thomas Stocker showed how far the study of tipping points had moved from a somewhat disreputable niche pursuit towards being a serious subject of mainstream research.

RISK ASSESSMENT FOR HEADS OF GOVERNMENT

With the climate science community showing signs of increasing interest in risk assessment, my team and I tried to reawaken the idea of a climate change risk assessment for heads of government. It would have to be short, holistic, and fearless in its communication of the worst that could happen.

We had the benefit of a prototype, produced by Chatham House as part of the third generation of the UK–China climate risk project that we had started in 2013.[11] This included some punchy figures. It said that if global emissions followed the trajectory set by countries' current targets, there would be a less than 1% chance of meeting the internationally agreed target of limiting warming to below 1.5°C. More than ten million people a year were likely to be exposed to heat stress exceeding the survivability threshold (likely to die outside), in the 2030s. The probability of synchronous crop failure in the top four maize producing countries, with devastating impacts for global food security, would rise from near zero now to an almost 50% chance of occurring at some point during the 2040s. The cascade of risks through natural and human systems was expected to drive unprecedented levels of crop failure, food insecurity, and migration, as well as increases in infectious diseases, political instability, and regional and international conflict. These and other nuggets of necessary bad news were packed into a dozen pages of plain English text and colourful charts.

The prototype did not pretend to be perfect, but it served two useful purposes. Where our contacts allowed, we used it to communicate climate risk to the top levels of government. At the same time, we used it to begin discussions in many countries, and between international institutions, about why a climate risk assessment for heads of government was needed and what it should look like.

Once again, we found that to many people in the climate change community, the need for risk assessment was not self-evident. I heard all the same objections that I had heard when I started out in 2013: 'Governments are more interested in the economic opportunity.' 'A negative message will just turn people off.' 'If you talk about bad things that will happen to other countries, they'll be offended.' And most reliably, 'Surely this exists already. Governments already know as much as they need to about the risks of climate change, don't they?'

Once again, I found an ally in a former government chief science adviser – someone who knew what it meant to bear the responsibility of communicating risk to a head of government faced with decisions on matters of life and death. This time it was Peter Gluckman, who had held that position in New Zealand from 2009 to 2018. When we asked for his support in a new initiative to improve the communication of climate change risk to heads of government, he immediately agreed. He recounted the experience of expert advice being given to his country's Prime Minister at the time of the Kaikoura earthquake in 2016 which had characteristics suggesting it was a foreshock for a larger quake which might affect the capital, Wellington. An expert had begun a detailed explanation of the situation, giving at once too much information, and too little. The Prime

Minister cut the discussion short. All he wanted to know was how serious was the threat, and what level of response was required. Should he tell people to stay at home, should he authorise some limited precautionary measures, or should he evacuate the entire city? In such a situation, the idea that the experts would withhold information on worst-case scenarios for fear that it might somehow be demotivating was obviously ridiculous.

Peter was now President of the International Science Council – an organisation whose several hundred members make up the world's largest network of scientific unions, associations, academies, and research councils, and that describes its aim as being to advance science as a global public good. His backing helped bring others on board. The World Meteorological Organization, the International Network for Government Science Advice, the World Climate Research Programme, and various other prestigious international and national groups joined the gang.

On 9 November 2021, 'Science and Innovation Day' at the UN climate change Conference of the Parties (COP26) talks in Glasgow, this new coalition of the willing committed to work together to improve the assessment and communication of climate change risk to world leaders. The Woodwell Climate Research Center, a US-based group of scientists with a long-standing commitment to informing decision-makers, bravely agreed to support this coalition in producing an annual climate change risk assessment for heads of government.[12]

Though little noticed as an outcome of COP26 – by that point in the second week of the conference, the media was already bored with new announcements – this could be the start of a process that is long overdue. Never before has such an authoritative group of institutions committed to properly communicate the risks of climate change to heads of government.

The task will be a difficult one. Cultural barriers in the science community are still strong, practices are ingrained, co-production is difficult, and coordinating academic institutions to produce something together is a tricky business at the best of times. On top of all that, the voices telling us that a risk assessment is unnecessary, counter-productive, or already available (and sometimes all three at once) will not go away.

Often when I hear these voices, I am reminded of a moment half-way through that first risk assessment project, when my bosses at the Foreign Office told me to give a written update to our Minister, Baroness Anelay, and ask her to decide whether we should continue. They were worried that if my ad hoc international coalition with its shoestring budget did a bad job on the report, we might be criticised for a poor use of public money, and equally worried that if we did a good job, it might be so shocking that other countries would complain at how their vulnerability to disaster had been exposed. They were quite right to tell me to bring these risks to the attention of Ministers, but to me this seemed like a no-win situation, so I was apprehensive. After all that work, drawing on the goodwill of so many scientists, philanthropists, and experts in other countries, would it all be called to a halt? I need not have worried. The response from Baroness Anelay's Private Office came through to my clunky civil service Blackberry as I sat on a train coming back from a visit to climate scientists at the Potsdam Institute in Germany. 'The Minister has read your submission. She considers that the greatest risk would be not to proceed.'

The same is surely true now. A risk assessment for heads of government may well be criticised, it might be unwanted, it can never be enough ... but why not try?

Reflecting on the intelligence community's failure to anticipate the terrorist attack on the World Trade Center, the 9/11 Commission wrote, 'The methods for detecting and then warning of surprise attack that the US government had so painstakingly developed in the decades after Pearl Harbor did not fail; instead, they were not really tried.'[13]

The same could be said, so far, about the communication of climate change risks to heads of government. That is the message of Part I of this book. In many fields, including public health, national security, finance, and engineering, principles and practices of risk assessment have been painstakingly developed. These have not failed in their application to climate change; instead, they have not yet really been tried. Instead of looking up at the dam, we are still making excuses for looking the other way.

If we want our leaders to respond adequately to the threat of climate change, then we should spare no effort in assessing and communicating the full scale of the risk. Undoubtedly, this will not on its own be enough to give us the five times faster decarbonisation of the global economy that we need. But without it, what hope can we have?

The pink boat at Oxford Circus was right: we should tell the truth.

PART II

ECONOMICS

9

WORSE THAN USELESS

The first part of this book was about how we understand the problem of climate change. The remaining two parts are concerned with what we do about it. Before we shift our focus completely, we will take a brief look at how economics has tried to build a bridge between problem and solutions. This involves a question of value: given our understanding of the problem of climate change, how hard is it worth trying to solve it?

Economics has tried to answer this question with an approach of beguiling simplicity. It works like this. Climate change will have costs, and the more climate change there is, the greater those costs will be. Limiting climate change also has costs, and the more we try to reduce global emissions, the more costly this will be. Cutting emissions is worth the effort as long as the cost of this action is less than the cost of the climate change it avoids. Beyond this point, it's not worth it. The point where the cost of a little more action to cut emissions is exactly equal to the cost of climate change it would avoid represents the 'optimal' response to the problem. For the best economic outcome, we should make this much effort, and no more.

The economist William Nordhaus is famous for this kind of analysis. In 2018, the economics profession gave him a Nobel Prize for it. His conclusion, though, is an odd one. He has estimated the 'optimal' level of effort in cutting emissions to be one that results in around 4°C of global temperature rise by the early decades of next century.[1] The IPCC describes the risks of this degree of climate change as 'high to very high', and as including '*substantial species extinction, large risks to global and regional food security, and the combination of high temperature and humidity compromising normal human activities, including growing food or working outdoors in some areas for parts of the year*'.[2] The World Bank has described the consequences of a 4°C temperature increase as 'devastating'.[3] Clearly, that is not quite the same as 'optimal'.

Climate change activists, when they first find out about Nordhaus's work, sometimes assume he is in the pay of fossil fuel companies and part of a global campaign of disinformation. I am quite sure he is not. But if he was trying to prevent action on climate change, he could hardly have done the job any more effectively.

Nordhaus reached a perverse conclusion because he made a perverse calculation. Let's take a look at his workings and see what he did.

ESTIMATING THE COSTS OF CLIMATE CHANGE: SPURIOUS PRECISION AND ARBITRARY CHOICES

In Part I of this book, we saw that many of the risks of climate change are deeply uncertain. The impact of a $3°C$ temperature increase on rice yields in Pakistan could be plus 23% or minus 24%, for example. Sea levels could rise ten metres in a few hundred years, or in a few thousand years. We might pass a tipping point that wipes out the Amazon forest and accelerates warming, or we might not. Scientists are unsure how likely these different outcomes are, and they disagree amongst themselves. No scientist would pretend they can put a precise number on any of those probabilities. If the scientists don't know, then the economists cannot possibly know.

If the direct impacts of climate change are uncertain, the indirect or systemic risks are even more so. If climate change makes parts of the world uninhabitable, will there be a globally managed relocation scheme for affected populations, or will there be wars? Security analysts will tell you what they think, but they won't pretend to know the magnitude or the probability of any of the possible outcomes. If the security analysts can't do that, neither can the economists.

Faced with these fundamental uncertainties, what does Nordhaus do? One of his earliest papers shows his approach most transparently. In a table of the costs and benefits of climate change, entries include a range (the impact of climate change on farming: from minus ten billion dollars to plus ten billion dollars), several precise estimates (less use of 'non-electric space heating': a benefit of $1.16bn), and five entries without a number: three question marks, one 'small plus or minus', and one 'plus'. Amazingly, Nordhaus adds up all these entries and comes out with a precise answer: an estimated total net cost to the US economy of $6.23bn, or 0.26% of GDP.[4]

You do not have to be a mathematics teacher to know that you can't add up question marks. When I was preparing my first lecture on this subject, I asked my daughter, then seven years old, to add up two numbers and a question mark. 'It doesn't make sense' was her prompt response.

A mathematics teacher would be even more critical, because stating your answer with this degree of precision implies you have a lot of confidence in it. If you say your estimate of the cost of climate change to the US economy is \$6.23bn, it means you are fairly sure that the true value is somewhere between \$6.225bn and \$6.235bn. But just one of the entries in the calculation, the impact on farming, was a range of minus ten billion to plus ten billion. And others were question marks. There is no justification for anything more precise than a question mark as the answer.

False precision in the face of uncertainty is not the only problem. Within this calculation, many hidden value judgements have been made. Climate change will cause the loss of species, the loss of lands that people call home, and the loss of human life. How should any of those things be valued? The economist can choose a method of valuation – for example, valuing an island country by the size of its GDP, or using the 'statistical value of a human life' to measure the cost of deaths – but there are many possible approaches to valuation, and the choice between them is unavoidably arbitrary. There is no means of objectively measuring these things; their value depends on your point of view.

Similarly, how should we value the future compared to the present? Economists use a discount rate to value things in the future less than things in the present. There may be objective ways to decide this rate if you are a business considering an investment. But if you are a society considering the future habitability of the planet, or a parent considering the prospects of your children, this rate can be anything you want. You might decide you value the future more highly than the present.

The Harvard economist Martin Weitzman showed that if you take into account the possibility of catastrophic outcomes of climate change, and allow for a diversity of preferences in regard to how much those outcomes should be avoided, then there is no upper limit that can be placed on the costs.[5] The total cost of climate change is somewhere between nought and infinity, and you or I or the bus driver have as much authority to pick a number in the middle as does William Nordhaus. Weitzman readily admitted that this conclusion was obvious, but he took the trouble to prove it using economic theory and algebra, for those who would find that more convincing.

ESTIMATING THE COSTS OF ACTION: MORE GUESSWORK

What about the costs of action to avoid dangerous climate change? These are uncertain too. A decade ago, almost nobody predicted what the costs of solar and wind power would be today. Today, we cannot say what the costs of zero-emissions industry and agriculture will be in future.

Economists like Nordhaus have assumed that reducing emissions will necessarily be costly, and that the more we reduce, the greater the costs will be. Our experience so far tells a different story. Solar panels and wind turbines now generate electricity more cheaply than gas or coal. To begin with, developing those technologies cost a lot of money. But now that we have them, they will go on giving us cheaper electricity forever.

Some economists now think that on balance, the whole global transition to a zero-emissions economy will have more benefits than costs, even if we assign no value to avoiding dangerous climate change. The debate is not settled, so for now we must admit that we do not know whether this side of the equation is a plus or a minus. Nordhaus's estimates of the cost of action are as unreliable as his estimates of the cost of climate change are meaningless.

THE 'OPTIMAL' RESPONSE

Even if we were confident in our estimates of the costs of climate change and of the actions to avoid it, putting them together as Nordhaus does to determine our 'optimal' level of effort would not actually make sense.

If you look at the statistics for house fires in your area, you can work out the likelihood of your house burning down in the next year – assuming you are as careful as your average neighbour. You can also estimate how much losing your house and belongings would cost you. Multiplying these two numbers together gives you an expected loss for the coming year. If you compare this to the cost of insurance, the cost of insurance will definitely be higher than your expected loss. We know this must be true, because otherwise the insurance companies would not make money. The conclusion of a cost–benefit analysis, therefore, is that you should not buy insurance.

So why do we all buy insurance? As the economist Frank Ackerman has pointed out, decisions about risk management are usually based more on the assessment of worst-case outcomes than on central estimates. We buy insurance in full knowledge that we will probably lose money on it, because we want to avoid an outcome that we would consider intolerable. The same could be said for decisions about large opportunities: people buy lottery tickets despite expecting to lose money, because the good outcome, if it happened, would be transformative.

Climate change is a risk management problem, so we should approach it the same way we do insurance. That means understanding the risk and deciding what we are willing to pay to reduce the risk to whatever level we consider tolerable. A cost–benefit analysis, even if it were possible, would be irrelevant.

In summary, Nordhaus reached his conclusion about the 'optimal' level of effort to make on climate change by taking an arbitrary number and an unreliable number and combining them in an inappropriate way. No wonder the result is perverse. It is obviously useless, but does it matter?

WORSE THAN USELESS

I believe it does matter. This kind of economic analysis is unhelpful to the public, to policymakers, and to the economics profession itself.

It is unhelpful to public understanding of the risk of climate change because it trivialises the problem. Nicholas Stern, one of the most famous climate change economists, has explained why.[6] First, economic models measure what is measurable. The largest risks are the most uncertain, and they are often simply left out of the calculation. Second, what data we do have on the costs of climate change relate mainly to the present, or to the near future. To estimate the costs at higher degrees of climate change, we have to somehow extrapolate. This is done using an entirely made-up equation.[7] (As the physicist Doyne Farmer once said, 'Economists pull these equations out of their arses.') Normally these equations err on the side of underestimating the risk. Third, the models typically assume that economic growth will continue unaffected by climate change – despite the plentiful evidence that climate change could damage land, labour, and capital, and leave us all poorer in future than we are now. Under this assumption, the economic costs of climate change will always appear trivial, because humanity will always be assumed to be many times richer in future.

In other words, when economists estimate the costs of climate change as a proportion of global GDP, they are taking an unrealistically small number (near-term costs of climate change), extrapolating from it in an arbitrary way (to get future costs), and then dividing it by an unrealistically large number (supposedly unaffected future GDP). Hence the Organisation for Economic Co-operation and Development (OECD) tells us that the costs of inaction on climate change 'could be as high as 14% of average world consumption per capita'.[8] Similarly, the IPCC has said that annual economic losses from 2°C of climate change could be between 0.2% and 2% of global income – which is roughly equivalent to saying that the total economic impact of climate change of 2°C would be the world reaching a level of prosperity in 2051 that it would otherwise have reached in 2050. If these estimates were correct, we would have no need to worry about climate change at all. Stern concludes that '*Many scientists are telling us that our models are, grossly, underestimating the risks. In these circumstances, it is irresponsible to act as if the economic models currently dominating policy analysis represent a sensible central case.*'

Unfortunately, many people still take this sort of economic analysis at face value and assume it is sensible. I have met philanthropists who concluded on this basis that climate change was relatively unimportant as a cause, and that they should instead concentrate on the risks of artificial intelligence. In government, I have seen estimates such as that of the OECD repeatedly included in briefings to ministers. As a civil servant, it is easier to cite the findings of an authoritative institution than to argue that they are bullshit.

If this kind of analysis is unhelpful to the public, it is even less helpful to policymakers. Not only does it trivialise a catastrophic risk; it also pretends to tell us the precise level of effort that we should put into all our policies. Nordhaus's model and others like it have been used to calculate the 'social cost of carbon'. This is what you get if you divide the total costs of climate change by the number of tons of carbon emissions to be avoided, at the 'optimal' level of action. It supposedly tells us the value to society of reducing each ton of carbon. This value has been used by many governments to assess the cost-effectiveness of policies to reduce emissions – in other words, to help them decide whether to do something or not.[9]

The problem, as we have seen, is that this value is entirely arbitrary. In November 2013, the Whitehouse Council of Economic Advisers updated its official estimate of the social cost of carbon from $38 per tonne to $37 per tonne, saying that this had been reached through a process of 'rigorous evaluation of costs and benefits', 'using the best science available'. But at the same time, the best science available was saying that the social cost of carbon could be anything between nought and infinity, depending on your point of view. A made-up number is no help in designing policy. It does not tell us whether a carbon tax set at that level would have any useful effect. We might just as well roll some dice. If we believe that this number is telling us anything meaningful, we are likely to make mistakes.

Finally, never mind the public and policymakers, analysis such as this is unhelpful to the economics profession itself because it undermines public trust. When people see spurious precision, they smell a rat.

When I joined the Department of Energy and Climate Change, the UK was in the middle of one of the most contentious public debates in living memory: whether or not to leave the EU. Much was perceived to be at stake: trading relations with our closest neighbours, control over migration, and the political and cultural identity of the country. The government of the day tried to win the argument for staying in the EU using economic analysis. The Treasury published reports that it asserted were 'rigorous and objective', saying the cost of leaving would be £4,300 per year for the average British household, that unemployment could rise by up to 820,000 people, and that house prices could fall by up to 18%.[10] The OECD published similar estimates.[11]

Just like Nordhaus's economic analysis of climate change, these apparently precise estimates covered up huge uncertainties. What new trading agreements would the UK manage to negotiate, and how long would this take? How would the gain of being able to make more policies independently compare to the loss of influence in setting standards within the world's largest market? In all honesty, nobody knew whether the economic consequences of Brexit would be large or small, positive or negative.

In the final month of campaigning ahead of the referendum, the then Justice Secretary, Michael Gove, famously commented that 'people in this country have had enough of experts'.[12] His words caused a storm of criticism from those who felt he was endorsing a descent into populism. But a survey conducted eight months after the referendum suggested that he was at least half right.[13] Whether old or young, male or female, northern or southern, rich or poor, Labour or Conservative supporting, Leave or Remain voting, the British people distrusted economists. People in almost every demographic gave economists a negative trust rating, mostly somewhere between minus 10% and minus 30%. Did this represent a rejection of all forms of expertise? Not at all. The same survey found high levels of trust in scientists, with scores of plus 40% to plus 70%. The people of this country had not had enough of experts, but they had, apparently, had enough of economists.

These three problems – trivialisation of risk, arbitrary guidance of policy, and undermining of public trust – all lead me to agree with the assessment of the MIT economics professor Robert Pindyck: that economic models such as those of William Nordhaus are not just bad, they are 'worse than useless'.[14] As Pindyck says, analyses based on these models 'create a perception of knowledge and precision that is illusory, and can fool policy-makers into thinking that the forecasts the models generate have some kind of scientific legitimacy'.[15] Personally, I would prefer that none of us were fooled.

WHY THE WILD GOOSE CHASE?

In many important areas of personal life and public policy, we accept that important decisions must be made under conditions of uncertainty. We fund our armed forces, despite not knowing if they will fight any wars. We pay for our children's education, whether through our taxes or privately, without any certain knowledge of the benefit they will derive from it. In both these cases, we have to make some decision about the level of resources to commit, but we do not expect there to be any 'optimal' level that can be magically divined.

Climate change need not be any different. We could rely on scientists and others with relevant expertise to inform us of the scale of the risk, as described in Part I of this book, without trying to express that risk as a single number. We could (and we do) discuss how much we care about this risk in public debate, with all perspectives on value considered explicitly, not resolved implicitly by an arbitrary equation in a model. We could decide the level of effort to go into each policy based on what each policy is intended to achieve, with no need for a magic number as a reference point.

Given this, why have some economists felt the need to go on the wild goose chase of trying to quantify the unquantifiable, and to find the perfectly objective solution to an inherently subjective problem? Why, when the fallacy of Nordhaus's approach was fully exposed as early as 1994,[16] did the economics profession give him a Nobel Prize more than twenty years later? And why have institutions like the OECD and the White House Council of Economic Advisers continued to present this analysis as authoritative, and governments continued to use it to inform policy, when experts such as Nick Stern have said it would be irresponsible to treat it as sensible?

To answer these questions, we have to dig into the muddy ground of economic history, to find the roots of Nordhaus's thinking. This is the subject of the next chapter. Unearthing those roots is useful, because we can see where else they lead.

10

THE ALLOCATION OF SCARCE RESOURCES

In the late 1850s, while John Tyndall was discovering the greenhouse effect and establishing the basics of the science of climate change, Léon Walras, a Frenchman who had failed in attempts to become a mathematician, an engineer, and a novelist, began laying the foundations of what has become the dominant form of economics. While Tyndall's discovery has stood up to scientific scrutiny, Walras's theories have not. Despite this, they have gone on to exert a pervasive influence on economic thought. Right now, these ideas are getting in the way of an effective response to climate change.

My account of how this has happened and where it has led us will be brief, and undoubtedly oversimplified. Economics is a diverse field, and a huge amount of good and helpful work is being done by economists. My criticism, given from the perspective of a recipient of economic advice, is aimed at a specific set of ideas which I believe are mistaken and unhelpful, at least when they are applied to the problems we face in dealing with climate change. I will call this set of ideas 'equilibrium economics', because a label is useful as a point of reference, and because I believe the idea of equilibrium is at the centre of our problems.

Some readers, especially those educated in economics, are likely to see this equilibrium economics as a straw man, a caricature that is unrepresentative of the state of the discipline. I must emphasise: the state of the discipline is not my primary concern. My concern is with what is being used – what kind of economics is influencing policy. If you are inclined to think that equilibrium economics is a straw man, then I ask you to suspend your disbelief while we look at what this straw man is doing. He does not represent the diversity of academic research, but he does claim authority, set the terms of public debate, and directly influence the decisions of governments. In the next few chapters, I will outline how his influence is actively unhelpful in our efforts to counter climate change. If after considering these examples you have no interest in defending this effigy, then I will invite you to join me in throwing it onto the bonfire, the compost heap, or another receptacle of your choice.

Another way of looking at it is that the ideas of equilibrium economics work well enough when they are applied within the appropriate domain: situations where it is reasonable to assume that nothing about the structure of the economy is going to change. When they are applied outside their appropriate domain, they give us the wrong answers – as we shall see.

***

THE ECONOMY AS A MACHINE

The economists who have done the most to shape our current understanding originally set out to describe the economy as a machine. This was no accident.

In the seventeenth century, Isaac Newton showed how a set of fixed laws could explain the motion of the Sun, Moon, and planets, as well as the behaviour of objects on Earth. These discoveries and others like them were so profound that they led not only to a revolution in science, but also to a new philosophy. People began to see the Universe as a great machine, no longer unknowable, but understandable and predictable with precision. God was imagined no longer as a shepherd, but as a clockmaker.[1]

Further advances in physics reinforced this mechanistic worldview. Theories of electricity and magnetism allowed more natural phenomena to be explained and predicted, and enabled the creation of new technologies and industries. As the first industrial revolution unfolded in the late eighteenth and early nineteenth centuries, the spread of machines into everyday life made the idea of God the clockmaker all the more plausible.

This was the landscape of ideas that surrounded Léon Walras when he turned his attention to economics in 1859. Walras thought it ought to be possible to create a theory of economics as scientific and precise as the theories of physics. If the Universe was a giant machine, then the economy must be a machine too. Why should we not be able to understand and predict its behaviour?

Walras borrowed a concept from physics to use as the basis for his theory of a mechanistic and predictable economy. The concept was that of equilibrium.

In physics, equilibrium is a state of balance. A hot mug of tea will cool until it is the same temperature as its surroundings; a state of thermal equilibrium will then exist between the tea, the mug, and the air. Water in a valley will flow to the lowest point, collecting there in a lake if there is no outlet to the sea. The water in the lake is stationary because it has reached a point of stable equilibrium with its physical surroundings. The Earth is in a form of equilibrium as it circles the Sun: the attraction of gravity is just enough to keep it at a constant distance, neither falling into the Sun nor flying off into outer space. In these physical examples, the concept of equilibrium helps us make predictions: we know what temperature the tea will reach; we can predict where the water in the valley will end up; and we can calculate the speed of the Earth's orbit.

Walras thought that the concept of equilibrium could be similarly useful for economics. He proposed that an equilibrium must exist in a market, balancing the forces of supply and demand. If people in the market did not have exactly what they wanted, they would trade with each other until this balance was reached. If the quantities of supply and demand for any product in the market were known, then the price at which that product would be traded could be predicted.

As Eric Beinhocker describes in *The Origin of Wealth*, contemporaries of Walras, and others who followed, built on this idea.[2] William Stanley Jevons showed that if people had different preferences and finite resources, then trade between them would inevitably lead the market to equilibrium. Vilfredo Pareto argued that if everyone in the market entered into any trades that would make them better off (or at least as well off as they were before), and if nobody made any trades that would leave them worse off, then the equilibrium that the market reached would represent a kind of 'optimum'. From this state, nobody could be made better off without making someone else worse off. This must therefore represent the best possible allocation of economic resources. Strikingly, this theory tells us a market will reach its best possible state automatically and inevitably.[f]

Neoclassical economists took these ideas further over the following century. In 1954, Kenneth Arrow and Gérard Debreu showed that Walras's idea of 'general equilibrium' could be applied not just to a single market, but to the whole economy. Because some goods can be replaced with others, and some are more useful when brought together with others, all markets are linked. With the assumption of certain conditions, Arrow and Debreu showed that markets would inter-act in a way that inevitably led the whole economy towards an 'optimal' equilibrium state.

---

[f] For this and the summary of the development of the ideas of equilibrium economics contained in following paragraphs, I draw on Eric Beinhocker's *The Origin of Wealth*, Ch. 2.

While the early development of equilibrium economics was motivated by a desire to be scientific, other cultural forces supported its later entrenchment. During the Cold War, some political leaders and public intellectuals were attracted by the notion that these theories proved that free markets were the best way to achieve economic success, inevitably better than anything communism or socialism could offer. Others may have seen an opportunity to justify a hands-off approach to government that would not disturb the patterns of distribution of wealth from which they benefited. For these and other reasons, the conclusions of equilibrium economics have been overstated and over-interpreted, put to uses for which their originators cannot fairly be held accountable.

We find ourselves now in a situation where the set of ideas launched on the world by Walras has achieved a remarkable position of dominance. Central banks and finance ministries rely on equilibrium models. Debates within the pages of the world's most prestigious economics journals take place largely within the equilibrium paradigm. Universities teach the set of ideas of equilibrium economics as the foundation of the discipline, and typically consign alternative perspectives to courses on the history of economics.[3] Equilibrium economics dominates the policy analysis done for governments and by governments, although the extent of this dominance varies between countries. In the UK civil service, an economist applying for a new job or a promotion will have to answer questions on the application of economic theory to policy. The 'correct' answer according to equilibrium economics must be given, for the candidate to pass the test.

Policy on climate change is no exception. The work of William Nordhaus that we reviewed in the previous chapter follows in the intellectual footsteps of Walras. Nordhaus assumes that economic problems have an optimal solution that can be calculated objectively and precisely, just like the speed of the Earth around the Sun. This is why he goes on the wild goose chase of searching for the optimal social response to climate change. He finds his solution at the point where the costs of further reducing emissions are perfectly balanced by the benefits of avoiding further climate change – a state of equilibrium. The acceptance of this set of ideas runs so deep that Nordhaus is awarded the Nobel Prize, despite the obvious fallacy of his methods and the perversity of his conclusions.

The ideas of equilibrium economics have become so pervasive that we may no longer even notice that we are applying them, or that we are making important decisions based on the assumption that the economy is like a machine.

THE LANGUAGE OF SCIENCE, BUT NOT THE METHOD

In seeking to make economics more 'scientific', Walras adopted the language of science, but not the method.

The language of science, much of the time, is mathematics. Walras was determined in his efforts to make economics more mathematical, and in this he succeeded. Whereas previously the discipline had been known as 'political economy', and many of the greats had taken a philosophical approach to theorising, from Walras onwards mathematical equations took up a more prominent place.

The intellectual descendants of Walras have tended to share his admiration of mathematics and his disregard for verbal reasoning. Robert Lucas, regarded as the leading theorist of neoclassical macroeconomics, wrote in his memoir, 'Like so many others in my cohort, I internalised [the view] that if I couldn't formulate a problem in economic theory mathematically, I didn't know what I was doing. I came to the position that mathematical analysis is not one of many ways of doing economic theory; it is the only way. Economic theory is mathematical analysis. Everything else is just pictures and talk.'[4]

To make the mathematics solvable, Walras and his followers had to continually make assumptions about how the economy worked. Walras's original theory of equilibrium relied on the assumption that people acted in a deterministic way with the sole aim of maximising their economic welfare. He also had to assume that an auction took place to determine the prices of all the goods in the market. Jevons's proof that the market would automatically reach equilibrium relied on assumptions about 'diminishing returns' – the idea that each additional input to production yields a progressively smaller increase in output. Pareto's argument that this equilibrium would represent a best possible state required the assumption that nobody would ever make a trade that left them worse off.

As the scope of the equilibrium theory expanded, ever more unlikely assumptions were needed to support it. Arrow and Debreu's proof that the whole economy would inevitably come to a perfect equilibrium state required the assumptions that every participant in the market has at least some of every commodity, that they know the probabilities of all possible future states of the world, and that they decide what to do by computing the best economic outcome for themselves from among all these possible states. It also had to be assumed that futures markets, where the right to buy or sell a commodity could be traded, existed for all products and services.[5]

Generally speaking, nobody believes these assumptions are true. Walras knew perfectly well that there was no celestial auctioneer governing all the trading in the market. Early critics of equilibrium economics recognised that people do not make decisions by performing elaborate computations to calculate the best possible option among all possible alternatives. In 1910, the economist E. H. Downey wrote:

> Deliberation, reasoned choice, plays but a minor part in the affairs of men. Habit, not calculation, governs the greater part of all our acts.... Calculation is difficult work. It is much easier to act on a suggestion than to weigh alternatives. The path of least resistance in buying a necktie is to enter a shop where neckwear is attractively displayed and select the cravat insinuatingly recommended by the engaging salesman. To make an exhaustive canvass of shapes, colors, prices, and of alternative uses of the purchase-money is far more tedious and wearisome.[6]

I could not agree more, as my wife will testify. Downey's observations have since been rediscovered by behavioural economics.

Similarly, nobody believes that people really know the probabilities of all possible future states of the world; on the contrary, they have deep uncertainty about many things, and total ignorance about others.[g] Nobody thinks that futures markets exist for all products. Most people recognise that power, as well as price, matters in the economy: sometimes a worker accepts a wage cut, or a bill-payer accepts a rate increase, even though they would rather not. Since the 1930s if not before, we have known that the 'law' of diminishing returns does not always hold. The aircraft engineer Theodore Paul Wright found evidence of an opposite effect: the more aircraft he produced, the fewer hours of labour he needed to make each one. Many businesses in the modern economy, including social media and technology firms, experience increasing returns to scale.

The method of science involves forming a hypothesis, identifying predictions that logically follow from it, and testing these against observations. If the hypothesis turns out to be contradicted by the observational evidence, it must be abandoned. If a theory depends for its validity on certain assumptions, and those assumptions are contradicted by the evidence, the theory should be dropped.

Walras and his followers should have known this. Once it became clear how far their assumptions differed from reality, they should have abandoned the theory that depended on them. In any situations where

---

[g] As the evolutionary economists Richard Nelson and Sidney Winter have pointed out in *An Evolutionary Theory of Economic Change*, if everyone did have perfect knowledge about the future, there would be no need for economic analysis.

those assumptions did not hold, there was no reason to believe that markets or the economy existed in a state of equilibrium. There was no reason, in fact, to believe that the economy was deterministic and predictable, like a machine.

But Walras preferred the language of the science to the method, and on top of unrealistic assumptions, he constructed made-up equations. These were designed to be self-consistent and solvable, not to reliably describe reality. When Walras wrote to a scientist he admired, Henri Poincaré, to ask for feedback on his work, Poincaré wrote back to him to say that his theory contained 'arbitrary functions', and that any conclusions deriving from these arbitrary functions would be 'devoid of all interest'.[7] Over a century later, this criticism is echoed by the economist Robert Pindyck in his observation that developers of economic models of climate change 'simply make up arbitrary functional forms'.[8] Pindyck's view was the same as that of Poincaré: any conclusions derived in this way would be useless.

One of the most famous and influential economists of the twentieth century, Milton Friedman, strayed so far from the scientific method that he argued it did not matter how unrealistic assumptions were, as long as the theories on which they were based made correct predictions.[9] This is obviously absurd. Suppose I have a theory that assumes the Earth is flat, and I use this to predict that people in all parts of the world will feel themselves to be standing the right way up. The prediction is successful, but this does not mean my flat-Earth theory is correct. Observation that the Earth is spherical shows that the assumption is false. My theory therefore has no explanatory power and should be abandoned.

Lack of understanding of the scientific method persists in economics today. Some economists argue that unrealistic assumptions are necessary aids to understanding, like the simplified diagram of the London Underground rail system in its official map.[10] This confuses simplification with misrepresentation. The fact that the map shows the rail lines as straight instead of wiggly, and that it has spaced them out to make them easier to see, instead of showing their exact geographical paths, is a simplification: it does not affect the validity of what the map sets out to explain. I can still successfully plot a course from my home to the office. If the map showed the lines meeting each other in the wrong places, if it showed stations that did not in fact exist, if it implied that tube trains could fly, or arrive instantaneously at their destinations, these would be misrepresentations. The map would no longer have explanatory power, and if I tried to follow it, I would get lost.

The untruth of the basic assumptions of equilibrium economics – or at least, their inapplicability in the majority of situations – is so readily acknowledged that rather than defend the theory, some economists now seem to suggest it is irrelevant to their work. In a debate carried out in the pages of British newspapers and magazines in 2018, one economics professor wrote, 'I literally can't think of a single [academic economist] for whom the "tenets of neoclassicism shape their day-to-day work".... Most of modern economics is... empirical testing, often using new sources of data, addressing questions of immediate importance and relevance to policymakers, citizens and businesses.'[11] But theory and practice are not so easy to disentangle. As the historian of science Thomas Kuhn has documented, theories determine the questions that are asked in experiments, the methods that are used, and the way in which empirical findings are interpreted. Or as Einstein supposedly put it, 'It is the theory that decides what can be observed.'

The theory of equilibrium economics has made us see the economy as a machine. Looking at the world through this lens has made it far more difficult for us to clearly see the behaviours of the economy that are not machine-like: the processes of creation and change.

BLIND TO CREATION

The earliest economists recognised that their discipline must consider at least two quite distinct problems: wealth creation, and wealth allocation. The problem of allocation is that of how to 'divide up the pie'. The problem of creation is that of how to make the pie in the first place.

The Greek scholar Xenophon addressed these two challenges in his book *Oeconomicus*, written around 2,400 years ago, which gave its name to the field of economics. In the first half of his book, he concentrated on the question of how a household should manage the resources it has. In his view, this had much to do with how a gentleman should teach his wife to manage a budget, do the shopping, and control the slaves. In the second half of the book, he focused on the question of how the household could increase its resources. This had mainly to do with farming, since that was assumed to be the business of a gentleman.

The economist Jesus Huerta de Soto defines these two challenges as different forms of economic efficiency. 'Allocative' or 'static' efficiency refers to how well existing economic resources are used at a fixed point in time. 'Dynamic' efficiency refers to how well new resources are created over time, through processes such as innovation, improvement, investment, and growth.[12] He writes that 'the tradition of clearly distinguishing between the two different concepts of efficiency, the static [allocative] and the dynamic, survived even until the Middle Ages', but that thanks to Walras's remodelling of economics on mechanical physics, after the nineteenth century 'the idea of dynamic efficiency was almost entirely forgotten in economics'.[13]

It seems likely that this forgetting had to do with the determination to express economics in the language of mathematics.[14] Problems of allocation have mathematical solutions: if five people want to share an apple pie equally, I can work out how much each of them should get. Problems of creation do not lend themselves so easily to mathematical description. There is no set of equations that can describe how to make an apple pie successfully. Important steps in the process will need to be described qualitatively. The creation problem has no optimal solution: we can make better or worse pies, but there is no such thing as the best possible pie. Faced with this problem, Walras set the challenge of creation to one side. He assumed that the set of goods existing in the economy was fixed and unchanging. Instead, he concentrated on the challenge of allocation: what prices would be set, and what trades would take place, to balance supply and demand.[15]

What was set aside was no small thing. The set of goods in the economy is not fixed; on the contrary, it is constantly changing, and constantly growing. New technologies, goods, and services are being created all the time. These new possibilities are what lead to the improvement of our living standards over time. We surely have a great interest in understanding how this process of creation works, and how it may be steered or strengthened.

The phenomenon of economic growth has not, of course, been ignored. But it could be said to have been more taken for granted than actually explained and understood. It is beyond the scope of this book and, thankfully, not necessary for our purposes to explore in detail the validity of economic growth theories. Suffice it to say that the modern era's two leading theorists of economic growth both seem somewhat dissatisfied with the state of their art.

Robert Solow created the neoclassical model of economic growth by assuming that the economy remains in a state of equilibrium, while growth is injected into it by the external factor of technological progress. The theory does not explain how that technological progress comes about. Solow has acknowledged that there is 'some truth' in the criticism that the neoclassical model 'is a theory of growth that leaves the main factor in economic growth unexplained'.[16,h]

---

[h] Solow has expressed support for the principles of endogenous growth theory – where growth is recognised to come from inside the economy – but commented in his 1987

Paul Romer, a former Chief Economist of the World Bank and the leading architect of endogenous growth theory (where growth comes from inside the economy), seems even less happy. He writes that macroeconomics has gone backwards for the past three decades, and describes the current approach to the discipline as a 'pseudoscience' and 'post-real' on account of its 'noncommittal relationship with the truth'.[17]

This failure to explain the processes of creation matters to our ability to address climate change. Reducing global emissions will require fast and widespread technological innovation. By one estimate, around half of the necessary reduction will need to be achieved using technologies that have not yet been commercialised.[18] An economic theory that does not understand the process of creation cannot give us reliable guidance on how such rapid innovation can be achieved.

BLIND TO CHANGE

Change in the economy is as ubiquitous as creation. Not only do prices change, as demand and supply fluctuate; technologies, goods, and services come in and out of existence. Business models change, infrastructure changes, regulations change, markets change, societies change.

Nobody is able to predict these future changes, or even to know the full range of future possibilities. The presence of this uncertainty makes it impossible for a person or a business to calculate a perfect solution to an economic problem. As the economist Brian Arthur has put it, 'there cannot be a logical solution to a problem that is not logically defined'. The best anyone can do is to form a belief or hypothesis about which strategies are likely to be successful, and then to constantly adapt, discard, and replace strategies as new information becomes available. Each person's actions affect the context encountered by others, so uncertainty generates further uncertainty, change leads to more change. Disequilibrium is the natural state of the economy.[19]

For an analogy, consider a game of football. In this carefully structured activity, the rules are fixed, and the entities on the pitch – ball, goals, and players (ignoring substitutions) – are unchanging. Even in this relatively

Nobel Prize lecture that, in practice, all the models of endogenous growth 'rest at some key point on an essentially arbitrary linearity assumption, on the claim that the rate of growth of this is a function of the level of that. . . . Of course, such a claim can be true, but the ones I have seen have been neither empirically verified nor overwhelmingly plausible *a priori*.'

static environment, the players and the teams never stop trying new strategies and tactics in their attempts to beat each other. A '*situation in which nobody has any immediate reason to change their actions, so that the status quo can continue*' – as the state of equilibrium is defined in economics[20] – never arises.

Similarly, trading in the financial markets never stops, and the invention of new financial strategies never stops, as traders keep trying to outperform the market. And in the even less structured game of the open economy, entrepreneurs, innovators, businesses, and investors never stop searching for new ways to create opportunities, exploit advantages, and beat their competitors. The turbulent reality of the economy bears little resemblance to the static and predictable machine imagined by equilibrium economics.

Change in the economy, like growth, has not been ignored, but neither has it been well understood by the mainstream. Those who pioneered thinking about structural change in the economy – such as Keynes, with his theories about how government spending could influence employment; Schumpeter, on technological change; and Hyman Minsky, on financial instability – did so by departing from the equilibrium paradigm. The dominance of equilibrium economics over recent decades has meant that we have made less use of their ideas, and less progress in building on them, that we could have done.

The economist Nicholas Stern, writing about the economics that informs public policy, says that 'The study of public economics has not, in its foundations, ignored processes of change but I think it is fair to say that they have been either on the margins or much less central than they should have been.' He writes that the standard approach has been one of 'comparative statics', comparing predicted equilibrium outcomes under different policies. It has not been a study of dynamics, which would look at how change happens, how it affects people along the way, and how it influences what is possible in the future.[21]

Leaving the study of change on the margins was not helpful when it came to anticipating the global financial crisis of 2007–2008. Most governments, central banks, and academic economists failed to see it coming. They were not helped by their most commonly used models, which assume the economy is in a state of general equilibrium and are therefore incapable of simulating or predicting any other possible states that it might be in. To make these models produce anything roughly resembling realistic behaviour, they have to be subjected to arbitrarily defined and randomly generated external 'shocks'. Paul Romer, the growth theorist cited above who was formerly Chief Economist of the World Bank, has described these 'imaginary forces' in the models as 'trolls', 'gremlins', and 'phlogiston', to highlight how they are entirely made-up.[22] None of these models could predict a global financial crisis because their design had already excluded its possibility.

By analogy, imagine you had a weather model that predicted every day would be sunny and windless, with the same atmospheric pressure and temperature. The only variations in your model happened as a result of you randomly poking it with a stick. You would not expect this model to be able to predict a thunderstorm.

The structural changes that we need to make in the economy to avoid dangerous climate change are far deeper than anything that happened as a result of the global financial crisis. We need what the IPCC has described as '*rapid and far-reaching transitions in energy, land, urban and infrastructure (including transport and buildings), and industrial systems ... unprecedented in terms of scale*'.[23] This could not be further from a 'situation in which nobody has any immediate reason to change their actions, so that the status quo can continue'.

Government policy will be critical to achieving these changes. Policy will be informed by economic analysis, and this analysis will be shaped by economic theory. How we understand the economy therefore matters to the future of human civilisation. And to be clear, what matters in this context is not the cutting edge of academic research – whether somebody somewhere is replacing one of Paul Romer's trolls or gremlins with something less arbitrary is scarcely relevant. What matters is how theory is understood, interpreted, and put into practice to inform policy decisions.

As we enter the age of the Anthropocene, where human activity is becoming the dominant force that shapes our environment, we are still seeing the economy as a machine. Theory that should have been discarded a century ago is still being used to inform policy decisions. Economic efficiency is defined in allocative terms – how to share out the pie – while the understanding of creation and change has been left on the sidelines.[24] The models used to guide governments in responding to climate change are ones in which large, structural changes, 'the guts of the story, are essentially assumed away'.[25]

This cannot be satisfactory. What do we have to do to put the guts back in?

11

THE CONFIGURATION OF ABUNDANCE

If the economy is not a machine after all, then what is it? For economics to help us understand creation and change, we will need a different metaphor. In this chapter, I describe a new way of understanding the economy, which I believe holds great promise. We will then explore in following chapters how the shift from the old to the new understanding of economics results in entirely different conclusions about how best to confront the threat of climate change.

THE SEEDS OF A NEW APPROACH

The first indications that we might not be living in a clockwork Universe came from physics itself. Newtonian mechanics had proved immensely successful in explaining and predicting the motion of objects, including the planets. But as well as answering old questions, Newton's work opened up new ones. How, for example, could you predict the motion of three interacting gravitational objects of comparable mass?

Two centuries after Newton defined the question, the nineteenth-century French mathematician Henri Poincaré – he who had responded disparagingly to Walras's made-up equations – arrived at a surprising answer: that there was no answer. Poincaré proved that the problem has no analytical solution. The best you can do, if you want to predict the motion of the three objects, is to simulate it – to calculate positions and forces again and again, in an iterative process that has no end.[1] This was a profound discovery, as it showed that not everything in the Universe was predictable.

Nearly a century later, in the 1960s, the American meteorologist Edward Lorenz discovered the same problem in his efforts to predict the weather. He found it was impossible to make long-term predictions. Immeasurably small differences in initial conditions led to completely different outcomes after a relatively short period of time, and weather systems could go on changing indefinitely without ever repeating themselves. No analytical solutions existed; simulation was the best form of prediction. We are used to this now. We know our weather forecasters cannot tell us precisely what the weather will be at any point in the future, but with the aid of some large computers, and over a short enough time horizon, they can simulate its behaviour and tell us what it is most likely to do.

At the same time, Lorenz noticed that there were patterns in what he was seeing. Although the new field of research that his work inspired was known for a while as 'chaos theory', he saw that the behaviour of the weather was not completely random. It displayed recognisable patterns, structures, and forms of order. This meant that while it might be impossible to predict precisely or over long time-periods, it was not necessarily impossible to understand.

A decade later, biologists found that with the new mathematics discovered by Lorenz, they could understand for the first time why the size of some animal populations appeared to alternate between high and low values. Previously they had been looking for equilibrium solutions, and none had been able to explain what was observed. Now, by studying the internal dynamics of the population, they could see how its unstable behaviour naturally arose.[2]

Lorenz's discovery of 'chaos' led to the emergence of a new field of study of complex systems. A 'system' is a set of entities that, through their interactions, form an identifiable whole. A 'complex' system is one that has many interacting components and as a result, has behaviour that is difficult to predict. Examples include a living cell, the human brain, an organism, a forest, a hurricane, a transport network, a city, three big lumps of rock in space, and the Universe.

This new way of thinking about the world has not only revolutionised physics and biology; it has also changed our understanding of the nature of the Universe. We now know that if there is a God, he is not a clockmaker. The old idea that he is a shepherd may, perhaps, be nearer the mark.

If just three similarly sized lumps of rock in space are a complex system, then the economy – with many more interacting lumps of rock and other things, including some that have minds of their own – is surely also a complex system. In fact, the economy is a complex adaptive system, because actors within it adapt their behaviour in response to the conditions in which they find themselves. Their actions go on to cause further changes to the system itself, creating an additional dimension of complexity. The economy, therefore, is not like a machine. Neither is it quite like the weather. It is like an ecosystem.

In the early twentieth century, economists such as Thorstein Veblen and Joseph Schumpeter had the intuition that change in the economy could be the result of an evolutionary process. By the 1980s, thinkers such as Richard Nelson and Sidney Winter had developed these ideas into a new branch of the discipline: 'evolutionary economics'.[3]

In parallel, from the 1950s onwards, computer scientists and researchers of organisational management, led by Professor Jay Forrester at the Massachusetts Institute of Technology, had been developing a practical approach to working with complex systems: 'systems thinking'. This concentrated on mapping the feedbacks created by interactions between system components. In Chapter 5, we saw how feedbacks were important to the behaviour of the climate system. Reinforcing feedbacks accelerate change, such as when rising temperatures melt sea-ice, and exposed sea water absorbs more heat, causing temperatures to rise further. Balancing feedbacks, acting like the thermostat in your house, tend to slow or prevent change. Forrester and his colleagues found that by mapping the feedbacks in a complex system, they could understand the system's behaviour. They could also make qualitative predictions about what it was likely to do, and identify effective ways to change its behaviour.

The introduction to economics of these new ways of thinking received an enormous boost in the 1990s, with the end of the Cold War. Eric Beinhocker, the foremost chronicler of what has become known as 'complexity economics', describes how the sudden cuts in defence spending in the US and USSR released a small wave of the world's best nuclear physicists, advanced mathematicians, and rocket scientists onto the labour market.[4] With financial markets newly liberalised and booming, many of them took up jobs on Wall Street. There, as they increasingly noticed the discrepancy between textbook descriptions of how the markets should work, and their own observations of what was really happening, some of them began to take an interest in economics. The complexity science that was transforming physics and biology gave them a new starting point for economic theory. The arrival of powerful computers provided a new tool for simulating the behaviour of economic systems. The publication in 2013 of Brian Arthur's paper 'Complexity economics: a different framework for economic thought' marked the distillation of this work into a clear and coherent vision of how the economy works, capable of explaining processes of creation and change. This was a vision of the economy as an ecosystem.

THE ECONOMY AS AN ECOSYSTEM

With the benefit of hindsight, we may now think it obvious that the economy is an ecosystem. We humans are an animal in an ecosystem. We depend for our survival on the animals and plants that we eat, the air that we breathe,

the water we drink, and all the biological, chemical, and physical processes that continually recycle these things so that they are always available.

Like some other animals, we pick things up and use them. Like the chimpanzees that use stones as hammers, the elephants that use branches as fly swats, and the dolphins that use sea sponges to stir up the sand and uncover prey at the bottom of the ocean, we take things from our environment and modify them to suit our purposes. We have simply gone further than other animals in creating new things, exchanging them, and combining them to make more new things. These things are what we call technologies, goods, and products, and some of the uses we put them to are called 'services'. The pattern of activity that involves making these things and exchanging them for money is what we call 'the economy'.

This subset of our activities that we call the economy is no less a part of our ecosystem than any other of our activities. It is no less subject to the processes of evolution.

Throughout our history as a species, our physical, cultural, and technological evolution has been intertwined. Research suggests that after we discovered the 'technology' of using containers to carry water, our bodies evolved a greater ability to sweat, as this cooling mechanism could now be employed with less risk of dehydration. The improved cooling capability allowed us to run for longer without overheating, and that made us more successful hunters. When we discovered the technology of fire and learned to cook the food we had hunted and gathered, our bodies needed less energy for digestion, and we made use of the surplus energy by evolving larger brains. These larger brains helped us develop ever more ingenious tools, and ever more complex cultures and practices to put them to use.[5]

Now that our tools are so many, they seem almost to have taken on a life of their own. Technologies, products, goods, services, and businesses are all competing, combining, adapting; some growing, others declining; all evolving together in the ecosystem of the economy.

When we understand the economy as an ecosystem, we can see all kinds of ways in which it is not like a machine. These have important implications for how we make decisions.

The first thing we can see is that unlike a machine, the economy is not fixed in its shape and structure. Like an ecosystem, it is constantly changing, and constantly growing in diversity and complexity. As Eric Beinhocker has pointed out, the Stone Age human economy had perhaps a few tens of goods and services. We now have billions, maybe tens of billions. That is at least a hundred-million-fold increase in diversity, compared to the economy of our hunter-gatherer ancestors. Over the long term, this persistent and explosive growth in diversity is perhaps the most striking feature of the economy.

It is commonplace, and true, to say that the Stone Age did not end because we ran out of stones. Neither did the Bronze Age end for a shortage of bronze, nor did the age of agricultural economies end for lack of agriculture. Hopefully, the fossil fuel age will not end because we run out of fossils. It need not. In each of those past transitions, we moved away from reliance on one set of tools and resources because we discovered how to harness other resources that were already present in abundance. We can surely do the same again. The sunlight falling on the Earth carries seven thousand times as much energy as we currently use to run our global economy. The biosphere produces hundreds of times as much matter each year as we produce in plastics.

The challenge of wealth creation has gone by many different names since Xenophon wrote the first book on economics. These days it is most commonly called 'growth', as distinct from the problem of 'distribution'. Brian Arthur has named it 'formation', as distinct from 'allocation'. I may be biased, but I think my father, Bill Sharpe, a computer scientist turned strategy consultant and thinker about ways to think about the future, has proposed the definition that best helps us understand the nature of the game. If the challenge of economics at a moment in time is 'the allocation of scarce resources', then the challenge of economics over the course of time is 'the configuration of abundance'.[6] The resources are all out there, and always have been. We just have to figure out how to bring them together in new and useful ways.

As we contemplate this challenge of configuring abundance, we see that the economy, unlike a machine, has an unlimited range of future possibilities. A clock has only so many positions that its hands can point to, and a car engine has only a limited number of gears. An ecosystem, in contrast, can evolve in any of an effectively infinite number of directions. Its constant evolution and tendency to increase in diversity over time means that the number of possible states increases faster than it can possibly explore them. It will never be all the things that it could be.

The theoretical biologist Stuart Kauffman has illustrated this with a thought experiment about proteins. A protein is a molecule made up of a lot of amino acids (which are smaller molecules) strung together in a chain. Many different proteins are possible, using different combinations of amino acids. Kauffman asks: how long would it take the Universe to create all possible proteins of length 200? With a back-of-the-envelope calculation, he finds that even if all the particles in the known Universe were reacting with each other at the fastest possible rate, ignoring any distances they might have to travel, then it would still take 10^{67} times the current lifetime of the Universe to create all such proteins. That is ten million trillion trillion trillion trillion trillion times the current lifetime of the Universe.[7]

If the life of the Universe is too short to explore all possible proteins of length 200, then it is certainly too short to explore all possible states of the human economy. Our economy is considerably more complex than a protein. It will realise only an infinitesimally small sample of its possible future states. Knowing this tells us that when we make decisions that affect the path of the economy's evolution, there is no such thing as an optimal choice, a best of all possible ways forward. We had better not waste our time by searching for it. Neither should we imagine that the economy will automatically find it. The poet Antonio Machado was right when he wrote: 'Traveller, there is no path. The path is made by walking.' The best we can do is choose a direction that seems to suit our interests, and guide the economy's evolution that way if we can.

Whichever way we choose, we will open up a unique set of new possibilities and close off many others. A machine is not path-dependent: whichever gear my car's engine is in, I can change it to any of the others. An ecosystem is different: the options at any moment in time depend on what has happened before. Humans could only evolve because apes came before us; and there will be no evolutionary descendants of the dodo now that the dodo is extinct. We see this path dependence at all levels of the economy. In the UK, our network of major roads still closely resembles that laid out by the Romans two millennia ago. The junctions between those roads have influenced the positioning and development of cities. The choices a century ago that led to those roads being used by fossil -fuel-powered cars have influenced the growth of the global oil industry, which in turn has changed the Earth's climate, and now climate change is affecting our choices of which new technologies we should develop.

Just as the arrival of a new form of bacteria once brought about the oxygenation of the Earth's atmosphere, transforming the environment of all the other lifeforms, so our invention of semiconductors is bringing about the digitisation of the global economy, transforming the environment of all other technologies. The ecosystem emerges from its inhabitants, and the economy, as Brian Arthur has said, emerges from its technologies. This means we should be alive to the effects of all our choices, even those that appear small. In the ecosystem, no action is neutral. Any policy will unavoidably advantage some technologies over others, and we cannot assume this will be without long-term consequences. The best we can do is to choose consciously and not accidentally.

As we try to understand and guide change in the economy, we see that just like an ecosystem, it has many possible dynamic states. It can grow, crash, oscillate, bounce, and lurch. It is rarely, if ever, in a perfect state of balance, or equilibrium.

Feedbacks will make the economy behave in a way that is unlike the behaviour of any of its individual components.[8] In an ecosystem of rabbits and foxes, the rabbits will follow their instinct to reproduce, and the more rabbits there are, the more baby rabbits there will be. Meanwhile, the foxes will follow their instinct to eat the rabbits. The more rabbits there are, the more foxes there are likely to be, which will in turn result in fewer rabbits. The interaction of these two feedbacks, one reinforcing, the other balancing, can cause either of the two animal populations to grow exponentially, to crash, to oscillate, or to plateau, depending on their relative strengths. These population dynamics cannot be explained by studying the behaviour of individual rabbits and foxes. Similarly, we cannot explain the dynamic phenomena that we see in the economy – such as financial bubbles, crashes, fashions, and the spread of new technologies – by studying the behaviour of an individual person. Understanding the feedbacks, in the economy just as in the ecosystem, is central to understanding how and why change is happening.

If we are choosing between different options – different policies – for changing something in the economy, there is little use in comparing them based on their predicted outcomes at a moment in time. This 'cost–benefit analysis' might be useful in a machine-like economy where each input leads to a precise, predictable, and final output. But in the ecosystem economy, which never stops evolving, there is no final outcome of any action. Like Poincaré's three rocks in space, there is no analytical solution, only continued movement. The only useful way to weigh up our options is to compare their likely effect on the dynamics of the system, on the processes of change within it. If we provide a new food source for the foxes, for example, it may weaken the relationship between the fox population and the number of rabbits being eaten. We cannot predict the precise outcome, but there are likely to be more rabbits.

In the ecosystem, cause and effect are often disproportionate. The famous illustration of this is the 'butterfly effect': the idea that because weather systems are so sensitive to small changes, the flapping of a butterfly's wings in Brazil could set off a tornado in Texas. Less famously, the same is true on a planetary scale. The astrophysicist Scott Tremaine writes that 'shifting your pencil from one side of your desk to the other today could change the gravitational forces on Jupiter enough to shift its position from one side of the Sun to the other a billion years from now'.[9] The only difference between these two examples is the timescale: Tremaine says that 'For practical purposes, the positions of the planets are unpredictable further than about a hundred million years in the future'; whereas the weather becomes unpredictable after about a week. The same disproportionality of cause and effect is visible in the economy, on many scales. One example is the bankruptcy of the investment bank Lehman Brothers in 2008, the 'straw that broke the camel's back' that set off a global financial crisis followed by an economic depression. Knowing this tells us that if we want to change something quickly and effectively, we should not limit ourselves to looking for the most efficient 'marginal gains' that save a few pennies here or there. We should be looking for points of leverage, like the tipping points in the climate, where a small push has an outsized effect.

It should be obvious by now that in the ecosystem of the economy, unlike in a machine, there is much uncertainty. We cannot predict future technologies, the actions of other people, or exactly how the economy will respond to all our complex interactions. We cannot assign probabilities to all possible future outcomes of our actions because we do not even know all the possible outcomes that exist. Comparing quantifiable costs and benefits, as we saw Nordhaus try to do for climate change in Chapter 9, is therefore not enough. If we only measure what is measurable, we will leave important things outside our calculation, making the analysis either irrelevant or misleading. We need to keep the qualitative information in view. In the presence of uncertainty, comparing risks and opportunities is the best we can do.[10]

Finally, as we consider risks and opportunities, we must realise that we do so from a particular perspective. A machine may be built for a single purpose, and a component within it – such as the windscreen wipers on a car – may have only a single function. The machine can succeed or fail in its purpose, and the component can be valued according to how well it fulfils its function. The ecosystem is different. It has no overall purpose, and so can neither succeed nor fail. The many actors within it have many different purposes of their own. The value of any component of the ecosystem depends on who is valuing it, for what use, and in what context. For example, think of a clump of seaweed in a marine ecosystem. For some microscopic bugs, it might be their home. For a small fish, it might be a place to hide from predators. For a bigger fish, it might be a refreshing vegetarian lunch. For another creature, it could be any one of those things depending on the time of day. What is the value of the seaweed? It depends on who you ask, and when you ask them.

The economy is like the ecosystem. Imagine a park in a city. It may be a home to a homeless person, an exercise ground for joggers, a playground for children, and a place of work for the park-keeper. It may help to keep the air cleaner for the residents of the city. What is the value of the park? It depends on who you ask. Nothing in the economy has a single, inherent value. The value of anything is contingent on its user, their use for it, and their context.[11] This means that when we compare options, our view will be limited if we convert all possible outcomes into the single metric of money. We cannot do this without choosing our method of conversion arbitrarily. We will see our choices more clearly if we keep different perspectives on value visible, and do not confuse the analytical process with the political process.

When we see the economy as an ecosystem, we see our own role differently. We are not mechanics, fixing the machine when it fails. We are something more like gardeners, tending and shaping the ecosystem so that it grows in ways that we find beneficial.[i]

THE ECOSYSTEM PERSPECTIVE IN PRACTICE

This new understanding is already beginning to be put into practice, in various fields.

In the late twentieth century, Donella Meadows developed the ideas of Jay Forrester into the practice of systems thinking, a form of analysis based on the understanding of feedbacks. She showed, for example, how feedbacks in a manufacturing supply chain could mean that actions intended to maintain a steady level of stocks could instead lead to an oversupply or a shortage.[12] Her methods are now used in business management, and occasionally in government.

New economic models have been constructed, free from the constraints of equilibrium, that are able to simulate processes of creation and change in the economy. The Bank of England has used one such model to understand instability in the UK housing market.

---

[i] Jean-Francois Mercure, other colleagues and I have proposed 'risk–opportunity analysis' as an approach to decision-making that can reflect all of the principles discussed above. In the same way as equilibrium is a special case of the dynamics of a complex system, cost–benefit analysis can be seen as a special case of risk–opportunity analysis, appropriate for use where uncertainty is low and change is marginal.

Although it was not much noticed until it was too late, at least one model of the economy as an ecosystem provided advance warning of the global financial crisis. The Australian economist Steve Keen built a model that was simple in design, but which, by replicating feedbacks in the economy, could simulate all kinds of complex behaviour.[13] It showed that rising debt and inequality were likely to lead to a crisis, and it also showed something unexpected: that the crisis was preceded by a period of apparent tranquillity, in which volatility in unemployment and wages diminished. So in the years when many economists saw a 'Great Moderation' as evidence of the success of their theories,[14] when politicians such as Gordon Brown, then the UK's Chancellor of the Exchequer, hailed the 'end of boom and bust' as evidence of the success of their policies, and when Robert Lucas, then President of the American Economic Association, claimed that the 'central problem of depression-prevention has been solved, for all practical purposes, and has in fact been solved for many decades',[15] Keen warned that what we were seeing was the calm before the storm. Keen could see this because his model, unlike most of the others, did not exclude by design the possibility of a storm.

These are promising beginnings, but there is a long way to go. Few people in government are aware of the existence of systems thinking, and fewer have taken the training needed to put it into use. Few of the models used to inform policy depart from the constraints of equilibrium. Economics students are still taught to see the economy as a machine, and economic analysts still advise government as if we were mechanics, using cost–benefit analysis to weigh up our options as if they had precisely knowable outcomes.

DECIDING HOW TO DECIDE

In the coming chapters, I will show how this choice – between seeing the economy as a machine or as an ecosystem – directly affects our ability to make good policy on climate change. Before going forward, I will return to a caveat I hinted at in the previous chapter, to avoid being unfair to the currently dominant form of economics.

It may be that in some circumstances, it is reasonable to treat the economy like a machine – a system that is fixed, or in equilibrium. It is, perhaps, a question of what we are trying to achieve, over what scales of time and space.

Over a timescale of minutes, in a given place, it may be safe to assume the weather is unchanging. For most purposes, we could treat it as being in equilibrium. Over a few days, the weather is changing, but its behaviour will be roughly predictable. More than a week or two ahead, it becomes largely impossible to predict. As we saw, the same could be said for the motion of the planets, except that the transition to unpredictability takes place after around a hundred million years. In an ecosystem, we may be certain that a forest standing today will still be standing tomorrow, but we cannot say where a colony of ants will go looking for its next meal, and neither do we know whether the forest will still be there in a century's time. In the economy, we can observe that some structures change slowly, such as the UK's road networks that still bear signs of their Roman ancestry, while others evolve quickly, such as the contents of my local computer shop.

If we do not intend to bring about any structural change, if we are acting with one simple purpose in mind, and if the scales of space and time involved are such that we can be fairly certain of all the outcomes of our actions, then we may be safe to think of the economy as a machine. For example, if we need to fix a broken light, and are choosing between one lightbulb that is cheaper and another that will last longer, then a simple cost–benefit analysis may be good enough to do the job.

If, on the other hand, any one of those conditions does not hold – if we intend to achieve structural change; if more than one purpose or perspective is likely to be affected; or if the scales of space and time involved are such that there is significant uncertainty around where our actions may lead – then we had better think of the economy as an ecosystem. If we want to bring about a change in the kind of lightbulbs that are made and sold to every household, then we will need to choose our policies using all the principles described above, acting in our role as gardeners, not as mechanics.

For any policy to do with addressing climate change, it is clear which side of this line we are on. To make ourselves safe, we need transformational change at a fast pace on a global scale. Structural change is the aim of the game. This cannot avoid affecting many interests of many people, and it comes with multiple uncertainties. If we want to have a chance of making good climate policy, we had better shelve our spanners and put on the gardening gloves.

12

NOT JUST FIXING THE FOUNDATIONS

The shift from seeing the economy as a machine to understanding it as an ecosystem changes our view of many individual policy choices. Before we look at some of those choices, we will in this chapter consider a larger issue: how this shift in understanding affects our view of the role of government itself.

When I began working on the UK government's new industrial strategy in 2017, the most surprising thing I found was that most economists could not give us a convincing reason why we should *have* an industrial strategy.

We consulted everyone. Businesspeople, non-government organisations, and the public welcomed the government's decision to develop an industrial strategy. They had no trouble in telling us why it was needed, and no hesitation in suggesting what it should do. But economists, as a group, seemed more conflicted.

The problem was crystallised for me when I saw a presentation that one economist from a prestigious university had given to our department. A PowerPoint slide asked the question 'What's a sensible industrial strategy?' and proceeded to set out three possible answers. They were:

(i) *Orthodox economic view: only sensible strategy is no strategy*
(ii) *More recent view: government should help in sectors with comparative advantage*
(iii) *More enlightened view: governments should help in specific sectors if that addresses some kind of market failure*

It seemed to me at the time that none of these answers was quite right.

It is not hard to see how the 'orthodox economic view' comes from the equilibrium economics of the 1870s. If the economy automatically and inevitably finds its way to an 'optimal' state, then the best thing to do is sit back and watch. Any intervention by the government would, by definition, take the economy out of its optimal state and into something less good. Even without having considered the nature of the economy as we did in the last chapter, this feels like an uncomfortable conclusion. Can the best strategy really be to have no strategy at all? There are few areas of life where this feels like a winning approach.

The 'more recent view' that government should help in sectors where the country has a comparative advantage comes from the work of David Ricardo, an influential classical economist of the early nineteenth century. Ricardo proposed that countries would benefit from unrestricted international trade because it would allow them to concentrate their productive efforts on the industries that they were relatively good at, while still obtaining all the goods and services that they needed.

There is some logic to Ricardo's insight, and whether or not it is a good guide to trade policy (a debate we do not need to have here), plenty of countries have indeed become richer through international trade. But when it comes to guiding industrial strategy, there is a problem. Comparative advantage is a backward-looking metric.[j] It tells us what we have been good at doing in the past. If the economy never changed, it would be fine to keep doing the same thing. But if the future will be different from the past, this might not be a good strategy.

The economic historian Erik Reinert has pointed out that if South Korea had followed the advice of international financial institutions after it emerged poverty-stricken from civil war in the 1950s, it would have focused its efforts on continuing to produce and export rice, since this was what past data 'revealed' it was good at. Fortunately for South Koreans, their government ignored that advice, and chose instead to focus its efforts first on heavy industries such as shipbuilding, and later on high-technology industries such as computing. This industrial strategy helped South Korea make more progress from poverty to wealth than almost any other country during the twentieth century. For six years running, between 2014 and 2019, it was ranked by Bloomberg as the most innovative country in the world.[1]

The 'more enlightened view' that governments should 'help in specific sectors if that addresses some kind of market failure', like the orthodox view, comes from equilibrium economics. 'Market failure' is defined as a situation where the market alone cannot achieve an optimal allocation of economic

---

[j] The standard method is to calculate a 'revealed comparative advantage' by dividing the share of a certain good in a country's exports by the share of the same good in total world exports. If the result is higher than one, it means the country is more competitive in producing this good than it is at producing most others. The only data on which this can be calculated is past data, so it is a backward-looking metric.

resources.[k] Standard theory recognises many reasons why this can happen. There are 'public goods', such as clean air, that private actors are not sufficiently incentivised to provide. There is imperfect information that does not allow buyers, sellers, and investors to interact efficiently. There are moral hazards, where businesses can gain from actions that force others to bear the costs. There is the exercise of market power, where powerful organisations abuse their position to limit competition. And there are 'externalities', where the actions of an individual person or firm create costs or benefits for others.

Unlike the orthodox view, the market failure view provides at least some rationale for government policy. However, it only justifies action up to a certain point: the point at which an optimal allocation of economic resources is restored. Beyond this point, any further action would cause a 'distortion', diverting resources from their best possible uses, and necessarily incurring net costs. This view can therefore be thought of as a form of permission to do the minimum necessary.

The three rationales for industrial strategy listed above therefore cover the range from 'do nothing' to 'do the minimum'.

THE 'DO THE MINIMUM' APPROACH TO CLIMATE POLICY

This restricted view of the role of government translates directly into policy advice on climate change.

Following the logic of equilibrium economics, climate change can be seen as a kind of market failure. Specifically, it is an 'externality': actions that benefit individuals (such as driving cars or using electricity) have wider costs to society (dangerous climate change) which are not accounted for in the market. The solution is clear: put a price on carbon emissions that reflects their cost to society. This will bring those costs inside the market and align individual incentives with the public interest. The market will be restored to its state of optimal allocation of economic resources.

A similar case can be made for supporting research and development of new technologies. Research generates a 'public good', in terms of economic

---

[k] At the time when the UK Industrial Strategy was being developed, the UK government's official guidance on policy appraisal defined market failure as '*where the market mechanism alone cannot achieve economic efficiency*'. Economic efficiency was defined as a Pareto-optimal allocation of resources: '*Economic efficiency is achieved when nobody can be made better off without someone else being made worse off.*'

benefits that are greater than the returns to the individual actors involved. This is another market failure that policy is justified in fixing.

Crucially, any actions beyond the scope of what is needed to restore equilibrium cannot be justified. Pricing the externality is seen as the most efficient way to fix the market failure, so any other policies are regarded as second-best. The 'enlightened approach' to climate change is therefore to put a price on carbon, invest in research and development, and do nothing more.

Any good economist reading this is likely to be shouting at this point, 'That is not what I recommend! Read my work, and the work of my colleagues! We recommend doing all kinds of things to address climate change!' And they will be right. Good economists do tell us we should be taking many different actions to address this problem. They have provided a huge amount of helpful advice to governments, from which I and others have benefited.

However, there is unhelpful advice too. Equilibrium economics has become so well established that prominent economists use it to make bold assertions on things they are entirely clueless about. This can be confusing and misleading for governments, and for the public, with unfortunate consequences.

An example is the 'Economists' Statement on Carbon Dividends' published in the *Wall Street Journal* in January 2019. Its original signatories include twenty-seven Nobel Laureate economists, four former chairs of the US Federal Reserve, fifteen former chairs of the US Council of Economic Advisers, and two former secretaries of the US Department of Treasury.[2] This undoubtedly deserves praise as a bipartisan effort to advocate action on climate change in the US, and the policy it recommends – a carbon tax, with the revenue ('dividends') returned to the public – has many advantages. However, in several ways the statement is unhelpful. It asserts that a carbon tax is the best of all policy options, 'the most cost-effective lever to reduce carbon emissions at the scale and speed that is necessary'. It suggests that a carbon tax is enough to do all that is needed: 'By correcting a well-known market failure, a carbon tax will send a powerful price signal that harnesses the invisible hand of the marketplace to steer economic actors towards a low-carbon future.' And it describes other policies, such as regulations, as 'cumbersome' and necessarily 'less efficient'.

All three of those assertions follow directly from the theory of equilibrium economics. All three have exerted a powerful influence on government policy, in many countries. All three, as we will see in coming chapters, turn out to be wrong.

The authors of the statement are not alone in their view. The World Bank advises that carbon pricing provides the 'least-cost way' for society to meet its environmental goals.[3] The International Monetary Fund has advised that 'of the various mitigation strategies to reduce fossil fuel CO_2 emissions, carbon taxes – levied on the supply of fossil fuels . . . are the most powerful and efficient, because they allow firms and households to find the lowest-cost ways of reducing energy use and shifting toward cleaner alternatives'.[4] Even researchers at the Institute for New Economic Thinking at the University of Oxford have confidently asserted that 'Putting a price on carbon is the most effective economic tool for meeting the goals of the Paris Agreement on mitigating global climate change.'[5] It is not uncommon for economists to oppose other climate change policies on the basis that they would not be as efficient as carbon pricing.

For the avoidance of doubt, I am not against carbon taxes. On the contrary: when the right level of tax is levied, in the right circumstances, it can be extremely effective (as we will see in Chapter 16). However, I believe the view that a price on carbon is necessarily the most efficient policy is mistaken. The suggestion that it is enough on its own to get the job done (fast enough) is far from the truth. The advice that amounts to a recommendation to 'do the minimum' to fix the market failure of climate change is deeply unhelpful. When this advice is repeated by authoritative international organisations and respected academic institutions, it is not surprising if it becomes lodged in the minds of many policymakers and influences many of their decisions. And, given the nature of this advice, it is not surprising if it results in far less action being taken than might be desirable.

A MISSION-ORIENTED APPROACH

An entirely different rationale for industrial strategy was put forward by the economist Mariana Mazzucato. Among the thousands of responses to our public consultation, hers stood out. She proposed that an industrial strategy should be organised around solving problems that mattered to society. If we chose problems that were 'grand challenges', relevant to many people in many parts of the world, over many years, then it was likely that any solutions developed in the UK would be useful globally. Investments in new technologies, goods, and services would pay off as the UK became more competitive in the global economy of the future. Finally, I was delighted to find, here was a forward-looking rationale for industrial strategy.

This 'mission-oriented approach' makes sense based on our new understanding of the economy as an ecosystem. (An industrial strategy is concerned with change over time, so it is clearly the ecosystem view, not the machine view, that is appropriate.) As we saw in the last chapter, the economy is constantly evolving over time. It can go in any of an effectively infinite number of different directions. It could become more or less digitised; more or less automated; more or less modified by genetic engineering or nanotechnology; more or less carbon-intensive; more or less equal; as well as more or less of an unlimited number of technological dimensions that we have yet to discover. There is no optimal path, and no correct choice about which direction to follow. The best we can do is to choose a direction that seems to suit our interests. And if we wish to be competitive in the economy of the future, then we have to anticipate the choices that will be made by others.

Mazzucato showed that industrial strategies had been highly successful in the past when governments had chosen a direction and then followed it with determination.[6] Her classic example was the mission to put a man on the Moon, pursued by the US government in the 1960s. President Kennedy set out the strategic goal in 1961 of 'landing a man on the Moon and returning him safely to the Earth' before the end of the decade. The purpose of setting this mission was to give the US the upper hand in its geopolitical competition with the Soviet Union. The effect of the government's intensive investment in solving the problems involved in this mission was to catalyse innovation in multiple sectors of the economy, including aeronautics, robotics, textiles, and nutrition. In later decades, sustained investment by US government agencies, mostly for the purposes of national defence, was instrumental in the development of the Internet and many of the technologies now used in mobile phones.

Mazzucato found similarities of approach in successful industrial strategies in fields as diverse as space, defence, public health, agriculture, and energy. After choosing a direction, governments had not just done the minimum to fix market failures. Quite the opposite: they had done the maximum to accelerate innovation and growth in the desired direction. Not only had they invested in research and development to 'push' new technologies into the economy, they had also used the full range of policy levers available – subsidy, tax, public procurement, regulation, and investment – to shape markets in a way that would 'pull' the same technologies into the economy. And they made sure to support the new technologies at every stage, from invention, through demonstration and first commercialisation, to expansion into the mass markets.

A similar story is visible in studies of great technology transitions of the past, many of which have been documented by the innovation expert Frank Geels. Entrepreneurs invented and innovated, but government action of all kinds was a critical determinant of the pace of change. The shift from sailing ships to steamships was catalysed in the 1830s by the British government's subsidy of faster but more expensive steamships to carry mail across the oceans, as a way of improving communication within the Empire. The creation of this subsidised market allowed engineers to develop their skills in steam technology and iron working, and to improve their steamships until they were incontestably the better option.[7] A century later, the US government acted as midwife to the birth of civil aviation in a similar way, supporting airlines through the subsidy of cross-continental airmail, while investing in airports and refuelling infrastructure, and creating new institutions to ensure safety and security. The intensification of agriculture in the UK was supported by grants and loans for tractors and land drainage, the fixing of wheat prices to incentivise investment, and training programmes for farmers. In the shift from horses to cars, while the businessmen invested in factories and the mechanics worked on their motors, governments wrote the highway code and built the roads. They did not just put a tax on horseshit and hope for the best.

Again, this 'market-shaping' approach makes sense from the perspective of the economy as an ecosystem. Nothing about the economy's evolution can be taken for granted. If we want it to evolve rapidly in a particular direction, there is no reason to believe that a single action will do the job. The more points of the system we act on, the more chance we have of achieving the desired effect, and of achieving it quickly. Moreover, cause and effect in the ecosystem are often disproportionate. A poorly chosen intervention could expend a lot of effort while achieving nothing noticeable; a set of well-aligned actions can achieve more than the sum of their parts. In this context, it makes sense to do the maximum.

In the process of working on our industrial strategy, I spent time with Mariana Mazzucato thinking through how we could apply a mission-oriented approach, writing a paper about this together,[8] and discussing it with colleagues in government. It was fun to work with her as she was fearless in challenging the orthodoxy, and could get away with saying rude things about established practices thanks to some combination of Italian charisma and academic credibility. (I could never be sure which was more important, but without having either myself, I appreciated both.) In these discussions, the question most often raised in objection was: 'We can't have a mission-oriented approach to everything. Resources are limited. How can we know what to choose?'

This is a fair question. I think the first answer to it is that we must recognise there are no definitively correct choices when it comes to long-term strategy. Nobody can foresee the future, and nobody should pretend to be able to. We should not ask economists to act as if they were astrologers.

The second answer is that we have to use our judgement. When we choose a direction, we can look at long-term trends in the economy that have their own momentum, such as demographic change, urbanisation, or the spread of digital technologies. We can look at actions being taken now that have implications for future markets: for example, if countries all over the world are installing intermittent renewable electricity generation, it is likely that in future there will be demand for energy storage. And we can look at societal need: if a problem affects many people in many countries and is getting worse over time, then there is likely to be rising demand for products and services that contribute to its solution. Climate change is a prime example.

At the same time, we can consider the plausibility of our country becoming competitive in a given area by looking at the extent to which we have the relevant expertise, natural resources, industrial supply chains, institutional capabilities, or opportunity to gain an advantage by being a first-mover.

Judgement will be needed again when we choose the policies to implement, and the technologies to develop. We can support the choice of policies by mapping out the feedbacks in the part of the economy we are dealing with, and looking at how potential interventions would affect the processes of change. We can take a view on technologies using expert knowledge of their technical potential, and the societal consequences of their use.

Of course, we can still make bad choices. We can always get it wrong. But the alternative to using our judgement to make the best decision we can is not that the market automatically finds us the perfect economic future. The alternative to deliberate choice is accidental choice.

When we take the machine view of the economy, the accidental choice we are most likely to make is inaction – because if there is no market failure, the theory tells us there is no reason to act. Doing nothing is most likely to benefit incumbent industries and mature technologies, because markets have grown around them and put them in a position of power. At the same time, we may lose ground to competitors who are more proactive in shaking up the status quo and stimulating innovation. When we see the economy as an ecosystem, we realise that inaction means standing still while the economy evolves around us, and this carries its own risks.

The approach we settled on with our industrial strategy was a forward-looking one. Not the 'do nothing' of the old orthodoxy; not the backward-looking approach of doubling down on what worked for us in the past; and not the 'do the minimum' approach of fixing market failures. The strategy set out a more positive view of the role of government: '*A truly strategic government must do more than just fix the foundations: it must also plan for a rapidly changing future, look to shape new markets and industries, and build the UK's competitive advantage.*'[9] It was organised around four 'grand challenges' based on trends that were likely to shape the global economy in years to come: the shift to a clean economy to address climate change; the move to new forms of mobility in a context of rapid urbanisation and worsening congestion; the increasing need for health services in an ageing society; and the spread of artificial intelligence across many areas of economic activity.

A NEW PARADIGM FOR CLIMATE POLICY

Our industrial strategy cast climate change policy in a new light. For years, the mantra had been 'decarbonisation at least cost'. Climate change was seen as a market failure, and the job of policy was to fix this with the minimum effort, the least cost, and the smallest possible 'distortion' to the economy.

Two years earlier when I joined the Department of Energy and Climate Change, I had worked as head of private office for the Minister of State, Andrea Leadsom. She had seen how thousands of British workers were losing their jobs in the oil and gas industry, as the North Sea fields gradually dried up. Meanwhile, new jobs were being created as government policy brought into being the largest offshore wind market in the world, around the shores of the UK. She constantly asked her officials: 'Given that we are investing billions of pounds every year in these clean technologies, can't we do more to make sure that some of the jobs go to British people?' It was a good question, but she faced an uphill struggle. Our policymaking was firmly aimed at achieving decarbonisation at least cost, while maintaining energy security. Following the logic of equilibrium economics, we had no particular aim of creating jobs in the new clean economy. In the imaginary world of perfectly allocated economic resources, deliberately stimulating job creation in one part of the economy just means taking workers away from somewhere else – an artificial and inefficient distortion.

The industrial strategy gave us a chance to look at the problem differently. We saw that the response to climate change was one of the highest-likelihood, highest-impact economic trends that anyone could identify. The risks of climate change were guaranteed to keep increasing over time. The trends of political engagement, social pressure, shifting investment, and technological development were all pointing in the same direction. Decarbonisation would affect many economic sectors, over many decades, in all countries of the world. Seen this way, it was obvious that we should want to be competitive in the face of this trend.

One part of the economy already being affected was the automotive sector. Car manufacturing employed hundreds of thousands of people in the UK, and contributed significantly to our GDP and our exports. The direction of change in this two-trillion-dollar-a-year global industry was about as clear as the future ever can be. Sales of electric vehicles were rising exponentially, and their share of the global market was projected to increase from about 1% then, to around 50% after the next two decades. We could do the minimum to fix the market failure of emissions from road transport, but there was no reason to believe this would be enough to win the UK a larger share of this global market as it evolved, or even to be sure that after the transition we would be left with a car industry at all.

On the other hand, if we made more of an effort, there was no reason to assume that the transition to zero-emission vehicles could not result in a net economic gain, rather than a cost. The new electric cars were already becoming cheaper to run than the old ones that burned expensive petrol and diesel (and this even in a period of relatively low oil prices). The time would come when they would be cheaper to buy too, as well as having higher performance, being quieter, and being less polluting. On top of all that, if we got ahead of the game, we could emerge from the transition with a larger market share. We realised that 'decarbonisation at least cost' was too narrow an objective. The larger challenge was to move to the clean economy at maximum gain.

It is not hard to imagine that the 'do the minimum' principle led to slower progress on emissions reduction than might otherwise have been made. Many good policies that could have been adopted were not, and others were weakened, in the name of decarbonisation at least cost. The tragedy is that this was not an inevitable consequence of political decisions about the level of priority to give to climate change. Within a framework of politically agreed climate change goals, it reflected what was thought to be an economically efficient way of achieving them. If we had had a more realistic understanding of the economy at an earlier stage, we could have made faster progress on climate change and generated more wealth for our country, with exactly the same level of political will.

**

Whether our aim is to create jobs and strengthen competitiveness in clean technologies, or just to decarbonise quickly and cost-effectively, in the ecosystem economy a 'do the maximum' approach is likely to serve us better than a 'do the minimum'. But the question raised by my colleagues still stands. We cannot do everything. Resources are limited. Where should we direct the effort?

Even in a 'do the maximum' approach, priorities must be chosen, and policies must be carefully designed. In the next three chapters, we will see how the old logic of equilibrium economics and the new understanding of the economy as an ecosystem lead us to different choices and policy recommendations. We will take three of the main forms of government policy in turn: investment, regulation, and tax.

13

INVESTING WITH OUR EYES OPEN

Investment has brought us our most outstanding successes so far in the battle against climate change. These would never have happened if we had followed the advice of equilibrium economics.

In 2014, *The Economist* magazine wrote that 'solar power is by far the most expensive way of reducing carbon emissions . . . the carbon price would have to rise to $185 a tonne before solar power shows a net benefit . . . governments should target emissions reductions from any source rather than focus on boosting certain kinds of renewable energy'.[1] Michael Grubb, a professor of energy and climate change who has followed debates around energy policy for decades, recalls that this advice reflected a long-standing view of many economists who assumed the economy was in equilibrium, saw the challenge of policy as 'decarbonisation at least cost', and thought that directly subsidising renewable power was 'economic madness'.[2]

Only six years later, the world already looked rather different. Solar and wind power had become the cheapest sources of electricity in over two-thirds of all countries, and their costs continued to plummet. They were becoming the technology of choice for all governments, regardless of concern – or lack of it – for climate change. In 2020, they accounted for three-quarters of the new electricity generating capacity added throughout the world.[3] This spectacular success came about not because governments followed the dominant economic advice, but because they ignored it.

The recommendation that we should 'target emissions reductions from any source rather than boosting certain kinds of renewable energy' means that our main, or only, policy should be to put a price on carbon. As we saw in the last chapter, the view that this is the most cost-effective way to reduce emissions has been put forward by the World Bank, the International Monetary Fund (IMF), and any number of Nobel Prize-winning economists.

The logic for this view is now familiar. The market failure of climate change needs to be fixed to allow the market to return to its state of perfectly allocated economic resources. Putting a price on the 'externality' of carbon emissions is the most efficient way to do this because it allows the cuts in emissions to be made wherever they can be made most cheaply.

The mistake in this logic is the unspoken assumption that the economy will never change. In a static, machine-like economy, the cheapest thing to do at a moment in time is the same as the cheapest thing to do at any time. But the ecosystem of the economy is changing: technologies, markets, and industries are constantly evolving. The cheapest thing to do at one moment in time may not be the most cost-effective way to guide this evolution in a desired direction.

Decarbonisation is not simply a problem of the 'allocation' of economic resources. It requires innovation and structural change. Our aim is to achieve this change over time in a cost-effective way. In other words, the challenge is not allocative efficiency, but dynamic efficiency.

To choose the most dynamically efficient policies – those that do a good job of accelerating change in the desired direction – we have to start from an understanding of the structures, processes, and relationships in the part of the economy we are dealing with. For the problem of decarbonising the power sector, we can look at the structure of electricity markets, the process of technological innovation, and the relationship between industry and political influence.

MARKET STRUCTURE

When I worked at the Department for Energy and Climate Change, our ministers were concerned about the rising bill for renewable energy subsidies. The government was spending over £4bn a year on these subsidies, which felt like a lot. Although household energy bills were actually lower than before thanks to energy efficiency improvements, ministers wanted to be sure that we were not wasting money or increasing consumer costs unnecessarily. Newspapers were not shy of bashing the government if they thought it was spending more than it should. Although I cared more than anything about making progress on climate change, I was acutely conscious of the need to help ministers find the most cost-effective way of meeting our goals.

I was a relative newcomer to energy policy. Having read *The Economist* magazine for many years and absorbed the narrative of equilibrium economics that permeates so much of public debate, I assumed it was true that carbon pricing was the most efficient policy for reducing emissions. So I asked my analyst colleagues: why didn't we just raise the carbon price, instead of giving out wasteful subsidies for renewable power?

The analysts sat me down and explained how the electricity market in Great Britain works. In the wholesale market, electricity is traded between the firms that generate it, and the firms that supply it to customers. Some of this trading takes place through a process that works like an auction, and it is this process that effectively sets the price for the whole market. The supply of electricity comes from a range of different sources: coal, gas, nuclear, wind, solar, biomass, hydropower, and even facilities that take energy from the burning of rubbish. Each of these has different operating costs. In the auction process, the different sources of electricity supply are taken up in order of cheapest first, up until the point where supply matches demand, within a given short period of time.[1] At this point, the price is set, and then the same price is paid for electricity from all sources. In recent years, it is usually gas power that has supplied the 'marginal unit' of power – the last unit needed for supply to match demand – and set the price for the whole market.

If renewables such as solar and wind are more expensive than power from coal and gas, as they were until recent years, then they will not be able to play a role in the market at all without some sort of policy support. With this market structure in mind, we can compare the costs of two policies: carbon pricing and renewable subsidies.

A carbon price can allow renewables to compete by making electricity from coal and gas more expensive. If gas is the price-setting technology, then this will increase the price of electricity for the whole market. This means that consumers pay a higher price for every unit of electricity, while suppliers of electricity from all sources that generate more cheaply than gas, such as nuclear, make larger profits. A renewable subsidy has a more targeted effect. It only needs to increase the revenues earned by renewables enough for them to be competitive; it does not need to raise prices across the whole market, and does not result in consumers giving away money to suppliers using any of the other technologies. The result is that a subsidy for renewables can achieve the same effect as a carbon price at a much lower overall cost. Figure 13.1 illustrates this difference.

---

[1] This ranking of sources of generation that determines the order in which they supply to the market, from those with the lowest operating costs to those with the highest, is known as the merit order. In the words of the UK's fourth largest generating firm, Drax, the merit order 'is not set by any regulator, economist or even by traders. Rather it is a naturally occurring, financial occurrence that explains what sources of electricity generation are feeding power onto the grid day-to-day.' In other words, it is an emergent phenomenon. https://www .drax.com/energy-policy/market-decides-great-britain-gets-electricity

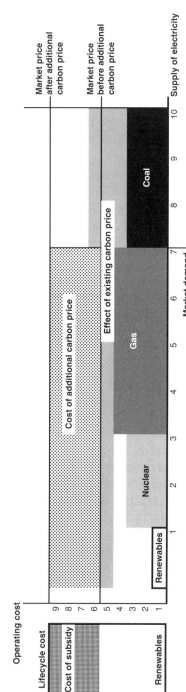

Figure 13.1 Illustrative comparison of tax and subsidy needed to enable the deployment of renewables within the UK power system. Area represents total cost to the market. Since gas is the price-setting technology, the market price increases by the same amount as the carbon price increases the cost of gas power. (Coal is shown here as not supplying the market, because the carbon price has made it more expensive than gas.)

This is a simplified representation. Deploying renewables is not the only way to reduce emissions. Our existing carbon tax had in fact already done a good job of cutting emissions by forcing a switch from coal to gas (a point to which we will return in Chapter 16). In principle, it might be possible for a higher carbon price to cause gas to be burned more efficiently, but there was no evidence to suggest any substantial emissions reductions could be found in that way. In practice, with coal already having been pushed into terminal decline, the only way to decarbonise the power supply further was by replacing gas with some form of zero-emission generation. The logic for subsidy being more efficient than a higher carbon price applied as much to new nuclear power as it did to renewables. A caveat is also needed in relation to 'cost': a carbon price sends resources from industry to government, while subsidy does the reverse; the economic effects are not exactly equivalent. But in the UK's electricity system, utilities pass the cost of the carbon price back to consumers, and the government passes the cost of subsidy back to consumers, so from the consumer's point of view, they are pretty much the same. If we leave aside the question of who pays, we can simply say that the subsidy achieves the same effect as the carbon price with a much lower transfer of economic resources.

This conclusion is strengthened if we take account of the role of finance. Renewable power sources tend to have very low operating costs (because they do not use fuel), but relatively high capital costs (they cost a lot to build in the first place). As a result, the cost of finance can play a large part in determining their overall cost. Historically, the financing costs for renewables have been high because investors were uncertain about the returns that could be made from these new-entrant technologies. This is still the case in many developing countries. Subsidies for renewables can do a lot to bring down the costs of capital, because they give investors certainty about the returns they will make. Carbon prices do not guarantee returns to any particular technology, so are less able to achieve the same effect.

After having these issues of market structure explained to me by my analyst colleagues, I was reassured that we had roughly the right policy. At least, having an increased carbon price instead of the renewable subsidies would have been worse, not better. It was only later that I came to appreciate the even greater importance in this policy choice of the processes of innovation.

INNOVATION PROCESS

In 1930s America, Theodore Wright, an aircraft engineer, found that every time total aircraft production doubled, the labour time needed to make another aircraft fell by 20%.[4] He saw that this relationship was surprisingly constant over time. Progress in renewable power technologies is following the same pattern, which we now know as Wright's Law. For every doubling in cumulative global deployment of solar panels, their cost falls by around 28%. For wind turbines, every doubling leads to a cost reduction of about 15%.[5] Over time, this leads to spectacular advancement. Solar panels now cost less than a three-thousandth of their (inflation-adjusted) cost half a century ago.[6]

This progress is driven by reinforcing feedbacks in the processes of technology innovation and diffusion. One of these is in the process of research and development: each discovery provides knowledge that leads on to further discoveries. Another is known as 'learning by doing': the more something is made, the more we learn how to make it better. As the product is improved, demand for it rises, leading to more of it being made. Another comes from economies of scale: the larger the volumes of production, the less it costs to make each individual unit. As costs come down, demand for the product increases, leading to further increases in production volumes, and further cost reductions. All of these reinforcing feedbacks give a self-accelerating momentum to technological progress. Figure 13.2 illustrates how they each reinforce each other. Their combined effect is enormously powerful.

In one study, a group of researchers has looked in detail at exactly where the cost reduction in solar photovoltaic modules came from, over a period of three decades.[7] First they looked at how much cost reduction had been achieved in each of the solar panel's specific components and materials. Then they looked at how each of these cost reductions had come about.

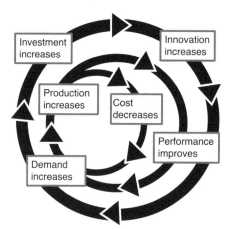

Figure 13.2 Reinforcing feedbacks in the processes of technology innovation and diffusion.

Those that involved doing something in a laboratory or a change in production techniques were attributed to research and development. Those that were incremental improvements achieved through routine manufacturing activity were attributed to learning by doing. Those that resulted from increases in the size of the manufacturing plant were categorised as economies of scale.

The researchers found that during the first two decades, research and development was the strongest driver of cost reduction, whereas in the third decade economies of scale became the most important factor. Learning by doing made a smaller but still significant contribution in both periods.

Finally, the researchers attributed these drivers of cost reduction to two generic forms of public policy support. Economies of scale, learning by doing, and private sector research and development were all considered to have resulted from market-shaping policies. This was a reasonable judgement to make, since without those policies the market for solar modules would not have existed, there would have been no production to scale up, no 'doing' from which to learn, and no reason for private companies to invest in this technology.[m] Public investment in research and development was the other form of policy support.

The results showed that over the thirty-year period, market-shaping policies accounted for around 60% of the cost reduction, while public research and development provided around 20%. The rest came from the 'spillovers' of progress in other parts of the economy, such as the semiconductor industry.

These market-shaping policies, identified as the main catalyst of cost reduction, were the subsidies and mandates 'boosting certain kinds of renewable energy' that *The Economist* so opposed. They worked so well because they strengthened the reinforcing feedbacks that were the drivers of progress. By creating or increasing demand for solar panels, they led directly to larger production volumes, greater economies of scale, accelerated learning by doing, and faster cost reduction.

A carbon price has a much less direct effect. It may incentivise some investment in renewables, but this is by no means guaranteed. It may instead

---

[m] Consumers of electricity receive the same product – 'the same electrons', as many have pointed out – regardless of how it is generated. When solar power was vastly more expensive than coal or gas, there was no possibility of selling it without policy support. Without dedicated support in the form of subsidies that guaranteed a market, there would have been no reason for any business to invest in researching or developing solar modules, or to build a factory to produce them. Without those investments, none of this dramatic technological progress would have been made.

incentivise fossils to be burned more efficiently, or cause one kind of fossil fuel technology to be used in place of another, or simply lead consumers to pay a higher price for the same fossil-fuelled goods and services. These are in fact the more likely outcomes early in the transition, when the cost of renewables is relatively high. In that case, the carbon price will do nothing to strengthen the reinforcing feedbacks in the development of new zero-emission technologies. It will not give society the benefit of any of that self-accelerating momentum. It may reduce emissions temporarily, but will not contribute to the innovation and structural change that is needed to bring a zero-emission economy into being. And let's not forget, a zero-emission economy, as fast as possible, is what we need. With any continued emissions, the world will continue to warm, and the risks of climate change will continue to increase.

When we consider the feedbacks at play, it is obvious that subsidising renewables is the more dynamically efficient policy. Carbon pricing, by comparison, is inefficient and wasteful. We would expect this to be true not just in the power sector, but in any sector where progress in clean technologies is a possibility.

INDUSTRIAL INFLUENCE

Technologies do not exist in isolation. They are designed, made, and sold by industries, using factories, tools, and skills developed for those purposes. A technology transition is therefore also an industrial transition: it involves a reallocation of resources to different people, making different things, in different places. This transfer of wealth and power will inevitably be con-tested: incumbents (such as fossil fuel companies) will fight off disruptors (such as renewable energy) for as long as they can.

In the early stages of a transition, the disruptors – inventors or produ-cers of the new technologies – will be relatively weak. They do not have piles of cash from past profits to invest in product development or advertising, and do not benefit from the confidence of investors. They have only a small share of the market, and so have little power to influence either buyers or suppliers. Since they have so few resources, a little support can go a long way. A government grant could allow for a new technology to be demonstrated and tested for the first time. A subsidy could create the first market for the product. These targeted interventions can set in motion the reinforcing feedbacks of innovation and improvement, which develop their own increasing momentum over time.

The situation of incumbents at the start of a transition is the opposite. They enjoy market power, political influence, low financing costs, large production capabilities, sometimes large cash reserves, and usually a supportive policy environment. These resources can be marshalled in defence against anything that threatens their dominance. Defence strategies can include funding public campaigns that spread misinformation about new technologies, lobbying governments against policies that could change the status quo, and buying up new entrants to prevent the growth of new business models.[8] These strategies act as balancing feedbacks in the political economy: the more pressure there is for change, the more resources are mobilised to resist change. Consequently, taking the forces of incumbency head-on is likely to be a bad way to begin. Effort spent in this way is all too easily wasted.

A simple analogy is the physics equation, pressure equals force divided by area. This equation is the reason that banging a stake into the ground is easier if it has a pointy end. If your economic resources allow you to exert a certain amount of force, you will create much greater pressure for change if you concentrate this force in a small area (for example, the 10% of a market occupied by a new technology) than if you spread it over a large area (the 90% of the market occupied by the incumbent). Thinking about the structure of industry in this way makes it obvious that early in a transition, the more dynamically efficient policies will be those that help to grow the new industries, not those that put pressure on the old. Towards the end of a transition, when the old technologies have been reduced to a minority share, the opposite may be true.

Germany is one of the countries that has done the most to accelerate the global transition to clean power, and it is a good case study to illustrate this choice. The academics Anthony Patt and Johan Lilliestam explain that when Germany first started supporting solar photovoltaics, the cost of solar power was around fifty US cents per kilowatt hour more than the cost of electricity from coal.[9] This was the difference that policy had to overcome, to give solar a chance.

The subsidies solar needed were high for each unit of electricity it generated, but because there was so little solar power to begin with, the total amount of financial support was trivial in relation to the overall economy. These subsidies allowed the new industry to take root, and set in train the rapid technological improvement from which we are all now benefiting.

If Germany had instead tried to overcome the same cost differential by putting pressure on the incumbent technology, Patt and Lilliestam estimate that this 'would have required an initial carbon price of roughly $700 per tonne of CO_2, applied to fossil-based generators that then supplied more than 90% of the power market, and possibly to other sectors such as steel and cement. This would have crippled German industry and dramatically raised consumer prices. It was, rightly, a political non-starter.'

***

In summary, the policy recommendation of equilibrium economics does not stand up to scrutiny. Consideration of market structure, innovation process, and industrial influence all point to the conclusion that subsidising renewable technology is a more cost-effective approach than carbon pricing for decarbonising the power sector, and more likely to lead quickly to the result we need – the fossil fuels staying in the ground. The last two of these factors suggest the same should be true in any other sector, at least in the early stages of a transition.

By ignoring the advice of equilibrium economics, governments made much faster progress than they or anyone else expected. The total global deployment of solar power capacity in 2020 was over ten times as much as was projected for this year back in 2006.[10] Reinforcing feedbacks, it turns out, are powerful things.

This pattern has been visible in other sectors too. Stephane Hallegatte and Julie Rozenberg, forward-thinking economists at the World Bank, wrote in 2019 that 'Today, renewable energy is cheaper than coal in many places in the world, all major car manufacturers are working on several electric car models, and cities are starting to switch to electric buses. All of this was achieved with policies focussed on new investments, not with carbon taxes.'[11]

It is time we stopped finding this surprising. It is intuitive that success comes more easily when we first build up something new, before trying to push out something old and well established. When we understand the economy as an ecosystem, we can draw on a substantial body of theory and analysis that confirms this intuition. Beyond the power sector, there are many more sectors that we need to decarbonise, including agriculture, buildings, cars, trucks, steel, cement, shipping, and aviation. We will have a much better chance of achieving this quickly and cost-effectively if we stop thinking that any success from strategic investment is a lucky result from a second-best policy, the exception to the rule, and start recognising that this is actually the best thing to do.

THE ILLUSION OF TECHNOLOGY NEUTRALITY

If the case for strategic investment is accepted, an important question follows: in what should we invest?

Equilibrium economics tells us that we should aim to be 'technology-neutral'. We should set policies that determine the required outcome, and then leave the market to decide the technologies to which resources should be allocated.

As we saw in Chapter 11, however, in the ecosystem economy, no action is neutral. Any intervention will affect its evolution, advantaging some of its inhabitants and disadvantaging others.

Recall the marine ecosystem, with the seaweed whose value depended on who you asked, and when. Imagine we sent down a diver and pulled up all the seaweed. We might think this was a 'fish-neutral' intervention, because it was not intended to target any one species more than any other. But the small organisms that used it as a home, or those that hid within it, might be left dangerously exposed by its absence, while the large fish that used to eat it for lunch might have plenty of other options. To have an identical effect on every one of the thousands of species in the ecosystem is all but impossible. Biology has no concept of a level playing field.

The economy is no different. People who work with technology – researchers, engineers, and entrepreneurs – know this. Research and development cannot be done in a 'technology-neutral' way. Something has to be researched, and something has to be developed. A choice is unavoidable. Policymakers ought to know it equally well. Any policy, including the policy of inaction, will benefit some technologies and disadvantage others. And since the economy is an expression of its technologies,[12] these apparently small choices will together shape the economy of the future.

The story of decarbonising electricity in the UK gives an example of how these choices are unavoidable, and why they matter.

To satisfy the requirements of EU competition law, the UK's support for renewable power was designed to be 'technology-neutral'. This involved some interesting regulatory and intellectual contortions. Renewable power technologies were sorted into different categories: one for those that were more established, such as onshore wind and solar; one for those that were less established, such as offshore wind and biomass; and another one that nobody I met ever understood. Within each category, each technology was assigned a different maximum level of subsidy that it could receive. This was then used as a 'strike price' in an auction for fixed-price power generation contracts. To ensure each technology received an equivalent level of support, the strike price for each was set at a level estimated to result in the deployment of the same proportion of its maximum possible deployment. For example, if the market could deploy 10 billion watts (gigawatts, GW) of solar and 20 GW of wind at the maximum, then if 50%

were chosen as the common proportion, the strike prices would be set at the levels estimated to bring forward 5 GW of solar and 10 GW of wind.

If reading that paragraph gave you a slight headache, you are not the only one. I witnessed many people struggling, and failing, to make sense of this particular aspect of our policy.

The problem, as our Chief Scientific Adviser at the time Sir David MacKay pointed out, was that nobody knew what the 'maximum possible deployment' of any technology was.[13] The numbers were guesses, plucked out of the air by a consultant. If these numbers were arbitrary, then so were all the other numbers derived from them, including the strike prices. The policy was not technology-neutral; it was technology-blind: making choices accidentally instead of deliberately.

Fortunately, that was not the only way the policy was being decided. First, the decision to create more than one category within which renewable technologies would compete against each other was a strategic choice, aimed at giving 'less established technologies' such as offshore wind the chance to establish themselves in the market. Second, within each category there were multiple policy decisions that would support one technology or another, and these were not taken blindly.

Within the category of less established technologies, an important choice was between offshore wind and biomass.

Offshore wind was not the favoured choice of equilibrium economists. In 2014 *The Economist* magazine wrote that 'unfortunately, offshore wind power is staggeringly expensive', and quoted the economist Dieter Helm describing it as 'among the most expensive ways of marginally reducing carbon emissions known to man'.[14] (Helm, apparently, overlooked the fact that neither the reduction of emissions, nor the structural change in the economy, was ever intended to be marginal.)

On the other hand, offshore wind had several attractions. The UK had exceptionally good natural resources for it: a long coastline, a wide continental shelf with shallow seas, and winds from the Atlantic and the North Sea that rarely cease to blow. UK industry had many of the right capabilities, such as expertise in underwater engineering developed by a world-class offshore oil and gas industry. And UK society seemed to have the right set of preferences: strong support for action to address climate change, combined with dislike amongst some communities for land-based wind turbines that spoiled the scenery.

Biomass appeared more attractive to those who favoured least-cost marginal emissions reductions. A 2014 analysis suggested that converting coal power plants to run on biomass (that is, burning woodchips) was considerably cheaper than generating power from offshore wind.[15] On the other hand, the lifecycle emissions reductions of a process that involved cutting down trees in North America, chopping them into wood pellets, shipping them across the Atlantic, trucking them to converted coal power stations, and then burning them, were rather dubious. It was equally doubtful whether the practice of burning wood – not exactly one of human civilisation's most recent discoveries – was a good way to generate technological progress, jobs, and opportunities for UK industry.

Whether by luck or by judgement, considerations of geography, technology, and politics came out above those of equilibrium economics. Offshore wind was the path taken. The government invested in its research and development, supported its first commercialisation, gave it access to the continental shelf and connections to the electricity grid, and created a market for it using subsidised fixed-price contracts. At one point our 'technology-neutral' market design looked likely to accidentally choose biomass for a big slug of extra subsidy. Ministers were worried; civil servants scrambled to come up with a solution; and rules were changed to give the market a friendly shove in the right direction.

The results were a huge success. The cost of offshore wind power has fallen by over two-thirds within the past decade. The most recently agreed contracts are leading to offshore wind plants selling electricity at below the market price. This means that instead of the industry receiving a subsidy from the government, the government will be receiving a subsidy from the industry.

A colleague and I commissioned an independent report to look at what had brought about this dramatically successful fall in costs, so that we could share the lessons learned with other countries. The report estimated that around 80% of the cost reduction achieved in the past decade came as the result of market-shaping policies.[16] Just as in the case of solar power, these policies had driven the reinforcing feedbacks of learning by doing and economies of scale.

As the costs of offshore wind have come down, its market has grown, and so have its industry and supply chains, which now support over thirteen thousand jobs in the UK. Many of these high-productivity jobs are located in less wealthy parts of the country. This growth has encouraged further policy support: whereas six years ago we were aiming for 20 GW of offshore wind to be installed by 2030, now we are aiming for 50 GW – more than double the original target – by the same time. Subsidising offshore wind when it cost three times the market price must have required guts from ministers, especially when influential newspapers gave a platform to economists who ridiculed the policy. Now that the reinforcing feedbacks have taken on their own momentum, the task is getting ever easier.

A growing number of countries are now deploying offshore wind, and many are looking to learn from the UK. There appear to be good prospects for further cost reduction for the countries that use the technology, and further growth in jobs and exports for those that produce it. It is hard to argue that burning wood pellets, once the cheaper option, would have been a better bet.

***

If these successes have been achieved despite the recommendations of influential economists, imagine how much more could be achieved with advice that was more consistently helpful. We have no way of knowing how many investments in clean technologies have been withheld because governments chose to implement only carbon pricing instead, or how many technology choices have been made badly because they were made blindly.

It is hard to imagine a more strategic investment for humanity to make than the development of technologies that help us keep a safe and stable climate. We should not be deterred from making this investment by a mistaken understanding of the nature of the economy. And when we do make this investment, we should do it with our eyes open.

14

REGULATING FOR A FREE LUNCH

There is no doubt that 'regulation' has a bad name. In the public discourse on economics, it has an even worse reputation than 'subsidy', often being accompanied by adjectives such as 'costly' or 'burdensome', or replaced with the irritating cliché 'red tape'.

There are some understandable reasons for this. There is no shortage of examples of regulations that have been obstructive or misguided, or had damaging unintended consequences. In the most extreme cases, countries that have attempted to run 'command and control' economies have strangled their businesses in bureaucracy. That is nobody's idea of economic efficiency.

On the other hand, sometimes regulation is the best way of getting things done. It sets rules of the road that ensure safety, fairness, and functioning systems. Take, for example, the rule that tells you which side of the road you are allowed to drive your car on. This not only makes the roads safer; it makes the traffic system function. Nobody proposes that instead of requiring people to drive on the correct side of the road, we should merely incentivise them to do so. Obviously, this would be a weaker and less effective policy. Neither does anyone propose we should abolish this regulation so as to 'cut red tape'. Clearly, if we did, the system would become vastly less efficient, not more.

If regulation has a worse reputation than it deserves, then equilibrium economics has something to do with it. If we think the economy is in a state of optimal allocation of resources, then we must believe that any regulation will move it into a less perfect condition. If we decide that there is a market failure and some action is needed to fix it, then we would still prefer to avoid regulation if possible. A price-based instrument, such as a tax, can in principle 'price an externality' precisely, returning the economy to its perfect state of balance. A regulation, in contrast, seems ham-fisted: it sets an inflexible requirement rather than an incentive, so cannot be deployed with the same precision.

Whatever deeper and more nuanced understanding of regulation exists within the economics profession, as it undoubtedly does, the crude view that 'regulation is inefficient' remains widespread. Authoritative economists and institutions continue to promote it, and governments cannot help hearing it.

The field of climate change policy is no exception. Recall the 'Economists' Statement on Carbon Dividends', from Chapter 12. It casually refers to regulation as something to be avoided – 'substituting a price signal for cumbersome regulations will promote economic growth' – and even goes as far as to suggest, with no hint of irony, that lack of regulation 'will provide the regulatory certainty companies need for long-term investment'.

The International Monetary Fund is similarly negative. Its report on the economics of climate change tells us that regulations 'tend to be inflexible and difficult to coordinate cost-effectively across sectors and firms'.[1] A carbon price, it suggests, would be more efficient.

I have seen the government I worked for, and governments of other countries, be influenced by these views. The strong presumption that regulations are inefficient makes us less willing than we otherwise would be to use them as a policy tool to decarbonise the economy. But is this presumption justified?

GETTING THINGS DONE

In the ecosystem view of the economy, there is no presumption against regulations. Whether they are an efficient policy or not depends on what part of the economy we are trying to change, and how it works.

Experience shows us that in some circumstances, regulation can be the best way to get decarbonisation done, more effective and more efficient than alternative policies. This is perhaps most clearly the case in situations where people are satisfied enough with their current conditions not to change them, even when a change would leave them better off.

The classic example is energy efficiency in buildings. People often fail to make energy efficiency improvements to their houses even when the savings from reduced energy use would more than offset the initial outlay. As behavioural economics recognises, we are not all profit-maximising calculators. Sometimes we just look at the hassle involved in gaining some additional wealth and decide we can't be bothered. Risk aversion, habits, short-term thinking, as well as laziness, can all deter us from actions that are apparently in our economic best interests. In these situations, since cost is not the factor that is preventing change, a price-based policy is likely to be an inefficient way to achieve change. Regulation can be much more efficient, by simply removing an option that is both economically and environmentally worse. This is one reason why organisations with expertise in the buildings sector, such as the Global Alliance for Buildings and Construction, recommend mandatory standards as the best way to improve the energy efficiency of buildings.

Lighting provides a similar example. The energy policy expert Michael Grubb writes that by around 2010, light-emitting diode (LED) technology had advanced enough for these lightbulbs to be cheaper than the traditional incandescent sort, as well as ten times more energy efficient. Despite this, some people continued to buy incandescent bulbs, perhaps because of their familiarity. Research and development, standards, and government procurement had all played a role in advancing the transition to more efficient lightbulbs, but cost advantage was not enough to complete it. At that point, many governments decided to complete the transition by banning incandescent bulbs from the market. This was a simple and efficient way to stop people wasting money on unnecessarily expensive and climate-damaging products.[2]

It is not only individuals whose behaviour can be effectively changed by regulation. Sometimes this is the best way to influence firms' behaviour too.

The lack of energy-efficient houses in the UK is not only the result of the laziness of homeowners like me. It is also a consequence of the dynamics of the property market. It would be easier for everyone if houses were built to a high standard of efficiency in the first place, so that there was no need for homeowners to face the hassle and expense of upgrading them. But in the UK as in many other countries, property developers face high costs to acquire land, and then must sell houses at prices that compete with those of all the existing houses on the market. This creates a strong pressure to minimise the costs of construction.[3] Building poorly insulated houses is one of the ways that the industry responds to this pressure. Regulations that remove this option are a highly effective way to change the industry's behaviour.

There is also evidence that regulations are currently the most effective policy for accelerating the transition to zero-emission vehicles. Car manufacturers are investing heavily in the development of electric vehicles since this is clearly the direction the market is moving in, but most of them would prefer to delay the transition for as long as possible. Petrol and diesel cars are still much more profitable. Converting factories to manufacture electric motors instead of combustion engines requires a high capital outlay, and most firms don't want to do this until they really have to.

Pricing carbon, for example by taxing fuel, does relatively little to change this situation. If the industry has not converted its factories and only petrol cars are in the dealers' showrooms, people have no choice but to pay more for their petrol. The UK's taxes on vehicle purchase and fuel are together equivalent to a carbon price of around £300 per tonne of CO_2 (nearly ten times the 'social cost of carbon' recommended by the Whitehouse Council of Economic Advisers). This may have incentivised consumers to spend less on fuel, but for years it had no impact on the likelihood of anyone switching to an electric vehicle.[4]

In contrast, regulations that limit the allowable emissions per kilometre driven, or that require a rising proportion of cars sold by each firm to be zero-emission, are proving to be highly effective in forcing manufacturers to switch their investment to the new technology. Such regulations are central to the transitions now under way in Europe, China, and California.[5]

As we saw in the last chapter, an understanding of the structure of markets and industries can help us identify the most dynamically efficient policies. Sometimes this understanding, and our experience, point to regulation as the best option.

THE FREE LUNCH HYPOTHESIS

Even when regulation is acknowledged as necessary to solve a problem, it is usually assumed to come with a cost. An alternative view, however, has been around for some time.

In 1991 Michael Porter, an economist at the Harvard Business School, argued that well-designed environmental regulation could actually increase innovation and competitiveness. This ran counter to the traditional assumption that businesses were already doing all they could to maximise their profits, and so any regulation that restricted their options would inevitably reduce those profits.

Porter suggested that regulations could signal to companies where resource inefficiencies might exist, and where technological improvements might be found. Regulations could also encourage investment by reducing uncertainty, and create pressure that would motivate innovation and technological progress. In many cases, though not all, the additional innovation could more than offset the costs of compliance. As others have paraphrased it, Porter's claim was not that regulation is always a free lunch, but that 'there may be a free lunch in many cases'.[6]

In 2011 a group of academics looked at how well Porter's hypothesis had stood up to twenty years of theoretical scrutiny and observational evidence.[7] They concluded it had done pretty well: the theoretical arguments that justified it were 'more solid than they appeared at first'; and the empirical evidence that backed it up was now 'fairly well established'.

A few years later, a new contribution to this debate was made by a group of researchers including Steven Chu, a Nobel Prize-winning physicist who had gone to work as Energy Secretary in the US government, under President Obama.

Chu obviously cared about climate change, and he wanted to use his time in government to make some progress. One of his aims was to strengthen energy efficiency standards, but he found this to be a tough challenge. 'Regulations are hard to get through – even no-brainers,' he once told an interviewer. 'You know, the Department of Energy regulates appliance standards. And the bar is that with the regulation in place, the cost of owning and operating the appliance should be cheaper than not. That's the hurdle you have to satisfy. And even then, there's resistance.'[8]

Resistance came mainly from businesses that were hostile to regulations because they would face the costs of compliance, while consumers would enjoy the benefits. But the economic analysis of the Department of Energy did not help Chu make the case for his regulations as much as it could have.

Chu was surprised to discover that when the department was considering new energy efficiency standards, its analysis of their economic implications did not include any assessment of the potential for technological learning. The prices of the products in question were assumed to stay flat. 'This is kind of weird,' he recalls thinking. 'Because every time there was an estimate of how much that would cost to implement these standards, it seemed to be consistently overestimating.'[9]

Chu cared enough about the possibility of a regulatory free lunch that he began a research study in his spare time. After making his name in physics, this would be his first paper on economics. As the results started to come in, he found the food on offer was even better than expected. 'You really can have your cake and eat it too,' he told a journalist. 'You get higher performance. You get lower cost. And you're saving tons of money. And by tons of money, I mean the cost of ownership going down threefold, four-fold. Really dramatic.'[10]

The study carried out by Chu and his co-researchers looked at historical data on the energy efficiency and costs of refrigerators, clothes washing machines, and air conditioners. The costs of all of these appliances had been gradually falling over time, as the technologies improved. In each case, the data showed that after energy efficiency standards were imposed, the rate of cost reduction had accelerated. The effect was striking: the acceleration in cost reduction was significant and sustained.[11]

In discussing their results, Chu and his colleagues noted the discrepancy between their observations and the 'classical regulatory impact analysis picture', in which standards 'bring the market to a new equilibrium where appliances have higher prices and lower operating costs'. Their findings, they concluded, contributed to a growing body of evidence that standards could accelerate innovation and push prices not up, but down.

AN EVOLUTIONARY EXPLANATION

Equilibrium economics has always struggled to explain innovation. Equilibrium, after all, is defined as a 'situation in which nobody has any immediate reason to change their actions, so that the status quo can continue' – a situation, in other words, where there is no reason for innovation to take place.[12] Walras's model of an equilibrium economy took the existence of goods and services for granted, assuming they were already present within the market. Modern equilibrium models assume a certain amount of technological progress is happening, but they do not simulate it, and cannot explain how it happens.

The ecosystem view of the economy lends itself more easily to explaining the processes of innovation and change, and can help us understand the 'free lunch' effect that Porter hypothesised and Chu observed.

Ecosystems change through the process of evolution. Evolution involves variation, selection, and replication. For example, a population of beetles may include some that are green and some that are brown – a form of variation. One variant turns out to be more successful than the other: green beetles get eaten by birds more often – a form of selection – and so brown beetles survive longer and reproduce more often. The beetles pass on their colour genes to their offspring – a form of replication. Over time, the population evolves in the direction of the more advantageous trait, of being brown.[13]

Evolution operates continuously. The outputs of one round of variation, selection, and replication are the inputs for the next. As Charles Darwin discovered, it can explain the creation of novelty, the origin of species, and the growth of diversity and complexity. It is a powerful formula.

As we discussed in Chapter 11, the economy is part of our human ecosystem: a collection of our tools and practices. We should surely expect it to evolve, just as other aspects of our culture have. Technologies and business models undergo constant variation, the market imposes selection, and those that are successful are widely replicated. As the economy reconfigures itself around one set of technologies, it changes the conditions of success for the next. Over a century ago, the Austrian economist Joseph Schumpeter recognised the patterns of evolution at play in the economy.

More recently, researchers have shown that the same mathematical equations that describe the competition of different species within an ecosystem can also describe the competition of different technologies within a market.[14]

In an ecosystem, the rate of evolution of a given species depends on how well adapted it is to its environment. The less 'fit' a species is for its environment, the more intense the selective pressure – the 'survival of the fittest' – will be. The more intense the selection, the faster the rate of evolution.[15]

If we understand innovation in the economy as occurring through an evolutionary process, and we wish to speed it up, this gives us two options. We can increase variation by supporting research and development, bringing more new ideas and technologies into the economy. Or we can increase the intensity of selection, by changing the market so that its current occupants become less well adapted to their environment.

Steven Chu's energy efficiency regulations were an example of the latter approach. The regulations altered the environment. Products that did not pass the energy efficiency fitness test would not survive. The businesses that made them had to adapt to the new conditions, and this made them innovate more quickly than they had done before.

Equilibrium economics can justify support for research and development, because of the 'public good' market failure: the benefits to society from research and development are greater than those to the firm, so firms do not invest in it as much as would be socially optimal. But the equilibrium logic provides less justification for reshaping the market. If resources are optimally allocated, apart from the effects of any market failures, then a change to market conditions that incentivises more innovation in one part of the economy is assumed to result in less innovation in another part of the economy. The net effect is expected to be zero.[n]

The ecosystem understanding is different. As we have seen before, in a context of perpetual change, limitless options, and fundamental uncertainty,

---

[n] An exception to this may be found if innovation in one part of the economy creates more 'spillovers' – technologies or improvements that turn out to be useful in sectors other than that in which they were discovered – than does innovation in another part of the economy. Following this logic, researchers at the London School of Economics compared the relative intensity of knowledge spillovers from 'clean and dirty technologies' in energy, cars, fuel, and lighting. They concluded that because the clean technologies appear to generate more spillovers than the dirty ones, this can justify stronger public support for investment in clean technology research and development. https://www.lse.ac.uk/granthaminstitute/wp-content/uploads/2013/10/WP135-Knowledge-spillovers-from-clean-and-dirty-technologies.pdf

there is no such thing as an optimal allocation of resources – not for the whole economy, not for a firm, and not for an individual. We are all having to muddle along as best we can.

One choice that we all face is how much of our resources we should devote to 'exploitation' of our current environment, and how much to 'exploration' for something new. On an individual level, this can be the choice between maximising the benefits of a current job (either for career advancement, or for an easy life), and spending time and energy looking for a new job. For a firm, the choice can be between spending more on advertising their current products, or investing more in the research and development of new products.[16]

The implications for the economy are not zero-sum. When Albert Einstein decided to spend less time being a patent clerk and more time developing the theory of relativity, there did not have to be someone else making the opposite move to keep the economy in equilibrium. His decision caused a net gain in innovation for humanity. Similarly, a business can decide to concentrate less on milking the benefits of incumbency and more on finding the next disruptive innovation, without forcing any other firm to do the opposite. Regulations that reshape the market can cause a net gain in innovation within the economy.

My colleague Mark Taylor gave me an example of this which is purely anecdotal, but I think interesting because it comes from a part of the economy where most of us would assume innovation is happening at top speed all of the time: Formula 1 motor-racing. Mark spent twelve years as a Principal Aerodynamicist at McLaren Racing, one of the most successful teams in the history of the sport. Formula 1 racing teams spend huge budgets on innovation, perfecting every detail of the cars so as to reduce lap-times by hundredths of a second. The sport's governing body sets rules for the design of the cars that aim to ensure safety, fair competition, and an exciting spectacle. The size of the cars' engines, the width of their tyres, and the dimensions, functions, weight, and materials of various components are all subject to these regulations.

Sometimes several years go past without any significant changes to the regulations. At other times, when the authorities deem the racing to have become either too dangerous or too boring, they make large changes to lots of regulations at once. I once asked Mark, 'When do the teams innovate the fastest? The years when the regulations stay the same, or the years when they change?' 'What do you think?' Mark said. 'Of course, it's the years when they change.' Necessity, after all, is the mother of invention.

***

Our new understanding of the economy as an ecosystem promises to rescue an unloved policy instrument. Regulation, it turns out, can be an effective and efficient means to achieve decarbonisation and a way of accelerating innovation at the same time. We should embrace it more enthusiastically than we have done so far. This can only be good news for the battle against climate change.

The coming together of evolutionary theory, economic modelling, and practical understanding of industries and policies is still in its early stages. Governments surely have much to gain from supporting a more rapid development of this understanding. Those that learn how to shape a market to accelerate innovation will be better placed to support the competitiveness of their national economies than those that stay stuck in the mindset of the economy as a machine.

15

STUCK IN FIRST GEAR

It is time to talk about tax, or more specifically, carbon pricing – economists' favourite climate change policy. As much as it is praised by economists of the traditional mindset and by the many policymakers they have convinced, carbon pricing is despised by many activists and academics who know that it cannot on its own be enough to win us the battle. As a result, it is almost certainly the most widely talked about and written about of all climate change policies.

Carbon pricing has also been at the centre of political struggles, notably in the US, where proposed legislation to implement a carbon price was long seen as the test of Congress's willingness (or as it has turned out, lack of willingness) to deal with climate change; in Australia, where it has featured prominently in several elections and prime ministerial back-stabbings; and in France, where it helped to spark mass demonstrations and the most violent riots in half a century.

Is it worth all the fuss? In the last two chapters, we have already seen that investment and regulation can often do a better job. Does carbon pricing even matter? Despite the disproportionate level of attention it gets, I think carbon pricing is both worse than, and better than, most people realise. It depends, of course, on how it is done.

There are two main ways that governments can implement carbon pricing. One is a tax; the other is a cap-and-trade system.

A tax is relatively simple. The government charges a fixed amount for each ton of carbon emitted. Usually this is paid by businesses operating within a sector of the economy that needs to be decarbonised, such as the power sector.

A cap-and-trade system is more complicated. Businesses operating in the part of the economy covered by this policy have to buy permits for their carbon emissions. Permits can be bought from the government at the start of each year and can be traded between businesses during the year. Their supply is limited by a cap, which is usually reducing over time. The carbon price emerges from this market in permits.

The two policies can be varied in several dimensions. They can cover just one sector of the economy, or several. They can vary in stringency: how high the tax is set, or how quickly the cap is set to fall. The revenues they generate, through the tax and the sale of permits, can be either kept by the government or reinvested in the same part of the economy they came from. Many other detailed aspects of their design can be fine-tuned. Generally speaking, however, a carbon pricing policy is usually identifiable as one or the other of these two approaches.

EQUAL IN EQUILIBRIUM

So, which one is better?

The equilibrium economics view is that both approaches are, essentially, equally good. The Harvard University economist Robert Stavins explains why, in a comparison of the two options.[1]

Stavins writes that there are two basic rationales for carbon pricing. One, we have already discussed: environmental pollution is a 'negative externality' – an activity whose costs to society are not reflected in the market. This market failure can be corrected by putting a price on the externality. A carbon tax is therefore a natural solution to this problem.

The other rationale is based on the idea that environmental pollution is a property rights problem. We all want to enjoy the activities that cause pollution, but the environment can only take a limited amount of it. Therefore, we should establish a market so that the 'right to pollute' can be sold to the highest bidder. When the problem is seen this way, a cap-and-trade system – which sells permits to pollute – is the natural solution.

Importantly, as Stavins makes clear, at a deeper level these two economic rationales are the same. Both lead us to put a price on the cause of pollution (for us, carbon): directly in the case of a tax; indirectly in the case of cap-and-trade. In both cases, theory predicts that firms will reduce their emissions as long as it is cheaper to do so than to pay the carbon price. They will take all of the opportunities for emissions reduction that cost less than the carbon price, and none of those that would cost more.

Both approaches are seen as cost-effective because they offer the same price for reducing emissions to all actors and all activities (at least, those within the scope of the policy).° This allows the cheapest emissions cuts to be made first. No specific actor is forced to take any specific action. Under

---

° Formally speaking, both approaches equate marginal abatement costs across all sources of pollution.

the tax, each business can change its activities in whichever way allows it to reduce emissions most cheaply. Under the cap-and-trade, the market ensures that emissions are cut by the businesses that can do it most cheaply, who will sell their permits to those that would find it more expensive. Either way, the result is that emissions are reduced wherever this can be done most cheaply. Economic resources are optimally allocated, and we achieve the Holy Grail of climate policy: decarbonisation at least cost.

On this basis, following a detailed theoretical comparison, Stavins concludes that a carbon tax and a cap-and-trade system are 'perfectly equivalent' in terms of three critical measures of their performance: how much they incentivise emissions reduction; what the total costs of reducing emissions will be; and any effects on competitiveness of the businesses they affect. He takes the view that in other ways the policies have differing pros and cons – the tax likely to be administratively simpler, while the cap-and-trade may be more easily linked to policies in other jurisdictions – but ultimately he concludes that 'the specific designs of carbon taxes and cap-and-trade systems may be more consequential than the choice between the two instruments'.

This is not a conclusion unique to Stavins; it is the mainstream view. I have cited Stavins only because he has expressed it most clearly.

THE MAJORITY CHOICE

Many governments have acted on economists' recommendations and put in place some form of carbon pricing. According to the World Bank's count in 2020, a total of 61 carbon pricing policies have been put in place worldwide, covering economic activity that generates over a fifth of global emissions.[2]

Informed by the equilibrium view that the two approaches to carbon pricing are economically equivalent, the choice of policy has been seen as one of preference. Governments can choose either to have certainty over the costs, but uncertainty over the rate of emissions reduction (in the case of the tax), or certainty over the emissions reduction but uncertainty over the costs (in the cap-and-trade). Stavins finds that environmental interest groups have tended to show 'a strong preference for cap-and-trade over taxes, in part because these interest groups prefer policies that help obscure the costs, but make benefits transparent and visible'.[3]

If we simply count up the instances of the two policies, then they appear to be running neck and neck. Worldwide, there are 31 cap-and-trade schemes and 30 carbon taxes either operating or scheduled for implementation.[4] However, if we look at the size of the economies involved and the amounts of emissions covered by each policy, it is clear which one is ahead. Cap-and-trade systems, preferred by the EU, China, and California, cover a much larger proportion of global emissions than do carbon taxes. If we disregard all the policies with carbon prices of less than $10 per tonne, which may be considered token gestures, then the difference is even greater: about five times as many emissions are covered by cap-and-trade schemes as by carbon taxes.

Is this the right choice?

A FLAW IN THE LOGIC

The equilibrium view of the two carbon pricing policies rests on an important assumption. It considers the two policies to be equivalent because they each allow emissions cuts to be made wherever they can be made most cheaply, at each moment in time. The aim of policy, of course, is to reduce emissions cost-effectively *over the course of time*. The two policies are equivalent if we assume that doing the cheapest thing at each moment in time will lead inevitably to the lowest costs over the course of time.

If the economy never changed, this would be a fair assumption. The menu of emissions cuts tomorrow would be the same as it is today. We would take the cheapest items from the menu first, and keep doing so until we had collected all the emissions reductions we needed.

If the economy is changing over time, however, this assumption does not hold. One way of cutting emissions today might make it easier to do more tomorrow, by generating some momentum for change. Another way of cutting emissions might have a less helpful effect. Recall the UK's choice of technologies for clean electricity that we discussed in Chapter 13. Supporting offshore wind helped set in motion the reinforcing feedbacks of technology innovation, which reduced costs by more than two-thirds over the course of a decade. If we had instead subsidised the burning of wood pellets, we would not have seen the same effect.

By analogy, imagine you are riding your bike. At any moment in time, you can ride the bike with least effort by cycling in first gear. But if you want to ride around the block with least effort, first gear will not be ideal. You would do better to select a higher gear and generate some forward momentum. Although at some moments in time this will take more effort, overall, over the course of time, it will take less effort.

Minimising effort at a moment in time, and minimising effort over the course of time, are not the same. Allocative efficiency and dynamic efficiency, as Xenophon realised but Walras forgot, are not the same. Policy needs to know which one it is trying to achieve. Otherwise, we will be pedalling furiously but going nowhere fast.

DIFFERENT IN THEIR DYNAMICS

The challenge of cutting emissions is all about changing the economy structurally over time – moving from fossil-fuelled technologies, products, and systems to completely different clean alternatives. Doing this quickly and cost-effectively is a challenge of dynamic efficiency. As we have already seen, for this purpose it is no use thinking about the economy as if it were a machine, sitting still in equilibrium; instead, we have to think about it as an ecosystem. To choose the best policies, we need to think about the feedbacks that can either drive change or keep things the same.

James Hansen is someone who naturally thinks about feedbacks. For over two decades, he was Director of the NASA Goddard Institute for Space Studies. After leading research on the atmosphere of Venus, he later realised he could use some of the same techniques to study what was happening to the Earth's atmosphere. This led him to take a strong interest in climate change, and he became one of the first scientists to bring the matter to the centre of political debate with his briefing of the United States Congress in 1988. He was particularly concerned by the feedbacks in the Earth system that could accelerate warming and push humanity into a dangerous future.

Hansen has become something of a climate change hero for his fearless telling of truth to power, and his perseverance despite sometimes intense political intimidation. When I was first getting interested in climate change, his was one of the first books I read. Interestingly, I found that apart from his clear explanations of climate science and inside account of US politics, Hansen had something unusual to say about climate change policy. When he looked at policies, he was instinctively interested in the dynamics they would create. Comparing the two approaches to carbon pricing, he realised their effect was not the same.[5]

In a cap-and-trade system, any company that cut its emissions would have less need to buy permits. Since the supply of permits was fixed by the cap, this lower demand would lead to a lower price. The lower price would mean that there was less incentive for other companies to cut their emissions. In summary, any action to cut emissions led to less pressure for further action. In other words, the system created a balancing feedback. It was inherently self-limiting.

A carbon tax does not have the same effect. Each company has to pay the same charge for each ton of its own emissions, regardless of what any other company is doing. Under this policy, no balancing feedback is created. Hansen suggested that if the tax revenue were given back to companies as a dividend, shared out equally among all companies in the relevant sector, then the opposite would happen. If one company were to cut its emissions, it would pay less tax, and so decrease the total revenue. Other companies would receive a smaller dividend as a result, while still paying the same tax per ton of their own emissions, meaning that their net tax would increase. In this case, any action to cut emissions would lead to more pressure for further action. A reinforcing feedback would have been created, with a tendency to accelerate change.

Based on this logic, Hansen concluded that the two approaches to carbon pricing were fundamentally distinct. Given that reinforcing feedbacks tend to accelerate change, while balancing feedbacks tend to prevent change, he argued that tax-and-dividend would be the best policy, and cap-and-trade was the worst.[P]

In government, I tried several times to influence policy discussions on carbon pricing using Hansen's argument. I never succeeded. A major obstacle was that often, the people I was talking to did not know what a feedback was. (This is not unique to the UK – I have been asked what a feedback is by officials in other countries' governments too.) This is just one example of how the knowledge that most strongly influences policy is often not the latest findings of academic research, nor even best practice within government, but the legacy of our basic education and the ideas of earlier times. How many of us were taught about feedbacks when we were at school?

On one occasion, a senior economist kindly sat down with me to try to understand why I was so bothered about our choice of carbon pricing policy. After I had made my case, he took out a pen and paper and started sketching some supply and demand curves. Starting from first principles, he began, think about what needs to happen for the market to be in equilibrium ...

Having bashed my head against this particular brick wall for longer than was comfortable, I was delighted when I came across a study done by a Dutch researcher, Emile Chappin.[6] For his PhD thesis, he had built a model to compare the effects of a carbon tax and a cap-and-trade system on power

---

[P] Hansen uses individuals rather than companies to illustrate the difference. I have used companies here to be consistent with other descriptions of the two policy approaches in this chapter. The change does not affect the logic of the comparison. Hansen does not explicitly consider the option of tax without dividend, but its place in the order of preference can be inferred from his description of the other options.

sector prices and emissions. His experiment was unusual because of the kind of model he used: an agent-based model.

Agent-based models are very different from the equilibrium models used so often by central banks and governments. Unlike an equilibrium model, an agent-based model makes no assumption at the outset about how the system will behave. Like a weather forecaster's model, it does not assume that every day will be sunny and windless; instead, it makes some assumptions about how parts of the system interact with each other; then it simulates those interactions and discovers how the system behaves.[q] This allows for all kinds of dynamic states to be observed and predicted. Equilibrium is one state that could occur, but only one of many. Agent-based models have successfully simulated economic phenomena including asset bubbles and crashes, technological innovation, and the growth of inequality.[7]

Chappin used his model to simulate the behaviour of companies in an electricity market making decisions about which power generating technologies to acquire and use. He compared what happened under the two approaches to carbon pricing: a tax, and a cap-and-trade system. To make sure it was a fair comparison, he ran the cap-and-trade simulation first, and then used the average carbon price that it generated as the level for the carbon tax. That meant the two policies were being compared at levels of equal stringency.

The results were striking. The carbon tax outperformed the cap-and-trade system in three respects. It reduced emissions more quickly. It produced a lower cost of electricity over the period of operation. And it caused

[q] Agent-based models (ABMs) simulate the behaviour of individual 'agents', such as people or companies, within an environment. The rules by which the agents make decisions are specified in advance – they are inputs to the model – although in some models it is possible for the agents to learn and adapt their decision-making rules over time. A reasonable criticism of ABMs is that if the decision-rules are not realistic, then the system behaviour that emerges from the model will not be realistic either. This is true, and so designers of ABMs must aim to make their decision-rules as realistic as possible, based on the best evidence available. ABMs are unlikely ever to settle to equilibrium, and so do not give precise 'optimal' values as the solution to a policy problem – unlike equilibrium models. But as Andrew Haldane, the former Chief Economist of the Bank of England, has said in arguing for greater use of ABMs within macroeconomics, 'for most problems in macroeconomics, the accuracy in how a problem is posed is likely to be a far larger source of error than the lack of precision in the numerical solution of that problem' (Haldane and Turrell, 2017). Equilibrium models aim for numerical precision but achieve this at the cost of a huge assumption that determines 'how the problem is posed'. ABMs, on the other hand, offer a way to discover the nature of the problem. As the saying goes, it is better to be roughly right than precisely wrong.

a larger shift in market share from incumbent to new technologies, meaning that the market was better placed to achieve continued emissions reductions after the period of comparison. Chappin's model had confirmed Hansen's intuition.

DECARBONISATION AT MAXIMUM COST

Hansen's systems thinking and Chappin's agent-based model suggest that the approach to carbon pricing taken by governments of most of the world's largest economies is the wrong one. It is slower and more expensive than the alternative approach. Given the urgency of action to address climate change, this is a mistake that we cannot afford to make.

But is it even worse than that? Now that we know that a cap-and-trade system does not give us decarbonisation at least cost, it seems worth examining it more critically.

Let's think about what actually needs to happen to decarbonise the power sector. Putting it simply, we need to move from a system that runs on coal and gas to one that runs on sun and wind. The main economic challenge of this transition is to build all the infrastructure: the solar panels, wind turbines, batteries, grids, and clever bits of kit to balance electricity supply and demand. If we assume the operating costs of the new system are the same as those of the old (a conversative assumption, as they are likely to be cheaper), then the cost of the transition is the cost of replacing the old capital stock with the new. To a rough approximation, we can think of this as a single lump sum that needs to be spent.[r]

As we have seen, the cost of the new technologies falls rapidly once they start being deployed, but at first it is very high. Early in the transition, a ton of emissions can be saved much more cheaply by burning coal more efficiently, or by switching from coal to gas, than by installing wind or solar power. A policy that makes the cheapest emissions cuts at each moment in time will therefore tend to focus effort, early in the transition, on making the fossil-fuelled system more efficient. From the long-term perspective, this

---

[r] There are, of course, many caveats to this extremely rough approximation. Most obviously, there is a limit to how quickly learning can take place. A new system cannot be installed instantaneously. In addition, there will be what are sometimes known as 'adjustment costs', such as the costs of accessing skilled workers and scarce capital, and these may be higher if a transition is faster. Vogt-Schilb, Meunier and Hallegatte make these points in a discussion of this approximation in their paper 'Climate policy: when starting with the most expensive option makes sense'.

is wasted effort. If we need to replace all that fossil infrastructure stock with zero-emission technology, why bother making it more efficient before we throw it all out? It's like replacing the windows in a block of flats that is about to be demolished. Every dollar spent is a dollar wasted.

By painstakingly incentivising only the cheapest emissions reductions at each moment in time, the cap-and-trade policy delays the expensive but necessary task of replacing the capital stock for as long as possible. This maximises the time in which money will be wasted on making the fossil system more efficient. Over the full course of the transition, it gives us decarbonisation at maximum cost.

For a least-cost transition, we would need to do the opposite: focus all of our effort on deploying the zero-emission technologies. This will require the most effort at the beginning, and gradually less effort over time as the technology costs come down. The sooner we get on with replacing the capital stock, the less money we are likely to waste on tinkering with the old system. Of course, if we really care about cutting emissions, we should do both at once – force the fossil system to operate as efficiently as it can, at the same time as replacing it as quickly as we can – but here I am focusing on the comparison between the cost-effectiveness of the two opposite approaches.

In an economy of limitless possibilities, there is of course no such thing as a worst possible pathway through time any more than there is a best possible one. We can imagine policies that would be more expensive than a cap-and-trade system. We could, for example, build a new coal power plant every Tuesday and blow it up every Thursday, just for fun. In this context, 'decarbonisation at maximum cost' is an overstatement. However, within the rough boundaries of a set of reasonable policy options, I think the criticism is a fair one. When the most cost-effective approach to a transition is to take the measures requiring maximum effort at the beginning, then a system designed to achieve the opposite is about as unhelpful as it could be. To return to our cycling analogy, cap-and-trade is like being permanently stuck in first gear.

COMPOUNDING THE ERROR

So far, we have only talked about how a cap-and-trade system might affect one sector of the economy, in one country. But advocates of the policy usually have grander ambitions for it than this.

The logic of equilibrium economics recommends expanding cap-and-trade schemes to cover as many economic sectors as possible, and even linking them internationally to include as many countries as possible. The broader the area of economic activity they cover, the more opportunities there will be to find the very cheapest of all possible ways to reduce emissions, at each moment in time.

The World Bank reports that governments are following this advice, expanding their cap-and-trade systems across economic sectors and national and state boundaries. In the past year, Switzerland linked its cap-and-trade system to that of the EU, and the US states of New Jersey and Virginia joined up with the Regional Greenhouse Gas Initiative, a regional carbon market operated by a collection of states in the northeast of the country.[8]

I suspect it is not only economic logic that drives this expansion. Policies that involve a great deal of bureaucracy to administer, as cap-and-trade does, constantly suck in civil servants to work on them. Many of those officials form an attachment to the policy they have worked hard to implement, and continue to advocate it after they have moved on to other jobs within the organisation. This feedback – perhaps evidence that not all reinforcing feedbacks in climate policy are helpful – gives the policy a self-perpetuating and expanding tendency, and makes it extra hard to get rid of. UK government officials have not only diligently implemented cap-and-trade in our own country; they have also enthusiastically promoted it abroad.

We have seen enough now to know that all this market linking and expansion is likely to achieve the opposite of what is intended. Chasing allocative efficiency is a mistake when the aim is to change things effectively over the course of time. The more opportunities to find cheap emissions cuts there are, the longer the more expensive but necessary steps will be delayed, and the more money will be wasted on unnecessary interim measures.

When cap-and-trade is applied across sectors, the availability of cheap emissions reductions in the 'easier' sectors such as electricity will keep the carbon price much lower than is needed to incentivise the deployment of clean technologies in 'harder' sectors like steel. For the whole of the time that it takes to decarbonise electricity, the carbon market will only incentivise the steel industry to spend money on making its fossil-fuelled infrastructure more efficient. Although this reduces emissions temporarily, it does not contribute to long-term change. In the big scheme of things, it only adds to the cost of the transition. If the carbon markets covering the two sectors were kept separate, then at least they could both proceed at their own pace: steel would not have to wait for electricity, and overall, less money would be wasted.

When cap-and-trade is applied across different countries, the effect will be similar. More difficult decarbonisation actions will be postponed in the more advanced countries, in favour of easier actions being taken in countries that are further behind. This may seem attractive to the advanced country that is able to temporarily spend less to claim a given level of emissions reduction, but from a global perspective it is simply delaying needed investments and increasing the overall cost of the transition.

On top of that, the balancing feedback will act as a further discourage-ment: actions taken in one country to accelerate decarbonisation will only lower the carbon price, reducing the pressure on other countries to follow. I remember this being pointed out once at the Department of Energy and Climate Change when we were considering some new policies for industrial decarbonisation. At the time, the UK was part of the EU Emissions Trading Scheme, a large cap-and-trade system that covers energy-intensive industries and the power sector across all of the EU's Member States. We knew that the policies we were considering could help UK industry to reduce its emissions. But we also knew that if they succeeded, they would only make it cheaper to burn coal to generate power in Poland. That wasn't an encouraging thought.

The broader the geographical expansion, the worse these effects are likely to be. In her studies of the great technological revolutions of the past, Carlota Perez finds they have generally started wherever the 'industrial core' of the global economy was at that time.[9] Then they propagated outwards, eventually reaching the countries on the economic periphery. The first industrial revolution – that of iron machinery, the mechanised cotton industry, water wheels, and canals – started in Britain in the 1770s before spreading outwards. The age of steam and railways began in Britain in the 1830s, and spread first to Europe and America, and then to the rest of the world. In the revolution that launched the age of steel, electricity, and heavy engineering, the USA and Germany took the lead. Then in the twentieth century, the revolutions first of oil, the automobile, and mass production, and then of information and telecommunications, each started in the USA and then travelled outwards via Europe to the rest of the world.

In each of these cases, the technological capability and financial capital of the world's most industrially advanced countries were the driving forces behind the revolution. If we want the clean technology revolution to pro-ceed quickly, we surely need the same to happen. Sucking the pressure for change out of the industrial core countries, and diverting it to countries on the periphery, would not be a helpful thing to do.

We can see this by analogy with one of the technologies used in that first industrial revolution: the water wheel. A river that flows across a plain is free to find its path of least resistance. It spreads out broadly, meanders around, and flows slowly. A water wheel placed in the river at this point would generate a minimal amount of energy. But when the river is forced into a narrow channel, it accelerates into a powerful torrent. A water wheel placed at this point will spin quickly, generating a large amount of useful energy.

Industrial investment is like the flow of the river, and policy shapes its landscape. A policy that allows investment to follow the path of least resistance will lead to a minimum rate of change in the desired direction. To achieve rapid change, policy needs to force investment into a narrow channel, to build up pressure, and to ensure the only outlet is through economic change in the desired direction. Any policy that lessens this pressure, by giving investment more places to flow, will be unhelpful.

***

We began this chapter by asking what kind of carbon pricing policy is likely to be most effective – an important question, since carbon pricing is the climate change policy most strongly advocated by many economists and economic institutions. We have seen that the form of carbon pricing most widely used in the world, cap-and-trade, is the least effective of the available options. It creates a balancing feedback, leading to a slow transition accompanied by high costs.

More fundamentally, we have found reason to believe that the basic premise of this policy – that minimising effort at a moment in time will minimise effort over the course of time – could not be more wrong. Following this logic only leaves us stuck in first gear. And the further we follow it, the more firmly we are stuck.

16

RUNAWAY TIPPING POINTS OF NO RETURN, REVISITED

When I was at school, we often used to push back in our chairs, pivoting them on their back legs with the front legs up in the air, so that we could sit with a more relaxed attitude. Every now and then, someone would tilt their chair a bit too far backwards and fall onto the floor with a crash, to be laughed at by the rest of the class (and reprimanded by the teacher). Occasionally, someone would feel their chair about to fall backward, and desperately grab the desk in front of them to prevent it. They would then do their best to look as if nothing had happened.

That place where the chair balances perfectly on two legs, where it could go one way as easily as the other, is the tipping point. At this point, the tiniest push can take the person-on-chair system into an entirely different state: from respectable uprightness to humiliating collapse.

As we saw in Chapter 5, the climate is full of tipping points, and from our point of view, these are bad news. We want to keep the climate as close as possible to how it has been for all the time that our civilisation has developed. Tipping points are dangerous because they threaten to take us far into new territory. The point at which the Greenland ice sheet becomes committed to complete disintegration, giving us an extra six metres of sea level rise, is one we would really rather not cross. This is probably the main reason why countries of the world are now aiming to keep global warming below 1.5°C instead of just below 2°C.

In the economy, our interest is the opposite. To eliminate emissions, we need to make changes on a massive scale, and to do so as quickly as possible. That makes tipping points, where a small push can bring about a large change, great sources of opportunity. In two examples that I wrote about with Timothy Lenton, the tipping point expert we met in Chapter 5, it appears that tipping points have contributed to countries making the world's fastest transitions in large greenhouse-gas-emitting sectors of the economy.[1]

TIPPING COAL OUT OF THE POWER SECTOR

When I worked at the Department of Energy and Climate Change, I spent some time trying to understand what had been done that had led to such a rapid decarbonisation of our electricity generation. In most of the greenhouse-gas-emitting parts of the economy, the UK's performance was nothing to shout about, but in the power sector, we were the fastest decarbonising country in the world.[2]

Many of our policies were similar to those of other countries. Like everyone else, we were subsidising renewables, and as solar panels and wind turbines sprang up around the country, they gradually ate into the fossil fuels' share of electricity generation. Like many other rich countries, we had controls on air pollution that made it more expensive to run coal power plants. Together with all the other countries in the EU, and many other states and countries elsewhere, we had put a price on carbon in the power sector, to disincentivise the burning of coal and gas. None of these policies could explain why we had made progress more quickly than others.

The one thing that was different was our carbon tax. The EU's carbon price was levied through a cap-and-trade scheme, which, as we saw in the last chapter, has a built-in balancing feedback that usually means it has limited effect. In the UK, we had supplemented this with a fixed carbon tax that raised the costs of burning fossils by a more significant amount. I knew this policy must be important because industry groups often lobbied us to abolish it. In climate change policy, that is often a sign that you have hit on something useful.

One day I came across a set of charts that showed me why this tax was so important. In the wholesale market for electricity, the power plants that generate power most cheaply get to supply the market first. Successively more expensive power plants then come on in turn, in what is known as the 'merit order', until demand is met. For a long time, coal plants had been able to generate electricity more cheaply than gas, and so had had priority in the market. Beginning in late 2015, the carbon tax together with the cap-and-trade scheme caused a reversal: they made power from coal (the more carbon-intensive of the two fossil fuels) more expensive than power from gas. This switched the positions of the two fuels in the merit order so that gas had priority, and coal had to wait. A tipping point had been crossed: the relatively small push of a carbon tax at £18 per tonne had led to a structural change in the system, with the disproportionately large result of coal plants generating electricity – and revenue – for far fewer hours than before.

I searched online to see what had followed from this change. It was clear that even before this tipping point had been crossed, the use of coal in our electricity generation had been falling as renewables ate into its market share, and pollution controls and carbon pricing added to its costs. The switch in the merit order was the last straw. Together with those other factors, it pushed the system past a second tipping point: that of coal plant profitability. In April 2016, Peter Atherton, an analyst of utility companies, commented, 'The economics of coal have deteriorated dramatically over the last 18 months . . . the increase in the carbon tax . . . flipped the economics over from barely profitable to loss-making.'[3]

With coal plants becoming loss-making, utility companies had no incentive to continue to operate them. Many were closed and demolished, some with their giant cooling towers being blown up in spectacular style, to the delight of onlookers. The decline in coal's share of electricity generation accelerated. Having stood at around 40% in 2012, by 2020 it was less than 1%.

TIPPING PETROLEUM OUT OF TRANSPORT

If the UK has done well in the power sector, Norway has done even better in road transport. Across the world, nearly all cars run on petroleum or diesel. Electric vehicles are spreading rapidly, but in 2019 they made up only about 2–3% of global sales. In countries with stronger policies, the proportion was higher – for China it was nearly 5%. But when you lined up countries' electric vehicle share of car sales on a chart, Norway stuck out like a sore thumb: it had already reached well over 50%, around twenty times higher than the global average.[4]

Norway has many policies to support the growth of electric vehicles, but one of them is unique. A combination of taxes and subsidies makes electric vehicles cheaper to buy than the equivalent petrol-powered cars.[5] Not surprisingly, this seems to have activated a tipping point in consumer preference. When petrol cars were cheaper, people preferred to buy petrol cars; when electric vehicles became cheaper, people went for those instead. With a policy input somewhat stronger than that of other countries, Norway has achieved a disproportionately large outcome. The result is the world's fastest transition to zero-emissions road transport.

A SHORT-SIGHTED VIEW OF THE LANDSCAPE

This might not sound as if it needs a genius to figure out. Making clean technologies cheaper than dirty ones seems like a no-brainer. To many of us, this would be the natural thing to do. The surprise, then, is that these examples are so rare. The UK's performance in the power sector, and Norway's in road transport, are both exceptional.

The reason, I believe, is that policymakers guided by equilibrium economics are not looking for tipping points. When I spoke to the civil servants who had created the UK's carbon tax in the power sector, I asked if it had been deliberately designed to cross the coal-to-gas tipping point. Nobody said it had. In fact, the policy had originally been for the carbon price to be on a constantly increasing trajectory, rising to a much higher level. As far as I could tell, the fact that it rose just high enough to activate the tipping point – and so to become our single most successful decarbonisation policy – was a happy accident.

In the strange world of equilibrium economics, decarbonisation is the task of Sisyphus. In the Ancient Greek myth, the gods punished Sisyphus for his murderous and dictatorial ways by condemning him to an eternity of rolling a boulder up a hill, only for it to roll down every time it neared the top. The economic model of Nobel laureate William Nordhaus, and others like it, behave in exactly the same way. If we spend some money to cut some emissions one year, the effect is assumed to be only temporary: to save the same emissions next year, we will have to spend the money again. However hard we try to push the boulder up the hill of decarbonisation, it always rolls back down, and every year we start again from the same place.

Policymakers guided by this view of the economy face a grim prospect. Equilibrium economics does not recognise that the top of the hill exists. It assumes that the shape of the economy never changes, so if we find ourselves on the side of a hill now, we must always be on the side of a hill. Its advice is therefore that we should carry out our hopeless task with a minimum of effort.

Specifically, the traditional advice is that we should only move the boulder far enough for the effort of pushing it to be matched by the benefit of being slightly higher up. In the jargon, economic efficiency is achieved when marginal cost equals marginal benefit. Spend a bit more money, face a bit less risk of dangerous climate change.

The problem with this approach is that the outcome is entirely arbitrary. As we saw in Chapter 9, there is no objective way to value the whole of the risk posed to society by dangerous climate change. The models that attempt this put made-up numbers into made-up equations, and are rightly described by the experts who understand them as 'worse than useless'. If these models are used to calculate a supposedly 'correct' price to put on carbon, it is down to pure luck whether or not that price will achieve anything useful.

To give an analogy, let's return to our friend the frog in the slowly boiling pot of water. Having managed to get a risk assessment out of his science adviser, the frog now knows that he needs to get out of the water before it's too late. He turns to his chief economist and asks, 'What should I do?'

The chief economist whips out a pen and paper and gets to work. He estimates how much the frog is willing to pay to avoid each degree of temperature increase. He does this by looking at what the frog normally pays for his air conditioning at home. Then he estimates how much energy the frog would use to climb each centimetre of the side of the pot, taking him gradually further from the hot water. He works out the economic cost of this effort first by converting energy use into food consumption, and then by converting that into dollars based on the frog's typical weekly supermarket bill. Finally, he puts these two equations together to find the point where the additional effort of climbing the side of the pot is exactly offset by the additional benefit of being further from the hot water. He tells the frog, 'The most efficient solution is for you to climb 4.73 centimetres up the side of the pot.'

The frog does not understand all the equations, but they look impressive, and the precise answer sounds authoritative. He accepts the advice and climbs 4.73 centimetres up the side. After a short while though, he is worried. It's taking constant effort to stay part way up the side of the pot, and it hasn't actually solved the problem: although he is further from the water, it is still warming up. He risks being steamed instead of boiled.

The frog decides to take a different approach. He asks the chief economist how high the sides of the pot are. The chief economist measures the height and tells him: 10 centimetres. The frog gathers his strength and launches himself into an 11-centimetre jump. He clears the side, and lands in safety on a cool surface. Then he sits back and relaxes, and wonders what to do next.

FREEING SISYPHUS

Thankfully, the economy is no more fixed than the Earth is flat, and decarbonisation does not need to be the task of Sisyphus. There may be some ways to cut emissions that are only temporary, but there are others that are permanent. If we demolish a coal power station and build a wind farm instead, the wind farm can generate zero-emissions electricity for a couple of decades, and when it can no longer be repaired, it will probably be replaced with another wind farm.

Imagine you are pushing a large boulder up a hill in the real world, instead of in Hades. Most of the way up, it takes a lot of effort to move the boulder a short distance. If you give a great shove, the momentum carries it a little way, but it soon stops and tries to roll back. Gravity is constantly trying to return it to the bottom of the hill where you started. Somewhere near the top, however, the hill flattens, and it becomes easier to push the boulder forward. Then, you find the tipping point: one more small push sends the boulder over the top, and all the way down the other side. Resistance is replaced with self-accelerating change, and the boulder ends up in an entirely new place. You, or Sisyphus, can finally relax.

We can think of a technology transition as happening in a similar way, as shown in Figure 16.1. Early research and development of a new technology pushes the boulder off the plain and onto the lower slopes of the hill. This takes intensive investment. If at any point the investment is cut off (taking your hands off the boulder), the new technology is likely to die (the boulder rolls back to the start). Policy pushes the boulder further up: public procurement, subsidies, or regulation help the new technology get established and give it a growing share of the market. Still, while the new technology is not yet fully competitive, removing policy support will allow incumbents to take back full control of the market. If we persevere, though, we may find a tipping point. Then the new technology begins to spread unaided by policy. Investors abandon the incumbents and pour all their resources into the new way of doing business. The forces for change become more powerful than the forces of resistance, and the transition becomes self-accelerating.

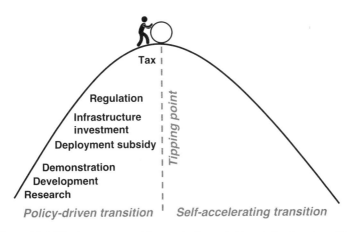

Figure 16.1 The journey to and from a tipping point in a technology transition.

This is a common phenomenon. Most successful technologies have at some point passed a tipping point, where they went from being niche curiosities to rapidly spreading tools of a 'new normal' way of doing things, displacing incumbents more suddenly than anyone expected. Tipping points can be crossed in competitiveness, consumer preference, or investor confidence; and of course, all of these elements interact. This is why, as the economist Rudi Dornbusch famously said, 'In economics, things take longer to happen than you think they will, and then they happen faster than you thought they could.'

Government policy is not always involved. In many areas of economic activity, society has no particular strategic interest in what happens next, and we are free to sit back and watch what the market serves up. In respect of climate change, though, we have a strong interest. We need clean technologies to take over from fossils, and we know they can only do this quickly enough if we give them some hefty help from policy.

Both of the above examples of fast decarbonisation took place in the context of global transitions, where a lot of groundwork had already been done. In the power sector, the decades of support for research and development made solar and wind into viable technologies, lifting them up the lower slopes. Policies supporting their deployment pushed them further up: subsidies, grid connections, and reforms to electricity markets that help them compete successfully against coal and gas power. As we push on further, the way becomes less steep: the more wind and solar we deploy, the better and cheaper it gets, and the easier it is to deploy some more. Now the boulder seems very close to the top of the hill, if not already over it. Solar and wind are now the cheapest forms of electricity generation in almost all countries, so their deployment is increasingly driven by purely commercial or economic interests. There are still some large bumps and dangerous chasms to negotiate on the way down the other side of the hill, but the transition has already acquired its own self-accelerating momentum.

Similarly in road transport: research has developed the technologies we need for electric vehicles; regulations have forced manufacturers to make them; subsidies have encouraged consumers to buy them; and investment in charging infrastructure has made it possible to use them. As the car industry shifts its investment into this new technology, its cost is falling rapidly. The boulder is not yet over the top of the hill. Electric vehicles are still more expensive to make than petrol cars, and are mostly sold at a loss; if all policy support for them were to be removed, it is likely that car firms would quickly abandon them, sending the market back to its starting point of petrol and diesel dominance (the bottom of the hill). But the summit is within sight.

With a few more years of pushing, we will reach the point where electric vehicles can compete unaided. Beyond that point, consumers will increasingly prefer to buy them, manufacturers will prefer to make them, and even governments that care nothing for climate change will want to support the transition in their own countries.

The boulder on the hill is a simplified analogy. Just as the Earth system has many tipping points on many scales – from the survival of a species of insect, to the sustainability of an ecosystem – so does any sector of the economy. This is a reason to be hopeful: there are many opportunities for things to change faster than we expect. Some of these tipping points will be easier to find than others, but what they all have in common, as points where a small push produces large results, is that they give us a lot of bang for our policy buck. Given how desperately we need to make faster progress in decarbonising the global economy, we would be crazy not to go looking for these opportunities.

SEEING MORE SUMMITS

Before setting out on our search for tipping points, there are some blinkers that we need to cast off. Not only have governments been blinded by equilibrium economics to the existence of the top of the hill, and advised to measure their steps by an arbitrarily determined 'correct' price of carbon, but they have also been misled by the recommendation to apply the same price of carbon across all sectors of the economy.[s]

As we discussed in the previous chapter, the idea has been that emissions should be cut wherever this can be done most cheaply. This would make sense in a flat-Earth economy where our surroundings never changed. A uniform carbon price applied to the whole economy would help us find the cheapest emissions cuts at any given moment in time. But in the ever-changing landscape of the real economy, this is a poor guide to navigation. The least-cost move now is not necessarily consistent with the least-cost strategy over a period of time. The next step that is easiest to take does not always lead to the best pathway for crossing the hills.

If we look around us, we can see that each greenhouse-gas-emitting economic sector has its own unique topography of decarbonisation. The power sector is a hill whose top we are near: in recent years, a carbon price

---

[s] This is a standard recommendation of equilibrium economics. To give just one example, it was a central recommendation of the Cost of Energy Review conducted for the UK government by the economist Dieter Helm in 2017.

of £18 per tonne had a dramatic effect in the UK; soon, none will be needed. Road transport has been a higher hill to walk up: for many years, taxes equivalent to a carbon price of £300 per tonne had almost no effect on the UK's transition to zero-emission vehicles, while in France, a fuel tax caused months of social protest without doing anything useful for decarbonisation. Steel is a cliff face that we have barely begun to climb. The buildings sector, where energy efficiency could save money as well as emissions, is more like a downward-sloping field, albeit with some tricky bumps to be negotiated.

In this landscape, as Figure 16.2 depicts, a uniform carbon price across the economy is hopelessly inefficient. A level sufficient to get the boulder over the hill in road transport would be much more than is needed in the power sector, and of no use whatsoever in steel. In the buildings sector, it is like pointlessly lifting the boulder up with a high crane to carry it across a field, when rolling would have been perfectly adequate. We can't afford to waste that kind of effort.

To channel our efforts more efficiently, we need a more calibrated approach. First, we should use targeted investment and all the other policies necessary to push the boulder up the hill in each sector. Then we should apply just the right amount of effort – which may be in the form of tax, or subsidy, or regulation – at the right moment, to push it over the top. Having used no more effort than was necessary, we can then stand back and watch with satisfaction as it rolls down the other side.

If we understand this to be the aim of policy, then the successes achieved by the UK in the power sector and by Norway in road transport

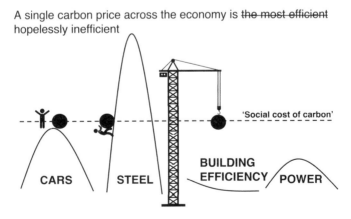

Figure 16.2 The dynamic inefficiency of a uniform economy-wide carbon price.

need not remain as exceptions. Now that we know what we are looking for, we can find many opportunities to replicate such rapid progress.

From where we stand, we can already see the tops of some of the hills around us. The view is not bad at all; we are definitely not in Hades. We can see tipping points where clean technologies could outcompete greenhouse-gas-emitting incumbents in several sectors, and some are not that far off. Electric aeroplanes could become cheaper than jet-fuelled planes on short-haul flights within the coming decade. Plant-based meat could taste the same as meat from animals and cost less, saving huge quantities of emissions from deforestation (as land is cleared for cattle grazing) and from the burping and farting of cows.[6] Hydrogen produced from renewable-powered electrolysis could become lower-cost than hydrogen from fossil fuels, creating new opportunities for decarbonised industry. Each of these tipping points can be targets for policy. Once investment has brought us close enough, then if we want to use carbon pricing, we can use it at just the right level to tip each of these sectors into self-accelerating transitions.

Across the landscape, businesses seeking to shift markets towards sustainability may be able to activate tipping points in investor confidence. Campaigners and NGOs may be able to find tipping points in public perceptions.[7] Some will be harder to see than others, and some will be difficult to reach. The best start we can make is to throw out our mental maps of the flat-Earth economy and all the navigational recommendations that they contain. If we set off in search of tipping points, we will find some of them. And as we move forward, more of the landscape will come into view.

FIVE TIMES FASTER?

If the change in economic understanding that I have called for is put into practice, will it be enough to give us the five times faster global decarbonisation that we need, to avoid dangerous climate change?

The UK's experience in the transition from coal to clean power is encouraging. Its combination of targeted investment, regulatory changes, and tax that activated tipping points resulted in a decarbonisation of the power sector that was, over the past decade, about eight times faster than the global average.[8] Norway has even more significantly outperformed the global average pace of transition in road transport. These two examples suggest that the kinds of policies that the new understanding of economics recommends can indeed bring a great acceleration of progress.

We must bear in mind, though, that these outstanding national performances were not independent of their global context. The UK's ability to deploy wind and solar power, and Norway's ability to put electric vehicles on the road, existed thanks to decades of efforts by many countries to make those technologies available. To put the whole global economy on track to decarbonise five times faster, it is likely that not only stronger national policies, but also stronger international action will be needed. That is the subject of Part III of this book.

17

REVOLUTIONARY

A transition of ideas may be much like a transition of technology. At first, new ideas are untested, unfamiliar, and often unwanted. They are likely to need a first niche for deployment – an issue on which they can prove their worth – before they can spread more widely through society or across our intellectual landscape. As they spread, they will meet opposition, particularly from those whose interests they threaten, and the lines of battle will be drawn along many fronts. Eventually, if the new ideas are strong enough to see off the incumbents, whole new systems of knowledge and patterns of activity will be reconfigured around them.

The shift from equilibrium economics to evolutionary (or 'complexity') economics is a transition of this kind.[t] The preceding chapters have, I hope, made it clear that the new ideas of evolutionary economics are considerably stronger than the old ideas of equilibrium: they are better at explaining what we see, and at predicting what will work. But this does not mean that they will be instantly accepted. The transition is still at an early stage. The new ideas hold only a small share of the market for economic analysis and advice.

Technology transitions can be moved forward by many different actors: inventors of new products, investors in new businesses, campaigners for new standards, and governments that change the rules of the economic game. When people at different places in the system act in ways that reinforce each other's efforts, change can happen surprisingly quickly. The same is likely to be true in the economy of ideas. In this chapter, we look at some of the actors who are gearing up for battle in the movement towards an evolutionary understanding of economics.

---

[t] The labels of 'evolutionary economics' and 'complexity economics' have been used by different groups of researchers at different times, with 'complexity' being more recent and encompassing other mutually compatible schools of thought. Both understand the economy as a complex adaptive system, in which processes of change are evolutionary in nature. Here I am using the terms interchangeably.

THE ACADEMICS

New ideas, like new technologies, are often made by combining existing ones in original ways. The academics pushing forward the boundaries of new economic thinking draw their inspiration from some of the intellectual greats of the past.

Erik Reinert, the economic historian and development economist we met in Chapter 12, gives practical advice to governments that draws on the body of economic thought produced before the year 1850 – the point where, in his view, the discipline took a wrong turn. Steve Keen, whose disequilibrium model predicted the global financial crisis, is one of the economists who describe themselves as 'post-Keynesian' – following in the footsteps of Keynes, who in the 1930s put forward pioneering new theories to describe the behaviour of an out-of-balance and ever-changing economy. Brian Arthur, the leading thinker of complexity economics, finds new insights by combining old ideas of political economy with the number-crunching power of supercomputers.

Because of the dominant position held by equilibrium economics – the incumbent in this ecosystem of ideas – these disruptive new thinkers are forced to operate at the margins, both figuratively and literally. Universities tend to attract funding in proportion to their perceived success. Success is judged mainly by the number of academic papers published in prestigious peer-reviewed journals. Publication depends on the approval of editors, and the editors of prestigious economics journals all tend to be adherents to the equilibrium school of thought. The more an academic economist departs from the orthodoxy, the less they will be able to get published in the right places and attract funding, and the more they will be pushed towards the academic sidelines. This balancing feedback loop prevents the discipline from changing (or at least, slows it down).

This is why Erik Reinert found himself studying economics with reindeer herders close to the Arctic Circle. It is why Steve Keen has removed himself from the university system altogether, and now uses crowdfunding to pay his own salary. It is also the reason why leading new economic thinkers at Oxford University (supported in that position by philanthropic funding) published their ground-breaking paper on 'sensitive intervention points in the post-carbon transition' not in an economics journal, but in the journal *Science*.

The good news is that while the academic world cares a lot about its prestigious institutions and journals, the rest of the world has other priorities. Mostly, the rest of us just want to get hold of the good ideas. We don't mind where they came from or where they were published, as long as we can use them and gain some advantage. So, the academics at the forefront of new economic thinking are finding niches for the first deployment of their ideas in some of the tough problems that the world wants to solve.

The problem of financial stability is one of these niches. As we saw in Chapter 10, theories and models that assume the economy is as still as a perfect summer's day are not much use when it comes to predicting or avoiding financial storms. Central banks, and others worried about instability and systemic risk in financial markets, are starting to notice the new thinking and take an interest. Doyne Farmer and his complexity economics colleagues found a willing customer in the Bank of England for their modelling work to explain and predict instability in the UK housing market. The UK's Institute and Faculty of Actuaries (IFoA), a bastion of the City of London's finance establishment, has commissioned research into the use of economics in the actuarial profession that highlighted the failings of the equilibrium economics paradigm and the need for more diversity of economic thought.[1] Steve Keen and other new economic thinkers have been involved in the IFoA's ongoing programme of investigation and discussion.

Industrial strategy and innovation policy is another niche. Many political leaders instinctively feel they should have a strategy to make their country competitive in the industries that matter, to attract investment, generate high-quality jobs, and increase exports to global markets. If for no other reason, governments often control large funds for public research and development, and need to decide what to spend them on. As I found when I worked on the UK's industrial strategy, equilibrium economics struggles to give convincing answers to the questions of why a country should have such a strategy, or what it should do. The word 'innovation' does not even appear in the UK government's guidance on policy appraisal, except briefly in an annex. Mariana Mazzucato and her Institute for Innovation and Public Purpose are exploiting this niche, telling the story of how an 'entrepreneurial state' can succeed, and making the case for mission-oriented policy. This has proved popular, with the EU, OECD, and UK government among those keen to put these new ideas into practice.

A third niche, and the one of most relevance to this book, is sustainability. The challenges of climate change, biodiversity loss, pollution, and depletion of essential resources are so great that they create demand not just for new solutions, but also for new thinking. Kate Raworth's *Doughnut Economics*[2] – a synthesis of new economic thinking about how to meet societal needs without crossing 'planetary boundaries', the environmental limits within which scientists believe humanity can live safely – has attracted huge interest from city governments, businesses, political leaders, econom-ics students, and concerned citizens around the world. Less visibly, disequi-librium modellers such as Jean-Francois Mercure, and experts in technology transitions such as Frank Geels, are beginning to find parts of governments grappling with the goal of net zero emissions that are taking an interest in their advice.

Within each of these niches, new economic thinking is being tested and improved. As it shows its worth, it attracts more interest and resources and develops further, increasing its readiness to break out into new areas and be applied on a wider scale.

THE STUDENTS

In the economy of ideas, students are important consumers. Many, at present, are unhappy customers. Students of technology, sociology, and environmental science may benefit from much of the best new economic thinking being pushed into those disciplines, but the economics students are the losers. The feedback loop that acts as an immune system within economics faculties, ejecting any ideas that are perceived as hostile, leaves these students with an increasingly barren intellectual landscape to explore. Many who begin their economics courses with dreams of learning how to solve real-world problems of poverty, inequality, and climate change are swiftly disillusioned when they find that instead, passing their degree will require three years of endlessly solving mathematics equations.

There is, of course, nothing wrong with solving mathematics equations. But those who want to study mathematics for its own sake can study math-ematics. Keynes famously said that an economist

> ... must be mathematician, historian, statesman, philosopher – in some degree. He must understand symbols and speak in words. He must contemplate the particular in terms of the general, and touch abstract and concrete in the same flight of thought. He must study the present in the light of the past for the purposes of the future. No part of man's nature or his institutions must lie currently outside his regard.

What happened to that?

A survey carried out by students concerned by the state of their discip-line found that in the final exams for core economics modules at several of the UK's top universities, the vast majority of the questions involved regur-gitating economic theory and applying it uncritically to a hypothetical situation, solving a preordained series of mathematics equations to come up with 'the answer'. Whether the theory was supported by evidence, the situation realistic, the model appropriate, or the answer useful, was not asked. Over three-quarters of the exam questions required 'no critical or independent thinking whatsoever'.[3]

Discontent with this situation has fuelled the growth of a student movement for 'Rethinking Economics'. After first stirrings in the 1990s, the movement has grown more rapidly since the global financial and economic crisis of 2008 – a time when students were astonished by the failure of their university courses to engage with the economic problems playing out on a grand scale in the real world. The movement puts pressure on university economics departments to reform their curricula, works to build international networks of critical thinking economists, and campaigns to increase diversity in the discipline. In some countries, it also lobbies for changes in the public funding formulae that influence universities' willingness to harbour heterodox thinkers. Branches of the movement are now active in over forty countries, spread across all the world's continents.[4]

In 2017, some of these students came together with academics in London to call for an 'economics reformation'. Inspired by the 500th anniversary of the Reformation in European Christianity, they drew parallels between the position of theology then and economics now. Neoclassical economics, they argued, had become a self-referential system of thought: a process of deductive logic flowing from foundational assumptions that were not themselves open to question. This made it more like a religion than a science. Like Catholic theology in medieval Europe, neoclassical economics in the twenty-first century set the terms for much of public debate, was carefully controlled by a priesthood that maintained the purity of the doctrine, was taught in a manner that encouraged repetition rather than critical evaluation, and served the interests of the powerful in society by effectively arguing 'that things are what they are because they have to be'.[5] In a tongue-in-cheek re-enactment of Martin Luther's defining moment, the student leaders, and Steve Keen dressed in a monk costume, 'nailed' a notice outlining the '33 Theses of an Economics Reformation' to the front door of the London School of Economics with inflatable hammers and Blu tack.

This episode was notable for starting an unusual debate about the nature of economic theory in the mainstream media. Sixty-five academics wrote a joint letter to *the Guardian* newspaper in support of the 33 Theses, saying, 'Ending the unhealthy intellectual monopoly within economics is not just about making the discipline more effective and democratic, it is essential to raise our collective chances of surviving and thriving.'[6]

Establishment economists came out to defend themselves, stating their commitment to solving real-world problems, asserting the diversity of their methods and fields of enquiry, and disputing the relevance of theory in a discipline which, as they saw it, was busy much of the time with statistical analysis.

The demand of the students that the economics establishment found hardest to disagree with was that in the economy of ideas there should be a competitive market, and not a monopoly. This has become the main organising principle of the student movement: to call for economic pluralism, instead of intellectual monoculture. It is a strong argument, and if it were acted on by, for example, the designers of university curricula or the regulators of university funding, these actions could have a significant impact. It is unlikely, though, to be enough. Market liberalisation alone does not sweep aside an old technology; there also has to be a new product. The same is true in the economy of ideas: an old way of seeing the world is not set aside, even if its failings are clear, until something more persuasive comes along.[7]

THE PHILANTHROPISTS

If the students' calls for pluralism stop short of giving full backing to the emerging ideas of evolutionary economics, the philanthropists may be willing to go further.

We might expect good ideas to beat bad ideas in a straight fight, but it is hard to have a straight fight if two sides have unequal resources. Money pays for time spent researching, developing models and theories, and gathering data to test hypotheses. It also pays for conferences to exchange ideas, and for intermediaries such as policy think-tanks to interpret and communicate ideas to new audiences.

The spread of equilibrium economics in the twentieth century was supported by targeted investment from those who wished to see it succeed. In the years after the Second World War, it was backed by businessmen in the US and Europe who worried their countries were drifting towards socialism, and were strongly attracted to a worldview that could be used to delegitimise trade unions and the welfare state and to justify arguments for a minimum of regulation. Corporate donors funded academic conferences to develop the free-market theories, university positions for sympathetic professors, books to communicate these ideas to the general public, and think-tanks to influence politicians and journalists. Some even invested in influencing the clergy. The Chicago School of economic thought, one of the most radical and influential centres of equilibrium economics, was brought together with the backing of a furniture manufacturer. Friedrich Hayek, one of its founding fathers, wrote later that if 'minority views are to have a chance to become majority views', financial support from wealthy individuals was a necessity.[8]

From these beginnings, the ideas of equilibrium economics appear to have benefited from the reinforcing feedback of increasing returns to scale. Funding helped their dissemination, leading to more support, and further funding. The think-tanks grew larger, more numerous, and more influential. With the elections of Prime Minister Margaret Thatcher in the UK in 1979 and President Ronald Reagan in the US in 1980, a political philosophy that took this understanding of economics as its starting point entered the mainstream of government. The success of the equilibrium economics worldview was such that it continued to guide the centre-left governments of the US and UK, led by Bill Clinton (President 1993–2001) and Tony Blair (Prime Minister 1997–2007) two decades later. It was no longer the focus of political debate; it was setting the terms of the debate.

If the American and European philanthropists of the 1950s saw communism as an existential threat to civilisation, many now feel the same about climate change. Large funders are beginning to see a change in economic thinking as being essential to address that threat, as well as for making better progress on other issues such as poverty alleviation, development, and public health. The Institute for New Economic Thinking, founded with a grant from George Soros in the wake of the financial crisis of 2009, sets out to challenge 'free market fundamentalism ... [that has] endangered economies, communities, and the planet as a whole', and to 'carefully incubate new economic thinking' by supporting research and public engagement.[9] The Hewlett Foundation announced in 2020 a commitment of $50 million to 'develop a new intellectual paradigm to replace neoliberalism', with a view to better addressing society's greatest challenges, such as climate change.[10] In 2021, the Bezos Earth Fund, a new foundation created to fight climate change with a $10bn grant, made clear its intention to do something similar by recruiting a Director for 'Economics of the Future'.

One can't help wondering, if some of the world's richest men share a disdain for the dominant description of how the economy works, is this a relationship of correlation or causation? At least in one or two cases, there may be a causal relationship between ignoring outdated theory and getting rich. Charlie Munger, a billionaire investor described by Warren Buffett as his right-hand man, cites this as one of the factors in his success: 'It really helped us to have everybody else believe in the efficient market theory in its hardest form. It was an interesting example of a learned profession going bonkers.'[11]

At the COP26 climate change talks in Glasgow at the end of 2021, I attended a private meeting convened by one of the philanthropic foundations to discuss the future of economics. One of the senior economists present joked that the economics profession in its current form had become a stranded asset – something in which money has been invested, but which is no longer useful. Others took up the metaphor, talking of the need for a 'just transition' with support for the retraining of equilibrium modellers. I was reminded of a conversation with a professor at a respected UK university who had developed a disequilibrium model, but who it seemed to me had done little to bring its advantages to the attention of my colleagues in government. When I asked him the reason for this apparent modesty, one of the reasons he gave was his anxiety about potential criticism from traditional modellers. He told me it took a great deal of time and money to build an equilibrium model, and once that had been done, its owners would need to put it to use in advising policy over a long enough period of time to make a satisfactory return. They would not welcome disruptive new entrants to the market.

This was a reminder, if one were needed, that in any transition there will be many sources of resistance. Overcoming them needs not only the 'push' of investment in new technologies or ideas, but also the 'pull' of a strong signal of demand.

THE GOVERNMENTS

Governments can create strong demand for new ideas, because their remit is to solve a large number of problems. Just as public procurement of a new technology can speed its progress from niche to mass market, so public procurement of new ideas can take them from the margins to the mainstream of public debate. For the new evolutionary understanding of economics to help put in place policies that make faster progress on climate change, it is going to have to be adopted by governments.

As the story of Steven Chu's fridges showed (Chapter 14), a political vision that does not rest on equilibrium economics can be frustrated by the institutions and processes of government that still work according to that paradigm. Steven Chu had to undertake an academic study in his spare time to disprove the assumptions of the economists in his own department.

I have seen the same phenomenon in the UK. I have already recounted how Andrea Leadsom, the energy minister I worked for in 2016, found it almost impossible to get any officials in her department assigned to work on the problem of maximising job creation through the transition to clean energy. Within the economic orthodoxy that set the terms for the policy debate, this simply wasn't taken seriously as an issue. (In equilibrium, creating more jobs in one part of the economy just means you are probably reducing the number of jobs somewhere else.) Two years later, the politics had moved on, and Prime Minister Theresa May made it a priority to develop an industrial strategy. Again, the fact that most of the economists in government did not believe in the need for an industrial strategy, especially not one that tried to do more than just fix market failures, was a serious impediment to translating that vision into policy.

More recently, Prime Minister Boris Johnson made one of his top priorities the 'levelling up' of economic conditions across different regions of the UK. His government, after hearing from many people that its own economic decision-making processes were at the root of the problem, instituted a review. One of the issues this exposed was a reinforcing feedback loop between public investment and regional economic inequality. The more productive a city or region was, the greater the value estimated to arise from infrastructure improvements there, and the greater its chances of being prioritised for further productivity-enhancing public investment. The review concluded that in situations where the aim of policy was transformational change, an assessment of system dynamics such as feedbacks and tipping points ought to be part of the decision-making process.[12]

Having seen up close this inertia in governments' use of economics, it seemed to me that two things needed to be sped up: the flow of new economic thinking from academia into government, and the application of the new theory to climate change policy.

In 2019, I was working in the part of the UK government that deals with international climate change. Since the UK accounts for only about 1% of global emissions, our future national security and prosperity depends on our ability to influence the rest of the world. Consequently, we have a directorate of a hundred-or-so people in London with a remit to do something about global emissions. Between 2016 and 2021, we had a budget of £5.8bn (our 'international climate finance') to support this work. To the government's credit, a small amount of this was reserved for experimental new approaches to addressing the problem. I decided to see if I could use this to do something about the problem of economics.

I began to put together the business case for a new project – one that would apply evolutionary economic thinking to decision-making on decarbonisation, in countries whose policies mattered greatly to global emissions.

I found several authoritative voices that I could cite in support. Nick Stern, a former top official at the UK's Treasury and a world-famous climate change economist, had written that we had economic models in which 'the guts of the story [of climate change] are essentially assumed away'. Angel Gurria, the Secretary-General of the OECD, had said that 'unless we employ systems thinking, we will fail to understand the world we are living in'. And Michael Grubb, a professor of energy and climate change who also chaired the government's panel of technical experts on electricity market reform, had complained that 'most economic models and many policy recommendations from economists continue to ignore what we know about learning and innovation'.

The case was coming together, but I needed to find out whether people in other countries agreed that this was a problem that needed solving. I already knew that climate change policymaking in the EU was strongly influenced by equilibrium economics; the UK, in fact, had on more than one occasion used our position as a Member State (before leaving in January 2020) to push the EU in this unhelpful direction. Academics who worked in the US told me the situation there was considerably worse than in the UK. But what about the large emerging economies, whose intellectual traditions of economics in the twentieth century were, for better or for worse, rather more varied than our own?

One of my early conversations in India was with Ajay Mathur, a former senior Indian government official, who at that time was the head of TERI, India's best-known climate and energy think-tank. I pitched the concept of the project: we would start from some real policy decisions that needed to be taken; apply evolutionary economics theory, models, and decision-making frameworks to assess different policy options; and compare the recommendations of this approach to those of the traditional equilibrium-based paradigm. Having set this out at some length, I paused with some nervousness; I had no idea how he would respond. Ajay's reply was stronger than I could have expected: this was definitely needed, he said. 'It would be revolutionary.'

In China, I had an unexpected echo of this conversation. Chinese contacts told me that whereas in the UK and US, new economic thinking might be on the rise, in China the trend was in the opposite direction: equilibrium economics had not yet peaked and was increasing its grip on institutions of government that had previously been more flexible in their thinking. At one institute with an influential role in climate and energy policymaking, I met thoughtful people who were worried that approaches such as cost–benefit analysis were leading them to the wrong policy conclusions. Despite all the differences in our countries' systems of government, our experiences of equilibrium economics getting in the way of good policy on climate change were surprisingly similar. As is often the way in such meetings, the most senior people did most of the talking. At the end of the meeting, as we stood up and pushed back our chairs, one of the most junior members of the team leant over to me. 'I hope we do this,' she said. 'This would be *ge ming xing*' – revolutionary.

Out of these and other similar discussions, a project was born: the 'Economics of Energy Innovation and System Transition' project, which has set out to apply evolutionary economic thinking to policy decisions that matter for emissions in China, India, Brazil, the EU, and the UK. I believe it is the first government-backed programme of this kind in the world.

At the COP26 climate talks in Glasgow, the project published its first report. This was a joint effort, with input from experts in all the participating countries. They had looked at some of the most outstanding successes in low-carbon transitions that each of these countries had achieved so far, to see what lessons could be learned.

The UK's proudest achievement was that it had brought down the cost of offshore wind power by about 70% within a decade, so that it was now becoming cheaper than power generated from gas. Brazil had grown its market for onshore wind more quickly than any other major emerging economy, cutting its cost to below that of power from gas or biomass, while creating an industry supporting 150 thousand jobs. Europe, led by Germany, and China could both claim credit for the enormous global progress in solar power, which had transformed it from a technology criticised as being 'the most expensive way of reducing greenhouse gas emissions' in 2014 to one hailed as providing 'the cheapest source of electricity in history' only six years later. India, meanwhile, had seen spectacular success in its transition to efficient LED lighting: it had cut the costs of LED lightbulbs by over 90% in less than a decade, increased their deployment several hundred times over, and used this to bring electric lighting to hundreds of millions of households for the first time.

Each of these stories had its own nuance and complexity, but two similarities stood out. First, in each case it was targeted investment that made the difference: subsidy, cheap public finance, and government procurement all played important roles, while carbon pricing was largely irrelevant. Second, in each case the policies most critical to success were implemented 'despite, and not because of, the predominant economic analysis and advice'.[13]

The report recommended a new approach: one that took the evolutionary nature of the economy as its starting point, used disequilibrium models to understand how policies would affect processes of change in the economy, and assessed not just quantifiable costs and benefits, but also important unquantifiable risks and opportunities. Looking ahead to difficult policy choices for the decarbonisation of transport and industry, it showed how this new approach could lead to different recommendations from those traditionally given by equilibrium-based analysis.

Almost as an afterthought, this international group of experts concluded that their findings had fundamental implications for international cooperation on climate change. In the equilibrium world, where deliberate change in the form of a low-carbon transition can only come at a cost, climate change diplomacy is a negative-sum game. If carbon emissions are unavoidably linked to economic welfare, then we must all fight for our slice of the carbon pie. In the disequilibrium world, a transition can be economically beneficial. Climate change diplomacy then becomes a positive-sum game: we can work together to increase those benefits and access them more quickly. We return to this subject in the next part of this book.

PUSHING FROM ALL POINTS IN THE SYSTEM

Like all of the transitions that we need to address climate change, the transition to a more helpful way of thinking about the economy needs to be sped up. Equilibrium economics took half a century to rise from a niche to the mainstream. We cannot afford for its replacement to take that long, if we want better economic advice for the transformational changes that are needed to reduce emissions now.

All of the actors mentioned in this chapter, and more, can play a part in accelerating the pace of change. Academics can lead the way in developing and testing new theories and models. Students can step up their campaigns for changes in how economics is taught. Governments can change the funding formulae for universities to break the feedback loop that disincentivises diversity in economics research. Governments can also procure disequilibrium models and analysis to inform climate and energy policy decisions; if these are used alongside traditional approaches, officials will be free to compare the two forms of analysis and decide which is more helpful for any given problem. Citizens can ask their elected representatives to ensure their governments are taking these actions.

NGOs can provide another source of demand for new economic thinking on climate change, and can be a channel of communication for its findings. In the past, some NGOs, like many of us in society, have taken equilibrium economics for granted; as a consequence, they have advocated climate and energy policies that followed from its logic. If they now develop the capacity to tell the difference, they will be able to use the new understanding to focus their efforts on campaigning for policies that will be more effective. Philanthropists can increase their funding for this work, supporting any of the academics, NGOs, or activists who are at the forefront of the movement.

But what, we might ask, if it all goes wrong? Many of those who backed equilibrium economics along its journey had good intentions. Not all of them wanted it to be used in an oversimplified form to justify a particular political philosophy. Even fewer of them would have wanted some of the think-tanks that its intellectual movement founded, with the aim of preserving individual freedom, to evolve into public relations vehicles for the defence of vested interests. Could the new evolutionary understanding of economics, or the movement to promote it, end up doing similar damage? Might we just, as the sign in my local coffee shop advertises, 'do stupid things faster and with more energy'?

My view is that we cannot know, and that this is a risk we have to take. Any advance in human understanding can be used for good or for bad. The evolutionary understanding of economics is only a tool. As Mariana Mazzucato says, it describes the economy with the mathematics of biology instead of the mathematics of mechanics. As a result, it has better explanatory and predictive power. Nobody thinks the challenge of climate change is easy, so we had better use the right tools for the job. We need a rapid rewiring of the global economy, and we can't do that if we only have a hammer.

PART III

DIPLOMACY

18

A FORESEEABLE FAILURE

My first experience of the United Nations climate change negotiations was in Doha, in 2012. I joined the crowds of negotiators, NGO activists, scientists, and many others who had settled for a fortnight in this island of oil wealth. Ferraris filled the hotel forecourts, while yachts bobbed in the bay. Newspapers reminded us daily of the Emir's leadership in the battle against climate change, while looking forward to the next prestigious international event that Qatar would host: the 2022 Football World Cup, expected to be held in air-conditioned stadia to protect the players against the extreme heat. On the night of the middle Saturday, the authorities laid on buses which took us for a long drive, past rows of glinting oil refineries, to a nondescript spot in the desert where we could attend the traditional 'NGO party' without our inevitable beer-drinking being visible to the locals.

I had offered myself as a spare pair of hands on the UK team so as to learn about the process. Like the rest of my colleagues, I divided my time mainly between the negotiating rooms, where I scrutinised documents and argued over changes in wording and punctuation, and our delegation office, where I ate biscuits and filed reports back to London. In the few gaps in between, I explored the side events and exhibitions, to see what the scientists and NGOs were saying.

What I saw was unlike any diplomatic talks I had previously come across. In my experience, formal talks usually focused on the substance of the issues they attempted to solve. Trade negotiations aimed to remove tariffs. Talks on counter-terrorism or cyber security discussed police cooperation and the exchange of intelligence. Human rights dialogues raised cases of political prisoners. But climate change negotiations, it seemed, were largely concerned with process. The most significant agreement reached in Doha in 2012 was that another agreement should be struck in 2015, which would come into effect in 2020.[1]

It was only among the scientists, NGOs, and other assorted experts in the outer corridors of the conference centre that I found talk of practical solutions to reduce the threat of climate change. Government representatives were

187

there too, displaying their own achievements and those of various development assistance projects – initiatives entirely independent of the negotiations. Substance, it seemed, had been relegated to a side-event. How had the diplomacy of climate change arrived in such a strange place?

****

Twenty years before my trip to Doha, the United Nations Framework Convention on Climate Change (UNFCCC) had been signed by 154 countries at the Earth Summit in Rio de Janeiro. This agreement set out a clear goal: to *'prevent dangerous anthropogenic interference with the climate system'*.

To make progress towards this goal, the Convention required a subset of its signatories – the most developed countries – to stabilise their annual emissions of greenhouse gases at 1990 levels by the year 2000. In this way, the Convention set the pattern that climate change diplomacy would follow for much of the next two decades. The idea was simple: climate change was caused by greenhouse gases; the aim of negotiations should therefore be to agree the amount by which each country should reduce its emissions, so as to keep global emissions within a safe limit.

While the climate change negotiations evolved over this time into a process of ever greater complexity, the attempt to agree long-term economy-wide national emissions targets remained their central focus, and so it is against this measure that in this chapter we will consider their success.

The first difficulty the process encountered was that countries could not agree any formula for the division of global emissions between them. Many different options were proposed, with one of the most popular being 'contraction and convergence' – the idea that all countries should converge on an equal level of emissions per capita, at the same time as reducing this level in line with a global emissions goal. This received at least rhetorical support in the negotiations from the Africa Group, China, and India, among others,[2] but neither this nor any other formula could be agreed. We should hardly be surprised. It may be an extreme analogy, but countries do not tend to resolve territorial disputes by agreeing an equal per capita allocation of land. To say that global power dynamics do not work that way, on issues that countries consider relevant to their core interests, would be an understatement.

A second and more serious difficulty was that some countries refused to even discuss the level of national emissions targets within the formal negotiations. The largest negotiating group of developing countries repeatedly called for the targets to be subject to discussion, but consensus for this could not be reached. Instead, the limited amount of reciprocal bargaining over emissions targets that took place – primarily between the US, the EU, and Japan – was carried out informally, outside the negotiations. With those partial exceptions, the emissions targets that countries committed to in the Kyoto Protocol of 1997 – the first major international climate change agreement – were set by each country independently, perhaps influenced to some extent by peer pressure, but not agreed through a process of negotiation.[3] As early as this, the substance had been moved to the sidelines.

The outcome at Kyoto was that thirty-seven industrialised countries agreed to quantified limits on their emissions, representing on average a 5% reduction compared to 1990 levels over the five-year period 2008–2012. Developing countries, including large emerging economies, did not commit to any quantified reductions of their emissions. How to judge the success of this outcome? The Kyoto Protocol has been credited with contributing to real emissions reductions in some countries, as well as to investments in low-carbon technologies, and to the establishment of practices for emissions accounting. On the other hand, to 'prevent dangerous anthropogenic interference with the climate system', we have to reduce global emissions to zero. A commitment by the world's most powerful countries to address 5% of the problem over the space of a decade does not feel like a resounding success. Neither does the fact that twenty-five years later, global emissions are still going up.

A further problem emerged over time: despite the modest nature of the emissions targets committed to in Kyoto, not all countries could be relied on to stick to them. In the US, even before the Protocol was agreed, the Senate had unanimously passed a resolution against signing any climate change treaty that would require cuts to emissions, unless it required cuts to the emissions of developing countries over the same time-period. While this effectively made US ratification of the Protocol impossible, the US might still be expected to act in line with its international commitments as long as the Clinton administration, which had signed the Protocol, remained in power. But when George W. Bush became President in 2001, he immediately made clear his opposition to the agreement. In a letter to Senators, he wrote, '*I oppose the Kyoto Protocol because it exempts 80 percent of the world, including major population centers such as China and India, from compliance, and would cause serious harm to the US economy. The Senate's vote, 95–0, shows that there is a clear consensus that the Kyoto Protocol is an unfair and ineffective means of addressing global climate change concerns.*'[4] In the same letter, President Bush cast doubt on the science of climate change, and stated that he would not impose measures to limit carbon dioxide emissions from coal power plants. With that, the world's largest emitter, with emissions nearly double the amount of China, the second-placed country at that time, confirmed its exit from meaningful participation in international negotiations.

In 2011, Canada announced it would withdraw from the Protocol the following year, after realising that it would fail to meet its 'legally binding' targets. Having committed to reduce its emissions to 6% below 1990 levels by 2012, Canada was instead on course for an increase of around 16% over that period.[5] The Canadian Environment Minister, Peter Kent, called the Protocol 'radical and irresponsible' and claimed that withdrawal was necessary to avoid the payment of $14bn in penalties for failing to achieve the targets. An opposition politician, Megan Leslie, countered that there were no penalties under the Protocol, and the government was withdrawing only to save itself from embarrassment. She told journalists, 'It's like we're the kid in school who knows they're gonna fail the class, so we have to drop it before that actually happens.'[6]

These events exposed a structural weakness of the Kyoto Protocol: there were no effective incentives for participation and compliance, or penalties for the reverse. As the international relations expert Scott Barrett has argued, both are usually needed for a treaty to be effective.[7] Without incentives and penalties to ensure compliance, countries can simply choose not to meet their commitments. Without incentives and penalties to ensure participation, countries can drop out of an agreement as an alternative to facing sanctions for non-compliance.

Under the Kyoto Protocol, countries that failed to meet their emissions targets could return to compliance by purchasing emissions permits or offsets from other countries. These were the 'financial penalties' that Canada's environment minister referred to. But these were ineffective in ensuring compliance because there were no penalties for non-participation. The US could fail to join the Kyoto Protocol, and Canada could withdraw from it, without facing any penalty other than international criticism. Free-riding – doing nothing to reduce their own emissions, while watching other countries attempt to tackle the global problem of climate change – was a more attractive option.

By way of analogy, we can consider the Nuclear Non-Proliferation Treaty (NPT), agreed in 1968. The NPT has two security objectives: preventing the spread of nuclear weapons; and promoting nuclear disarmament. It also has one economic objective: promoting cooperation in the peaceful use of nuclear energy.

The NPT contains a provision to incentivise participation and compliance with respect to its first objective, preventing the spread of nuclear weapons: only countries that are party to the agreement and subject to the safeguards of the International Atomic Energy Agency are eligible for trade in fissile material, and other forms of civil nuclear cooperation. In addition, the international community has acted when necessary to deter non-participation and non-compliance. After Iran was found to be failing to comply with its obligations, it was subjected to a series of sanctions imposed by the United Nations Security Council from 2006 onwards, including bans on the supply of nuclear-related materials and technology, travel bans on influential individuals, an arms embargo, and asset freezes and other financial restrictions applied to individuals and organisations. North Korea was subjected to similar sanctions after it withdrew from the NPT in 2003. Perhaps as a result, the NPT has been reasonably successful at preventing the spread of nuclear weapons. Whereas at the time of the treaty's agreement it was thought likely that many countries would acquire this capability, very few actually have. Apart from the five nuclear weapons states recognised in the treaty (the US, USSR/Russia, China, France, and the UK), the only other countries known to have done so are India, Pakistan, North Korea, and possibly Israel.

In contrast, the NPT contains no credible incentives or penalties to ensure compliance with its other security objective: disarmament. The five recognised nuclear powers committed to 'pursue negotiations in good faith on effective measures relating to cessation of the nuclear arms race at an early date and to nuclear disarmament, and on a treaty on general and complete disarmament under strict and effective international control'. Against this objective, the NPT has been much less successful. Although the US and USSR reduced their nuclear stockpiles significantly through a series of bilateral agreements, half a century after the agreement of the NPT none of its five recognised nuclear powers is showing any sign of disarmament.

My first job in the Foreign Office was in the 'sanctions team', where we designed restrictive measures to be implemented by the UN Security Council or the EU against governments or individuals that those self-appointed representatives of the international community deemed to be threats to international peace and security. While I worked on travel bans and asset freezes (of dubious effectiveness) to impose on Congolese warlords and leaders of Zimbabwe's authoritarian regime, my boss negotiated with the Russians, Americans, and other members of the Security Council to agree the measures to be taken against Iran and North Korea. As a result, I was familiar with this architecture.

When I later took up my first Foreign Office job on climate change, I could not help noticing how the problems of non-participation and non-compliance were similar to those that we faced in nuclear non-proliferation, but that our response in this case was very different. If the international community took the threat of climate change as seriously as it did the risk of nuclear proliferation, then we ought to deter non-participation in the UNFCCC just as vigorously as we deterred non-participation in the NPT. Logically, Canada should be subjected to some form of sanctions for its withdrawal from the Kyoto Protocol, just as North Korea was sanctioned for its withdrawal from the NPT. I pointed this out to my Head of Department, who tactfully suggested that I should probably not put this idea down in writing. We both felt a sense of outrage that a country could so casually disregard its climate change commitments, but it was obvious to both of us that correcting the structural flaws of the Kyoto Protocol was politically impossible.

With the election in 2008 of Barack Obama, a US President willing to act on climate change, hopes rose again that a global deal could be done. Although the structure of the negotiations was unchanged, it was thought that with a greater political push, it might be possible to achieve an agreement with enough parties committed to emissions reductions for the result to be meaningful. Ahead of the Copenhagen round of the climate change negotiations in 2009, the hope was that developed countries would agree quantified emissions reductions for the period after the Kyoto Protocol ended (2013–2020), and that major emerging economies such as China, India, and Brazil would commit to emissions reductions in the same period that would be less strict, but subject to some form of international verification.[8]

The Copenhagen conference failed on both counts. The US could not support a Kyoto-style agreement in which industrialised countries made legally binding commitments to reduce their emissions by specified amounts, as it was clear that this would not be ratified by the Senate. China refused to countenance the proposal that its emissions should be independently monitored and verified, and was so opposed to the idea of committing to reduce its emissions that it tried to remove all mention of such pledges from the public documents of the conference.[9] Consensus proved impossible to reach.

The eventual outcome of the conference – the Copenhagen Accord, negotiated by the US, China, India, South Africa, and Brazil, 'taken note of' by the conference, and later endorsed by other countries – was something rather different. Instead of binding countries in a reciprocal agreement specifying the amounts by which each would reduce their emissions, it explicitly allowed each country to determine its emissions target unilaterally. Whereas there had previously been attempts to make targets the subject of negotiation, and the Kyoto Protocol had at least taken the form of a mutual legal commitment, the Copenhagen Accord openly gave up the attempt. It only stipulated that countries would communicate their emissions targets to the secretariat of the talks by the end of the following January.[10] In other words, it was an agreement of process, not of substance.

The aim of negotiating agreed targets to reduce emissions did not quite die with Copenhagen. But by the time of my introduction to the UNFCCC process in Doha in 2012, the focus of diplomacy was shifting. The Doha meeting did, finally, agree a second period of implementation of the Kyoto Protocol, but it was increasingly irrelevant. Japan, Russia, and New Zealand, realising they had nothing to lose from non-participation, dropped out. That left only the EU and a handful of other countries – together representing less than 15% of global emissions – accepting quantified and legally binding emissions targets. The greater interest of most countries in Doha was in the process for reaching an entirely new agreement, to come into effect from 2020. It was increasingly clear that this new agreement would look more like the Copenhagen Accord than the Kyoto Protocol, allowing countries to determine unilaterally the course their emissions would take without either the substance or the form of mutual agreement. The attempt to negotiate a division of global emissions, which had faltered from the beginning, had effectively been abandoned.

Throughout this time, global emissions of greenhouse gases continued to rise. By 2012, annual global emissions of carbon dioxide were around 60% higher than in 1990, the base year of the international negotiations.[11] According to one analysis, while the Kyoto Protocol did reduce the emissions of participating countries, its overall effect on global emissions was 'statistically indistinguishable from zero'.[12]

One interpretation of this history is that failure could have been avoided if leaders had been bolder, and diplomats more skilful. As the historian William Sweet recounts in *Climate Diplomacy from Rio to Paris*, after the messy end of the Copenhagen conference, two main schools of thought quickly emerged: one that blamed the US for making agreement impossible by failing to take on its fair share of the burden; and one that blamed the Chinese and Indians for preferring to wreck the talks than to accept any need for their own countries to act. (The

Europeans, as I recall – I was working at the EU Delegation in Beijing at the time – were mostly upset with themselves for failing to have secured a seat at the table when the US and the big four emerging economies sealed the hasty deal to end the talks.) Sweet himself concludes: 'Copenhagen, in a nutshell, epitomised all that had been wrong in two decades of climate diplomacy. It was not the complexity of the issues or the unmanageability of the process. It was diplomatic pusillanimity on the part of every major participant, from the European Union and the United States to China, India, and the G-77 [a large negotiating bloc of developing countries].'[13]

Maybe I am just another pusillanimous diplomat, but I believe this is too simplistic a conclusion. Certainly, the positions taken by some of the most powerful players in the negotiations left much to be desired. The US administration of President Bush and the Canadian government of Stephen Harper (Prime Minister from 2006 to 2015) were both so captured by fossil fuel vested interests that they deliberately spread misinformation, casting doubt on the science of climate change as an excuse for inaction domestically as well as internationally.[14] China, while making legitimate points about its lack of historical responsibility for the greenhouse gases in the atmosphere and the needs of its poorer citizens, was determined to extract every ounce of benefit from its dual identity of 'developing country' and global industrial powerhouse. As for the Europeans, well, my friends in India taught me how annoyingly self-righteous we can seem to the rest of the world. With such players as these, reaching a strong and effective agreement was always going to be difficult. But then, the Soviet Union in the 1960s was hardly an easy customer for an arms control treaty. Vested interests and narrow-minded nationalism were not absent from global geopolitics during the Cold War. And yet, in the nuclear Non-Proliferation Treaty, a pragmatic deal was done. Why should an effective climate change deal be so much more difficult?

In a world where only a minority of countries are industrialised and wealthy, it is to be expected that the poorer majority will strongly resist making any commitments that they believe could limit their prospects for development. In a global economy that gets over 80% of its energy from fossil fuels, it is hardly surprising if the suppliers of those fuels exert a strong influence over the politics of their countries. What I saw first-hand in the climate change negotiations, and what I believe we all see when we read the history, is not weak-willed and timid diplomacy, but the opposite: countries, governments, and leaders that were bold and forthright in asserting what they considered to be their interests.

We have to deal with the world as we find it. The question we ought to be asking ourselves is whether the attempt to negotiate a division of global emissions ever really stood a chance. Or, given we could not change the players, should we have changed the game?

HOW TO GROW AN AGREEMENT

David Victor is a professor of international relations who specialises in issues of environment and energy. He attended the first and second 'Conferences of the Parties' of the UN Framework Convention on Climate Change, despaired at what he saw, and did not return until the twenty-first conference, two decades later. In the interim, he devoted his efforts to other ways of making progress on climate change, outside the formal negotiations.

David's view is that the first twenty years of international negotiations on climate change took an approach that was bound to fail. The fundamental mistake was to try to agree everything at once. What I have learned from David is that successful agreements take time to develop. They cannot be bought off the shelf; they have to be grown.

As David explained in a report that we and the systems transitions specialist Frank Geels worked on together, what works in international cooperation depends on the nature of the problem, and the interests of the parties.[15] Two factors can be thought of as fundamental in determining how parties see their interests and relate to each other: their degree of understanding of the problem at hand; and their degree of consensus about who should do what to solve it.

In the early stages of grappling with a problem, understanding of it is often low, and there is little consensus about who should do what to solve it. A strong and comprehensive agreement in these circumstances is unthinkable, but that does not mean nothing can be done. An 'experimentalist learning' approach to cooperation is most likely to be effective. This is where parties test possible solutions, share learning, and build experience and understanding.[16]

When there is a greater degree of consensus, a stronger form of cooperation is possible. This involves parties taking deliberately aligned or coordinated actions, taking up solutions that have been found to be viable and applying them across a wider scope.

When consensus is high, and understanding of a problem is well developed, international cooperation can take its strongest form: 'contracting'. This is where parties make detailed agreements setting out specific actions each must take, whose reciprocity may be guaranteed by law or by a set of credible incentives and penalties governing participation and compliance.

Crucially, understanding and consensus can both change over time. If they are carefully nurtured and developed, international cooperation can progress from its weakest to its strongest form. If experimentalist learning demonstrates viable solutions, it can increase the chances of consensus on action. If aligned actions are taken that scale up those solutions, yielding further information about what works and creating new constituencies in favour of those actions, then the possibility of a 'contracting' style of agreement can become real.

Together with this view of the need to build cooperation progressively over time, we can consider three dimensions that at any moment in time will affect the chances of achieving the understanding and consensus needed for an effective agreement.

First: the scope of the problem. The broader the scope, the harder it is likely to be to reach an understanding of the problem and its possible solutions. This means that very large and complex problems are more amenable to international cooperation if they are broken down into smaller and more manageable parts. For example, there is no attempt at an international agreement to end world poverty. It is simply too broad a scope to be manageable. International cooperation on debt forgiveness or fair trade is contentious and difficult, but these problems are at least bounded enough for international agreements occasionally to be sought. International development assistance that is focused on solving specific problems in specific places is more limited in its aims but can sometimes be successful.

Second: the number of parties. The more parties there are to a negotiation, the more diverse their interests will be, and the harder it will be to reach consensus. We all experience this in daily life – think of a family trying to agree what film to watch. Put another way, the more people there are who need to agree, the lower you have to go to find the lowest common denominator. (This is why families end up watching so many Disney films.)

Third: the length of time that is under negotiation. The longer the time covered by an agreement, the less confident the parties will be in their commitments. Each party knows exactly what it can and cannot do in the present, but it has less confidence in what it may be able to do in the future, and even greater uncertainty over what the eventual outcomes of its actions will be. This is why when you take out a mortgage, the lowest interest rate you can get will be the one that is fixed for the shortest amount of time. The longer the duration of the fixed rate, the greater the uncertainty, and the less generous the terms the bank is willing to offer.

Taking all these factors into account, it would seem advisable to start a process of international cooperation with the scope of the problem, number of parties, and length of time under negotiation all set at their minimum viable levels. Then as understanding and consensus are built up, the scope may be expanded, the number of parties increased, and the length of time under negotiation extended.

The application of these principles is visible in examples of successful international cooperation in environmental protection, security, and trade. Before going into those examples, let me give one that is closer to home.

An agreement is simply the formalisation of a relationship – two or more parties agreeing how they will behave in relation to each other on some issues of common interest. So consider a relationship between two people. At the beginning, mutual understanding is low – neither knows much about the other; consensus about any future they may have together is also low. An experimentalist approach is taken first: going on a few dates. At this point, the scope of agreement is narrow, and the time commitment is short: they agree to meet for a drink on Saturday night. This approach builds understanding, and if the two people like what they find, they may decide to take coordinated action that broadens the scope and duration of cooperation – for example, living together. If that goes well, and consensus develops further, they may move on to the strongest form of cooperation: contracting. In that stage, the scope and depth of cooperation is broadened considerably (financial interdependence; children); the duration of commitments is extended (to a lifetime); and reciprocal obligations of the parties are even defined in a legal agreement (a marriage contract). As we all know, there are many paths to a successful relationship, and at least as many routes to failure. But if we try to jump straight to contracting without going through any of the previous stages, most of us would not expect to reach an agreement. And as for reaching a similar agreement between more than two parties ... well, let's not go there.

When international cooperation has worked, in matters of security, trade, and the environment, similar patterns are visible in the gradual growth of agreements. I am again grateful to David Victor for the following examples, which are described in more detail in the report we published together with Frank Geels.[17]

International cooperation to restrict the testing of nuclear weapons began with the narrow scope of reducing the damage done by the weapons testing to the environment and public health. After a series of experiments confirmed it was possible to test the weapons (and detect each other's tests) underground, the Cold War superpowers agreed, in the Limited Test Ban Treaty of 1963, to no longer test them in the atmosphere and the oceans. Further experimentation and confidence-building led over time to agreements of greater scope, depth, duration, and participation. In 1974, the Threshold Test Ban Treaty limited the magnitude of underground nuclear weapons testing. In 1996, many governments signed the Comprehensive Test Ban Treaty (CTBT), which aims to ban nuclear weapons testing entirely. Although the CTBT has not entered into force as it lacks ratification by several important countries, together with its predecessor agreements it appears to exert a strong normative constraint. No country except North Korea has tested a nuclear weapon since 1998, and nearly all global testing of nuclear weapons has ended since 1991.

Trade agreements may be the area of international cooperation that most obviously takes a contracting approach. Agreements tend to be highly detailed, explicitly reciprocal, and accompanied by dispute-resolution processes and institutions that can penalise non-compliance. But the scope, depth, and complexity of trade agreements has developed over time: from relatively simple agreements focused on tariff-setting and government procurement, to highly complex agreements that cover a wide range of economic, social, and financial policies. This progress has been made through an iterative process of experimentation and learning. Countries have experimented with different trade measures, tested their legitimacy in dispute resolution fora such as the World Trade Organization, and gradually developed a consensus on how to distinguish between allowable actions to protect workers, the environment, or public health, and actions that constitute protectionism. With each advance in this consensus, broader and deeper agreements have become possible.

Of course, this is not a one-way process. International consensus on trade can weaken, and agreements can be ripped up. The direction of change is not inevitable. The point I am making here is that broad, deep, and effective international trade agreements did not come into being all at once. The possibility of such agreements only arose through a longer process that started with smaller ambitions, and gradually built understanding and consensus. Not only that, but at any time, it is generally easier to conclude a trade agreement of a given depth between two countries, or a small number, than between a large number of countries.

In the history of international cooperation on environmental problems, probably the most outstanding success is the Montreal Protocol, agreed in 1987 with the aim of ending damage to the ozone layer of the atmosphere.

The development of this cooperation progressed through each of the three stages described above.

At first, although the causes of ozone depletion were known – emissions of chlorofluorocarbons and other chemicals used in products such as refrigerators, aerosol sprays, and fire extinguishers – it was not clear what alternative materials or technologies could be used instead. Technical committees established by the Protocol brought together the producers and consumers of ozone-depleting substances in each economic sector to experiment with new products and processes, and learn what was possible. This shared learning laid a foundation for coordinated action. In each sector, the most influential governments and industry players coordinated around technology standards, quickly shifting global markets. Meanwhile, developing countries were helped by an international fund to support compliance, which they could access provided they established a national unit to plan and implement the phaseout of ozone-depleting substances in each sector. As technologies progressed and solutions became ever more clearly available, a contracting approach became possible. Provision was made for trade sanctions as a penalty for non-compliance, and parties to the Protocol agreed not to trade in controlled ozone-depleting substances with any countries that were not parties. This created such a strong incentive for participation that all countries joined. The Montreal Protocol, originally signed by forty-six countries, and its predecessor, the Vienna Convention, became the first universally ratified treaties in United Nations history.

The result of the Montreal Protocol was striking: it achieved a rapid turnaround, from sustained growth in emissions of ozone-depleting substances, to sustained decline. Kofi Annan, a former Secretary-General of the United Nations, has described it as 'perhaps the single most successful international agreement to date'.[18]

IGNORING THE LESSONS OF HISTORY

The first twenty years of climate change negotiations largely ignored these lessons from history. The scope for cooperation was set at its maximum possible extent: the whole problem of climate change, including all global emissions, not to mention the problem of adaptation, was supposed to be addressed within a single negotiating process. Participation, also, was maximised: virtually every country in the world had a seat at the table. The period of time under negotiation was long: it was not a country's immediate actions that were the subject of discussion, but its economy-wide emissions of greenhouse gases over a decade into the future. And despite a low degree of confidence in the future availability and cost of low-emissions technologies, and an even lower level of consensus in how the burden of solving this problem should be allocated between countries, an attempt was made to jump straight to contracting, with a legally binding agreement.

Viewed this way, it is not surprising the attempt failed. With such a broad scope and long timeframes, at a time of low confidence in solutions, it was inevitable that actions and commitments would be weak and that no compliance mechanisms could be agreed. With so many countries trying to agree so much, it was natural for the negotiations to end in acrimonious collapse. The game could hardly have been designed to make progress more difficult.

It can reasonably be argued that these two decades of diplomatic effort at least normalised the process of countries meeting regularly to talk about climate change, and to some extent encouraged practical cooperation. How much more progress could have been made, though, if all that political capital had been spent productively instead of burned up trying to achieve the impossible? What if we had structured the game so that the substance was not left on the sidelines?

****

At the end of two weeks of negotiations in Doha, Pete Betts, the head of our UK delegation and also chief negotiator for the EU, sank his head onto the table in exhaustion. A handful of us were sitting in a bar in the slowly emptying conference centre, sharing a few beers and an informal debrief. Pete, sitting next to his own boss, Ed Davey, the Secretary of State for Energy and Climate Change, made little progress through his pint before falling asleep.

Pete Betts is a legend of UNFCCC diplomacy. In that Doha conference, he had taken a stand at a decisive moment. Talks had drifted through the first week, making no progress. Then in a session to discuss the future of the 'Ad Hoc Working Group on the Durban Platform for Enhanced Action', when the Chinese negotiator appeared to be holding firm against all possibility of compromise, Pete made his point. 'Enough of this,' he said. 'We've come here to negotiate, not just repeat our positions!' He recalled the various compromises the Europeans had offered, which small island states and some other developing countries had supported, and challenged the Chinese to come forward with a more constructive response. When he finished speaking, applause sounded from around the room, and not just from the Europeans. A small huddle formed at the front of the room, as representatives of a handful of the most influential countries conferred.

A compromise was found. Text was agreed. A moment of breakthrough, after which the talks began to go somewhere. At the end of the conference, countries agreed the process by which this same 'ad hoc working group' would take forward negotiation of a new universal climate change agreement. The aim was for this to be agreed in 2015, and to enter into force in 2020.[19]

Pete's head on the table at the end of the fortnight seemed a metaphor for a tired process. But with his critical intervention, he had helped to open the way to a new stage of the game, one that for many would be cause for a reawakening of hope.

19

THE GREATEST PUBLIC RELATIONS GAMBLE
IN HISTORY

Fast-forward three years, and the conclusion of the 2015 climate change conference in Paris was celebrated by its chief negotiators not with heads on the tables, but with hands in the air. The Paris Agreement was immediately hailed by world leaders as a diplomatic triumph. The UN Secretary-General, Ban Ki-moon, called it a 'resounding success for multilateralism'. US President Barack Obama said it sent 'a powerful signal that the world is firmly committed to a low-carbon future'.[1] China's Foreign Ministry described it as 'comprehensive, balanced, and ambitious'.

The reactions of experts were more balanced, but still generally positive. Scientists welcomed it as an important step forward, while pointing out that we had already left it rather late to begin cutting emissions. The most grudging praise, not surprisingly, came from environmental NGOs. Kumi Naidoo, the head of Greenpeace, said, 'The deal alone won't dig us out of the hole that we're in, but it makes the sides less steep.'[2]

Personally, I was closer to the Kumi Naidoo end of the spectrum of opinion than the Ban Ki-moon end. I had worked hard on the agreement, as had so many others. But my knowledge of what was in it, and what was not, did not make me confident that the world would avoid dangerous climate change. Despite having won the office sweepstake with my lucky guess that the talks would over-run by twenty-seven hours, my feelings were mixed, at best.

THE EMPEROR'S NEW CLIMATE TREATY?

Here is a rough summary of what was in the Paris Agreement.

The first thing it did was establish some collective goals. Countries agreed that they would seek to limit the rise in global temperatures to well below 2°C, compared to the pre-industrial period, and to 'pursue efforts' to limit the rise to 1.5°C. To achieve this goal, countries agreed that they would aim to reach a peak in global emissions as soon as possible, and to reach net zero global emissions ('a balance between anthropogenic emissions by sources and removals by sinks') in the second half of this century. At the same time, the Agreement affirmed the collective goals of increasing adaptation and resilience to climate change, and of making financial flows consistent with a pathway of decreasing emissions and increasing resilience.

The second thing the Paris Agreement did was specify a set of processes. Countries agreed that they would individually submit 'nationally determined contributions' setting out their targets and actions to reduce emissions and build resilience to climate change. They agreed to come forward with new 'contributions' every five years, and to the principle that each time they did so, a country's new contribution should 'represent a progression' beyond its current one. They also agreed that the accounting of their emissions reductions should follow the principles of environmental integrity, transparency, accuracy, completeness, comparability, and consistency, and the avoidance of double counting.

The third thing the Paris Agreement did was encourage and endorse certain forms of cooperation. Developed countries would provide money to support developing countries in reducing their emissions and adapting to climate change. Parties agreed that they should strengthen their cooperation on adaptation, on emissions reduction, on technology development, and on the protection of carbon sinks such as forests. And they agreed that if countries wanted to, they could enter into voluntary arrangements for international emissions trading, such that emissions reductions achieved by one country could be accounted for by another.

The limitations of the Paris Agreement are not difficult to identify. Most obviously, agreeing a collective goal is not the same as agreeing individual actions to meet it. As the academic Scott Barrett said of the 2°C goal, 'The problem is that this is a global goal. Everyone is responsible for meeting it, meaning that no country is responsible for meeting it.'[3] The Paris Agreement agreed a strong set of collective goals, but left countries entirely free to choose by themselves the nature and extent of any actions they would take to meet them. The process was legally binding, but the substance was optional.

For a simple analogy, think of a tax return. Imagine that the government sets strict laws specifying the forms you must fill in, the information you must disclose and the evidence you must provide as proof of its accuracy, the accounting principles you must use in working out your sums, and the date by which you must submit the returns each year. But at the same time, the rate of tax you pay is entirely up to you. You can even claim net benefits if you like. There is a reason why tax returns do not work this way.

Systems of cooperation only work if they have some way of ensuring that individual behaviour is consistent with collective goals.

For a more sobering example, consider the Kellogg–Briand Pact of 1928, officially known as the General Treaty of Renunciation of War as an Instrument of National Policy. Signatories of the Pact, which included all the most powerful countries in the world at that time, agreed never to go to war, and to use only peaceful methods to resolve any disputes that might arise between them. The Pact was powerful as a statement of the common desire for peace, but it created no incentives, penalties, or infrastructure of cooperation to ensure that countries' individual actions were consistent with this goal. Ten years after it came into force, the world entered the Second World War.

It was perhaps with examples such as these in mind that our own Chief Scientific Adviser in the Department of Energy and Climate Change at the time of the Paris Agreement, David MacKay, wrote that 'Forty years of empirical and theoretical literature on cooperation confirms that individual commitments do not deliver strong collective action.'[4] If this were true, how could anyone expect the Paris Agreement to work?

Three possible ways by which the Paris Agreement can help the world make progress on climate change are often put forward. I will call them peer pressure, the process effect, and the self-fulfilling prophecy.

Peer pressure was what the climate change negotiations had always relied on in the past, in the absence of any significant financial incentives, trade sanctions, or other means of changing the interests of parties. Clearly, in the past this had not been enough. But the hope for Paris was that if emissions targets were explicitly 'nationally determined', countries would consider credibility on climate change to be a matter of national pride, and this would enable 'an upward spiral of ambition over time'.[5] If each believed that others would stay true to the spirit of the Agreement, then each would feel obliged to do their own fair share. Nobody I ever met justified the Paris Agreement with reference to the Kellogg–Briand Pact, but if they had wanted to, they could have argued that the Pact did exert a normative power, eventually serving as one of the legal foundations of the presumption that conquering another country's territory is unlawful.[6] The Paris Agreement was intended to achieve something similar.

The 'process effect' refers to the internal workings of governments. The argument was that if the Paris Agreement required countries to resubmit plans for emissions reductions every five years, then this would regularly force governments to review those plans. In that process of review, they would identify actions they could take, which if unprompted, they might not have considered. One academic told me he had witnessed this effect at work within the UK government, resulting from the five-yearly 'carbon budget' system created by the UK's Climate Change Act.

The self-fulfilling prophecy argument was that the Paris Agreement would send a strong signal to markets, to which investors would respond by reallocating capital away from fossil fuels and towards clean technologies. As those technologies improved, and the markets for them grew, governments would gain confidence in their ability to reduce emissions and would come forward with new and stronger targets – a reinforcing feedback.

This last argument was dominant in the run-up to Paris, at least in the UK, and it represented a huge gamble. It relied on one of two conditions being true. One condition was that countries would implement stronger national policies as a result of the Agreement and their nationally determined contributions than they would have done otherwise. This could only be explained by peer pressure or the process effect, so was in fact only a restatement of those potential mechanisms of change. The alternative condition was that businesses and investors would believe, contrary to the facts, that the Agreement was about substance rather than process, and change their behaviour accordingly.

Investors I met at an event in the City of London a few weeks ahead of the Paris Agreement seemed remarkably ignorant about its likely content. 'Would it agree a price to be put on carbon?' some of them asked me. 'Would it rule out the use of coal power?' If ignorance such as this could be maintained, perhaps there was still hope for us all. But surely all businesses and investors would eventually do their homework, and at least find out whether any policies had been adopted that would directly affect their own sectors. What then? Would they, like the child in the story of 'the Emperor's New Clothes', see the Agreement in all its nakedness, and laugh it out of the room?

The self-fulfilling prophecy argument and the peer pressure argument both told us that if everyone believed hard enough that the Paris Agreement was effective, then it would come to be true. This might sound crazy, but it is not impossible. Perceptions can shape reality. Confidence-building can lead to cooperation. Statements of policy intent can influence investors. The path-dependent nature of economic change means that even if at some point it is discovered that the initial confidence was misplaced, the actions already taken may still be enough to generate further progress.

If that sounds optimistic, it is. We are staking the future of human civilisation on a giant public relations gamble.

IS IT WORKING?

Six years have passed since the negotiation of the Paris Agreement, at the time of writing this book. Many people ask, 'Is it working?'

Experts who study trends in emissions and low-carbon technologies typically say, 'We are making progress, but nowhere near fast enough.' However we choose to measure progress, this judgement seems roughly right.

For a start, we can see that global emissions are still going up. Throughout the past decade, global emissions of carbon dioxide have increased on average by around 1% each year. This is similar to the rate of increase throughout the 1990s, but substantially lower than the average 3% per annum rate of increase that took place in the 2000s.[7]

The emissions targets that countries submitted as 'intended nationally determined contributions' under the Paris Agreement in 2015 implied that global emissions would continue to increase throughout the period that most of them covered – the decade from 2020 to 2030. However, the upward slope implied by the targets was less steep than the 'business as usual' trajectory that some analysts had previously estimated. This was seen by many as evidence of the Paris Agreement's effect.

More recently, there has been rapid growth in the number of countries setting themselves the target of achieving net zero emissions, typically by around the year 2050. The UK was one of the first, passing a law in June 2019 to upgrade its 2050 emissions target from 80% below 1990 levels to 100%, or net zero. In September 2020, China announced it would aim for carbon neutrality by 2060, giving the net zero movement a considerable boost. Japan, South Korea, and the US (after Joe Biden replaced Donald Trump as President) all followed, and by the end of 2021 the countries with net zero targets, mostly to be met by mid-century, covered 90% of global GDP.[8]

The net zero trend is encouraging, but as analysts and protesters alike have pointed out, there remains a huge discrepancy between these long-term goals and most countries' nearer-term targets and actions.[9] As of November 2021, countries' targets still appeared to imply a slight increase in global emissions over the decade to 2030.[10] At the same time, the yawning gap between the level of global emissions in 2030 implied by the targets and a level consistent with limiting warming to 2°C had barely changed since the Paris Agreement.[11] According to the UN Environment Programme, many countries were off track to meet even these inadequate targets, and some of their policies ran directly counter to them.[12]

A more practical way to measure progress is to look at how fast clean technologies are spreading through the economy. On this measure too, we are far off track. The International Energy Agency has estimated that only six out of a set of forty-six low-carbon technologies are being deployed at rates consistent with internationally agreed goals for avoiding dangerous climate change.[13] There are, however, some reasons to be hopeful. Global deployment of solar power in 2020 was more than ten times higher than experts had forecast only fifteen years previously,[14] and progress in several other technologies, including wind power, batteries, and electric vehicles, has outpaced experts' expectations.

THE ATTRIBUTION PROBLEM

All of this is consistent with the view that there has been some progress, but not nearly enough. To answer the question 'Is the Paris Agreement working?', however, we have to understand *how and why* progress has been made.

In climate science, there is a whole field of research devoted to the problem of attribution: understanding which changes in the climate, and to what extent, have come about as the result of emissions of greenhouse gases from human activity. Careful estimates are made of the effects on global temperatures of changing levels of volcanic activity, solar intensity, and air pollution, to separate these from the effect of greenhouse gas emissions. Measurements of the concentrations in the atmosphere of different isotopes of carbon dioxide help us to distinguish between the CO_2 that we have emitted by burning fossil fuels, and the CO_2 that is naturally present. When an extreme event such as a heat wave occurs, simulation models can be used to compare the likelihood of it happening in the current climate with its likelihood in the pre-warming climate that we used to have. All of these techniques help us understand how much the extreme weather we experience is due to climate change, and how much climate change is due to our activities.

If we want to understand how much of the change that we are seeing in the global economy is due to the Paris Agreement, then we ought to try to be equally rigorous in our approach to attribution. Our task is more difficult. In climate science, at least the study of cause and effect is untroubled by questions of motive. As the physicist Murray Gell-Mann reportedly said, 'Imagine how hard physics would be if electrons could think.'[15] That is the problem we face in political economy. Many causes and effects are wrapped up together, and why things were done as they were can never be known for sure. Still, we must analyse what we can.

(A) POLICY OR ACCIDENT?

When we compare emissions targets to 'business as usual' projections, a lot depends on what we expect 'business as usual' emissions to be. That depends heavily on expectations of economic growth – its rate, and its quality.

In the decade after the global financial crisis of 2008–2009, many countries experienced slower than expected economic growth. The EU grew so much more slowly than expected that it met its 2020 emissions target around eight years early. China's economic growth slowed too, from around 10% per year in the 1990s and 2000s to around 7% per year in the 2010s.[16] These and other developments contributed to the IMF revising downward its growth projections for the world economy every year from 2011 to 2016.[17] At the same time, throughout the past decade China's economy has been undergoing structural change, with growth shifting from heavy industry to much less carbon-intensive services. Since China is by far the world's largest emitter, this has a significant impact on global emissions. Altogether, this could account for a large part of the difference between the 'intended nationally determined contributions' trajectory of 2015 and the 'business as usual' trajectory expected previously. This was not policy, but accident.

On the other hand, the progress in development and adoption of low-carbon technologies is clearly attributable to policy. Governments funded the research and development of solar and wind power technologies for decades before they became commercially viable. No markets existed for them, until they were created by government subsidies. Similarly, regulations have driven progress towards more energy-efficient models and lower-carbon technologies in lighting, heating, cooling, buildings, and cars.

(B) TARGETS OR ACTIONS?

Where policies have driven progress, it is helpful to understand whether they were put in place in order to meet emissions targets such as those foreseen in the Paris Agreement, or for other reasons.

In the UK, we have a system of five-yearly 'carbon budgets', designed to ensure that our emissions in the short term are consistent with our long-term targets. Policies in the power, buildings, transport, industry, and land use sectors are implemented with the aim of meeting the carbon budgets. The EU has a similarly top-down approach: its members agree an overall emissions target, and then put in place policies jointly and separately to reduce emissions in line with that target. In the UK and EU, it is fairly clear that emissions targets drive policy action.

In most developing countries and emerging economies, things work differently. Very few have a system of carbon budgets, in which the need to reduce emissions overrides other policy priorities. In China and India, the uptake of renewable power and progress in energy efficiency have been driven mainly by the policy priorities of energy security, air quality (reducing local air pollution to protect public health), and industrial opportunity. Reducing emissions ranks around fourth on the priority list, at best. In countries such as these, economy-wide emissions 'targets' have generally been arrived at by estimating the emissions likely to result from policies that have already been put in place. In other words, it is policy actions – taken for reasons other than climate change – that drive emissions targets.

To illustrate this, consider China. It has an overall target to peak its emissions by around 2030. Most experts consider this target to be extremely weak – comparable to 'business as usual' for China, perhaps even business as usual plus a cushion. Within the narrower scope of the power sector, where China aims to become competitive in low-carbon technologies, cut its imports of coal, and clean up its urban air, experts have generally considered China's targets for deployment of solar and wind power to be impressive. But even these targets have been comprehensively blown out of the water by what has actually happened. The actions China has taken to deploy renewable power, such as subsidies for its production and consumption, reforms to markets, and connections to grids, have proved far more effective than it expected. It is these actions that have driven progress, much more than any targets.

This is an important distinction to make because it helps us understand what kind of diplomacy might work in different kinds of countries. Peer pressure on emissions targets may be effective in influencing countries where targets drive policies, but it is unlikely to have much impact in countries whose targets are just the forecast outcomes of policies. To influence the latter group of countries, assistance with policy development is likely to be more effective.

(C) PEER PRESSURE OR LEADERSHIP?

Where countries have set top-down emissions targets of the kind that drive policy change, we can ask whether these targets were set in response to pressure from international peers, or as independent acts of leadership.

The UK can make a reasonable claim to have acted with the intention of leadership when it established its Climate Change Act in 2008, with a target to reduce emissions by 80% by 2050 compared to 1990 levels. For a long time, the UK was the only developed country to have a target consistent with the international community's goals, together with a legislative framework designed to ensure that short-term and medium-term policies were in line with that target. The US administration of President Obama could also be considered to be acting primarily out of concern for the dangers of climate change when it forced through measures to cut emissions despite strong political opposition. Among developing countries, Costa Rica has long been recognised for its leadership on climate change, and in 2019 it set out a detailed plan to reach net zero emissions by 2050.

In many countries, domestic pressure from civil society – including, more recently, protests by schoolchildren – has helped motivate governments to adopt stronger emissions targets.

Within the EU, there is clear evidence of international peer pressure playing a role. Leaders of the EU's Member States have first agreed emissions targets for the EU as a whole, and then agreed how the necessary reductions should be apportioned between their countries. It is no secret that some Member States have been much less enthusiastic about this process than others and have come under significant pressure from their more climate-concerned peers.

China, India, and other countries whose policies have not been driven by top-down emissions targets have shown themselves to be highly resilient to international peer pressure on targets – so much so that the world's aggregate emissions targets for the next decade still point up, not down. But the recent movement towards net zero emissions targets, as mentioned above, suggests the emergence of a new international norm. This could be interpreted as evidence that peer pressure is beginning to play a more important role.

(D) PARIS AGREEMENT OR GENERAL GEOPOLITICS?

International peer pressure on climate change does not come uniquely from the Paris Agreement, or from the UN negotiations process. Leaders regularly discuss climate change when they meet in other fora, such as the G7 and G20, the UN General Assembly, and ad hoc climate change summits such as those hosted by the UN Secretary-General in 2019 and 2020. If governments care about international perceptions of their countries' positions on climate change, they may also be influenced by media reporting, which can happen at any time regardless of whether there are summits or negotiations.

Which of these processes are more likely to be successful in generating peer pressure? Is it the UN negotiations, where thousands of bureaucrats who typically have minimal influence over their countries' domestic policies haggle acrimoniously over the details of accounting rules, but from which agreements are produced that signify consensus and legitimacy? Or the summits, where leaders meet face-to-face, but sometimes give climate change no more than a fleeting mention? Or the media, where governments' policies may be praised or rubbished, forensically analysed or carelessly misrepresented? In truth, we do not know. It seems reasonable to assume that when peer pressure plays a role, it has arisen from a combination of these factors.

THE VERDICT

In summary, the Paris Agreement can be credited with some of the progress that we are seeing, but certainly not all of it, and probably not most of it. Accidents of economic development, policies adopted for reasons other than climate change, national leadership, and international peer pressure from other sources have all made significant contributions to global emissions being on a lower trajectory now than previously expected.

NO TIME TO GIVE UP

The Paris Agreement is often presented as a new and radical departure from the approach that preceded it, as epitomised by the Kyoto Protocol. Whereas the early aim had been to set emissions targets by mutual agreement, and Kyoto had at least maintained the appearance of doing so, the Paris Agreement openly renounced any such ambition. In one sense, after having tried and failed to secure a global agreement of maximal scope, the international community had gone to the opposite extreme, and settled on an entirely unilateralist approach. Countries would now set their climate change targets and policies entirely independently, with only the processes for accounting and reporting being the subject of agreement.

In another sense, however, the Paris Agreement was simply a continuation of what had been tried before. As the researcher of the international climate change negotiations Joanna Depledge has pointed out, the differences between Paris and Kyoto were more of style than of substance.[18] In each case, the reality was that countries had set their targets independently. The important constant was that throughout all this time, the unchanging focus of diplomacy was countries' long-term economy-wide emissions targets, and its main lever of influence was peer pressure. The change over time was less a radical departure, and more a progression: away from attempts at formal agreement, and towards greater acceptance of unilateralism.

This raises the question: could something else be tried?

History suggests a unilateralist approach will not be enough: individual commitments do not produce strong collective action. And as we saw in the previous chapter, there are reasons to doubt that diplomacy will be most effective when its scope is as broad as countries' long-term economy-wide emissions targets.

We can debate how much credit to give to the Paris Agreement, or to the past thirty years of negotiations, for the progress now being made – this is wide open to interpretation. What cannot be debated is that we desperately need to make progress *much more quickly*. Global emissions are widely predicted to continue rising for the next decade, or, at best, to stay roughly flat, whereas to limit global warming to below 1.5°C, they need to be halved within that time. Recall that while the past two decades have seen the emissions intensity of the global economy decrease by only 1.5% per year, this decade it must fall by around 8% per year – *five times faster*. Even if we choose to give the Paris Agreement all the credit for the progress we are making now, we obviously need to be considering all possible options for accelerating the pace.

Often when the effectiveness of the international negotiations process is questioned, the response is that it's 'the only game in town'. It is true that a process such as this creates its own institutional lock-in, and that finding new forms of cooperation will be difficult. In our current circumstances, though, to dismiss the possibility of other options without fully considering them would be inexcusably complacent, and dangerous.

Another argument I have heard for hesitation is that it's 'too soon to say whether Paris is working'. This is true: it will be many years, if not decades, before we can form a well-rounded view of the effectiveness of the Paris Agreement. But this is like the arguments of the climate deniers who said we should wait until there was more comprehensive scientific evidence of climate change before taking any steps to reduce emissions. Just as there was enough scientific evidence then to justify new policies to reduce emissions, there is enough historical evidence now – from the examples of successful international cooperation in trade, security, and environmental protection – to justify new approaches to climate change diplomacy. If we wait for more evidence, it will be too late to preserve any chance of meeting our collective goals.

****

Before we move on, we will pay one last visit to our friend the boiling frog. We find him this time in a pot together with a dozen other frogs. All have received risk assessments from their science advisers and know that they are in danger. Their chief economists have measured the sides of the pot, and they know how high they need to jump to get out. The problem is, the sides are too high: none of the frogs can manage to jump out.

Our friend the boiling frog turns to his chief negotiator. 'What shall we do?' he asks. 'Is there any way we can save ourselves?' The chief negotiator responds, 'Tell the other frogs to raise their ambition. They need to try harder. Maybe if they try harder, one of them will be able to get out and turn off the gas.' The frog tries this, but the other frogs react angrily, and tell him they are already jumping as high as they can, and he ought to try harder himself. An argument starts up about whose idea it was to get into the pot in the first place. The frog goes back to his chief negotiator, and asks, 'Is there anything else we can try?' 'No,' says the chief negotiator. 'This is the only game in town. Besides, we need to try it for longer to see if it will work.'

The frog feels unconvinced. He suggests to the others that instead of urging each other to try harder individually, there might be practical ways they could cooperate. What about standing on each other's backs? Most of the others ignore him, but a few are willing to give it a try. It turns out that when three of them sit on each other's backs, the fourth one can jump out of the pot. He clears the side with a heroic leap, turns off the gas, and saves them all.

Ok, so it won't be that easy. But between the two extremes of a universal treaty and unilateral action, a wide range of possibilities exists. Long-term economy-wide emissions targets do not have to be the focus. In the next chapter, we look at what forms of international cooperation on climate change might give us the best chance of making progress.

20

SYSTEM CHANGE, NOT CLIMATE CHANGE

The first solar cell was created by the Russian physicist Aleksandr Stoletov around the year 1890. Six decades later, solar panels began to be used in space, powering America's Vanguard I satellite, nicknamed the 'grapefruit' by Soviet Premier Nikita Krushchev. Another two decades on, in 1979 US President Jimmy Carter installed solar panels on the roof of the White House, as a statement of things to come. Three more decades passed, and in 2008 my parents were among the first wave of homeowners to put solar panels on their own roofs, with the support of government subsidies. One more decade on, and solar and wind power together made up over half of the world's new installations of electricity generating capacity each year.[1]

In the past half-century, solar power has progressed from being an expensive curiosity used in space to the cheapest source of electricity in most of the world.

Looked at one way, this is a story of how fast progress can be. Since that 1957 installation on the Vanguard satellite, the cost of solar panels has fallen to less than one three-thousandth of what it was.[2] This is impressive when we consider that over similar lengths of time, the costs of coal, oil, and gas have seen many fluctuations, but no sustained fall. Looked at another way, this is a reminder of how long change can take. It has taken us six decades from that first deployment to arrive at a point where solar and wind are now dominating the market for new power plants. Even now, because power plants have long lifetimes, most of the world's electricity is still generated from fossil fuels, and at the time of writing less than a tenth of it comes from solar and wind.

In the years to come, we will need to transform electricity grids to deal with the intermittency of renewable power. We will need to find ways to store large amounts of energy – not only from daytime to night-time, but also from summer to winter. Markets will need to work differently, so that they reward consumers for using more power when supply is plentiful, and less when it is scarce. Electrical appliances will need to be designed so that they can manage their energy use intelligently, so that consumers do not have to worry about it. All this change in the power sector will have social consequences too. In places where the coal industry is at the centre of economic activity, new sources of jobs, regional development, and government revenues will need to be found. In the transition to clean power, there is still a long road ahead.

SYSTEM TRANSITIONS IN THE GLOBAL ECONOMY

To understand how we can reduce global emissions more quickly, it helps to go back to first principles. What is it that we are actually trying to do? The Intergovernmental Panel on Climate Change has described the challenge as: '*rapid and far-reaching transitions in energy, land, urban and infrastructure (including transport and buildings) and industrial systems. These systems transitions are unprecedented in terms of scale, but not necessarily in terms of speed . . .* '.[3]

The unfolding story of solar and wind power taking over from coal and gas is that of a system transition. The 'system' is the global power sector, broadly defined: the pattern of activities that supports the production, governance, and use of electricity in society. This system includes the power stations that burn fossil fuels and convert heat into electricity; the infrastructure networks that transmit electricity over long distances and distribute it to homes and industries; the markets that balance supply and demand; and the regulators who ensure the markets function effectively. It also involves miners who extract the coal, utility companies that operate the power plants, and investors, both private and public, who allocate funds across technologies, companies, and regions, influenced by where they expect the profits to be made.

The 'transition' is not simply the replacement of the old technologies of coal and gas power with the new technologies of solar and wind. It involves changing everything around them too – related technologies such as batteries, smart meters, and intelligent appliances, as well as the markets, the infrastructure, the business models, the fossil fuel industries and the communities that currently rely on them. To make the move from coal to clean power quickly, we will need to anticipate, and act to bring forward, the necessary changes in each of these critical elements of the system. If we do not want the growth of renewables to be held back by the technical difficulty of balancing intermittent supply with demand, then we had better work hard at developing energy storage. If we do not want the decline of coal to be stalled by local governments that fear unemployment and social unrest, then we had better invest in regional development in the right places.

At the same time, it is important to recognise that the scope of this transition has its limits. To shift from fossil fuels to clean power, we do not

need to change the fashion industry, the water infrastructure, the functioning of the stock market, or consumer culture. Although everything in the
economy and society is interconnected, we do not have to change everything to accomplish a specific goal such as a transition to clean power. In
other words, we can draw a boundary around the edges of the system we are
trying to change.

The idea of a 'system boundary' is a useful one to keep in mind. It is
within the roughly defined boundaries of a system such as the global power
sector that new technologies can be developed and diffused, practices of
consumption and production changed, markets reformed, and infrastructure replaced. If we search for points of leverage within these boundaries, we
will have a reasonable chance of accelerating change. In contrast, if we focus
our efforts too narrowly, for example on single technologies, we are likely to
ignore elements of a system that are critical to its transition. Or if we focus
too broadly, such as at the level of the whole stock market, or the whole
economy, we are likely to waste effort or, at least, spread our resources too
thinly to be effective.

UNPRECEDENTED IN TERMS OF SCALE, BUT NOT NECESSARILY IN TERMS OF SPEED...

When we look at system transitions that happened in the past, we can see the
actions that helped them proceed more quickly. Frank Geels is one of the
world's best-known experts in the study of past transitions. His case studies
show that although each transition is unique, there are general lessons for
the role of government policy.[11]

In the earliest stage of a transition, known as the 'emergence' stage,
innovators are searching for new technologies, or new ways of doing
business. Governments can accelerate this process by investing in
research and development, and by setting clear goals that encourage
businesses and private investors to align their efforts. Governments can
also play a crucial role by creating 'niche markets' within which new
technologies can be deployed for the first time. These are like sheltered
nests for the new inventions, allowing them to grow and develop before
going out into the world to compete against the big beasts of incumbent technologies.

---

[11] This section summarises the explanation of the stages of a system transition and several
case studies that Frank Geels contributed to the report 'Accelerating the low carbon
transition', based on his academic papers.

The emergence of aviation provides an example of both these kinds of intervention.[4] Government investment in research and development dramatically accelerated progress in aeroplane technology during the First World War. Then in the 1920s and 1930s, public procurement and subsidy, including through the protected niche of US airmail, made it possible for a civil aviation industry to become established.

In the middle stage of a transition, known as the 'diffusion' stage, new technologies and business models are battling hard against incumbents as they struggle to spread through markets and society. The new technologies benefit from self-reinforcing feedbacks: as they improve, they gain market share, attracting more investment, leading to further improvement. Governments can accelerate this process by reshaping markets, tilting the battlefield in favour of the new entrants and against the incumbents. Targeted investments in the new technologies, taxes on the old, changes to regulations, installation of new infrastructure, and public communications campaigns can all be used for this purpose.

The diffusion of the technologies and practices of intensive agriculture in the UK in the 1940s and 1950s was supported in this way.[5] The government used capital grants and cheap loans for new tractors and land-dredging, training programmes for farmers, and market controls on wheat prices, to transform the sector within the span of a couple of decades.

In the final stage of a transition, as the new technology becomes fully established, all the social and economic systems around it are adjusting to accommodate themselves to this 'new normal'. This stage is known as 'reconfiguration'. Governments can help this happen more quickly by investing in the widespread installation of new infrastructure, or in the development of complementary technologies that enable the core technologies of the transition to become ubiquitous. They can also create new institutions, support the emergence of new professional standards, and even ban the use of old technologies, as ways of seeing the transition through to completion. The transition from horses to cars benefited from all these kinds of support, with governments investing heavily in both the physical infrastructure of road networks and the institutional infrastructure of driving tests, vehicle registration databases, and the highway code.[6]

In each of these stages, the roles of different actors can be mutually reinforcing. Campaigners who call for change can open the way for policy that favours innovators over incumbents. Innovators who demonstrate new technologies create the possibility of new business models. Entrepreneurs who invest in new business models give new options to consumers. Consumers who choose the new products over the old help to strengthen the hand of advocates calling for further change. In the transition from cesspools to sewers, doctors who highlighted public health risks, engineers who developed new pipeline technology, and governments that invested in new infrastructure networks all supported society's shift to a new system.[7] When actors share the goal of accelerating a transition, they can achieve far more together than any of them could alone.

THE GAINS FROM INTERNATIONAL COOPERATION

Within the modern global economy, countries are connected by flows of finance, technology, people, products, and knowledge. We invest, sell, travel, and communicate across borders. No man is an island, and neither, in the twenty-first century, is any national economy. In this context, systems transitions are ever more likely to be acted out on an international stage.

The story of the unfolding transition to clean power described above is a global one. The dramatic progress of solar and wind power over the past half-century is a product of early support for research and development in the US and Japan, incentives for their early deployment in Europe, and massive investment in their production in China. Thanks to international trade, cheap solar panels and wind turbines are now available all over the world, governments everywhere are reforming markets to remove barriers to their entry, and businesses and investors are moving to take advantage of this new opportunity.

The interconnected nature of our economies means that in each greenhouse-gas-emitting sector, the transition to zero-emissions systems can hardly avoid being global. And of course, it *must* be global, because nothing less will bring us to net zero global emissions. So, the starting point for climate change diplomacy should be to ask: how can countries best work together to accelerate system transitions in the global economy?

In 2019, David Victor, Frank Geels, and I teamed up to find an answer to this question. We brought Frank's understanding of system transitions and David's expertise in international relations together with the practical knowledge of leading experts in each of the ten sectors that contribute the most to global emissions.[8] We found there were enormous potential gains from international cooperation. These could be roughly grouped into three opportunities: faster innovation, larger economies of scale, and level playing fields where they are needed.

218

FASTER INNOVATION

Just as a university or a company might put more researchers onto a problem to accelerate the search for solutions, and a government might fund more universities for the same purpose, globally we can innovate faster if different countries align their efforts. The astonishingly rapid development of vaccines for the COVID-19 virus in 2020–2021 was a case in point. If we coordinate research and development internationally, we can discover new technologies more quickly. If we share the lessons from early testing, we can confirm what works at an earlier date. And if we create the first 'niche markets' for the same new technologies at the same time, these will be larger spaces than any country could create alone, and so likely to attract more investment, leading to faster development.

Of course, the economy is a competitive place. Countries want their own industries to succeed. However, experience from semiconductors to pharmaceuticals shows that it is quite possible for cooperation to take place in the 'pre-competitive' space, with countries exchanging information on what works at the same time as allowing companies to develop their own patents and build their own competitive positions.

The need for innovation to avoid dangerous climate change is intense. The International Energy Agency estimates that about half of the emissions reductions needed to reach net zero global emissions by mid-century will have to come from technologies that are not yet fully commercialised. This does not mean that we need to wait for new 'miracle technologies' to be invented. We already have most of what we need. It means that many technologies still have to go through a significant developmental journey: having already been proven in concept, they still need to be tested, improved, deployed in industry, and established in markets.

Most countries have barely begun to decarbonise the energy-intensive industrial sectors such as iron and steel, cement, and plastics that together account for about a fifth of global emissions. Eliminating their emissions will involve a combination of replacing coal and gas-burning with electricity or hydrogen, creating entirely new chemical feedstocks, and capturing carbon emissions and shoving them underground. None of these technologies have yet been tested at the scale of industrial production, let alone commercialised. The first pilot plants are only just being built.

The need for innovation in agriculture and land use is no less great. The burping and farting of cows, the use of fertilisers for crops, and a host of other activities involved in producing food together account for over a tenth of global emissions. We urgently need to develop low-emission fertilisers and ultra-resource-efficient methods of farming, not to mention climate-resilient crops and livestock so that our food sources survive the extreme weather events that are coming our way. We could all become healthier by moving to a plant-based diet, but if we want to continue to enjoy eating things that taste like meat, then we had better quickly develop alternative proteins that don't involve such enormous amounts of land and resources being given over to raising animals.

Even in the power sector, where the low-carbon transition is most advanced, we have not yet solved the problem of storing solar energy generated in summer to heat our homes in the dark nights of winter, or the challenge of installing enough zero-emissions generating capacity in a densely populated country with little space for solar farms and wind turbines. There are reasonable solutions to these problems that engineers can describe, but taking them from the drawing board to the national grid is no small task.

Across all sectors, developing the technologies we need at the pace we need them is a huge challenge. We will be far more likely to achieve this if we carefully and deliberately align our efforts, share learning, and build on each other's successes than if we each act independently, scattering our efforts in different directions.[9]

LARGER ECONOMIES OF SCALE

Just as government, business, and civil society can reinforce each other's efforts nationally to accelerate a transition, the same is true globally. In an internationally connected sector of the economy, the battle between new entrants and incumbents plays out on a larger scale than that of any individual country. If countries send similar policy signals about the direction and pace of a transition, they will more quickly incentivise investors to reallocate capital from the old technologies to the new, and companies to shift from old business models to new ones.

The reinforcing feedbacks that spread new technologies through markets and societies all benefit from scale. Larger markets attract more investment, stimulating faster innovation and improvement of the new technologies, enabling faster growth in their market share.

We can see this effect in the rapid progress of technologies such as solar panels, wind turbines, and electric vehicle batteries. Each time the world's total cumulative production of these technologies doubles, their cost falls by a constant fraction. (For solar power this is about 28%; for wind power, around 15%.) Roughly speaking, if twice as many countries of a similar size deploy the same technology at the same time, its costs will come down twice as quickly. Analysis has shown that critical clean technologies could be up to 45% cheaper by 2030, and up to 75% cheaper by 2050, if they are deployed quickly all over the world than they would be if we continue to make slow progress.[10]

This means that even if we disregard the threat of dangerous climate change, countries still have a strong shared interest in helping each other deploy clean technologies more quickly. We all benefit from the lower costs that come from faster collective deployment.

In the power sector, for many countries the challenge is to reform electricity markets so that they attract investment in renewables. Practical assistance with such policies, and with finding new economic opportunities for communities previously reliant on coal, is a way for international cooperation to accelerate the transition. We will discuss this in detail in Chapter 22.

In road transport, the transition from petroleum and diesel cars to electric vehicles is gathering pace, but still needs to go much faster to be in line with the Paris Agreement goals. The higher cost of electric vehicles is an obstacle, but with every increase in production, their cost comes down, and we get closer to the tipping point where they will outcompete the incumbents. Cars are traded internationally, so their manufacturers respond strongly to rules set in the largest markets. If the governments of these markets act together, they can push the global industry to shift its investment much more quickly towards electric vehicles, accelerating cost reduction and making them available and affordable to consumers all over the world at an earlier date. This is the subject of Chapter 23.

Buildings are a tricky sector to decarbonise. They have long lifetimes: my poorly insulated London flat was built by the Victorians over a century ago and is still going strong. This makes it difficult to replace them quickly. We can improve the buildings we have – sticking solar panels on the roof, upgrading the insulation, and replacing gas boilers with heat pumps – but for many of us, the upfront costs and the hassle are a strong deterrent. Government policy tends to be timid when it comes to interfering with people's homes. Unlike cars, buildings are not shipped across the seas in international trade; instead, they stay rather obstinately in place, and the supply chains of the construction sector are relatively localised. This makes it harder to use trade as a lever to accelerate the transition.

Even here, though, coordinated action can spread change more quickly across the world. If countries focus their subsidies for clean heating on viable zero-emission technologies like heat pumps, instead of squandering them on paying people to burn woodchips, as Europe does at present, these technologies will quickly improve and come down in cost. Coordination on standards for air conditioners, which are internationally traded, can quickly push up their efficiency and cut emissions. The development of comparable measures of building energy efficiency across countries can make it easier for international investors to put their money into genuinely low-carbon buildings, helping to grow the markets for more efficient methods of design and construction. All of this is essential to get right, as new buildings are being constructed globally at a rate equivalent to adding the floor area of Japan every year.

None of this is intended to oversimplify the challenge. In each sector, every government will have to grapple with its own problems. Engineers will need to be trained in the installation of heat pumps and the servicing of solar panels. Charging infrastructure will have to be built for all those electric vehicles, and financing models designed to enable the retrofitting of old buildings. New sources of revenue will need to be found to replace taxes on petroleum, and new sources of employment to replace jobs in coal mining. And yet, none of this detracts from the enormous potential of the gains from cooperation. Sporadic and loosely aligned international actions have reduced the cost of solar power to a three-thousandth of what it was, over half a century. Targeted, strongly coordinated and sustained action over the coming years could dramatically cut the costs of clean technologies and accelerate transitions in every sector.

LEVEL PLAYING FIELDS WHERE THEY ARE NEEDED

In almost all sectors, low-carbon technologies are expensive at first. In some, they are likely to remain so for the foreseeable future. In competitive international markets, this can create a formidable obstacle. First-movers will never move first if they expect to be immediately undercut by incumbents and put out of business. Transitions towards sustainability in several important sectors are being held back by exactly this problem. Countries can overcome this obstacle by working together to put in place comparable standards or carbon prices, specific to each sector, so that companies can adopt sustainable fuels, technologies, or business practices without putting themselves at a competitive disadvantage.

The need for such coordination is pressing in relation to the agricultural commodities whose production causes over half of global deforestation. Many governments want to protect their forests, but this is hard to do when businesses that engage in destructive practices are rewarded with high profits from international trade. Multinational businesses face some consumer pressure for sustainable sourcing of food, but the threat of losing out to competitors limits their willingness to act individually. Even when some businesses show leadership, they are unable to fundamentally alter the incentives driving deforestation if they only represent a small proportion of market demand. Only coordinated international action is likely to be able to solve the problem. We return to this issue in Chapter 24.

In shipping and aviation too, the task of transition is tough because of the role of international competition. Ships burn the dirtiest dregs of fuel left in the oil refinery after everything else has gone, almost literally scraping the bottom of the barrel. Planes are the most fossil-fuel-intensive form of transport. In both sectors, zero-emission fuels and technologies are being developed, but they are barely beginning to enter the market. Sustainable aviation fuel, electric planes, and ammonia-powered ships look likely to remain expensive for the foreseeable future. This means that airlines and shipping companies cannot deploy these technologies without losing business to their competitors, and ports and airports cannot require their use without risking traffic being diverted to rival hubs. Without coordination, there is no significant deployment of the new technologies. Without deployment, it is impossible for the reinforcing feedbacks of technology development to take hold, so we make little progress in bringing down their costs. We are stuck.

International cooperation can offer a way out of this impasse. Coordinated standards along international routes could require the use of sustainable shipping and aviation fuels and technologies without putting their users out of business. Coordinated investment in charging and refuelling infrastructure could ensure that the supply of clean energy is developed at the same time as demand, and ensure the first electric planes do not find themselves stranded at the end of their first journeys.

In heavy industry, as soon as viable zero-emission technologies are demonstrated, international cooperation will be critical to enabling their deployment. Rough estimates suggest that at first, zero-carbon steel could cost 20–50% more than the current product, and fully decarbonising cement could double its cost. In these highly competitive and cost-sensitive sectors, such increases in production costs are unthinkable. Even if you are a forward-thinking CEO who believes the future of the industry is low-carbon, there is no point being a first-mover if you will be instantly wiped out by the competition. The boss of one of the companies leading a pioneering low-carbon steel project in Sweden has reportedly told the Swedish government: 'We will definitely decarbonise steel production. Whether we still have a steel industry afterwards is up to you.'

International cooperation, through coordinated standards or carbon prices in each of the heavy industrial sectors, can ensure there is a market for zero-emission materials. This is essential to giving industry the confidence to invest in new production processes. Government procurement and subsidies will be able to get the first few pilot plants up and running, but commercial investment driven by market demand will be needed to scale up zero-emission production at the necessary pace. The first wave of small-scale pilot plants for low-carbon steel, planned for the early-to-mid 2020s, are expected to produce a few hundred thousand tons of steel per year. The industry will need to increase this production capacity ten-thousand-fold over the coming two decades, to decarbonise the sector in line with the Paris Agreement goals. Since steel plants take a while to design and build, planning for the plants that we want in the 2030s needs to be beginning now.

The scale of the challenge in cement, plastics, and other energy-intensive industrial sectors is no less great than in the steel sector. The need for international cooperation to support transitions in each of these sectors is clear, and urgent.

A MORE FOCUSED APPROACH TO CLIMATE CHANGE DIPLOMACY

The three major coordination gains – faster innovation, larger economies of scale, and level playing fields where they are needed – roughly map onto the three stages of the transition, as shown in Figure 20.1. This suggests that the focus of diplomacy should be different for each sector, at each stage of its transition.

The approach to climate change diplomacy suggested here is fundamentally different from the approach discussed in Chapter 18, that taken by the international community for the first twenty years, in important ways that make it more likely to succeed.

The scope of the problem is reduced to something manageable. Instead of attacking the problem of global emissions from all parts of the economy at once, we would deal with each emitting sector separately. This makes sense because each sector is different from the others in its technologies, industrial and financial structures, political economy, and influential actors. Shipping is not the same as steel, and agriculture is not the same as aviation. We have a better chance of moving each transition forward if we understand its unique structure and focus our efforts on its particular challenges and opportunities.

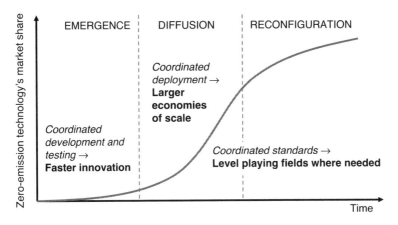

Figure 20.1 The Accelerating Transitions Framework, Victor, Geels and Sharpe (2019). System transitions generally happen in three stages: emergence, diffusion, and reconfiguration. At each stage, different policies, and different kinds of international cooperation, are likely to be effective in accelerating the transition.

The time under discussion is shortened: instead of trying to agree long-term targets, we would concentrate mainly on immediate and near-term actions. Bringing the focus of cooperation into the present instead of the future increases the confidence with which countries can approach it. We all know more about what we can do now than about what we can do in ten years' time, and it turns out that what we do now has enormous potential to shape our future options.

The focus on specific actions within individual sectors of the economy makes it possible to realise the coordination gains described above. These provide a form of incentive for participation and compliance in international cooperation because they relate to strongly held interests such as energy security, low-cost transport, and industrial jobs. Such incentives do not exist when the focus of cooperation is economy-wide emissions targets, since the only interest at play in that case is avoiding dangerous climate change – which, as we can all see, is not usually a strong enough driver of action on its own. In the minority of sectors where a 'free-rider' problem exists, cooperation to establish level playing fields in international trade can effectively create penalties for non-participation and non-compliance.

Finally, separating the global emissions problem into its constituent sectors means we can deal with the countries that matter most in each one. This can go a long way towards solving the participation problem in climate change diplomacy. There is no need to plumb the depths of the lowest common denominator of 197 countries.[v] A few countries working together can speed the development of a new technology. A critical mass cooperating can quickly spread it through global markets.

In the power sector, two countries, China and India, account for over half the global pipeline of planned new coal plants, and with another five countries (Turkey, Vietnam, Indonesia, Bangladesh, and Egypt) the share rises to three-quarters.[11] With the right support to these countries, it ought to be possible to swiftly cancel most of the world's plans for new coal plants and replace them with new investments in clean power.

In agricultural commodities, Indonesia and Malaysia together produce over 80% of the world's palm oil, and the EU, India, and China account for half of global imports. Brazil and the US together produce 70% of the world's soy, and China and the EU together import well over half of the global total. Côte d'Ivoire and Ghana together produce over half the world's cocoa, and the EU and US account for over two-thirds of global imports. Small groups of these producers and consumers, working together, could be well capable of shifting global markets to favour sustainable production of each of those commodities.

In transport, three jurisdictions – the EU, China, and California – write the rules for over half of the global car market. Coordinated action by those three could shift incentives for car manufacturers everywhere. In aviation and shipping, different countries act as nodes in the networks of international routes. The top twenty ports, located in just twelve countries and jurisdictions, control 45% of global container shipping freight. The Netherlands and Singapore have global influence in this sector far beyond the size of their national economies, due to their strategic locations. Just 5% of the world's airports host more than 90% of all international flights, with the top three for international passenger traffic being Dubai, London Heathrow, and Hong Kong.[12]

In buildings, even a small group of cities working together could help to establish a market for high-efficiency designs by taking a coordinated approach to zero-emission building standards. Brussels, New York, and Vancouver appear willing to lead in this way: all are setting regulatory trajectories for buildings that are consistent with global climate change goals.

---

[v] The 197 countries that have ratified the UN Framework Convention on Climate Change include all United Nations member states, United Nations General Assembly observers the State of Palestine and the Holy See, and UN non-member states Niue and the Cook Islands. The EU is also a party to the Convention.

In the heavy industrial sectors, low-carbon transitions are at such an early stage that any country with sufficient industrial capability, resources, and political will can make a globally significant contribution by demonstrating and testing zero-emission technologies. However, for these transitions to gain momentum and build up the potential to shift global markets, some of the big players will need to be involved. China leads the world, with India second, in both steel and cement production; the US and Germany lead in the global production of chemicals.

ORGANISING FOR SUCCESS

In each of the emitting sectors, if we focus our efforts carefully, we can grow international agreements of ever greater strength and depth, moving from experimentalist learning, through coordinated action, and eventually to contracting, as we progress through the transition. In this way we can emulate the pattern of successful cooperation in security, trade, and environment described in Chapter 18.

For this cooperation to take place, we need a crucial ingredient: institutions. Places for governments of different countries to meet, discuss, negotiate, and agree. When David Victor, Frank Geels, and I took stock of the state of climate change diplomacy in 2019, the most striking thing about it was that the institutions we needed were almost entirely absent.

There was a busy landscape of climate change cooperation, without a doubt. There were countless bilateral projects. There were business leadership groups, investor groups, 'high-ambition coalitions' of countries, and more alliances and partnerships than you could shake a stick at. Many of these were doing excellent work and making real progress.

Despite this, in many sectors it was clear that the institutions for serious cooperation did not yet exist. In some, business leadership was not matched by the engagement of governments. In others, Western Europeans and Californians had not yet been joined by the emerging economies whose growing industries and consumers were increasingly shaping the development of global markets. As each new Presidency country of the UN climate talks promoted a new set of priorities, the annual conferences resembled what one CEO called a 'festival of initiatives' more than a set of institutions for substantial and sustained cooperation.

On land use, there was no forum where the major producer and consumer countries of forest-risk commodities came together to agree actions to shift global markets towards sustainability. In agriculture, the most relevant forum was the Global Research Alliance on Agricultural Greenhouse Gases (GRA). The GRA supported collaboration on research, as its name suggests, but it did not discuss how the hundreds of billions of dollars spent each year in agricultural subsidies could be reoriented to incentivise the protection of ecosystems instead of their destruction. When the GRA was formed, such matters were decided to be out of scope because member countries considered the subject of agricultural policy to be 'too sensitive'. Discovering this made me recall my days in the sanctions team at the Foreign Office. If leading countries had decided that nuclear weapons policy was 'too sensitive' for discussion, would we ever have had the Six-Party Talks with North Korea, the Iran nuclear deal, or the Nuclear Non-Proliferation Treaty?

In transport, things were not much better. There was no forum in which the transport ministers of the three jurisdictions that wrote the rules for half the global car market sat down together and regularly discussed how they might cooperate on the transition to zero-emission vehicles. They had never yet had that conversation. In 2017, when the UK government was considering a phaseout date for sales of new petrol and diesel cars, some of the multinational car companies with factories in the UK threatened to move their manufacturing to other countries if we set too early a date. If we had been able to coordinate with other countries, we might have been able to leave the industry with nowhere to go, but there was no forum within which this discussion could be had. The UK is arguably more active in climate change diplomacy than any other country, with a global network of climate and energy attachés in our embassies that dates back over a decade. But without the right institution for cooperation, we were left to take this policy decision entirely unilaterally.

In shipping and aviation, there were well-established institutions, the International Maritime Organization and the International Civil Aviation Organization, where countries participated in collective rule-setting. However, these organisations were created for cooperation on issues of safety and security. Their almost universal membership (174 and 193 countries respectively) makes them ill-suited to the deep and focused collaboration needed to kick-start low-carbon transitions. Both have so far managed only shallow cooperation on climate change: goal-setting, measures to make fossil-fuelled ships more efficient, and a scheme to offset emissions from aviation as they continue to grow. The institutions for small groups of countries to cooperate on testing and deploying zero-emission technologies in these sectors – the critical steps needed to start transitions – had not yet been created.

In the heavy industrial sectors like steel, cement, and plastics, no effective intergovernmental groups had yet emerged to collaborate on the demonstration and testing of zero-emission technologies, or the creation of markets for their deployment. The Leadership Group for Industry Transition, formed by India and Sweden in 2019 with a cross-sectoral remit and the participation of a dozen countries, could become such a forum, but it was too early to tell.

In the power sector, which benefits from more climate change cooperation than any other part of the economy, several international organisations were active, including the International Energy Agency, the International Renewable Energy Agency, and Sustainable Energy for All. Despite this, as recently as 2013–2016, G20 countries and the multilateral development banks in which they hold influence financed $38bn in coal projects internationally, compared to only $25bn in renewables projects. Despite all the activity, there was no international forum dedicated to discussing how to turn this imbalance around, to make sure no further coal plants were built.

If we stand back and self-critically take stock, it is rather shocking that after forty years of international cooperation on climate change, begun with the World Climate Conference in Geneva in 1979, things were in this state: necessary institutions non-existent in most sectors; major economies acting unilaterally even where coordination gains would be easiest to access; policy in critical areas deemed to be 'too sensitive' for discussion; groups for focused collaboration in high-emitting sectors only beginning to emerge in embryonic form. To put it mildly, we seem to be missing a trick.

In some ways, the international community is working hard on climate change – developing consensus on global goals, pressuring each other on emissions targets, agreeing accounting processes, investing in bilateral cooperation, and campaigning, inventing, communicating, and sharing every imaginable practical solution. But in another way – when it comes to effective cooperation of a kind that could dramatically accelerate change in the global economy – we have barely begun to try.

The approach to diplomacy described in this chapter will not be easy. Real cooperation never is. But meeting our shared climate change goals any other way is likely to be far more difficult, if not impossible.

Making a low-carbon transition is like turning around an oil tanker: you have to overcome a great deal of inertia. Doing this quickly requires much effort and skill. It is a sobering thought that even in the sectors where low-carbon transitions are most advanced, so much acceleration is needed to bring progress into line with the Paris goals that some of the leading experts doubt its plausibility. Achieving low-carbon transitions in all the high-emitting sectors of the global economy as quickly as we need to is like trying to swivel a whole fleet of oil tankers all at once. At least, if the crews work together, we might just have a chance.

21

BETTER LATE THAN NEVER

At the first UN climate change talks I attended, there was a moment when the chair asked countries which of them wanted to host the next conference. No hands went up. Returning to our office, I asked our head of delegation and his right-hand man, 'What about us – could we do it?'

The UK had been one of the first countries to call for action on climate change at the United Nations. Our scientists had been central to the founding of the IPCC, and our economists had led the way in arguing that the costs of action were outweighed by the costs of inaction. We were the only rich country, at that point, to have fulfilled the promise to spend 0.7% of gross national income on international development assistance, and a significant chunk of that went on helping countries address climate change. We had what was widely recognised as the most active diplomatic service on climate change in the world, with dedicated climate and energy experts in many of our embassies. Why not us?

'Are you crazy?' they replied. 'No chance!' Hosting a UN climate change 'Conference of the Parties', or 'COP', would be expensive. It would be a logistical nightmare. As for the diplomacy, there was much more downside than upside. Any failure to reach consensus among nearly 200 countries, and the host country – the chair of the talks – was likely to be blamed, as Denmark had been for the perceived failure of the Copenhagen conference in 2009. Any success in reaching agreement was likely to be greeted with scepticism and criticism, since it would inevitably look weak compared to the scale and urgency of the climate change crisis.

Countries could volunteer to host a COP because of their interest in moving global cooperation on climate change forwards. Equally, they could do so in order to hold it back – using the position of chair to limit the risk of anything being agreed that they might find awkward. Or they could do it to prove their relevance on the international stage, a bit like hosting the Olympic Games. Previously, none of these had been compelling enough reasons for the UK to put itself forward.

231

By 2019, two things had changed. Domestically, the politics of climate change was in a more positive place. Social concern was rising, as was activism, with even children coming out onto the streets to protest as part of Greta Thunberg's Fridays for Future movement. Polling showed that women and young people, in particular, ranked climate change high on the list of issues they wanted government to address. Internationally, the UK's decision to leave the EU had raised questions about our commitment to multilateralism. It was hard to find a more suitable issue than climate change on which to reaffirm the UK's positive role in tackling global problems – an issue where our strategic interests were clear, our domestic record defensible, and our international relationships relatively good.

The hosting of COPs rotates between regions, and in 2020 it would be the turn of 'Western Europe and Others' – a region that might sound geographically vague but is well defined in the atlas of United Nations bureaucracy. Italy had already put itself forward, but, after a change of government, was no longer so sure that it wanted to play host. The UK came in as a late bidder but made a strong case. Even the European countries that were fed up with our antics on Brexit saw value in having the UK's diplomatic machinery take charge of what was generally regarded as an important moment for the climate talks – the first test of countries' commitment in the Paris Agreement to strengthen their emissions targets every five years. And so it was agreed, with some fudging to create a partnership with Italy, that we would host the twenty-sixth Conference of the Parties of the United Nations Framework Convention on Climate Change: 'COP26'.

PUTTING THEORY INTO PRACTICE

The formal responsibilities of the host country of a COP are to organise a big conference, and to chair the UNFCCC negotiations. Informally, but at least as importantly, the host country has an opportunity to influence the international debate on climate change. It has greater than usual convening power, and can use this to initiate some new international discussions, joint statements, or practical cooperation on the climate change issues that it cares about.

Soon after taking on the position as incoming Presidency country, we decided that alongside our formal responsibilities, we would run five 'campaigns'. These would bring countries together to try to make faster progress on the practical problems of adaptation and resilience, energy, nature, transport, and finance.

There were two reasons to do this. The negative reason was that we had to spread our bets. We would try our hardest to secure agreement in the formal negotiations, but there was no guarantee that we would not repeat the failure of the last two COPs to agree on the final rules for the implementation of the Paris Agreement. We would also lobby relentlessly for countries to come forward with stronger emissions targets in their nationally determined contributions, but our influence had its limits, and the targets were likely to be underwhelming. (This proved to be the case, as discussed in Chapter 19.) We needed a portfolio approach, to increase our chances of finding some form of success.

The positive reason was that we had a vision for the next stage of climate change diplomacy. Over the previous few years, we had been developing the 'Powering Past Coal Alliance', an international campaign to phase out coal power. This had shown us the benefits of bringing practical cooperation together with a clear narrative, focused political engagement, and coordinated actions among businesses, investors, and NGOs. We had also been heading the secretariat of Mission Innovation, a group of around twenty countries committed to working together on clean technology research and development. Conversation among the officials in this group was increasingly turning to the need to cooperate not just on research and development, but also on creating and growing global markets for the new technologies. Finally, a refresh of our international climate change strategy had embraced the approach described in the last chapter. Recognising global emissions as a problem of system transitions, we saw the need for focused cooperation in each emitting sector to accelerate progress. The problems of adaptation and resilience could similarly benefit from more targeted international efforts, as could the challenge of redirecting global flows of finance so that they better supported the international community's climate change goals.

I will not describe our efforts on adaptation and resilience, or finance, as the focus of my work, and so of this book, has been the problem of global emissions. As part of the UK government's 'COP26 Unit', my job was to create and run campaigns in three of the major greenhouse-gas-emitting sectors of the global economy. The next three chapters tell the story of those campaigns.

We limited ourselves to three emitting sectors because there was no point spreading our political capital too thinly. We would need to focus, to have any hope of making progress. We chose the sectors based on three criteria: the size of their contribution to global emissions; the potential to make faster progress through international cooperation; and the credibility of the UK as a convenor, taking into account our domestic policies and our international relationships. The three that emerged from the centre of this Venn diagram were the power sector ('energy'), road transport, and land use ('nature').

The intervention of the COVID pandemic, leading to the postponement of COP26 by a year, meant that what had been expected to be one year of campaigning became two. In the context of the slow evolution of climate change diplomacy over the past forty years, this was a tiny slice of time. Fully realising the potential of focusing international cooperation on system transitions is likely to take much longer. Still, without overinterpreting our experiences of this period, I hope that something useful can be learned from our attempt to start out in that direction – whether from its successes or from its failures.

To be clear, I am not suggesting that the UK was the first country to think that practical cooperation on climate change would be a good idea. At the very outset of the UN negotiations, the EU had advocated an approach based on agreeing specific policies and measures in each sector, but this had been strongly opposed by the US and failed to gain the support of most other countries, with the exception of the small island states.[1] In 2010, the US itself (under a different administration) led the establishment of the Clean Energy Ministerial, a group of the largest countries meeting entirely separately from the UN negotiations to focus on practical cooperation. For years, the top experts in China – the people pushing hardest within the Chinese system for strong action on climate change – had responded with frustration to foreigners' constant badgering about economy-wide emissions targets, asking us why we could not focus on practical action and cooperation instead.

Why had these efforts not previously taken centre stage? In the early negotiations, many countries were anxious to avoid any specific policies somehow being imposed on them.[2] For the reasons discussed in Chapter 18, a negotiation involving all countries in the world, discussing all sectors at once, was not a forum in which such an approach could be expected to succeed. Even in smaller groups of countries, it would take time to build the confidence and understanding needed to support coordinated action. Later, as the diplomacy of peer pressure and economy-wide emissions targets became ever more strongly established as the dominant approach, it acquired a self-reinforcing inertia. Some strong advocates of action on climate change, in governments and civil society, even became suspicious and wary of attempts at practical cooperation, believing they could be a distraction from the more important economy-wide targets. The cynical actions of governments such as the George W. Bush administration of the

234

US fuelled these fears, but the result was unfortunate: we failed to focus effort on an approach that could have been effective, so as not to distract attention from an approach that was largely ineffective.

As we entered into our COP26 Presidency in early 2020, some important contextual factors had changed. Consensus was beginning to grow on 'net zero' emissions by somewhere around mid-century as being a goal all countries could aim for – an emerging norm for which the IPCC and the UN negotiations process could each take some credit. Even if nearer-term emissions targets still pointed up and not down, this stronger consensus on the end goal created a larger political window for the discussion of 'how we get there'. Within the UN talks themselves, the need to move 'from negotiation to implementation' was becoming a repeated refrain. Perhaps most importantly, the dramatic progress in solar power, wind power, and electric vehicles showed that clean technologies could become cheaper and, in some ways, better than fossil-fuelled alternatives. This made the prospect of coordination gains from joint action more tangible than it had been in the past. If the logic for a focused approach to climate change diplomacy was as strong as ever, these contextual changes suggested it now had even greater chances of success. In any case, if this was the approach most likely to succeed, it was better to start late than never.

As COP26 finally arrived in November 2021, representatives from all the world's countries came together in a sprawling conference centre on the banks of the River Clyde, in Glasgow. Crowds of officials tramped the corridors eating sorry-looking sandwiches; oil-rich countries and reputation-conscious corporates showed off their latest technology in flashy exhibitions; and dogged activists marched through barricaded streets in the cold rain. Outside the conference centre, the skyline was dominated by the hulk of a giant old crane that used to lift steam engines onto ships. In a similar way, the landscape of media coverage around the event was dominated by the creaky old infrastructure of the United Nations negotiations. But less visibly, a little lower down, new foundations were being laid.

22

FROM COAL TO CLEAN POWER

Two hundred years before delegates to COP26 gathered on the banks of the River Clyde, this place had been the centre of the world's shipbuilding industry. From here, coal-powered vessels had crossed the oceans, helping to carry coal-powered trains and other machinery of the fossil-fuelled industrial revolution to all the world's continents. As much as anywhere, this could claim to be one of the birthplaces of the global economy's relationship with the dirtiest fossil fuel, from which it is only now just beginning to disentangle itself. In 2021, this same spot would host the first discussion among all countries in the world about ending the burning of coal for electricity generation – currently its number one use.

***

The power sector – electricity generation – consumes more coal and emits more greenhouse gases than any other sector of the economy. It accounts for about a quarter of all global emissions. Its importance to addressing climate change is even greater than this share suggests, because clean electricity is likely to be needed to replace the burning of fossil fuels in many other sectors, including parts of transport, industry, and heating.

Despite all the spectacular growth in solar and wind power across the world, global emissions from the power sector are still going up, not down. This is because demand for power is increasing, as a result of economic growth, faster than its supply is being decarbonised. Coal is at the heart of the problem: as the dirtiest fossil fuel, emitting the most carbon for each unit of energy, it accounts for over 70% of global power sector emissions.

To kick coal out of the power sector, there are two things we have to do. The first is to stop making the problem worse. Around forty countries are still planning to build new coal plants, which will belch out more emissions for decades to come. Even though renewable power is now cheaper, some countries are still attracted to coal power by its large scale, low cost of finance, and ability to supply a constant flow of electricity to the grid. The second task is to get rid of the coal plants we have, replacing them with some form of clean power. This is particularly difficult in places where coal is central to the local economy, often supporting large numbers of jobs, and sometimes also a high share of local government revenues.

These twin problems suggested corresponding aims for our campaign. To stop new coal plants being built, we needed to make sure that for every country considering a new coal plant, the opportunity of clean power investment was more attractive. It would also help if we could turn off the taps of international financing for new coal plants, so that the coal option became less attractive. To get rid of the existing coal plants, we would need developed countries to lead by example – they had the moral responsibility to do so, and with little if any demand growth, the greater ability. To help emerging economies move in the same direction, we would need to provide support that went beyond technical assistance for electricity market reforms, and that grappled with the real social and financial barriers to transition. Over what became the two years of our Presidency, we organised the campaign around these four tracks of action.

MAKING CLEAN POWER THE MOST ATTRACTIVE OPTION

One of my first meetings of the campaign was with Damilola Ogunbiyi, the Special Representative of the United Nations Secretary-General for Sustainable Energy for All. She was, in fact, meeting our ambassador to the UN, and I had joined as I happened to be around. Our ambassador followed the briefing notes she had been sent by officials in London, and asked Damilola how we could persuade African countries to come forward with stronger emissions targets ahead of COP26, as all countries were supposed to do. Damilola stiffened, and punted the ball back into the rich countries' court: Africa's emissions per capita were tiny, and poor people on the continent were already being hit hard by climate change; why couldn't the rest of the world do more to help? I tried out our campaign pitch: how about if we worked to ensure every country considering a new coal plant had access to assistance and investment that made clean power more attractive? Damilola's face lit up, and she leant forward in her chair. 'Yes! That's exactly what we need to do.' As we left the ambassador's office, she saw an empty meeting room and suggested we sit back down again. 'Right,' she said. 'I'm a practical person. Let's talk about how we're going to do this.'

Our work to put that vision into practice reminded me of the saying attributed to the writer Poul Anderson: 'I have yet to see any problem, however complicated, which when you looked at it in the right way, did not become still more complicated.' There was already a wealth of international assistance for the transition to clean power. In some ways, the problem was that there was too much of it. In fifteen developing countries that we worked with, we found over 600 ongoing programmes of international assistance in the power sector. Recipient governments clearly found it difficult to keep track of what was happening in the multiple overlapping initiatives. Donor governments often found it equally hard to know what they were achieving. In many cases, programmes spending tens of millions of dollars were engaging with governments only at the technical level, without any link to political dialogue about the pace of the transition to clean power.

We were certainly not the first to see the need for some coordination, but we did think there was room to build on previous efforts. Surely, the international community ought to be able to put together a more coherent offer of support, a clearer political ask to go along with it, and a more effective dialogue between countries that wanted help and those that offered it? Others seemed to agree, and so for this purpose we created the Energy Transition Council: a group of countries, multilateral development banks, and international organisations with energy expertise committed to working together to accelerate the transition to clean power.

Damilola was appointed co-chair of the Council, alongside incoming COP President Alok Sharma. Her previous experience as a recipient of development assistance was an important guide to its functioning. As head of Nigeria's rural electrification agency, she had needed concessional finance to start linking households and villages to sources of clean power. It had taken her eight years of trips to Washington, with minimal funding but plenty of form-filling, before she had been able to secure support on any substantial scale. Other developing countries' ministers told her that they too struggled with the complexity of processes to apply for support, and the associated uncertainty and delay. To try to overcome this, we created the Council's Rapid Response Facility. Countries and organisations that were members of the Council made funds and experts available so that when a developing country asked for help with something, support could be on hand within weeks, or at most a few months, instead of years. It was only a small fund, but it could also be used to help countries access support from larger funds over the longer term.

Over the course of several months, the Council held a series of in-depth discussions in developing countries. The wonderful thing to see in this process was that while all of the countries were participants in the same global transition from coal to clean power, each had its own unique way of contributing to that global transition, as well as its own particular needs for support.

Morocco had built the world's first concentrated solar power plant and was so confident in its abundant resources of sunlight that it was aiming to be one of the first countries to achieve 100% renewable power, committing to hit this target by 2030. It wanted help with smart grids, to integrate all that solar power. Bangladesh had already deployed a good deal of solar power but had limited land area, and so wanted help creating a market for offshore wind; so did Vietnam, which had rapidly growing demand for power and a long coastline. Laos had no coastline, but its mountains and rivers gave it huge hydropower resources; in the rainy season this allowed it to export electricity to its neighbouring countries, but in the dry season it had to be an importer of power. That made improving regional grid interconnection a high priority.

Nigeria had more people without access to electricity than almost any other country; it wanted help to close that gap through a massive solar homes programme, as an alternative to exploiting its significant reserves of coal. Indonesia had already built a lot of coal power plants, but was interested in repurposing them, perhaps with its unusually plentiful supply of geothermal energy. Pakistan had made a world-leading commitment to building no more new coal power plants and wanted support with energy storage to support clean forms of baseload power.

The best discussions were those where the participants gave each other – in a friendly and respectful way – a hard time. International donors pressed the question of whether those planned new coal plants really were needed. Developing countries challenged whether the support they were receiving really was effective. Experts differentiated between real and imagined problems, and local NGOs differentiated between national and corporate interests. Together, the community got closer to identifying the real obstacles, whether political, financial, or technical. We could then follow up with action, supported either by the Rapid Response Facility, or by new work within larger ongoing programmes.

The quick follow-up seemed to be useful not just for its practical benefit of providing help when it was needed, but also for building confidence in the value of the dialogue. It showed that the Council was not just a talk-shop.

When we brought all the countries and organisations back together for a joint meeting to take stock of progress, we found a notable shift in the discussion. At first, most countries had only been willing to talk about the challenge of increasing clean power, typically asking for help with mobilising private investment. Now, many of them were also talking openly about the challenge of moving away from coal. The economics were shifting: in the leading markets, it was becoming cheaper to install new solar and wind farms than to continue shovelling coal into existing power stations. Some countries wanted help with renegotiating long-term power purchase agreements so that they could procure power from renewables instead of from coal. Others responded enthusiastically when the Asian Development Bank floated the idea of a new fund to support the early retirement of coal plants. This led to the announcement at COP26 of the world's first deals to support early coal plant retirement, between the Asian Development Bank and Indonesia and the Philippines, marking a new milestone in the global transition to clean power.

A less talked about shift in economics was also taking place with interconnectors – the high-voltage cables that connect the energy systems of different countries to each other and enable the international trading of electricity. As the technology was improving, longer-distance connections were becoming economically viable. These connections could potentially help to balance electricity grids that were loaded up with variable renewable power, reducing the need for energy storage.

Many countries were interested in the opportunity, but none more than India. Prime Minister Narendra Modi had a vision he called 'One Sun, One World, One Grid': the Sun was shining somewhere on Earth at any time, so why not have solar power everywhere and connect it all up in one giant grid? A first step could be to connect the solar farms of the sun-drenched Arabian Peninsula to the energy-hungry population centres of South Asia. In a wonderful combination of grandiose vision and civil service incrementalism, my colleague Will Blyth commissioned a feasibility study, with the support of the World Bank, to see if this first step could work. The study found that yes, in principle, it could. At the same time, the African and Asian development banks had identified many opportunities for greater interconnection within their regions, but found that often these were stalled for lack of political engagement. These discussions culminated in the launch at COP26 of a new global 'Green Grids Initiative – One Sun, One World, One Grid', backed by over eighty countries, which will bring political, financial, and technical levers together with the aim of creating a more interconnected global grid.[1]

While all this work was going on to support the scaling up of clean power, we also needed to cut off the flows of international finance for new coal plants. Public finance was particularly damaging because it could link investment in new coal plants to bilateral diplomatic relationships, making it more difficult for a country to change its mind. At the start of our COP26

Presidency, only China, Japan, and South Korea still provided public international financing for new coal plants. By COP26, they had all committed to end it.

What worked seemed to be a combination of back-channel discussions between experts, and peer pressure in the run-up to international summits. Experts from the three countries gave each other some reassurance that they were travelling in the same direction: if one country jumped first, the others would not just steal its business. The summits offered countries the opportunity to show leadership, or the risk of isolation. South Korea took the leadership option, using a US-hosted summit in April 2021 to announce the end of its international financing of coal power.[2] One month later, Japan yielded to pressure and joined consensus on the issue at a meeting of G7 environment ministers.[3] That left China looking awkwardly isolated, a position it maintained for only four months before President Xi Jinping announced at the United Nations General Assembly that it 'will not build new coal-fired power projects abroad'.

Our campaign was riding the currents of the transition, giving the politics an extra push wherever we could to reinforce the gathering momentum of technological and economic change. Inspired by Pakistan's leading commitment to 'no new coal power', and a report from the International Energy Agency that made clear this should be the rule for all countries, we worked to align the messaging of as many partners as possible with this simple principle. Whether encouraged by the improving economics of clean power, the end of cheap finance for coal, or for other reasons of their own, a series of 'no new coal power' commitments started to build. After Pakistan, the Philippines; then Indonesia, then Malaysia, then Sri Lanka and Chile, and finally, another twenty or so countries at COP26. Some had caveats (Indonesia's commitment would only come into effect in 2023, and the Philippines described its commitment as a 'moratorium'), but a new global norm was visibly beginning to form.

POWERING PAST COAL

If the world was making progress in cutting back the pipeline of planned new coal plants, the bigger challenge was to get rid of the 2,000 GW of existing coal plants. For developed countries, our analysis showed that coal power needed to be phased out completely by 2030 to meet climate goals, so this was our ask.

The Powering Past Coal Alliance had been campaigning on this issue since 2017 and had managed to bring a significant number of countries, states, cities, electricity utilities, banks, and investors on board. In the run-up to COP26, we continued to grow the Alliance, with new joiners including Chile, Croatia, Peru, Singapore, Spain, HSBC, and Swiss Re. By the end of COP26, the Alliance included nearly two-thirds of OECD and EU governments, as well as developing countries in all continents, and financial institutions with over $17 trillion in assets.[4]

The big prize to aim for, though, was the G7: a handful of countries accounting for nearly half the global economy, whose actions could symbolise developed country leadership, or the lack of it. A G7 commitment to phase out coal power by 2030 was a real long-shot, but as the UK was chairing the G7 as well as the UN climate talks, it wouldn't hurt to give it a try. There were three of the G7 countries that we knew would find this difficult. Germany had committed to coal phaseout, but only by the late date of 2038. This had been agreed through a careful dialogue involving coal mining communities, unions, climate scientists, businesses, and local and national government. Germany was unlikely to bring the date forward unless it found itself isolated and under great pressure. Japan still planned to use large amounts of coal power for the foreseeable future, even though it was now nominally committed to achieving net zero emissions across the economy by 2050. It was struggling with uncertainty about the role of nuclear power, which had been central to its plans until dramatically losing public support after the Fukushima disaster of 2011. To get Japan over the line, we would need concerted pressure from the US.

In the US, coal plants had closed even more quickly under President Trump than under President Obama, despite the Trump administration's best efforts to encourage a coal resurgence. Coal power had fallen victim to a scissor movement from cheap renewables and cheap natural gas. The election of President Biden in November 2020 gave us great hope that the American government would once again be pushing in the right direction.

Biden's campaign pledge to achieve 100% clean power by 2035 logically implied a phaseout of coal power ahead of that date (unless accompanied by carbon capture and storage, which was always a caveat we applied). Unfortunately, with seats in the US Senate split 50:50 between Democrats and Republicans after the 2020 elections, Biden's administration could be blocked in its attempts to pass legislation by just one Democrat senator choosing to vote with the other side. This left US climate politics on a knife-edge. Joe Manchin, the Democrat senator from West Virginia whose family business sells coal to a power plant,[5] made it fairly clear where he stood. Not wanting to provoke opposition to their proposals for enormous investment in growing the clean economy, the US government decided it could not risk explicitly giving an end date for coal. A clear G7 commitment to phase out coal power would therefore have to wait. The closest we could get from the G7 in 2021 was a commitment to achieve 'overwhelmingly decarbonised power systems in the 2030s'. A reminder, if one was needed, of the many ways a transition can be held up. As Bill Clinton's campaign director should have said, 'It's the political economy, stupid.'

THE JUST TRANSITION TRANSACTION

Most of the large emerging economies were not yet ready to talk about coal power phaseout, but they were at least preparing to move in the direction of using less coal. China and India, as they set themselves ever higher targets for the deployment of renewable power, were interested in quietly discussing how to handle the loss of millions of coal jobs, an inevitable process that had already started. China was still letting its provinces build new coal plants at an alarming rate, which many were keen to do to keep their local construction industries busy, supporting jobs and generating tax revenues. But as China's coal plants already only run about half the time, and as the central government continues to deliberately reduce coal's share of electricity generation, this looks increasingly like a job-creation scheme building stranded assets. In October 2021, China responded to coal supply shortages by pushing through long-awaited electricity market liberalisation measures; these are expected to push up the price of coal power, making it even more expensive compared to renewables.[6]

South Africa stood out as a country that was ready to talk seriously about the coal transition, and that would challenge the international community to get serious about its support. Its circumstances were pressing. Eskom, the state-owned utility that generates about 95% of South Africa's electricity, was heavily loss-making, and its ballooning debt had led to it being described by Goldman Sachs as the 'biggest risk to South Africa's economy'.[7] Lack of investment, and the unreliability of its old coal power plants, contributed to frequent power cuts that hurt the country's industries. Some of the poorest parts of the country were highly dependent on the coal industry for jobs, but mechanisation of mining was already driving a long-term trend of job losses.

In September 2019, South Africa's President Cyril Ramaphosa threw down the gauntlet to the international community. At a climate summit hosted by the UN Secretary-General, he told the world that to reduce emissions over the coming decade, his country was developing a 'Just Transition Transaction'. It would consist of a blended finance vehicle and a just transition fund, and would include in its scope the decommissioning of old coal power plants, the addition of significant renewable energy capacity, the funding of large-scale regional development programmes, and the financial stabilisation of the electricity sector.[8] It was the boldest vision for getting out of coal that any national leader had yet put forward, and it included a clear call for international support.

The pieces of the jigsaw were all on the table, and it was possible to imagine how they could come together. Concessional finance could support the replacement of coal plants with renewable power. The cheaper renewable power could help Eskom return to profitability. The improved profitability could support a refinancing of the debt, potentially with lower interest rates. A portion of the savings, or profits, could be reinvested in regional development schemes to provide new jobs for communities moving away from coal. It made sense, but there were risks for everyone involved, both political and financial. Over two years, talks between South Africa and a small number of donor countries went through their fair share of ups and downs. At least on the UK side, what drove us on was the feeling that we wouldn't have a hope of decarbonising the global power sector unless we got to grips with the guts of the problem: the debts, the jobs, and the local politics of coal. And if the President of South Africa was bold enough to put out a plan and ask for help, then the international community had better rise to the challenge.

Finally, a deal was reached that could be announced at COP26. In the 'Just Energy Transition Partnership' with South Africa, the UK, France, Germany, the EU, and the US committed an initial $8.5bn of grants and concessional finance to support the holistic approach to the transition that Ramaphosa had proposed.[9] Ramaphosa himself described it as 'a watershed moment'. 'South Africa,' he said, 'has consistently argued that developed economies must support a just transition in developing economies. [This] represents a first-of-its-kind partnership to turn these commitments into reality, and a model for similar forms of collaboration globally.'[10] Celebration would be premature: it will take time to work out the details, and implementation of the partnership is likely to be a bumpy ride. But the deal has almost certainly expanded perceptions of what is possible. Ramaphosa was not the only one to see it as precedent-setting: we had barely got home from Glasgow before another major emerging economy was in touch with our embassy, asking how it could secure a similar agreement.

Less widely noticed, we and a few other donor countries had also supported the Climate Investment Funds, a collaborative initiative between six multilateral development banks (MDBs), to develop the first global programme dedicated to helping countries accelerate their transitions away from coal. It would aim to support economic and social development planning, reskilling of workers, and repurposing of coal infrastructure including land and power plants.[11] India, Indonesia, the Philippines, and South Africa were announced in Glasgow as the first countries to have stepped forward to take part in the programme. It was not on the same scale as South Africa's Just Transition Transaction, but it could well pave the way for more ambitious efforts in future – especially if it helps the MDBs focus their general development lending, which is vastly greater than their finance for clean energy, on new economic opportunities for the most coal-dependent communities.

DOWN BUT NOT OUT IN GLASGOW

Policy on climate change is an ongoing process. Most countries do not wait for international conferences before making their decisions. Despite that, a global event can sometimes act as a forcing mechanism, if the ground is prepared in advance. As we entered the final months of our campaign, we wanted to use COP26 to wring every last drop of political commitment out of global leaders. We couldn't know how much unspent political will for accelerating the coal to clean power transition was out there in the world; the only way to find out was to create a statement.

The art of a joint statement is to pitch it at the right level of difficulty. Too tough, and no-one will support it; too easy, and it will not move anything forwards. In our 'Global Coal to Clean Power Transition Statement', we set the dates for phasing out coal power as '*in the 2030s (or as soon as possible thereafter) for major economies and in the 2040s (or as soon as possible thereafter) globally*'.[12] This was a little less than meeting the Paris Agreement temperature goals would require, but a lot more than most countries had committed to. We heard of at least one major emerging economy where it prompted an argument between the prime minister and the energy minister, so we felt it was in the right zone. We also allowed countries to align themselves with different parts of the statement, so that those that could not bring themselves to commit to coal power phaseout could at least commit to 'no new coal'.

Two weeks ahead of COP26, we were still unsure if there would be enough signatories for the statement to be worth releasing. Then in the last week, the flow of emails confirming support accelerated. The day before 'Energy Day' at COP, Poland came on board; long the backmarker in EU climate policy due to its coal-dependent economy, Poland represented a major victory. Then, even more surprisingly, Vietnam – the country with the world's third largest pipeline of new coal plants committing to coal phaseout as well as no new coal. With our deadline for signatures long passed, and our press note already sent out, still more came in. Late at night: Indonesia; then over breakfast on Energy Day itself, South Korea. In the final count, forty-six countries supported the statement, and over twenty of these had made commitments for the first time to phase out coal power, including five of the world's top twenty coal power generating countries.

China Daily reported it as 'COP26 participants vow to "consign coal industry to history".' Chris Littlecott, a leading NGO expert and campaigner on coal, said it was 'definitely a big step forward, and would have been unthinkable a year or two ago'.[13] It certainly was more than we had expected. Some combination of the self-accelerating momentum of the transition, the political campaign, the practical assistance, and the forcing moment of COP itself seemed to have paid off.

Emboldened by this success, our negotiators decided to try something else that had previously been unthinkable, and threw a commitment to coal power phaseout into the formal negotiating text for agreement by all the world's countries. It was almost ludicrously unlikely. In all the pieces of paper produced during thirty years of UN negotiations, coal had never before even been mentioned. Just days ahead of COP26, an attempt to agree coal phase-out in the G20 had quickly been killed. Not surprisingly, the draft text did not stick. China, India, and a few others made sure of that. But for a moment, it had looked almost possible. The inclusion in the final text of a universal commitment to 'phase down' coal power, mirroring the language of China's national policy position, was still, in its own way, unprecedented.

Not everybody was impressed. There were two main criticisms of the COP26 outcomes on coal, one of which was more helpful as a guide to future action, the other less so.

The first criticism was that the commitments were not enough. The world had not agreed to coal power phaseout in the negotiated text, and the top three coal-burning countries, China, India, and the US, were all absent from the Global Coal to Clean Power Transition Statement. This was true. Those of us who had worked on the campaign might want to ask how much progress could realistically be expected to be made in two years after thirty years of inadequacy, but this would be missing the point. We have not yet solved climate change. There is still a long way to go to decarbonise the global power sector. To get the job done, we need to keep figuring out how to move faster, and how to land the bigger fish.

The second criticism was that the joint statement had 'no mechanism to hold governments to account'. This was also true, but in my view, it points us in an unhelpful direction. Never mind the question of what sort of 'mechanism' could actually work. The problem in the power sector transition so far has not been a failure to meet targets. The world had installed more than ten times as much solar power by 2020 than governments had committed to achieve by that date, fifteen years before. At the time of the Paris Agreement, governments were planning to build another 2,000 GW of coal power plants, about as much as the world already has, but since then they have changed their minds and cancelled over three-quarters of that planned new capacity.[14] The evidence suggests that when the right actions are taken, targets can be comprehensively beaten.

The challenge, then, is not so much to hold each other to account, as to help each other. To give each other more confidence, and more options. If we want the world to move faster, we need to help India realise its dream of intercontinental grid connections, help China figure out what its three million coal workers are going to do next, and help someone in the US figure out how to turf Joe Manchin out of the Senate. While we're about it, we can help the 770 million people without access to electricity benefit from clean power, which is now the cheapest power in history.

Steps forward matter, but learning to run is more important. To help each other more effectively, we need to invest in our institutions. We committed at COP26 to continue the Energy Transition Council for at least another five years, and formed a partnership between the Council and a large new philanthropic fund that aimed to help multilateral development banks act more quickly and take larger risks. Earlier in 2021, the twenty-plus countries of Mission Innovation also committed to work together for another five years, and the UK, China, and Italy agreed to jointly lead the 'innovation mission' to demonstrate cost-effective and secure power systems running on 100% renewables. Helping these and similar initiatives succeed should be at the centre of our efforts.

If in the coming five years we can cancel the rest of the new coal plant pipeline while helping countries all over the world scale up clean power instead; if we can do some more South Africa-style deals to support large emerging economies move more quickly away from coal; and if we can demonstrate the ability of energy storage, interconnectors, and flexible grids to integrate massive amounts of renewables, then it is *just possible* that by the second half of this decade, as solar and wind accelerate up the steepest part of the S-curve, we could see the global power sector on track for a Paris-aligned transition. That, without doubt, is what we have to aim for.

23

FROM OIL TO ELECTRIC VEHICLES

Road transport accounts for about a tenth of all global greenhouse gas emissions, a share that makes it one of the largest-emitting sectors. Two factors make it even more significant as a battleground for bending the curve of global emissions. It is becoming the largest global market for batteries; as these are improved and made cheaper through mass production, they may be able to help decarbonise the power sector by storing energy from the wind and the Sun. It is also the largest global market for oil. If we can shrink this market quickly, it will force the oil and gas companies to get serious about diversifying their investments and finding new opportunities in the clean economy.

These opportunities make road transport an exciting subject for a campaign. Despite that, it receives relatively little attention. NGOs prefer to encourage people to walk or cycle, or if they must, take the bus. Donors of international climate finance prefer to pour their funds into the larger-emitting sectors of power and land use; for transport they provide barely a trickle. One reason for this seems to be that many people expect the transition to zero-emission vehicles to happen by itself. I have repeatedly heard the assertion that policy is irrelevant to this problem. 'The industry is leading this transition, isn't it? Governments are struggling to keep up!'

Nothing could be further from the truth. Without government policy, no electric vehicles would be on the road. Electric vehicles are still more costly to produce than petrol or diesel cars, and at least until recently, major manufacturers have been making a loss on each one that they sell. Tesla may have achieved a market capitalisation higher than Ford or General Motors, but it was created with a loan from the US Department of Energy and only makes a profit because of subsidies from the state of California. In Europe, America, and Asia, car companies have only put electric vehicles on the roads because they were forced to by regulation.

The behaviour of the car companies can easily confuse onlookers. Are they not investing huge sums of money in the research and development of electric vehicle technology, and bringing out new electric models all the time? Yes, they are. Policy has made the transition inevitable, and so the companies are preparing for the future. None wants to be left behind the others. At the same time, however, most of them have been working hard to slow down that transition as much as possible. From their point of view, the longer they can make a profit from their existing technology, the better.

The history of car companies lobbying in Brussels for weaker regulation of the European market is legendary. In the UK, when we considered setting a clear date by which all new car sales must be zero-emission, at least two multinational manufacturers threatened to pull their factories out of the country, sack all the workers, and publicly lay the blame on government policy. (Thankfully, our ministers called their bluff.) In the US, when the state of California pushed forward with the transition despite the national government under President Trump moving backwards, General Motors, Fiat Chrysler, Toyota, and many others in the industry sided with Trump in suing to strip California of its right to set its own standards.[1]

The good news is that regulation can have a powerful effect. In Europe, ever tighter efficiency standards are now so hard to meet with conventional cars that they are forcing a shift to electric vehicles. The introduction of the EU's latest regulations on 1 January 2020 saw electric vehicles' share of car sales jump to 11% in that year, up from 3% in 2019.[2] California has a mandate that requires a fixed share of each company's sales to be zero-emission vehicles; this has helped the state achieve an electric vehicle share of car sales that is four times as high as that of the US as a whole.[3] In China, national regulations modelled on California's have been complemented by strong policies in major cities. Keen to lower their life-threatening levels of pollution, Beijing and Shanghai have made it difficult to get a new number plate for a petrol or diesel car; buying an electric vehicle can avoid years of waiting in a queue. At the start of 2019, there were more electric vehicles on the road in Shanghai than in the whole of the UK, and more in Beijing than in the whole of Germany.[4]

The even better news is that the effect of these regulations in major markets travels far beyond their own borders. Cars are a $2 trillion a year global industry, dominated by multinational companies, with high levels of international trade, and complex international supply chains. Manufacturers have to watch what is happening in the largest markets, and act accordingly. Companies in Japan have been known to stop making successful models because they could no longer comply with European regulations: if a car could not be sold to the EU, it was not worth making globally.

The future of the global industry is concentrated in the hands of a small number of regulators. Ten countries account for three-quarters of global car sales, and the rules for over half the global market are written by just three regulators: those in Brussels, Beijing, and California. (When there is a willing government in Washington DC, the proportion is even higher.) If these three, or enough of those ten, align their regulations towards 100% of new car sales being zero-emission vehicles by an early date, then they are likely to shift investment throughout the entire global industry. The economies of scale created by this rapid increase in production would quickly make electric vehicles cheaper all over the world.

This was the coordination gain that we set out to target with our campaign. When we began, the most optimistic projections said that roughly half of new car sales globally would be zero-emission vehicles by the year 2040. Analysis suggested that *all* new car sales would need to be zero-emission vehicles by that date, for the sector to make its contribution to meeting the goals of the Paris Agreement. So we needed to double the pace of the global transition. We aimed to convince as many of the major markets as possible, and other actors in the ecosystem of the global car industry, to align their targets and actions with this goal.

My first meetings on the campaign were at an electric vehicle conference in Beijing in January 2020. I spoke to regulators from China, California, and the EU, and asked each of them if they were considering setting a target for all car sales to be zero-emission by 2040 or earlier. All three said no. The main reason? Cost. Although the cost of electric vehicles was falling, it was still too high for most people, and none of the three governments thought it could bring its consumers along with a transition at that pace. I asked each of them if their governments had modelled what effect it would have on the costs if instead of committing to a fast transition alone, they did it jointly with the other two largest markets. Again, all three said no, but they agreed it was an interesting question.

I already knew the answer to another question: had the ministers responsible for writing the rules for the world's largest car markets ever sat around a table together and discussed what pace of transition was needed to meet the goals of the Paris Agreement? No, they hadn't. A few groups had been formed for countries to exchange best practice on zero-emission vehicle policy, but they met only at an official level, discussed technical rather than strategic issues, and had plenty of participants from small European countries and progressive North American states, but relatively few from major emerging economies.

To fill this gap, we created the Zero Emission Vehicles Transition Council. It might sound similar to the Energy Transition Council – deliberately so, since it was a plurilateral sector-specific group aimed at accelerating a transition – but its membership and focus were different. Reflecting the different points of leverage in the two sectors, while the Energy Transition Council concentrated primarily on practical assistance for developing countries, the top priority for the ZEV Transition Council was regulatory convergence among the major markets. Its founding members included the EU, California, India, Japan, Mexico, and around ten others, together covering about half the global car market. Germany joined a little later; the US joined after the Biden administration came into power; and China, having been cautious at first, eventually joined as an observer, taking the group's coverage to well over three-quarters of the global market.

THE PACE OF THE TRANSITION

The most important conversation for the ministers in the ZEV Transition Council to have was about the pace of the transition. We prepared for this by assembling the most persuasive evidence we could find. The UK's Committee on Climate Change (CCC), an independent body that monitors whether we are on track to meet our carbon budgets, did some helpful mathematics and modelling. The starting point was simple: to meet the goals of the Paris Agreement, major economies needed to reach net zero emissions nationally by around 2050. The typical lifetime of a car was fifteen years, so unless you want to pay people to take polluting cars off the road, you had better require all new car sales to be zero-emission by 2035.

The CCC showed that nothing much could be gained by a slower transition. Assuming a country was aiming to hit net zero by 2050, slower decarbonisation of road transport would only require faster decarbonisation in other sectors where it would be more difficult and expensive. Even without the constraint of a net zero target, the CCC showed that for the UK, a fast transition to zero-emission vehicles was cheaper than a slow transition. This was because although electric vehicles were more expensive to buy than petrol or diesel cars, they were much cheaper to run, and were already becoming cheaper in lifecycle terms (where purchase and running costs are combined). Once this tipping point was passed, the sooner a country moved fully to electric vehicles, the greater its savings would be – at least to a first approximation. For countries or regions that were net oil importers, such as China, India, Japan, the EU, and the UK, a faster shift to electric vehicles could also have great benefits for energy security and the balance of payments.

If it was true at a national level that a fast transition would be cheaper than a slow transition, then the same was even more true at the global level. Batteries are what makes an electric car cost more than a petrol or diesel car. The cost of batteries, just like the cost of solar panels or wind turbines, follows Wright's Law: it falls by a constant fraction, in this case about 20%, with each doubling of cumulative global production. A comparison by the researchers Daniel Kammen and Sergio Castellanos showed that in a fast global transition, aligned with the goals of the Paris Agreement, the stock of electric vehicles on the roads by 2030 would be about two-and-a-half times what it would be in the most pessimistic scenarios of a slow global transition.[5] That meant battery costs should be more than 20% lower by 2030 in the fast transition. By 2040, the fast transition would have seen more than two extra doublings of production, meaning battery costs could be over a third cheaper than in the slow transition.

Without doubt, for most of the ministers in the ZEV Transition Council, the competitiveness of their countries' car industries was a primary concern. They knew those that led the way in the transition were likely to come out of it with a larger share of the global car market than those that dragged their heels. What held them back more than anything was the fear that consumers would punish politicians who forced them to buy expensive cars. The coordination gain analysis showed that if we collectively committed to a fast transition, the costs would be lower for everyone. There was no reason we could not collaborate to grow the global market for zero-emission vehicles, at the same time as competing to supply it.

By the time we brought this discussion to the ZEV Transition Council, we had already been campaigning on it for over a year, sharing our analysis and making our arguments bilaterally and at conferences, often supported by the experts from the International Council on Clean Transportation (ICCT), one of the few NGOs with deep expertise on road transport decarbonisation. California had moved first, committing in September 2020 to make all new car sales zero-emission by 2035. Two months later, the UK had brought forward its own date for the phaseout of conventional car sales from 2040 to 2030, and requiring all new sales to be fully zero-emission by 2035. That meant we had one large market as an ally on the Council, alongside the smaller but more ambitious Norwegians, Dutch, and Swedes, who were already ahead of us.

The response of the Council was, not surprisingly, mixed. Countries that already had strong ZEV targets spoke up in support of the experts. Several ministers acknowledged the analysis but said it would be difficult for their industries to manage a transition at that pace. A few refused to engage with the question and waffled their way through lists of their own policies instead. None disputed the basic mathematics, and many seemed interested in the potential for cost savings. We carried on campaigning.

Attribution is always difficult in diplomacy, and we will never know if our campaign made a difference, but a few months later there came what we counted as a big win. The European Commission brought out its long-awaited proposals for bringing the EU's vehicle regulations in line with its 2050 net zero-emissions target. The headline proposal was exactly what we had been campaigning for: 100% new car sales to be zero-emission by 2035. Around the same time, Canada, another important market, came into line with the same goal.

Ahead of COP26, we prepared a joint declaration on accelerating the transition to zero-emission vehicles, to see if we could grow the emerging consensus on a Paris-aligned pace of transition a little bit further. Friendly countries, NGOs, and others all helped us lobby. In the end, the commitment to work towards all sales of new cars and vans being zero-emission globally by 2040, and by no later than 2035 in leading markets, was supported by over 35 countries, 6 major carmakers, 43 cities, states, and regions, 28 large vehicle-fleet-owning companies, and 15 financial institutions and investors.[6] Although there were many other countries whose support we would have liked to secure, it was a clearer marker than had ever been laid down before about the necessary pace of the transition. As such, it should help to shape the expectations of policymakers, investors, and manufacturers as they make their next set of decisions.

As with the coal to clean power statement, those close to the sector were pleased with the progress; those further away were more critical. The best measure of how far we had come was that countries representing 20% of the global car market were covered by commitments or proposals to make all new car sales zero-emission by 2035, up from only 5% in 2019. This was significant, but as people rightly pointed out, there was a lot still to do.

Member States of the EU still needed to agree to the Commission's proposals. The US government thought it was on track for 100% zero-emission car sales by 2035, but it was wary of its political adversaries and only willing to commit to 50% by 2030. China was far ahead of the US in its current electric vehicle share of car sales, but thought it had expanded its industry too quickly, achieving volume at the expense of quality; in its mood of retrenchment, it was only willing to go for 40% by 2030. All of these countries and others will need further encouragement in the years to come.

In another similarity to the power sector, criticism of these commitments for lacking means of 'accountability' or enforcement seemed to me somewhat wide of the mark. In 2016, the most optimistic projections were that 35% of new car sales globally would be electric vehicles by 2040.[7] Five years later, the same analysts were projecting 70% by 2040 – double their previous estimate.[8] Governments, industry, and analysts alike seem to be constantly surprised at the effect of the reinforcing feedbacks of technology development and diffusion. It must be hard to find many governments that have set targets for zero-emission vehicles and failed to meet them. If civil society is to hold governments accountable in this transition, it would be best to focus less on monitoring their progress towards targets, and more on their actions: what are they doing today to put the right policies in place?

If we want these leading markets to set themselves stronger targets and to beat them, then encouraging them to jointly take the opportunity of a huge coordination gain is one approach worth pursuing. Another, of course, is to support high-quality exchange of experience on what works.

As the experts from the ICCT showed the ministers in the ZEV Transition Council, the transition will be fastest when it is supported by a combination of regulations, incentives, infrastructure investment, and public communications. But if there is one policy that is proving more effective than any other, it is ZEV mandates: by forcing each manufacturer to meet a continually tightening target for the ZEV share of its sales, these regulations increase ZEV production in the most direct manner possible. This gives a direct boost to the feedbacks, bringing down costs, increasing demand, and incentivising further investment. The ZEV mandates also effectively force manufacturers to cross-subsidise between their models, making ZEVs cheaper at the expense of conventional cars, in order to comply. This makes it less necessary for governments to implement unpopular taxes, or for environment ministries to persuade finance ministries to give them money for public subsidies. Despite the proven effectiveness of this policy, so far it is only in use in California, China, and a couple of provinces of Canada. There is plenty of potential for its wider use to speed up progress in the global transition.

It would be wrong to move on from this discussion without a word more about the car manufacturers. Although we did not expect many to be our allies, we thought it worth doing what we could to encourage some to step out in front of the pack and state their commitment to a fast transition.

Nigel Topping, the UN High Level Action Champion for climate change, and a former employee of the motor industry himself, was an enthusiastic ally in this campaign.

Some of the car companies did show genuine leadership, most notably Volvo, which not only committed to make all of its vehicles fully electric by 2030, but also entered into agreements to procure zero-emission steel. Others showed an impressive ability to adapt quickly to changing political conditions: eight days after Biden replaced Trump in the US White House, General Motors stopped suing California and proclaimed itself a leader in lowering emissions, becoming one of the first global manufacturers to commit to 100% of the cars it made being zero-emission by 2035. At COP26, Volvo and General Motors were joined in support for our ZEV declaration by Ford, Jaguar Land Rover, and Mercedes Benz, among others. By that time, about a third of the global car market was covered by manufacturer commitments to go 100% ZEV by 2035, up from almost none of the market only a year earlier.

A few of the less committed companies decided to get their rebuttals in early. Two days ahead of 'Transport Day' at COP26, Volkswagen, Toyota, and BMW briefed the *Financial Times* on why they would not be supporting the ZEV declaration. Volkswagen let it be known that its refusal to sign was due to China's lack of commitment to phasing out coal power, and followed up after COP26 with a letter to *The Times* newspaper elaborating on the theme that there was no point switching to electric vehicles unless the power sector was decarbonised. This wilfully ignored the evidence that even in countries with the most coal-intensive power systems, switching to electric vehicles already cuts emissions because they are so much more efficient.[9] Toyota, known for its aggressive lobbying of developed countries to go more slowly in the transition, said that it could not commit because markets in Africa and Latin America might take longer to catch up. BMW blamed a lack of infrastructure, and said it believed – contrary to all the evidence so far – that the shift from combustion-engined cars would take longer than expected.[10]

I have already made it plain enough that I do not think lobbying car companies is the best point of leverage for accelerating this transition. We do not need to persuade them all. NGOs should lobby governments to put strong policies in place. Governments should regulate so that the power of the market drives companies to compete to get ahead in the transition and not to hang back. Then it will be up to the car companies to decide their own fate. Having said that, if investors in the companies less enthusiastic about the transition do not want to find themselves holding shares in stranded assets, they should start giving the CEOs of these firms a hard time.

TECHNOLOGY CHOICES

The second most important discussion for these countries to have, after the pace of the transition, was about technology choices. The largest economies of scale and fastest cost reductions will only be achieved if the same zero-emission vehicle technology is being developed in different markets around the world. And zero emissions will only be achieved if the technology in question really is zero-emission.

It may seem obvious which technology is winning the race: at the time of writing there are now over ten million electric cars on the road, compared to only a few tens of thousands of vehicles powered by hydrogen fuel cells, and none of the alternatives look plausible. However, industry lobbying can push policy in strange directions, and views on technology still differ between the governments of the largest car markets.

Analysis from the ICCT, presented to the ministers at the ZEV Transition Council, ran through the options. Only two technologies could plausibly enable cars to drive with zero emissions: battery electric, and hydrogen fuel cell electric vehicles. Either of these would be acceptable; in practice, the battery electric technology is already so far ahead in the market, and favoured by the presence of electricity infrastructure and relative lack of hydrogen infrastructure, that a 'technology-neutral' zero-emissions policy for cars is a de facto choice in favour of batteries. (Trucks may be different: hydrogen may have advantages there.) Hybrid cars, which use electric as well as petrol power, obviously cannot achieve zero emissions. Despite Toyota's best efforts to tell us that we should still be using 1990s hybrid technology in the 2040s, this is clearly not the way to go.

The worst option of all is biofuels: because their production can cause deforestation, they can sometimes lead to higher emissions than petrol. The world's supply of genuinely sustainable biofuels needs to be saved for the sectors where we have no better alternatives, such as long-distance aviation, and plastics.

A final option is synthetic fuels, produced by combining hydrogen with carbon dioxide. If the hydrogen is made from renewable-powered electrolysis, this can be a zero-emission technology. However, it is inherently inefficient: only about 16% of the solar or wind energy can be converted into powering the car's wheels this way, compared to about 72% in battery electric vehicles.[11] That means synfuels will always be a lot more expensive. A few carmakers such as Porsche like them because they can be burned in internal combustion engines, but any policy that encourages this will be unhelpful: it will only delay the necessary reallocation of the industry's capital from factories that build combustion engines to those that make electric vehicles.

Putting this evidence in front of the ministers at the Council certainly did not lead to consensus. Several countries' views on the issue bore a strong resemblance to the views of their leading manufacturers. However, sitting around the virtual table together, they could not avoid hearing each other's intentions. There is not much point encouraging your industry to make hybrid, biofuel, or synfuel cars if the regulators of your largest export markets do not plan to allow people to buy them. No government is likely to change its mind quickly, but I believe this was a useful discussion to have, and that it should be continued, both publicly and privately, until consensus is reached.

When the world first started to drive 'horseless carriages' over a century ago, the technology choice was between electric, petrol, and steam. At that time, motor racing played an important role in deciding which one would win. Although electric cars set early speed records, petrol cars did better in long-distance races, and this helped to establish their dominance.[12] Now, as the world chooses again, sport could again be influential. Formula 1 is used by some of the world's largest manufacturers as a testing ground for technologies, as its intense competition helps to drive rapid innovation. Some of the sport's recent innovations, such as the recovery and reuse of energy from braking, are already supporting the decarbonisation of road transport.

Early in our campaign I approached people in Formula 1 to see what role they thought the sport would play in the transition to zero-emission road transport. First, I learned that the sport was committed to achieving zero emissions in its logistics – nice, but not the point. Then I was told that the sport would have zero-emission cars by 2030. The technology for this had not yet been decided, except that it would not be electric. Apparently, fans of motor racing enjoy the sound of burning fossils too much for quiet electric cars to be an option.

I happen to be a fan of motor racing myself, and I think this is ridiculous. I have witnessed a thousand-horsepower hybrid car at Le Mans, using its electric power to storm past petrol cars with nothing but a menacing whine and a *whoosh*, and it is awesome. Formula 1, which I love, needs to stop being pathetic. It should set itself a mission-oriented goal: electric cars that can beat the laptime of the current petrol cars, and do a 200-mile race either on one battery charge or with 20-second pitstop recharges, within the next five years. That would help us win the race against climate change. Otherwise, what will be the sport's legacy and its future? If it invests in technologies that are only a distraction from the decarbonisation of road transport, then as well as being no help to society, it will lose its usefulness to the manufacturers. Like the manufacturers themselves, the sport can choose either to lead, or to be left behind.

MORE PROBLEMS TO SOLVE

Beyond setting the right regulatory trajectories for cars in the major markets, there are several other big problems that we will have to solve, to decarbonise road transport in line with our goals for avoiding dangerous climate change.

Developing countries will need to be supported in the transition; help with mobilising investment in charging infrastructure is likely to be an important priority. We will also need to deal with the many polluting vehicles already on the roads. Retrofitting could be a valuable option: once a mass market for the practice has been developed, it should be much cheaper to stick in a battery and motor where an engine used to be than to buy a whole new car. Regulations could require all cars to be retrofit-ready, starting from now. Batteries themselves will need to be made sustainable: we will need rules to limit their lifecycle emissions, and such rules will be more effective if they are coordinated across the major markets. Heavy goods vehicles will soon contribute more to global emissions than cars. We will need to take steps to deploy zero-emission trucks, and again, the economies of scale will be larger if we align internationally in our choice of technology.

In each of these areas, countries can do more together than they could alone: shifting investment through the global industry, bringing down costs, and putting in place a level playing field where it's needed. At COP26, the ZEV Transition Council published its 2022 action plan, with its members agreeing to work together on several of these issues.[13] The US announced it would co-chair the Council along with the UK, giving some extra confidence in the group's continuity. The Council is still an embryonic institution. It is crazy that it has taken thirty years of international talks on climate change before the ministers regulating the world's largest car markets got together to discuss the global road transport transition. We need sustained support and scrutiny from all sides, to make sure this effort succeeds.

PICKING OUR BATTLES

Climate change is such a huge and complex problem that it can be attacked from many angles. If you want to do something about it, then whether you are a government, an NGO, or a concerned citizen, you have to pick your battles. You cannot campaign on everything at once.

Throughout our road transport campaign, two campaigning choices frequently presented themselves. Both have relevance beyond the boundaries of this sector.

NGOs generally gave weak support to our campaign, because (with notable exceptions, such as the ICCT) they could not reconcile themselves to its unapologetic focus on cars. Many of them told us we should talk more about walking and cycling. In my view, the principle to apply here is that any actor should understand their points of leverage. If you are an NGO with strong influence at a local level, you may be well placed to encourage people to walk, cycle, or take the bus more often. If you are an urban planner, you may be able to redesign your city so that these options become easier for many people. If you are a government charged with holding an international conference on climate change, you need to think how best to use your convening power with countries. The potential for a few countries, through a few decisions, to transform a global market responsible for a tenth of global emissions and around a half of global oil consumption represents an incredible point of leverage. There is no equally strong mechanism by which habits of walking or cycling can be propagated internationally. We each have to understand the opportunities presented by our place in the system and do our best to exploit them.

Another choice is whether to focus on the supply of fossil fuels, or the demand for them. Since it has become clear that there are many more fossils under the ground than we can safely burn, support has grown for the call to 'keep them in the ground'. There is nothing wrong with this in principle. In practice, though, people who own ground with fossil fuels in it tend to be strongly motivated to dig up the fossil fuels and sell them. This is likely to continue to be the case as long as there is a market for fossil fuels anywhere in the world. The UK government was strongly criticised during our Presidency of COP26 first for allowing the opening of a new coal mine, and then for allowing the development of a new oil field. There is no doubt that these decisions hampered our campaigning, but the oil one at least was hardly surprising: the UK's policy on oil and gas in the North Sea is to 'maximise economic recovery' of the resources – in other words, extract as much as we can sell. Denmark was praised for saying it would not sell fossil fuels anymore, but only did so because it had more or less run out of them.

In contrast, people who use fossil fuels – all of us – tend not to care very much what kind of energy has been used, as long as we get the goods and services we want. That is why it is easier to keep coal in the ground by shifting to renewable power than by pressuring coal mines to close. Similarly, it is easier to keep oil in the ground by moving to electric vehicles than by asking oil companies or the Saudis not to sell the most valuable thing they own. All forms of campaigning have a place, but since we have so little time to solve this problem, we should surely focus our greatest effort on the strongest points of leverage.

24

FROM DEFORESTATION TO SUSTAINABLE DEVELOPMENT

The forests of the world are being lost at an alarming rate: an area the size of a football pitch every two seconds. It is all the more alarming because unlike in the energy and transport transitions, there are powerful reinforcing feedbacks that are working against us, accelerating change in the wrong direction. As the world heats up, pests and plant diseases change their ranges, increasing tree mortality. With hotter air and drier ground, forest fires become more frequent and intense. The loss of trees leads to less carbon being sucked out of the air, more left in the atmosphere, and so further warming. The more this continues, the harder it is to stop.

This makes the transition to sustainable land use a game of two halves played simultaneously: we have to change our economic systems as fast as we can, in order to prevent change in the natural systems. In the power sector transition, the Schumpeterian 'creative destruction' brought to the coal industry by the growth of renewables is a force that is hard to manage, but that is at least pushing us towards greater sustainability. In land use, climate change has unleashed similar forces in our ecosystems, and we have no wish to see where they lead.

The politics is different too. In energy and transport, low-carbon transitions can follow the pattern seen in many technological revolutions of the past: beginning in the industrial core of the world economy, and propagating outwards. The countries with the largest and most advanced economies can do most of the hard work to get these transitions started. When it comes to forests, by accident of geography and history, the largest and most carbon-rich ones – those most crucial to protect, if we are to avoid dangerous climate change – are concentrated in regions where many people are poor: the Amazon basin, southeast Asia, and central Africa. Deforestation in those regions is mainly driven by agricultural expansion, with a large part of this being for the production of internationally traded commodities.

In late 2018, the British supermarket Iceland worked with the NGO Greenpeace to make an advert highlighting its commitment to remove palm oil from all of its products. The advert showed a young orangutan that was sad because it had lost its home, as its forest was brutally destroyed to make way for palm oil production. Regulators banned the advert from television because it was too political, but it became an internet sensation. Like many parents, I found myself being told by my primary-school-aged daughter that I should no longer shop at any supermarket except Iceland. To many of us in Europe or North America, it may seem easy to identify the good guys and the bad guys in this story. To those in southeast Asia, it looks rather different. It appears that we have forgotten that we chopped down our own forests to make way for agriculture long ago; that we have no concern for the poverty of many of the farmers who produce the palm oil that goes into our food; and that we are ignorant of the fact that palm oil is much more efficient in calories per unit land area than many of the crops we grow ourselves.

Enthusiasm in rich countries for offsetting emissions has in some ways made the politics of deforestation even worse. Although forested countries would generally welcome any revenue stream that helps them protect their forests, there is something deeply distasteful about being tossed a few pennies as an excuse for carbon-intensive countries and companies avoiding the difficult decisions involved in their own decarbonisation. The international agreement on aviation in 2016, in which countries agreed that the sector could carry on growing its emissions while doing nothing more than purchasing some offsets, was a prime example of this abrogation of responsibility.[1]

For all these reasons, the task of halting and reversing the world's forest loss, essential to meeting our climate goals, is uniquely difficult. It is depressing, but not altogether surprising, that the global rate of loss of tropical forests has barely changed over the past two decades.[2] If anything, it has gone up more than down.

ELEMENTS OF A SOLUTION

The successes and the failures of past efforts to address deforestation have gradually made clearer what needs to be done. Early attempts were focused on the supply side: protecting forests through promoting sustainable land use practices, and better laws and enforcement, in the places where the forests were. This proved insufficient. The financial value of trade in the agricultural commodities whose production causes most risk to tropical forests is around 100 times the amount of finance devoted to the protection of those forests.[3] It is an unequal battle. Even the best-designed national governance systems will struggle to prevent deforestation if it continues to be rewarded so generously by global markets.

In a second phase of effort, attention turned increasingly to how action on the demand side could complement measures taken within forested countries. In 2014, under pressure from NGOs, many businesses that were large traders or consumers of agricultural commodities committed to eliminate deforestation from their supply chains by no later than 2020.[4] But when 2020 arrived, deforestation was proceeding as rapidly as ever. Despite isolated examples of progress, the systemic problem was obviously not solved. In discussions with our government, businesses explained that it was impossible for them to have a large enough impact on sustainability without government regulation to ensure that all in the industry, including consumer companies in emerging markets, played by the same rules.

An experiment in Brazil had shown what could be achieved at a national level when there was strong, government-backed action on both the supply and demand sides. The Soy Moratorium, begun in 2006, involved major soybean traders agreeing not to purchase soy grown on deforested land in the Brazilian Amazon, with compliance checked by a satellite and airborne monitoring system developed by industry, NGOs, and government partners. Over the period of its implementation, the proportion of soy expansion achieved through deforestation in the Amazon fell from nearly 30% to around 1%.[5]

A policy created by the EU had shown what could be achieved through international cooperation. The Forest Law Enforcement, Governance and Trade (FLEGT) initiative had combined a ban on the import of illegally logged timber with support for the establishment of licensing and traceability systems in producer countries, helping them meet the eligibility criteria for international trade. Along with measures taken by the US, Australia, Japan, South Korea, and later China, to prohibit illegally logged timber from entering their markets, this led to a measurable decline in illegal logging in a number of countries.[6]

FLEGT was a helpful precedent, but there were at least two significant ways in which it fell short. One was to do with participation. Its strength came from the way it was created in partnership: the EU and a timber-producing country such as Indonesia would agree on what was acceptable, so that this guided both the governance of production and the governance of trade. Measures on the supply and demand sides were then mutually reinforcing. The problem was that the EU was not the only important consumer market, and the others were not involved. Indonesia's timber exports were certified for the European market, but without similar recognition in other major markets it gained little economic advantage compared to producer countries that were less responsible. The second shortcoming was to do with scope. Not all defor-estation comes from the timber industry; a large proportion comes from the production of agricultural commodities such as soy, palm oil, beef, and cocoa.

This experience, and the logic of the problem, suggested a set of elements that must be part of the solution. Measures to address deforest-ation must cover all of the main forest-risk commodities. They must involve action on both supply and demand sides: governing trade as well as produc-tion. They would need to be agreed in partnership, and this would need to be a plurilateral partnership, involving the largest producers and consumers of the relevant commodities, in order to be effective. Implementation would need agreed systems of traceability and transparency, so that everyone could tell the difference between which commodities had met required standards and which had not. There would also need to be support to farmers, especially the smallholder farmers with few resources, to help them meet the standards expected by global markets.

CREATING FACTS ON THE GROUND

Despite the many positive efforts that had been made to address defor-estation in three decades of diplomacy on climate change, the group of countries that could collectively have a chance of solving this problem – the major producers and consumers of agricultural commodities – had never been brought together to discuss it. Putting the elements of a solution together would obviously need sustained engagement, but there was no international forum within which this was taking place.

It was for this purpose that we created the Forest, Agriculture and Commodity Trade (FACT) dialogue. Our status as incoming hosts of COP26 gave us some legitimacy to convene countries, and with advice from the Tropical Forest Alliance, an expert NGO, we carefully crafted an invitation to talks that we hoped conveyed our intention to respect all the participating countries' interests. The stated aim of the dialogue was not to 'save the rainforests' but to protect forests while promoting development and trade. The participants included the world's leading exporters of palm oil, Indonesia and Malaysia; major producers of soy and beef such as Brazil and Argentina; Ghana and Côte d'Ivoire as leading cocoa exporters; and the large consumer markets of the EU, China, Japan, Korea, and – after the replacement of Trump with Biden – the US.

Early meetings in Latin America, southeast Asia, and west and central Africa drew out the interests that countries would bring to the table.

Major exporters, naturally, were worried about the prospect of any restrictions on trade. Some were suspicious that sustainability would be used as an excuse for protectionism. Many had a considerable amount at stake. In Indonesia, the palm oil industry generates 4.5% of GDP, accounts for 15% of exports, and employs three million people. In Côte d'Ivoire, cocoa accounts for 10–15% of GDP and nearly 40% of export earnings, and provides a living for 5–6 million people, nearly a fifth of the population. For comparison, financial services, a sector that we fight hard for in international trade negotiations, accounts for around 9% of the UK's economic output and 3% of our jobs. Some of these countries had already sued the EU at the World Trade Organization when they felt it had unfairly discriminated against their agricultural commodities, and they were quite prepared to do so again.

At the same time, some of the countries that felt they were doing more than most to protect their forests called for a level playing field in global markets, to ensure that sustainable producers were not undercut by those less responsible. Equally, several of the exporters asked for consumer countries to take a coherent approach: it would be more efficient for producers to meet one set of standards than to have to satisfy different requirements in each of their international markets. Above all, openness to discussing trade came with a determination that any measures should be adopted through agreement, and not unilaterally imposed by consumer countries.

The other major strand of concern was about smallholder farmers. Millions were involved in the production of palm oil and cocoa who had the skills and equipment for only the most basic methods of farming, and who lacked access to any source of finance that could help them increase their productivity. For such people, clearing a new patch of land from the forest each time the last patch became degraded was sometimes the only viable way to keep going. If standards were set that they could not meet, these farmers would be shut out of global markets. As well as worsening poverty, this could be self-defeating if it meant that the incentives for illegal deforestation and trade remained high. Consequently, many of the countries in the group made clear that support to smallholder farmers must be a central part of the collective effort; without it, no solution would be either politically or economically feasible.

These early discussions largely confirmed the picture of the problem that the experts had drawn based on their past experiences, and brought the shape of the possible solution into sharper focus.

When we brought the whole group of nearly thirty countries together for the first time, an entirely unexpected issue nearly threw us off course. We had originally named our process the Sustainable Land Use and Commodity Trade dialogue. The name accurately described what the talks were about, but some of my colleagues decided that its acronym, 'SLUCT', sounded too inelegant. Whether they thought it sounded like slugs or sluts I am not sure, but they were unpersuaded by my arguments that boring names were good for institutions that wanted to be taken seriously, and that the acronym would be different in every language anyway. We renamed it the snappier-sounding Forest, Agriculture and Commodity Trade dialogue: 'FACT'. What all of us failed to consider was that any of the other countries might care. It turned out that for one of the important countries in the group, the unintended hint of a shift in emphasis could have implied a change in which department of government was considered responsible, and this in turn could have led to non-participation. As a result, our first 'global' meeting of the dialogue began with us receiving a telling off for our lack of consultation. It was an early sign of the level of sensitivity we were dealing with, and how careful a line we would have to tread.

As a confidence-building measure, we made it an early priority to agree within the group a set of 'principles for collaboration'. After a few rounds of discussion and redrafting, a list emerged that included principles of part-nership, collaboration and assistance, stakeholder participation, and respect for international commitments.[7] It also included two that went to the heart of the matter: 'sovereignty' – meaning that each country has a right to establish its own policies; and 'synergy' – the principle that we would 'work to align our efforts, including discussion on shared policies and standards, so that our collective impact is greater than the sum of its parts'. Finding constructive resolution to the inherent tension between these two principles would be crucial to the success of these efforts. Nobody would say the principles were world-changing, and it was easy to say they were unob-jectionable. On the other hand, they gave the group shared terms of refer-ence, and it was the first time anyone could remember that Brazil and Norway, at opposite poles in the international politics of deforestation, had put their names to the same statement on the issue.

As well as agreeing the principles, the first ministerial meeting of the dialogue confirmed the four main areas in which the countries would work together. Three were central to the original concept: trade and markets; traceability and transparency; and support to smallholder farmers. The fourth, research and innovation, underlined the importance to the forested countries that the transition to sustainable land use, just like low-carbon transitions in any other sector, must be a move towards greater prosperity. This is an obvious point, but when Western politicians or NGOs go into 'nature protection' mode, it is easily forgotten. In any country that still has its forests, the politics of sustainability cannot be solely about conservation; they must also be about aspiration.

Over the five months that followed, we worked to agree a shared 'Roadmap' that would set out actions to be taken together by countries in the group. We benefited from the advice of an expert taskforce including representatives of NGOs, businesses, Indigenous peoples' groups, and international organisations that had long experience and extensive networks in the field.

Discussions were always respectful, sometimes insightful, and often difficult. Anyone who has taken part in international talks on climate change will be familiar with the experience of listening to a meeting participant list their country's policies and achievements instead of engaging with the specific question intended for discussion. Sometimes the fault was ours, for not presenting a substantial enough proposal to serve as the focus of debate. In a few cases, there may have been an element of filibustering. Mostly, I believe the problem was that countries have not yet developed the habit or the capacity for serious international engagement on the substance of climate change. Without established international fora in which collaboration in each of the major emitting sectors is discussed, most governments have no people in the relevant policy areas for whom such engagement is their job.

Another familiar phenomenon that often held us up was what I call the 'linking game'. This is when somebody asks, 'Have you considered the link to X?', where X is some other international process or event. Usually, the question is accompanied by an earnest warning of the dangers of duplication, or of taking a 'siloed' approach. The implication, typically, is that further consideration is needed before agreeing to do something. The linking game can be played for the right reason, to genuinely ensure a coherent approach to an issue; for the wrong reason, as a disingenuous ploy to prevent progress when interests are felt to be threatened; or for the simple reason that the person cannot think of anything better to say. When a meeting includes participants with each of these motivations, it swiftly becomes a game of international agreement bingo. UN Framework Convention on Climate Change? Tick. UN Convention on Biodiversity? Tick. Sustainable Development Goals? Tick. World Trade Organization, Koronivia Dialogue, UN Food Systems Summit? Tick, tick, tick. The linking game can sap the energy and drain the time out of any meeting. Again, I believe the underlying reason for this problem constantly appearing in talks on climate change is the lack of appropriate institutions. Without recognised institutions in each emitting sector with the mandate and authority to coordinate action for system transitions, attempts to collaborate effectively will constantly have to battle against this kind of confusion.

Despite these and other difficulties that we grappled with together, the countries of the FACT dialogue eventually produced a Roadmap to launch at COP26. It included commitments to explore options for international markets' recognition of countries' national approaches to providing assurance of sustainability; to improve the availability of finance for smallholder farmers; to develop shared guidelines for governments' data-sharing on commodity supply chains; and to strengthen countries' institutional capabilities for international research partnerships.[8] Since it had not been possible to reach consensus on every point, the Roadmap took the form of a chair's statement, with the UK and Indonesia as co-chairs of the dialogue, and Colombia, Ghana, Malaysia, and Brazil as chairs of the various working groups, taking responsibility for summarising the discussion and outlining the way forward.

Many of us would have liked to have moved further and faster. It was not only climate change that was urgent; so was economic development, for many of the people in this sector. There were already examples of the right kind of work being done: business roundtables that voluntarily set high sustainability standards for palm oil and soy; a partnership between the Netherlands, Indonesia, Malaysia, and Nigeria that was successfully supporting smallholder famers; and an initiative in Ghana and Côte d'Ivoire to sustainably increase cocoa production while restoring degraded land. Compared to the pace of those ongoing initiatives, our talks often felt frustratingly slow.

This made me reflect on the reasons for slowness in government and in diplomacy. Decision-making in government is usually slower than in business or in an NGO, because it affects so many people and so must carefully balance their different interests. Diplomacy is even slower because it balances the interests of different countries, but with the exception of certain fields, there is no ultimate decision-making authority. Diplomacy has to work by building trust and exerting influence, and those are usually long games.

As we discussed in Chapter 18, there is always a trade-off in diplomacy between breadth and depth. If the aim is a strong global agreement, it is often best to start small and gradually grow outwards in participation, scope, and bindingness of commitment. This is especially likely to be true if the purpose is to accelerate an economic transition, since the further the transition proceeds, the more actors' interests become aligned with its continuance. That understanding must guide our approach to international cooperation in each of the emitting sectors of the economy. In this sector of forest-risk commodities, it means we must keep working to pitch our efforts at the point where they get traction: not expanding participation too quickly for the cooperation to be substantial, and not focusing too narrowly for the impact to be systemic.

However frustrating it may feel, we must not give up. One country acting alone will not be able to shift global commodity markets towards sustainability. Two hundred countries in a multilateral forum could talk for a decade without agreeing an agenda. Action must involve a critical mass. The FACT dialogue is the only attempt so far to bring a critical mass of countries to the table for this strategic discussion. The countries have shown each other goodwill and trust, and have mapped out the next steps they can take together. Bringing this to fruition will take considerable skill and sustained effort. I hope that governments, businesses, and NGOs will do whatever is in their power to help it succeed.

HALTING AND REVERSING

The most headline-grabbing outcome of COP26 on forests was not the FACT dialogue Roadmap, but the 'Glasgow Leaders' Declaration on Forests and Land Use'. In this joint statement, 141 countries that together contained over 90% of the world's forests committed to '*working collectively to halt and reverse forest loss and land degradation by 2030 while delivering sustainable development and promoting an inclusive rural transformation*'.[9] It had been agreed in advance through a painstaking process of consultation, beginning with the countries with the most forests and the largest land areas, before being opened out for all countries to consider.

The point of it was to establish a clear collective goal, and to set out an agenda for the work to achieve it. We felt the clarity of the 2030 goal was helpful. There is, after all, no other emitting sector in which virtually all countries in the world have agreed the necessary pace of the transition. Beneath the headline, the statement committed its signatories to working together on issues of trade, finance, the incentivisation of sustainable agriculture, and the rights of Indigenous peoples and local communities. As one friend with long experience in the NGO world told me, this could set the campaigning agenda on forests and land use for the coming decade.

Since all of the important forested countries were on board with the statement, what criticism there was focused on its credibility. Many countries had committed to a similar goal in the New York Declaration on Forests in 2014, but there did not seem to have been any measurable progress. Why should anyone believe it would be better this time? In particular, if President Jair Bolsonaro of Brazil, widely seen as reckless in his approach to the Amazon, had signed the statement, how could it be credible? Once again we were asked: how could we ensure accountability?

I share this concern, and I certainly would not say that because we have a political statement, it is all going to be fine. It is more difficult to be optimistic about forests compared to clean power or transport, because we cannot rely on reinforcing feedbacks to help us outperform our targets. We can now use satellites to monitor forest loss in great detail, and governments can be held accountable through democracy in their own countries and through peer pressure internationally, but this provides no guarantee of success.

As in the other sectors, holding each other accountable is not enough; we also have to help each other. Remember when you sit down for dinner in Europe and eat Chinese pork fed with Brazilian soy, your consumption is part of a global system that can only be changed by countries working together. If there is any reason to be more optimistic now than in 2014, it is that collective efforts towards system change are becoming more serious. The FACT dialogue is one of those efforts, and so were the commitments at COP26 of financial institutions to eliminate from their portfolios investment in activities linked to deforestation; the promise of a dozen companies that manage over half the global trade in forest-risk commodities to come up with a joint plan for sustainable supply chains; and the public and private commitments of finance to restore degraded land, improve governance systems, and advance the land tenure rights of Indigenous peoples and local communities.[10] If we want to be more confident of meeting the goal of halting and reversing forest loss by 2030, these are the efforts that we need to continue to grow.

As for Brazil, we have to remember that, like any other country, it is not one entity with one set of interests; it is a collection of actors with competing interests. There are miners engaged in illegal deforestation, and agribusinesses concerned about access to international markets. There are business lobbyists, environmental campaigners, and politicians of all persuasions at national, state, and local levels. There are civil servants, and there are voters.

In a paper published a year ahead of COP26, the academics Michaël Aklin and Matto Mildenberger argued that for decades the problem of climate change diplomacy has been fundamentally misunderstood.[11] It was assumed that each country was held back from stronger action by the concern that other countries might not do their fair share. This created a 'prisoner's dilemma' situation, where each country acted selfishly, and all were worse off as a result. The academics argued, though, that there was no evidence for this being true. In fact, evidence suggested that in any country, the strength of action on climate change is mainly determined by the outcome of domestic battles between those whose interests are in favour of low-carbon transitions, and those whose interests are against. This certainly fits with my experience in the UK, and with everything I have seen of the other countries I have dealt with over the past decade. The implication for diplomacy is that we should build international cooperation of a kind that strengthens the hand of those in favour of transitions. Rather than seeing any country as friend or foe, we should look for interests aligned with our aims, and help each other win our respective battles.

Aklin and Mildenberger titled their paper 'Prisoners of the wrong dilemma', reflecting the likelihood that if we continue to misunderstand the nature of the problem of climate change diplomacy, we will remain stuck on the wrong path. They were right. We have been prisoners for too long, and it is time to break out – or break through, into a new paradigm.

25

THE BREAKTHROUGH AGENDA

Businesses know that the policies that matter to emissions happen within specific sectors of the economy. Electricity utilities in the UK did not suddenly start replacing coal plants with solar farms when the Climate Change Act was passed, or when our first five-yearly economy-wide emissions targets were set. They did it when taxes made coal unprofitable, subsidies made renewables attractive, and regulations reformed the market so that a shift from coal to clean was inevitable.

Not everyone in the climate change community fully recognises this. At least, they often act as if they don't. For thirty years, international negotiations have focused on economy-wide emissions targets to such an extent that to those at the centre of this game, these targets can seem to be the only thing that matters. To those with this perspective, initiatives in specific sectors look like a nice-to-have optional extra. They are often assumed to be nothing more than an exercise in public relations, there to 'demonstrate progress in the real economy'. Along with this goes another common assumption: that any sector-specific initiative must be business-led, because the job of intergovernmental diplomacy is to discuss economy-wide emissions targets.

This is a set of assumptions that we have to change. None of the sector-specific challenges discussed in the last three chapters are optional. Without new economic opportunities for coal workers, power sector emissions are not going to go away. Without regulations forcing a faster shift of investment throughout the car industry, and then doing the same for trucks, ships, and planes, transport emissions will keep going up and not down. Without a shift to sustainably produced agricultural commodities, we can carry on waving goodbye to our forests. There is no magic economy where we set emissions targets and then all this happens by itself. The 'real' economy is the only one we have; governments are indispensable actors within it; and if we want to reduce global emissions, this is the dirty work that we have to do. This is not about how we demonstrate progress; it's how we *make* progress.

The question for diplomacy is how much it can help. For a long time, many of the policymakers doing the difficult work of regulatory reform in emitting sectors, not to mention the businesses active in those sectors, have felt that the process of climate change diplomacy is irrelevant to them. If we want to achieve the goals for avoiding dangerous climate change that we have agreed in these international meetings, then we cannot let this continue.

As the International Energy Agency has estimated, without international cooperation, the transition to net zero global emissions could be delayed by decades.[1] There is great potential for diplomacy to make a real difference. Coordinated action can lead to faster innovation, larger economies of scale, stronger incentives for investment, and level playing fields where they are needed. All of these can help countries reduce their emissions more quickly, more easily, at lower cost, and at greater gain. All of our emissions come from global systems of economic activity that operate across borders; if we work together, we can change these systems more quickly.

Bringing that new paradigm of climate change diplomacy into being was one of our aims for COP26. Our Presidency campaigns on power, road transport, and land use served a dual purpose: to make as much progress as possible in each of their sectors, and to demonstrate a new working model – to show what it looked like to get serious about working together within sectors. We knew, though, that this was unlikely to be enough. The campaigns could easily be seen as an ad hoc collection of activities. Two years was scant time to make progress in any of them. Countries involved in one might not be involved in others, since we were deliberately only convening the most relevant countries in each sector. Many of the discussions needed to be closed-door to build trust, and this made it difficult to build a strong media narrative around them. Somehow, on top of the individual campaigns, we needed to make the overarching case for the new approach.

The overarching narrative began with the incoming COP President Alok Sharma's speech in December 2020, where he closed a climate change summit of world leaders by setting out his 'four goals' for COP26. Three of these were goals that were already enshrined in the Paris Agreement, and that could trace their roots back to the UN Framework Convention on Climate Change of 1992: 'mitigation' (meaning emissions reduction); adaptation; and finance (support to developing countries). Nobody could question any of those. The fourth goal was 'collaboration'. 'Enhanced international collaboration,' he argued, was the only way to deliver the transition at the pace required.... By working together, we can innovate faster, we can create economies of scale, and drive stronger incentives for investment. But we will only access those gains, if we tailor our approach to every challenge, and to each sector. And our COP26 campaigns aim to do just that.... All [are] aimed to help reduce emissions while meeting other needs, like affordable energy, clean transport, and green jobs. Targeted practical collaborations like these are vital. And they should form a central theme to our efforts over the next decade.[2]

Over the following months we made this argument through all the channels we had: in bilateral meetings; at ministerial conferences; within groups where countries already worked together in a practical way, such as Mission Innovation and the Clean Energy Ministerial; and in back-channel talks with experts from the largest emitting countries. We found considerable support, especially among officials or experts with longer experience in the field. At a conference we co-hosted with the International Energy Agency in 2021, we secured agreement from twenty-three countries to the principle that stronger mechanisms for international coordination were needed within sectors, as an important means of meeting net zero targets.[3]

We also encountered indifference, from those in the community who held the view that such practical collaboration was a nice-to-have optional extra, and some scepticism. Those who were sceptical had two main criticisms. The first was that 'collaboration' sounded like 'motherhood and apple pie' – something so self-evidently good that there was no need to make an argument for it. There was some truth in this as a criticism of our communications, and it made us think about how best to describe what we were advocating. However, we did not think it was valid as a criticism of the substance. The coordination gains that could be had in each sector were very real; there were specific ways that countries needed to work together to access those gains; and at the moment, the countries were not working together in those ways.

The second criticism was that it was naïve to imagine countries such as China and the US could work together on the specifics of transitions in each sector, when they were competing with each other both industrially and geopolitically. Again, there was truth in this in the sense that countries' wariness of each other made collaboration more difficult. But it did not make it any less necessary. In fact, the opposite is true: it is precisely because of the international competition in sectors where clean technologies are more expensive than fossil fuels, such as steel, cement, shipping, and aviation, that we need international competition to establish level playing fields and incentivise investment. With the right cooperation, industrial competition acts as an accelerator of progress instead of a brake.

Those who agreed with our argument wanted to know what was next. Beyond supporting the individual campaigns, how could they support the attempt to put collaboration within sectors at the centre of climate change diplomacy for the coming decade?

Our first instinct was to try to agree between countries the main forum for collaboration in each of the emitting sectors. It could be the Energy Transition Council in the power sector; the ZEV Transition Council in road transport, and so on. But we found this was not possible. The debate was not yet mature enough, or to put it another way, most governments simply had not thought about what the criteria were for an institution to support effective international collaboration within an emitting sector. An underlying problem was that in most countries, there is nobody in government whose job it is to come up with a strategy for global emissions. There are officials working to reduce emissions domestically; there are chief negotiators concerned with the formal UN process; and there are climate envoys, who represent their country on any climate change issues it considers important. But even in most of the largest countries, there is nobody whose job it is to think strategically about how to get global emissions going down instead of up, and to engage other countries on this issue.

Within the G7 group of countries, which the UK happened to be chairing in 2021, the most we could achieve was a collective recognition that this was a problem, and an agreement to work together to begin sorting it out. The environment ministers of the G7 said in their joint communique:

> We recognise that delivering and accelerating the transition to a net zero global economy will require scaled-up international collaboration. The institutional architecture to enable this should be structured and strengthened appropriately. . . . We will convene to review the pace of the transition required in each sector to meet the Paris Agreement goals, and the international landscape of institutions and sectoral fora to decarbonise major emitting sectors, with a view to strengthening collaboration in key sectors up to COP26 and beyond.[4]

This was progress, but it was clear that we would not have agreement on the main institution to work through in each sector by the time of COP26. In any case, the G7 was not enough: important emerging economies like China and India needed to be involved in shaping this new landscape for collaboration; otherwise, they would be unlikely to feel compelled to participate.

As an alternative way to use the political moment of COP26 to advance this agenda, we decided to seek countries' agreement to a set of goals. These would not be the kind of targets that we were already lobbying countries to commit to within our individual campaigns, such as phasing out coal power by 2030 or making all new car sales zero-emission vehicles by 2035. Instead, they would be goals that could only be met through international collaboration. They would be framed, as closely as international consensus would allow, in terms of tipping points – points at which clean technologies would gain the upper hand over fossil fuels. This could serve to focus international collaboration on achieving the conditions that would lead to the greatest acceleration of progress.

Working through existing or emerging international fora in a handful of emitting sectors, we agreed goals with some of the countries that were already most interested in working together. In the power sector and road transport, we would aim to make clean power and zero-emission vehicles the most affordable option in every part of the world by the end of the decade. We would aim to make near-zero-emission steel the preferred choice in global markets, and make affordable renewable hydrogen available globally, by the same date. In agriculture, the aim would be for climate-resilient, sustainable agriculture to be the most attractive and widely adopted option for farmers everywhere by 2030.[5]

Ahead of COP26, we asked presidents and prime ministers to sign a statement committing their countries to work together in this way. So that the statement would not be an empty gesture, a country's name could only be added if it also specified at least one of the goals that it would actively work on, and if it participated in at least one of a shortlist of initiatives for international collaboration relevant to meeting that goal.

We worried it was an overly complex proposition, and countries did not have long to consider it. We found, though, that each country saw in it something they could gain. India recognised the power sector goal as being in line with Prime Minister Modi's vision of One Sun, One World, One Grid, and our new jointly led global Green Grids Initiative. China saw the alignment with the partnerships it had through Mission Innovation, and was particularly interested in collaboration on hydrogen. The US was strongly motivated by the need to work together on the decarbonisation of heavy industry, an issue on which it had pushed us to be more ambitious in our Presidency of the G7. The European Commission was preparing a package of policy proposals to cut EU emissions by 55% by 2030 and could see that collaboration with other major economies could make it easier for these policies to be agreed and implemented. Nigeria recognised how this approach could translate into stronger and more coherent support to developing countries, as it had experienced in the Energy Transition Council.

In the end, the leaders of over forty countries, together covering over 70% of global GDP, put their countries' names to the statement launching what we called the Breakthrough Agenda. It was an unapologetic endorsement of the vision of positive-sum diplomacy, implicitly ditching the decades-old paradigm of a negative-sum world in which we were condemned to argue forever over how to divide up the pie of a shrinking global carbon budget, and taking a step forward from the pure unilateralism of the Paris Agreement. Countries would *'work together in each sector ... to make the global transition to a clean economy faster, lower cost and easier for all, while making solutions to adaptation more affordable and inclusive'*. The challenge was not burden-sharing, but opportunity-sharing: to catalyse the growth of markets and jobs in the clean economy globally to meet objectives of development, health, and climate change. At the heart of it was a mission statement, similar in its ambition to President Kennedy's famous 'moonshot': the countries would work together to *'make clean technologies and sustainable solutions the most affordable, accessible and attractive option in each emitting sector globally'* before the end of this decade.[6]

After the World Leaders Summit at the start of COP26 set out this vision, events throughout the fortnight of the conference helped to give it substance. Our campaigns on power, road transport, and forests showed countries working together to get to grips with the issues, and making progress where they could, as described in the last three chapters. Days focused on finance, and on adaptation and resilience, also highlighted a growing willingness of public and private sector actors to work together internationally to bring about systemic change.

There was progress in other emitting sectors too. In the largest ever global initiative of its kind, a group of fourteen countries agreed to work together to double the energy efficiency of energy-intensive appliances including lighting, refrigerators, air conditioning, and industrial motor systems. This might not sound glamorous, but these four types of appliance together account for over 40% of global electricity consumption, so doubling their efficiency could cut a huge chunk out of global emissions at the same time as cutting people's energy bills.[7] Since these appliances are traded internationally, coordination by this group of countries may well be able to effectively set standards on a global scale, kicking the most wasteful products out of the market. If Steven Chu noticed, I hope he celebrated with a beer from his highly efficient fridge.

On agriculture, there were agreements by groups of countries not only to work together on research and development, but also to reorient their subsidies and other forms of public policy support to incentivise a shift towards sustainability.[8] At present, only around 5% of the $700bn spent annually in agricultural subsidies is targeted to encourage practices that regenerate ecosystems; much of the rest continues to incentivise their destruction.

On industry, a small group of countries agreed to coordinate on the public procurement of low-carbon steel and cement.[9] This is likely to be a critical step towards getting transitions in those sectors started. The fossil-fuelled production processes of steel and cement are still the cheapest, so companies will only make the large investments in low-emission production facilities if governments assure them that there will be a market for the low-emission but higher-cost materials. In the countries taking part in this initiative – India, Germany, Canada, the UK, and the United Arab Emirates – public procurement represents 25–40% of the domestic market for steel and cement. By coordinating their efforts, they will have more chance of jointly creating a market for low-emission materials that is large enough to incentivise the necessary industry investment.

Even on shipping, for a long time one of the more depressing sectors of climate change diplomacy, there was at last a chink of light. Shipping is one of only two sectors, the other being aviation, that has an international institution with clear authority to discuss its decarbonisation. Unfortunately, as discussed in Chapter 20, this institution – the International Maritime Organization – was created for other purposes, and its wide multilateral membership makes it poorly suited to the narrow and deep cooperation needed to get a technology transition started. Through the International Maritime Organization, countries have so far only agreed measures to make fossil-fuelled shipping more efficient. The emissions this saves are likely to be offset by the industry's growth, and it will do nothing to start the necessary transition to zero-emission technologies.

To get a transition started, a niche has to be created: a place where the new technology can be deployed for the first time. After that, the reinforcing feedbacks kick in, making the technology better, cheaper, and more widely adopted. Just like the steel industry, shipping is a competitive sector where fossil fuels will be the cheapest option for some time, so policy measures are needed to create the niche market where the first zero-emission ships can operate. Two centuries ago, a global transition from sailing ships to steamships was kicked off first by the use of steamers as tugboats in canals and harbours, and then by the British government's subsidy of ocean-going steamships for the transport of mail.[10] Now, analysis by expert NGOs suggests the most viable niches for zero-emission shipping will be subsectors with high market concentration (and where the major shipping operators are willing to cooperate with governments), along routes close to plentiful supplies of cheap renewable energy with which to make green ammonia (a new zero-emission shipping fuel), running between countries that share a commitment to climate policy and an interest in the shipping industry.

This vision was put forward by the NGOs, notably the Global Maritime Forum and the Energy Transitions Commission, and championed by industry leaders such as Maersk. At COP26, a group of twenty-two countries, including the US, the UK, Japan, Chile, Australia, and the Marshall Islands, committed to putting it into action. In their 'Clydebank Declaration', they announced an aim to establish at least six 'green shipping corridors' by the middle of this decade, and more in the following years.[11] This is exactly what we need to be doing, to start the shipping transition. Ideally, we would have started this a long time ago, but still ... better late than never.

The UK was an active instigator of several of these initiatives, but we were not the only one. The US and EU led a multi-country commitment to reduce emissions of methane, a greenhouse gas that is shorter-lived in the atmosphere than carbon dioxide, but highly potent in its warming effect. The UAE, a country that imports about 90% of its food supplies, built widespread support for a renewed push on innovation for climate-resilient and sustainable agriculture.

In many sectors, and in the Breakthrough Agenda itself, we worked in partnership with the UN High Level Action Champions on Climate Change and their team. The 'Champions', Gonzalo Muñoz of Chile and Nigel Topping of the UK, had a UN-mandated role of mobilising stronger action on climate change by connecting the work of governments with that of cities, regions, businesses, investors, and NGOs. Organising such a diverse and distributed set of actors would have been impossible, but Gonzalo and Nigel put forward an overall vision which, on emissions, encouraged all actors to set net zero targets and to work together for systems change in their sectors. Their team of NGO activists from around the world put pressure on banks to end finance for coal power, on car companies to set phaseout dates for petroleum, and on supermarkets to do their bit on deforestation. Wherever the feeling of progress being made was strongest, there was often evidence of strong alignment between the efforts of governments, businesses, and civil society.

There were still some who thought all of this was no more than an exercise in public relations. According to one NGO commentator, 'the UK government cunningly curated announcements throughout this fortnight so that it seemed rapid progress was being made'.[12] But a more widespread view was that something important was changing, in a good direction. As Naoyuki Yamagishi, energy and climate director for WWF Japan, put it, 'The meaning of COP is shifting. It is no longer just about formal decisions. We're seeing a changing phase of the Paris Agreement from rulemaking to implementation.'[13]

For me, the lasting memory of COP26 will be the comments of the activists, businesspeople, and policy officials who told me they felt the sector whose decarbonisation they had been bashing away at for years was being taken seriously for the first time. I heard it was 'the first COP to be all about energy'; 'the first COP to put nature front and centre'; 'the first COP to take transport seriously', and I lost count of how many others. Some people saw the pattern. It was a COP that took the economy seriously; one that took system change seriously.

Whether history takes this view or not is likely to depend on what we do next. As part of the statement on the Breakthrough Agenda, countries agreed to commission an annual report from independent experts that will advise them on how they can work together in each sector to make faster progress. Ministers will meet to consider its findings. The UK has committed to bringing together the different initiatives in each sector to help inform the first expert report, and to working with international partners to establish this as an ongoing annual process – with the aim of 'keep[ing] this at the top of the international political agenda throughout this decade'.[14]

That aim can only be achieved with widespread support. If we do want 'system change, not climate change', as the placards at the protests say, then we need to build a stronger common understanding than ever before of which systems to change, and how to change them. We will need governments to appoint people to engage internationally in each of the emitting sectors, breaking down the divide between domestic and international policy. We will need NGOs to challenge governments and companies not just on how they are meeting their own targets, but also on how they are interacting with others in each sector to accelerate the transition. We will need academics, philanthropists, journalists, and leaders of all kinds to point to this practical, positive-sum, plurilateral collaboration as the best hope we have for meeting our collective goals.

Inertia in the economy means that COP26 will almost certainly show up as another point on the rising line of global emissions over time. But if we can make it the point where we changed our way of working together, we might just see a bend in the curve of emissions before long after.

26

TIPPING CASCADES

In this section on diplomacy, I have argued for a new approach that would give us a greater chance of success: targeted collaboration within each of the emitting sectors, to make low-carbon transitions faster, less difficult and lower-cost for all countries. As the previous chapter described, this approach has recently gained some support, building on foundations laid by earlier efforts. However, it remains far from certain that it will secure the serious engagement of governments and support from all parts of the climate change community that it needs to succeed.

At COP26 in Glasgow, alongside the emergence of new attempts at practical collaboration, there was also a doubling down on the unilateral target-setting approach that has dominated climate diplomacy since the Paris Agreement. Countries agreed that since the 2030 emissions targets they had set in 2021 were, collectively, so far from adequate, they would consider them again in 2022. Many commentators welcomed this agreement and expressed hope that the reconsideration of targets would become an annual event, instead of happening once every five years as previously envisaged. This puts faith in peer pressure and the 'process effect' described in Chapter 19: the idea that governments will set tighter emissions targets when an international process prompts them to think about it.

The process effect may indeed be helpful, but we have to recognise that it is a reminder, not an enabler. Setting your alarm clock to go off every five minutes does not make it easier to get out of bed. Receiving an email from a charity every month asking you to increase the size of your donation does not give you more money in the bank, or fewer alternative things to spend it on. Being asked to set a new emissions target every year does not make reducing emissions any easier.

As we saw in Chapter 7, the greatest failures in risk management are sometimes failures of the imagination. If we do not consider a catastrophic event possible, we do not take action to avoid it. Similarly, failing to imagine a good possibility can mean we miss the opportunity to act in a way that could achieve it. In this last chapter on diplomacy, I want to set out a way in which I could imagine us meeting our internationally agreed goals on climate change. It is a stretch – unavoidably so, given how late we have left it to get serious. It may sound speculative, and to some extent it is. But I have not yet heard an alternative that to me sounds plausible. I describe it here because aiming for it, even if we did not realise it in full, would surely help to bring us closer.

CASCADES OF CHANGE

Chapter 16 discussed the evidence for tipping points in the economy – points at which a small input can trigger a disproportionately large response, sending a system into a qualitatively different future state. We saw that the world's fastest power sector decarbonisation, in the UK, and the world's fastest transition to zero-emission vehicles, in Norway, both owed a significant part of their success to tipping points having been crossed.

I first learned about tipping points from Tim Lenton, Director of the Global Systems Institute at Exeter University, who studies their presence in the climate system. When I went to see him in the spring of 2020, he told me he was increasingly thinking about the possibility of tipping cascades. We realised this concept could apply to the global economy as much as to the global climate. What follows is based on a paper we wrote together on this subject.[1]

Sometimes, in interconnected complex systems, the activation of one tipping point can increase the likelihood of triggering another, which in turn increases the chances of activating another. Together, this creates a 'tipping cascade'. The easiest visual metaphor for it is a line of dominoes arranged so that when the first one is tipped, all of them fall down. A tipping cascade does not have to have the same inevitability of outcome as the line of dominoes – it is enough that crossing each tipping point increases the likelihood of activating the next.

In the line of dominoes, each tipping point creates an event of the same scale as the previous one – as all the dominoes are the same size. But in more complex systems, this does not have to be the case. As a tipping cascade unfolds, changes can take place over increasing or decreasing scales. When each change takes place at a larger scale than the last, we call it an 'upward-scaling tipping cascade'.

For those who care about both etymology and gravity, this may be a disconcerting term: 'cascade' is from the Latin 'casicare', meaning 'to fall', and falling rarely occurs in an upward direction. But Tim and I could think of no better term, and in our defence, 'scale' in this context can be thought of in several dimensions: either in time (towards a greater degree of permanence), in space (expanding to affect a larger geographical area), or in terms of system boundaries (for example from a product, to an economic sector, to an economy of many sectors).

Upward-scaling tipping cascades can cause rapid change on very large scales. For example, the global financial crisis of 2008–2009 followed this pattern: home-loan defaults triggered devaluation of collateralized debt obligations, which triggered bank and insurer insolvency, which led to a credit crunch, an economic depression, and wider consequences still felt today. In ecosystems, upward-scaling cascades can be triggered by the removal or introduction of a single 'keystone species'– for example, the reintroduction of wolves to Yellowstone National Park in the US led to a cascade of changes in populations of various animals and plants, and signs of recovery at the level of the whole ecosystem.[2] Tim Lenton's research has also found that upward-scaling tipping cascades are possible in the climate system.[3]

Equally, several past 'socio-technical transitions' started with disruptive technological innovations in small niches that cascaded upwards through tipping points to society-wide change. For example, the invention and refinement of the steam engine triggered a massive expansion of coal mining and the creation of a rail transport network, propelling the industrial revolution in England. At the start of the twentieth century, the transition from horse-drawn carriages to fossil-fuelled cars happened in just over a decade in US cities. In fact, each historical transition in primary fuel supply – from wood through coal to oil and gas – was of this type.

As we discussed in Chapter 13, new technologies diffusing through markets and societies tend to benefit from many reinforcing feedbacks. These include learning by doing (the more something is made, the better it can be made), economies of scale (the more it is made, the more cheaply it can be made), and the emergence of complementary technologies (the more something is used, the more technologies emerge that make it more useful). As a result, technology diffusion is self-generating, self-accelerating, and over time becomes increasingly difficult to reverse. Any tipping point that gives a new technology a substantial new advantage – such as greater market share, easier access to finance, or broader social acceptability – is likely to strengthen these reinforcing feedbacks, further amplifying its effect.

Technology diffusion feedbacks can interact with social contagion – reinforcing social feedbacks and tipping points in the adoption of norms, behaviours, and new products. These include tipping points in social convention, in which a population-wide consensus can be overturned by a group with a minority viewpoint once it reaches a critical mass.

All of this suggests the possibility that not only tipping points, but tipping cascades, could be deliberately activated for the purpose of accelerating low-carbon transitions and reducing global emissions. From a policymaker's perspective, if a tipping point converts a small change in input to a disproportionately large change in outcome, then an upward-scaling tipping cascade could in principle offer the maximum possible 'bang for your buck'.

Tim and I outlined a possible route by which each of the two tipping points we had identified at the national level might be converted into upward-scaling tipping cascades.

A TIPPING CASCADE THAT STARTS WITH CARS

In Chapter 16, we saw that Norway had used tax and subsidy policy to make electric vehicles cheaper to buy than the equivalent petrol car, crossing a tipping point in consumer behaviour. This helped electric vehicles achieve a share of car sales in Norway ten times higher than in almost any other country, and twenty times higher than the global average.

If any governments of large countries follow Norway in activating this tipping point within their own markets, they will greatly strengthen the feedbacks of diffusion: shifting more industry investment into electric vehicle technology, leading to its faster improvement and cost reduction, and further growth in its market share. As we discussed in Chapter 23, if countries with the largest car markets were to act together, for example by coordinating regulatory trajectories towards all new sales being zero-emission vehicles, they could have an outsized effect, shifting investment decisively throughout the global market. This would bring forward a second tipping point: the point where electric vehicles are cheaper to buy than equivalent petrol cars even in the absence of policy.

This second tipping point would have more permanence than the first. When preference for electric vehicles depends on subsidy, progress can be reversed if subsidies are stopped. But when electric vehicles reach cost parity with fossil-fuelled cars without assistance from policy, the increasing returns of the new technology will dominate the behaviour of the system. Consumers will increasingly prefer to buy electric vehicles, manufacturers will prefer to make them, and investors will be more willing to invest in charging infrastructure. A return of the system to its old fossil fuel state will soon become unimaginable.

The second tipping point also leads to change on a greater geographical scale. As electric vehicles become cheaper and more attractive than fossil-fuelled cars, even governments that care nothing for climate change will have reason to support the transition in their own countries. The transition will still require investment, but for most countries this will be more than offset by the economic benefit of reducing oil imports. Tipping points in consumer behaviour, of the kind seen in Norway, could then be expected to cascade across countries, but this time without the need for taxes or subsidies.

The crossing of the second tipping point could in turn increase the chances of activating important tipping points in other sectors. First, the massive scaling up of batteries and electric drivetrain technology within the automotive sector would bring down the costs of zero-emission trucks, buses, and other larger vehicles, eventually making them cheaper than fossil-fuelled alternatives. Second, a rapid transition in road transport would deprive oil companies of their largest market, strongly incentivising the diversification of their investment, potentially into hydrogen or synthetic fuel production – critical for the decarbonisation of industry, aviation, and shipping. Third, accelerated growth of battery production and reduction in battery cost would make cheaper energy storage available for the power sector, supporting cost-effective integration of renewable power into electricity systems. This could help to tip the power sector – where emissions are still growing – into an irreversible transition. Figure 26.1 illustrates this tipping cascade.

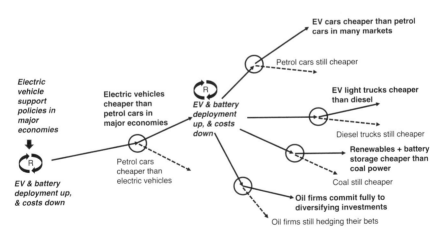

Figure 26.1 A tipping cascade that starts with cars. EV, electric vehicle. Reprinted by permission from Elsevier Science and Technology, from Sharpe, S. and Lenton, T., 2021. Upward-scaling tipping cascades to meet climate goals: plausible grounds for hope. *Climate Policy*, 21(4), pp. 421–33.

A TIPPING CASCADE THAT STARTS IN THE POWER SECTOR

In Chapter 16 we saw that the crossing of two tipping points had helped to give the UK the fastest power sector decarbonisation in the world – about eight times as fast as the global average. First, the carbon price had made coal more expensive than gas, flipping their positions in the 'merit order' by which different technologies are called on to generate electricity. This meant that coal plants would generate revenue much less of the time. Together with other factors that were reducing coal's revenues and increasing its costs, this led to the crossing of a second tipping point, where coal power moved from being profitable to unprofitable. The result was the accelerating closure of coal plants, a precipitous drop in coal use – by around 75% over five years – and a large fall in emissions.

As in the cars example, the first of these tipping points could be reversible: either a change in policy, or a rise in the price of gas compared to coal could send the market back to its earlier state. The second tipping point, though, acted at a larger scale – affecting not just the electricity market, but the economics of coal power – and in a more permanent way, since it involved the closure and destruction of coal power stations.

The strong results achieved at the national level were, I believe, critical in giving the UK government the confidence to launch an international campaign in 2017 to phase out unabated coal from the global power sector – the Powering Past Coal Alliance (PPCA), and later to make the transition from coal to clean power a priority in our COP26 Presidency.

The PPCA's growing membership, now covering nearly two-thirds of OECD and EU governments as well as thirty-three financial institutions, could reasonably claim to be influencing investor and policymaker expectations about the global future of coal power. Along with the commitments on the way to COP26 of China, Japan, and Korea to end the remaining public international financing for new coal plants, this is likely to continue pushing up the cost of capital for new coal plants globally.

Meanwhile, policy reforms, financial de-risking instruments, and concessional lending can reduce the financing costs of renewables, which in many developing countries are a significant barrier to investment. With stronger support of this kind from the international community, as the Energy Transition Council is working to mobilise, and a greater corresponding willingness from recipient countries to implement the necessary market reforms, the cost of capital of renewables could be brought below that of coal in all of the countries that are currently planning to build new coal plants (as is already the case in much of the developed world).

Such a global tipping of the relative financing costs for coal and renewables would be likely to accelerate the trend of cancellations of planned new coal plants. If current plans to build a further 450 GW of coal power capacity were to be replaced with plans for more renewables, global power sector emissions would finally begin to go down instead of up.

Meanwhile, each time a country succeeds in reforming its markets to enable faster growth of renewables, it adds to the reinforcing feedbacks of diffusion operating at the global level. With each increase in global deployment of solar and wind power, their costs fall further, and they become economically attractive in a wider range of countries and sectors. In some countries, this process is already beginning to trigger a fourth tipping point, as it becomes cheaper to invest in new renewables than to continue shovelling coal into an existing coal power station. As this point is crossed, it will be increasingly attractive to close coal plants early, even when they are still technically capable of operating for many more years.

Given that solar and wind currently contribute less than a tenth of global power generation, there is enormous potential for greater deployment of these technologies and for further reduction in their costs. Ultra-low-cost clean electricity could transform the feasibility of the decarbonisation of large parts of transport, heating and cooling, and industry. With progress in all of those sectors, we can begin to contemplate a global low-carbon transition at the economy-wide scale.

CASCADES IN ALL DIRECTIONS

In many sectors, it is possible to foresee a tipping point where a clean technology or sustainable solution becomes cheaper than the fossil-fuelled incumbents. In others, we can imagine a tipping point in investment towards clean technologies when a critical mass of countries set regulatory requirements for their use.

Although each sector is different, all are connected to each other within the global economy, meaning that there are many directions in which tipping cascades can potentially run. The contributions of different sectors to global emissions are often shown on a pie chart, but we can visualise this potential more easily if we see the causes of emissions less as a pie, and more as a flow of ingredients: from primary energy resources, through conversion into various forms of useful energy, then conversion into materials or products, and finally into services of use to people. This is how they are shown (with the exception of land use, which is not included) in Figure 26.2, a Sankey diagram.

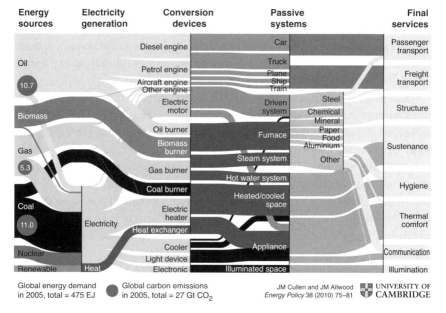

Energy sources	Electricity generation	Conversion devices	Passive systems	Final services

Global energy demand in 2005, total = 475 EJ ● Global carbon emissions in 2005, total = 27 Gt CO$_2$

JM Cullen and JM Allwood *Energy Policy* 38 (2010) 75–81 — UNIVERSITY OF CAMBRIDGE

Figure 26.2 Sankey diagram showing the flow of energy through the global economy in 2005, in exajoules (EJ, billion billion joules). The thickness of each line represents the size of the energy flow. Numbers in circles represent annual global direct carbon emissions in 2005, measured in gigatonnes (Gt, billion tonnes) of CO$_2$. Reprinted with permission from Cullen, J. and Allwood, J., 2010. The efficient use of energy: tracing the global flow of energy from fuel to service. *Energy Policy*, 38(1), pp. 75–81.

We can imagine tipping cascades running in several directions across this flow of energy, technologies, products, and services. They may be:

- **Up-and-down:** Technologies for storing, carrying, and managing energy are likely to be important to transitions in many sectors. If action in one sector scales up their production, improves them, and brings down their costs, then they become better able to accelerate transitions in other sectors. As in the example above, batteries scaled up in light road transport will be helpful in the power sector. 'Smart systems' for energy management that can be scaled up in the power sector may be useful in decarbonising buildings.
- **Right to left:** Where products or services are easier to decarbonise than the sectors that supply them, actions in 'end-use' sectors can catalyse change back through the supply chain. For example, lifecycle emission standards for buildings or cars that restrict the emissions generated in their construction could either help to create markets for decarbonised steel, cement, and plastics, or stimulate a switch towards less energy-intensive materials.

- **Left to right:** Developing new technologies for the supply of zero-emissions energy, and bringing down their costs, can support transitions in many sectors. Zero-emission power could decarbonise large parts of light transport and heating. The development of cheap zero-emission hydrogen, which could be scaled up first in fertilisers and refining, could help to decarbonise trucks, shipping, and many of the industrial sectors. Sustainable biofuels or synthetic fuels could be important to transitions in aviation and plastics.

TAKING PART IN THE TIPPING

These cascades of change are by no means inevitable. Many obstacles exist, which will need many actions to overcome. The point is not to predict whether these tipping cascades will happen; the point is to make them happen. Visualising the potential for tipping cascades in this way can help us think about where each of us can intervene with the greatest effect.

Any government that wishes to contribute to activating tipping cascades can start by identifying the sectors in which its country's interests are most strongly aligned with the transition, and where it has the greatest global influence – which could come from its technological capabilities, market power, political power, or strategic location. It can then look for other countries that share these qualities, and institutions that are active in these sectors, and work with them to build or strengthen the foundations for effective collaboration.

Diplomacy is likely to be most effective when it is targeted within sectors that have: a large share of global emissions coming from broadly one kind of product (like electricity, or cars); a high chance of interests being aligned with the transition (more the case at the right-hand end of Figure 26.2, where consumers care little about where the energy has come from, than at the left-hand end, where owners of fossil fuels have a strong interest in selling them); and a high level of international connectedness (more the case at the left-hand end, where commodities and products are traded across borders, than at the right-hand end, where decisions on, for example, urban planning are inherently local, and social norms around flying and eating are not easily exportable). Combining these criteria suggests that the best places for us to work together internationally to try to start tipping cascades in the global economy are likely to be mainly in the middle-right area of the figure – the sectors where energy is consumed in the creation or use of some kind of product.[4]

As discussed in the previous chapter, international organisations, NGOs, and philanthropists can all help to establish and maintain the institutional structures for effective international cooperation. The more effectively these structures operate, the more chance they will have of propagating cascades of change in the global economy.

Businesses can think about their contribution to generating tipping cascades in the global economy by identifying where in this system they can exercise the greatest leverage. Some will be able to change their own sectors by developing a new low-carbon technology or product that has a greater competitive edge over fossil-fuelled incumbents. Many others will have more chance of exercising leverage through their buying power, using this to help reshape other sectors. The 'RE100', 'EV100', and 'EP100' initiatives, where businesses commit to using only renewable power for their electricity supply, to buying only electric vehicles for their car fleets, and to doubling their energy productivity (through use of technologies such as heat pumps, for example), respectively, will all strengthen the reinforcing feedbacks that enable those low-carbon technologies to take growing shares of the markets in their sectors. Similarly, coalitions of firms in the freight sector can use their buying power to help create initial demand for zero-emission shipping; and companies that spend a lot on business-class air travel could do the same for aviation. (This would have a much more positive effect than buying offsets.) And although not shown on this diagram, companies that buy and sell agricultural commodities have an important part to play in protecting forests.

Cities often have different levers, and different interests, from those of national governments. In China, cities like Beijing and Shanghai have made huge contributions to the transition to zero-emission vehicles through policies that make it easier for their residents to purchase, register, and drive them, compared to petrol or diesel cars. In countries where the automotive sector has a strong hold over the national government, cities that are geographically removed from these vested interests may be freer to implement strong policy to advance the transition. Cities may also have special leverage in their ability to deploy zero-emission buses, potentially one of the most viable initial niches for hydrogen technologies which could then spread into heavy goods vehicles and industry. Of course, urban planning can also help people move to lower-emission forms of transport, including walking and cycling. Some cities have the power to set building regulations, which can grow the market for heat pumps and begin to shrink the market for gas.

Experts can contribute to this process by identifying the nature and location of tipping points, and the policies most likely to activate them.

A tipping point is an easily understandable concept, but that does not mean tipping points are always easy to find. Often the policies best able to activate tipping points will be different from those recommended by equilibrium-thinking economists. As we saw in Chapter 16, even in the power and transport sectors, the experiences of the UK and Norway are the exceptions, not the rule. Tipping points in industrial or agricultural sectors may be more difficult than these to locate and to activate.

Experts can also help by mapping out the potential routes of tipping cascades through sectors. This could be particularly important for the family of technologies around zero-emission hydrogen, including electro-lysers and fuel cells. There is already widespread awareness of the potential for hydrogen to act alongside electricity as a second carrier of energy in a zero-emission economy. But the 'hydrogen economy' will not be developed quickly unless we clearly identify the first niches for its deployment and invest in those niches in a manner that reflects their significance to a potential global cascade, not just the immediate emissions reductions that might be achieved. For the longer term, there is a similar challenge with bioenergy carbon capture and storage (BECCS). Most economy-and-climate models imply the use of this negative emissions technology (where carbon is taken *out* of the atmosphere) on an enormous scale in the latter half of this century, as this is the only way they can make the numbers add up so that a 2°C or 1.5°C global emissions pathway is still possible. But in which sectors, if any, will this be an economically viable technology, and how will it be scaled up?

NGOs and other campaigners can act at many points in this system. Many have great skill in finding their points of leverage. One way they can increase the chances of activating tipping cascades is to advocate policies well suited to bringing about transformational change, not marginal change. Some NGOs still advocate cap-and-trade schemes – creating new ones or extending existing ones to cover more sectors. As I argued in Chapter 15, this is one of the slowest and least efficient ways, both politically and economically, to advance a low-carbon transi-tion. It would be better to devote campaigning resources to encour-aging governments to make the strategic investments or regulatory changes that shift resources to zero-emission technologies and scale them up more quickly. If experts have identified where tipping points exist, NGOs should urge governments to implement the policies most likely to activate them.

Each of us, as citizens, can think about where our own professional knowledge, social connections, or democratic rights allow us to intervene with the greatest leverage.

A GLOBAL PHASE CHANGE

As change cascades through the global economy in different directions, low-carbon transitions will increasingly overlap with each other. Zero-emission technologies, business practices, and societal norms that have cross-sectoral application, acting as links in the network of transitions, will become increasingly frequent. This increasing density of interconnection will create a growing possibility of economy-wide change.

The economist Eric Beinhocker gives the following example to illustrate the potential for rapid change within networks.[5] 'Picture a thousand buttons scattered on a hardwood floor. Imagine you also have in your hand pieces of thread; you then randomly pick up two buttons, connect them with the thread, and put them back down. As you first start out, the odds are that each button you pick up will be unconnected, so you will be creating a lot of two-button connections. As you work away, however, at some point you will pick up a button that is already connected to another button and you will thus be adding a third. Eventually, as there are fewer and fewer unconnected buttons, you will get more and more little clusters of three buttons, and then some four- and five-button clusters will begin to form, like little islands scattered in a sea of buttons. Then, as you keep stringing together buttons, isolated clusters of connected buttons will suddenly begin to link up into giant superclusters – two fives will join to make a ten, a ten and a four will make fourteen, and so on.'

Beinhocker gives the example of water changing to ice at $0°C$, or to steam at $100°C$, as instances of this phenomenon of 'phase change', where a sudden change takes place in the character of a system. In this example, it is the connections between molecules that are the links in the system. As an example that may have involved a similar process of change in the economy, he cites the Internet: after being invented in the 1960s, it 'percolated along in obscurity for twenty years, used mostly by academics'. But then, with faster and cheaper modems, and better user interfaces, it became attractive to more people. The more people and businesses that used it to connect to each other, the more useful it became to everyone else. At some point in the late 1990s, perhaps when the density of these connections passed a critical threshold, use of the Internet exploded across society and the economy, quickly becoming ubiquitous.

We can speculate that a phase change towards sustainability may be possible in the global economy. We are already beginning to dismantle the structures of the fossil fuel economy. We can imagine a zero-emissions economy, centred on solar, wind, hydrogen, and regenerative agriculture. Further into the future, we may be able to imagine an economy where not only all energy, but also all materials, are created from renewable flows instead of finite stocks, and where natural stocks are not just protected, but regenerated. As we make progress in this direction, might there be a point when our islands of sustainability suddenly link together to become super-clusters? Or even a point where the superclusters join, and just as the last link of thread enables all the buttons to be picked up at once, the whole system begins to move as one towards its new, regenerative state?

In Chapter 5, we asked whether a 'point of no return' might exist in the Earth system beyond which climate change could become self-sustaining, carrying us to an ever less hospitable planet. Scientists are unsure. Most think it unlikely that a single such point exists, but they cannot rule out the possibility. At the same time, they are confident that many tipping points exist, and that the more the world warms, the more of them we are likely to cross. In the warming world, there seem to be more reinforcing than balancing feedbacks, causing change to accelerate. Perhaps for this reason, the Earth system has proved more sensitive than expected to climate change.

I believe we should think about the economy in the same way. We do not know whether there is a single point beyond which the transition towards a regenerative economy will become self-sustaining, but it is possible. We can be confident that there are many tipping points in the economy, and that the more our low-carbon transitions advance, the more of them we are likely to cross. In the early stages of these transitions, there are more reinforcing than balancing feedbacks, and these will help us on our way. This is surely why the global economy has proved more sensitive than expected to policy change – with solar capacity growing ten times faster than we expected, and wind, batteries, and electric vehicles all similarly outpacing expectations.

So we are in a race. As my colleagues and I wrote at the conclusion of the climate change risk assessment described in Part I of this book, 'The risks of climate change may be greater than is commonly realised, but so is our capacity to confront them. An honest assessment of risk is no reason for fatalism. If we counter inertia with ingenuity, match feedback with feed-back, and find and cross the thresholds of non-linear change, then the goal of preserving a safe climate for the future need not be beyond our reach.'

Winning this race will not be easy. Could well-targeted diplomacy, on top of more effective national policy, give us the additional boost that we need for a five times faster decarbonisation of the global economy? I do not know. It might – just. The fact that large and rapid changes have happened in the economy before, and the real possibility that we could make such changes happen again, do, I feel, give us plausible grounds for hope.

27

EPILOGUE

I have argued for a change in the way we approach the science, economics, and diplomacy of climate change. In each of these fields, I have shown how old ideas are holding us back, and different ways of thinking are needed to help us move forward.

I have said that without proper climate change risk assessments that make clear to heads of government the full extent of the threat, we cannot expect our leaders to have the political will to take on the difficult tasks of transition as determinedly as they must.

I have proposed that with a better understanding of how the economy really works, we can put more effective policies in place more often, yielding faster progress for whatever level of political will our leaders are able to muster. In isolated cases where a country has implemented the kinds of policies this new economic understanding recommends, decarbonisation of the relevant sector at more than five times faster than the global average pace has already been achieved.

Finally, I have made the case that if diplomacy is targeted within each emitting sector of the global economy and international agreements are grown carefully over time, we can work more effectively with countries' diverse national interests and bring about much faster global progress.

I have suggested that if we do all of these things, then meeting our overall goals – decarbonising the global economy five times faster, limiting global temperature increase to below 1.5°C, and avoiding dangerous climate change – might just conceivably be possible.

Along the way, we have seen some of the difficulties involved in moving away from the old ways of thinking. The cultural values of the science community that are so different from those needed for risk assessment. The system lock-in achieved by equilibrium economics, with its dominance of academic journals and university research funding. The inertia of the UN climate change negotiations process, whose ever-expanding complexity makes it ever more impenetrable to outsiders. Are these blockages in our intellectual plumbing just random accidents, or is there anything that links them? And how can we best unblock them quickly?

The obstacles to new thinking in the science, economics, and diplomacy of climate change, are, I believe, connected. To some extent at least, they share a common root. That root is reductionism: the approach of trying to understand something by breaking it down into its constituent parts.

Reductionism has dominated Western science since the Enlightenment, 300 years ago. Its enormous success in explaining the natural world in terms of physics, chemistry, and biology has helped it become dominant as a way of thinking. The idea of God the clockmaker spread from physics to philosophy, on to economics and beyond. We have all learned that to understand a clock, you must take it apart and study each piece.

The reductionist approach has many advantages, but it also has limitations. The behaviour of systems often cannot be deduced from the behaviour of their components. The possibility of a hurricane cannot be discovered by studying the properties of a water molecule. Neither can the workings of a democracy be known by studying the actions of an individual person. The system itself has to be studied, to understand how it works.

We can see how reductionism has limited our understanding, and our ability to act effectively, in each of the three fields we have discussed. The limitation is most severe in economics. Treating the economy as if it were exactly the sum of its individual parts has forced us to assume it is like a machine. This has prevented us from understanding all the dynamic phenomena, such as innovation, structural change, and technology transitions, that only occur at the level of the system – and that are critical to our interests.

Our reductionist view of the economics of climate change has been translated into the diplomacy. Countries have been seen as if they were entirely separate entities, each having full control over their own emissions. This has made it harder for us to see how, with the right kinds of collaboration, we could accelerate systemic change in the global economy.

Science led the way into reductionism, and is now leading us out of its constraints, by giving us a new understanding of complex systems and new ways to think holistically. Still, our appreciation of the risks of climate change is limited by the way our academic institutions encourage each researcher to focus on their own narrow area of expertise. To understand the risk that climate change poses to global food security, we need to know more than how it affects individual crops.

A side effect of taking a system apart to study it is that we forget we are a part of it. Our own actions, intentions, and ideas all influence it. And as the system evolves, it influences us in turn, changing our ideas, our interests, and our actions. In our determination to be objective, we forget that we have agency.

In science, this practice of putting ourselves outside the picture is preventing us from finding out what we need to know. Good risk assessment always starts from an understanding of our interests: knowing what it is that we wish to avoid.

In economics, we have become blind to our own powers. Governments ask consultants to predict what clean technologies will cost ten years into the future, as if this was preordained by some external force, instead of realising it is their own actions that will be the determining factor. We have forgotten that the path is made by walking.

In diplomacy, we have made ourselves 'prisoners of the wrong dilemma' by assuming that our own interests, and those of our counterparts in other countries, are fixed and immutable. We have overlooked the way that changes in our environment feed back into changes in what we want, and in what we do.

In summary, we have spent too long looking at the pieces of the clock. We have become so stuck in our reductionist ways that we have forgotten how to tell the time.

A TRANSITION OF IDEAS

Changing our ways of thinking may be difficult, but it is not impossible. We have done it before and can do it again.

Examples of the new thinking we need are already present. Recall the study in the IPCC report that took as its starting point the mass death of corals, and then showed so plainly the reality of this risk. Recall the policies in Norway that made electric cars cheaper to buy and more convenient to own than petrol cars, and so achieved an electric vehicle market share ten times higher than that of most other large economies. Recall the Energy Transition Council, in which countries have come together, recognising their interest in acting collectively to accelerate a global transition to clean power. These examples show that we are quite capable of thinking holistically, and of remembering our own agency.

The problem, as always with climate change, is one of urgency. The weakness of our response over the past few decades has left us in a desperate situation. We cannot afford to wait for our collective understanding to advance 'one funeral at a time', as the physicist Max Planck is paraphrased as complaining that it did. We need to speed the process up.

I suggested in Chapter 17 that we can think of a transition in ideas as being similar to a transition in technology. Our mental maps, after all, are as much a part of our ongoing evolution as our physical tools.

If this analogy holds, then we should apply the same principles to accelerate the transition. In the early stages, we should not waste too much effort criticising the incumbent ideas. Nobody will abandon them until they can see something more compelling to move towards. We should instead concentrate on creating the first niches where new ideas can be demonstrated and tested.

In science, we can conduct studies of individual risks where we first identify an impact of concern, and then assess how the likelihood of experiencing it will change over the course of time. The more of these examples we have, the more their value will become clear. As we compile more of these studies of individual risks, it will become easier to put together the big-picture risk assessments that are needed by heads of government.

In economics, we can identify positive tipping points, encourage governments to take the actions that will cross them, and celebrate it when they do. The more these examples become visible, the more others will be tempted to give it a try. Appreciation of tipping points will naturally open the way to a broader consideration of the dynamics of complex systems, and how they can be manipulated to our advantage.

In diplomacy, we can give our support to the most promising examples of practical collaboration focused within a sector, sustaining these examples long enough for them to bear fruit. The more the gains from cooperation become apparent, the more countries will be willing to invest in it seriously. Eventually, enough will be invested in these efforts that they become the centre of attention. Substance will no longer be left on the sidelines.

The new ideas, just like the new technologies, will benefit from reinforcing feedbacks. Successful demonstration will encourage communication, which will encourage others to put them into practice. Complementary ideas will emerge, which reinforce the original ones. We can strengthen these feedbacks by investing in any of their components: the ideas' development, their demonstration, and their communication.

If we do this well, the new ways of thinking will spread quickly, eventually becoming pervasive. With them will come new ways of acting, and a faster transition to a sustainable and regenerative economy.

At some point along the way, we may also find that our society has changed. If an economy is, as Brian Arthur said, an expression of its technologies, in the same way as an ecosystem is an expression of its inhabitants, then perhaps a society is an expression of its ideas.

I said at the beginning that we did not need a moral revolution to solve climate change. But perhaps solving climate change will, after all, bring one about.

That is for us to discover.

Acknowledgements

My deep thanks go to the many academics and experts who have generously given their time to teach me what they knew, and to answer my questions. Many have gone beyond the call of duty in doing so. I am as grateful for their public spiritedness as for the knowledge they have shared.

I am especially grateful to all the friends and colleagues who contributed to three projects whose development informed much of the content of this book. To David King, Daniel Schrag, Zhou Dadi, Qi Ye, Arunabha Ghosh, and the many others involved in our 2013–2015 climate change risk assessment project and its successors. To David Victor, Frank Geels, our friends at the Energy Transition Commission, and others who gave expert input to our 2019 report, 'Accelerating the low carbon transition'. To Jean-Francois Mercure, Michael Grubb, our friends in Oxford and Cambridge, and our partners in China, India, and Brazil, on the ongoing Economics of Energy Innovation and System Transition project. Similarly, I thank Mariana Mazzucato and the team at Institute for Innovation and Public Purpose for their partnership in our work on the UK's industrial strategy. I also thank Bryony Worthington, Eric Beinhocker, Tim Lenton, and Oliver Bettis for the inspiration they have repeatedly provided.

I have also learned much from my colleagues in government, and thank them for their comradeship, commitment, and tolerance. Especial thanks to my tireless COP26 campaigns team, and to all our partners on the campaigns. I am sincerely grateful as well to my counterparts in other countries' governments, for their openness and willingness to work together to move things forwards, whatever our political circumstances.

I am grateful to my agent, Maggie Hanbury, and my editor, Matt Lloyd, for helping to make a reality of this book. I give a special thanks to my parents, whose ideas and conversations over the course of time have influenced this work more than anyone except themselves can know. Above all, I thank my wife and my daughter for supporting me in this project even when it consumed a large amount of our precious holiday time.

Notes

1. INTRODUCTION

1. Based on global GDP data and 2030 forecast from OECD (available at: https://data
.oecd.org/gdp/gdp-long-term-forecast.htm), emissions data from Netherlands
Environmental Assessment Agency (PBL) (available at: https://www.pbl.nl/en/p
ublications/trends-in-global-co2-and-total-greenhouse-gas-emissions-2020-report),
and 1.5 degree scenario emissions data from IPCC (available at: https://www
.ipcc.ch/report/ar6/wg3/). Thanks to James Foster and Sam Karslake for this
calculation.

2. LOOKING UP AT THE DAM

1. Brulle, R., 2013.
2. Stern, N., 2013.
3. King, D., Schrag, D., Zhou, D., Qi, Y., and Ghosh, A., 2015.
4. Diamond, J., 2011. p. 436.

3. KNOWING THE LEAST ABOUT WHAT MATTERS MOST

1. Young, O. and Steffen, W., 2009.
2. IPCC, 2014a.
3. Smith, K. R., Woodward, A. D., Campbell-Lendrum, D., et al., 2014. p. 736.
4. Sherwood, S. and Huber, M., 2010.
5. Global Challenges Foundation analysis of content of IPCC Fifth Assessment Report
(AR5), Working Group II Summary for Policymakers. [online] Available at: https://
static1.squarespace.com/static/59dc930532601e9d148e3c25/t/59fb3d8df9619
a5600a70cdf/1509637522365/Briefing-on-IPCC-AR5-WGII-and-WGIII.pdf
[Accessed 23 June 2022].
6. *AVOID – Providing key advice to the UK Government on avoiding dangerous climate
change.* [online] Available at: http://ensembles-eu.metoffice.com/avoid/
[Accessed 23 June 2022].

7. European Commission. *Final Report Summary – HELIX (High-End cLimate Impacts and eXtremes)*. [online] Available at: https://cordis.europa.eu/project/id/6038 64/reporting [Accessed 23 June 2022].

8. *IMPRESSIONS: Impacts and risks from high-end scenarios: strategies for innovative solutions.* [online] Available at: http://www.impressions-project.eu/news/0_3_ 2014_8_2014 [Accessed 23 June 2022].

9. *IMPRESSIONS.* [online] Available at: http://www.impressions-project.eu/ [Accessed 23 June 2022].

10. IPCC, 2013. p. 17.

11. Lubchenco, J., 1998.

12. De Meyer, K., et al., 2018.

4. TELLING THE BOILING FROG WHAT HE NEEDS TO KNOW

1. UK Government Cabinet Office, 2017.

2. IPCC, 2014a.

3. Sharpe, S., 2019.

4. Hoegh-Guldberg, O., Cai, R., Poloczanska, E. S., et al., 2014. Figure 30.10.

5. King, D., Schrag, D., Zhou, D., Qi, Y., and Ghosh, A., 2015.

6. Andrews, O., Le Quéré, C., Kjellström, T., Lemke, B., and Haines, A., 2018.

7. Bettis, O., 2014.

8. Horton, B. P., Rahmstorf, S., Engelhardt, S. E., and Kemp, A. C., 2014.

9. Church, J. A., Clark, P. U., Cazenave, A., et al., 2013. p. 1190.

10. Environment Agency, 2012.

11. Reeder, T., Wicks, J., Lovell, L., and Tarrant, T., 2009.

12. Sutton, R., 2019.

13. De Meyer, K., et al., 2018.

5. RUNAWAY TIPPING POINTS OF NO RETURN

1. Schmidt, G., 2006.

2. Lovejoy, T. and Nobre, C., 2018.

3. IPCC, 2021.

4. Wunderling, N., Donges, J., Kurths, J., and Winkelmann, R., 2021.

5. National Snow and Ice Data Center. *Frozen ground and permafrost.* [online] Available at: https://nsidc.org/learn/parts-cryosphere/frozen-ground-permafrost/why-frozen-ground-matters [Accessed 10 September 2022].

6. Dickens, G. and Forswall, C., n.d.

7. Lowe, J. and Bernie, D., 2018.

8. Kriegler, E., Hall, J. W., Held, H., Dawson, R., and Schellnhuber, H. J., 2009.

9. Lenton, T., 2020.

10. *Eos. The emotional toll of climate change on science professionals.* [online] Available at: https://eos.org/features/the-emotional-toll-of-climate-change-on-science-professionals [Accessed 23 June 2022].
11. Steffen, W., Rockström, J., Richardson, K., et al., 2018.
12. Betts, R., 2018.
13. Sutton, R., 2019.
14. Wolff, E., Shepherd, J., Shuckburgh, E., and Watson, A., 2015.
15. Wunderling, N., Donges, J., Kurths, J., and Winkelmann, R., 2021.
16. Committee on Climate Change, 2017.
17. O'Neill, B., van Aalst, M., Zaiton Ibrahim, Z., et al., 2022.
18. Oppenheimer, M., Campos, M., Warren, R., et al., 2014. p. 1053.
19. Lenton, T., 2011.

6. THE MEANING OF CONSERVATIVE

1. King, D., Schrag, D., Zhou, D., Qi, Y., and Ghosh, A., 2015. p. 22.
2. Ibid. p. 47.
3. Ibid. p. 22.
4. IPCC, 2014b. pp. 17–18.
5. Porter, J. R., Xie, L., Challinor, A. J., et al., 2014. p. 498.
6. National Research Council, 2009.

7. MORE THAN SCIENCE

1. Climate Action Tracker, 2015.
2. Kean, T. and Hamilton, L., 2004.
3. *The 9/11 Commission Report: Final Report of the National Commission on Terrorist Attacks Upon the United States, Executive Summary.* [online] Available at: https://govinfo.library.unt.edu/911/report/911Report_Exec.pdf [Accessed 23 June 2022].
4. CNA Military Advisory Board, 2014.
5. Tero Mustonen, in King, D., Schrag, D., Zhou, D., Qi, Y., and Ghosh, A., 2015. p. 111.
6. Jose Marengo, in King, D., Schrag, D., Zhou, D., Qi, Y., and Ghosh, A., 2015. p. 111.
7. Kelley, C. P., Mohtadi, S., Cane, M. A., Seager, R., and Kushnir, Y., 2015.
8. Femia, F. and Werrell, C., 2012.
9. Otto, F. E. L., Massey, N., vanOldenborgh, G. J., Jones, R. G., and Allen, M. R., 2012.
10. Femia, F. and Werrell, C., 2013.
11. PwC, 2013.
12. Adger, W. N., Pulhin, J. M., Barnett, J., et al., 2014. p. 779.

13. *The 9/11 Commission Report: Final Report of the National Commission on Terrorist Attacks Upon the United States*, p. 344. [online] Available at: https://govinfo .library.unt.edu/911/report/911Report.pdf [Accessed 23 June 2022].

14. *A brief history of CNA*. [online] Available at: https://www.cna.org/about/history [Accessed 23 June 2022].

15. King, D., Schrag, D., Zhou, D., Qi, Y., and Ghosh, A., 2015. pp. 121–122.

16. Climate Home News. *War gaming the climate: how global warming could trigger nationalism*. [online] Available at: https://www.climatechangenews.com/2015/1 2/24/war-gaming-the-climate-how-global-warming-could-trigger-nationalism/ [Accessed 23 June 2022].

17. Ibid.

8. TELL THE TRUTH

1. Bank of England Prudential Regulation Authority, 2015.

2. Scientific Advisory Board of the United Nations Secretary-General, 2016.

3. *Record-breaking heat in Canada*. [online] Available at: https://www.rmets.org/m etmatters/record-breaking-heat-canada [Accessed 23 June 2022].

4. ScienceBrief News. *Explaining heatwaves and extreme temperatures*. [online] Available at: https://news.sciencebrief.org/explaining-heatwaves/ [Accessed 26 June 2022].

5. *The lesson from German floods: prepare for the unimaginable*. Climate Home News. [online] Available at: https://www.climatechangenews.com/2021/08/20/les son-german-floods-prepare-unimaginable/ [Accessed 23 June 2022].

6. World Weather Attribution. *Heavy rainfall which led to severe flooding in Western Europe made more likely by climate change*. [online] Available at: https://www .worldweatherattribution.org/heavy-rainfall-which-led-to-severe-flooding-in -western-europe-made-more-likely-by-climate-change/ [Accessed 23 June 2022].

7. *Climate scientists shocked by scale of floods in Germany*. [online] Available at: https:// www.theguardian.com/environment/2021/jul/16/climate-scientists-shocked- by-scale-of-floods-in-germany [Accessed 23 June 2022].

8. Church, J. A., Clark, P. U., Cazenave, A., et al., 2013. p. 1140.

9. IPCC, 2021.

10. Boers, N. and Rypdal, M., 2021. See also: Boulton, C., Lenton, T., and Boers, N., 2022

11. Chatham House, 2021.

12. *Science and innovation critical to climate change solutions*. [online] Available at: https:// www.gov.uk/government/news/science-and-innovation-critical-to-climate-chang e-solutions [Accessed 23 June 2022].

13. *The 9/11 Commission Report: Final Report of the National Commission on Terrorist Attacks Upon the United States*. p. 347. [online] Available at: https://govinfo .library.unt.edu/911/report/911Report.pdf [Accessed 23 June 2022].

9. WORSE THAN USELESS

1. Nordhaus, W., 2018.
2. IPCC, 2014b. p. 14.
3. World Bank, 2014.
4. Funtowicz, S. and Ravetz, J., 1994.
5. Weitzman, M., 2011.
6. Stern, N., 2013.
7. Pindyck, R., 2017.
8. OECD, 2012.
9. Rogelj, J., Shindell, D. K., Jiang, K., et al., 2018. p. 151.
10. *HM Treasury analysis shows leaving EU would cost British households £4,300 per year.* [online] Available at: https://www.gov.uk/government/news/hm-treasury-analysis-shows-leaving-eu-would-cost-british-households-4300-per-year [Accessed 23 June 2022].
11. OECD, 2016.
12. *Financial Times. Britain has had enough of experts, says Gove.* [online] Available at: https://www.ft.com/content/3be49734-29cb-11e6-83e4-abc22d5d108c [Accessed 23 June 2022].
13. Haldane, A. and Turrell, A., 2017.
14. Australian Financial Review. 2015.
15. Pindyck, R., 2017.
16. Funtowicz, S. and Ravetz, J., 1994.

10. THE ALLOCATION OF SCARCE RESOURCES

1. McGrath, A., 2018.
2. Beinhocker, E., 2010.
3. Earle, J., Moran, C., and Ward-Perkins, Z., 2017.
4. Lucas, R. E., 2004.
5. Beinhocker, 2010. p. 38.
6. Downey, E., 1910.
7. Beinhocker, 2010. pp. 48–49.
8. Pindyck, R., 2017.
9. Friedman, M., 1966.
10. *Prospect Magazine*, 2017.
11. Ibid., 2018
12. Huerta de Soto, J., 2014.
13. Huerta de Soto, J., 2009.
14. Arthur, W. B., 2013.
15. Beinhocker, 2010. p. 32.
16. Solow, R., 1994.
17. Romer, P., 2016.

18. IEA, 2020.
19. Arthur, W. B., 2013.
20. Black, J., 2003.
21. Stern, N., 2018.
22. Romer, P., 2016.
23. IPCC, 2018.
24. At the time of writing, the UK government's official guidance on policy appraisal, respected internationally as a prime example of its kind, defined economic efficiency in allocative terms, with explicit reference to Pareto optimality: '*Economic efficiency is achieved when nobody can be made better off without someone else being made worse off.*' https://assets.publishing.service.gov.uk/government/uploa ds/system/uploads/attachment_data/file/685903/The_Green_Book.pdf
25. Stern, N., 2018.

11. THE CONFIGURATION OF ABUNDANCE

1. Physics Central. *Chaos rules*. [online] Available at: https://www.physicscentral .com/explore/action/chaos.cfm [Accessed 24 June 2022].
2. Ibid.
3. Nelson, R. and Winter, S., 1982.
4. Beinhocker, E., 2010. p. 390.
5. Henrich, J., 2015.
6. Sharpe, B., 2013. p. 111.
7. Kauffman, S., 2003.
8. Anderson, P. W., 1972.
9. Tremaine, S., 2011.
10. Mercure, J., Sharpe, S., Vinuales, J., et al., 2021.
11. Sharpe, B., 2010.
12. Meadows, 2008. p. 51.
13. Keen, S., 2017.
14. IMF, 2010.
15. Krugman, P., 2009.

12. NOT JUST FIXING THE FOUNDATIONS

1. *Germany breaks Korea's six-year streak as most innovative nation.* [online] Available at: https://www.bloomberg.com/news/articles/2020-01-18/germany-breaks-korea- s-six-year-streak-as-most-innovative-nation [Accessed 24 June 2022].
2. Economists' Statement on Carbon Dividends Organized by the Climate Leadership *Council.* 2019. [online] Available at: https://www.econstatement.org [Accessed 24 June 2022].

3. World Bank. *Pricing carbon.* [online] Available at: https://www.worldbank.org /en/programs/pricing-carbon [Accessed 24 June 2022].
4. IMF, 2019a.
5. Funke, F. and Mattauch, L., 2018.
6. Mazzucato, M., 2018.
7. Geels, F. and Schot, J., 2007.
8. Kattel, R., Mazzucato, M., Ryan-Collins, J., and Sharpe, S., 2018.
9. Department for Business, Energy & Industrial Strategy, 2017.

13. INVESTING WITH OUR EYES OPEN

1. *The Economist*, 2014b.
2. Grubb, M., McDowall, W., and Drummond, P., 2017.
3. IRENA, 2021.
4. Wright, T., 1936.
5. Henbest, S., 2020.
6. Beinhocker, E., Farmer, D., and Hepburn, C., 2018.
7. Kavlak, G., McNerney, J., and Trancik, J., 2016.
8. Geels, F., 2014.
9. Ibid.
10. Beinhocker, E., Farmer, D., and Hepburn, C., 2018.
11. Hallegatte, S. and Rozenberg, J., 2019.
12. Arthur, W. B., 2013.
13. MacKay, D., 2015.
14. *The Economist*, 2014a.
15. Appleyard, D., 2014.
16. Jennings, T., Andrews Tipper, H., Daglish, J., Grubb, M., and Drummond, P., 2020.

14. REGULATING FOR A FREE LUNCH

1. IMF, 2019b.
2. Grubb, M., McDowall, W., and Drummond, P., 2017.
3. Ryan-Collins, J., Lloyd, T., and Macfarlane, L., 2017.
4. Watson, J., 2012.
5. International Council for Clean Transportation, 2019.
6. Ambec, S., Cohen, M. A., Elgie, S., and Lanoie, P., 2010.
7. Ibid.
8. Drollette, D., 2016.
9. *POLITICO Pro.* [online] Available at: https://subscriber.politicopro.com/art icle/eenews/1059965900 [Accessed 25 June 2022].
10. Ibid.

11. Van Buskirk, R., Kantner, C., Gerke, B., and Chu, S., 2014.
12. Black, J., 2003.
13. *Natural Selection – Understanding Evolution.* [online] Available at: https://evolu tion.berkeley.edu/evolibrary/article/evo_25 [Accessed 25 June 2022].
14. Mercure, J., Pollitt, H., Bassi, A., Viñuales, J., and Edwards, N., 2016.
15. Smith, J., 1976.
16. Beinhocker, E., 2010.

15. STUCK IN FIRST GEAR

1. Stavins, R., 2020.
2. World Bank, 2020.
3. Stavins, R., 2020.
4. World Bank, 2020.
5. Hansen, J., 2009. p. 214.
6. Chappin, E., 2011.
7. Arthur, W. B., 2013.
8. World Bank, 2020.
9. Perez, C., 2014.

16. RUNAWAY TIPPING POINTS OF NO RETURN, REVISITED

1. Sharpe, S. and Lenton, T., 2021.
2. Staffell, I., Jansen, M., Chase, A., Cotton, E., and Lewis, C., 2018.
3. *Guardian. Solar power sets new British record by beating coal for a day.* [online] Available at: https://www.theguardian.com/environment/2016/apr/13/solar-power-sets-new-british-record-by-beating-coal-for-a-day [Accessed 26 June 2022].
4. IEA, 2019.
5. *Norwegian EV policy.* [online] Available at: https://elbil.no/english/norwegian-ev-policy/ [Accessed 26 June 2022].
6. Systemiq, 2020.
7. Farmer, J. D., Hepburn, C., Ives, M. C., et al., 2019.
8. The carbon intensity of the UK power sector decreased by 8.9% per year between 2010 and 2019 (Drax: Electric Insights Quarterly, July–September 2020. Available at: https://www.drax.com/wp-content/uploads/2020/11/201126_Drax_20Q3_005.pdf [Accessed 23 June 2022]), while the global average power sector carbon intensity fell by 1.1% per year over the same period (International Energy Agency: Tracking Power 2021. Available at: https://www.iea.org/reports/track ing-power–2021 [Accessed 23 June 2022]).

17. REVOLUTIONARY

1. Institute and Faculty of Actuaries. *Economic modelling.* [online] Available at: https://www.actuaries.org.uk/learn-and-develop/research-and-knowledge/actuarial-research-centre-arc/recent-research/economic-modelling [Accessed 27 June 2022].
2. Raworth, K., 2018.
3. Earle, J., Moran, C., and Ward-Perkins, Z., 2017. p. 51.
4. Rethinking Economics. *About us.* [online] Available at: https://www.rethinkeconomics.org/about/ [Accessed 27 June 2022].
5. New Weather Institute, 2017.
6. *Guardian* | Letters. *Delving deeper into an economics reformation.* [online] Available at: https://www.theguardian.com/business/2017/dec/19/delving-deeper-into-an-economics-reformation [Accessed 27 June 2022].
7. Kuhn, T., 1970.
8. Mirowski, P. and Plehwe, D., 2009.
9. Institute for New Economic Thinking. *Our purpose.* [online] Available at: https://www.ineteconomics.org/about/our-purpose [Accessed 27 June 2022].
10. *Hewlett Foundation announces new, five-year $50 million Economy and Society Initiative to support growing movement to replace neoliberalism.* [online] Available at: https://hewlett.org/newsroom/hewlett-foundation-announces-new-five-year-50-million-economy-and-society-initiative-to-support-growing-movement-to-replace-neoliberalism/ [Accessed 27 June 2022].
11. BBC Radio 4. *Think with Pinker,* 25 November 2021.
12. HM Treasury, 2020.
13. Grubb, M., Drummond, P., Mercure, J. F., et al., 2021.

18. A FORESEEABLE FAILURE

1. UNFCCC. *The Doha Climate Gateway.* [online] Available at: https://unfccc.int/process/conferences/the-big-picture/milestones/the-doha-climate-gateway [Accessed 27 June 2022].
2. *Transcript of UNFCCC debate 11 December 1997.* [online] Available at: http://www.gci.org.uk/COP3_Transcript.pdf [Accessed 27 June 2022].
3. Depledge, J., 2022.
4. George W. Bush Whitehouse archives, *Text of a Letter from The President.* [online] Available at: https://georgewbush-whitehouse.archives.gov/news/releases/2001/03/20010314.html [Accessed 27 June 2022].
5. *Greenhouse gas emissions.* [online] Available at: https://www.canada.ca/en/environment-climate-change/services/environmental-indicators/greenhouse-gas-emissions.html [Accessed 27 June 2022].
6. *Canada first nation to withdraw from Kyoto Protocol.* [online] Available at: https://www.thestar.com/news/canada/2011/12/12/canada_first_nation_to_withdraw_from_kyoto_protocol.html [Accessed 27 June 2022].

7. Barrett, S., 2008.

8. Sweet, W., 2016. p. 152.

9. Ibid. p. 149.

10. UNFCCC. *Copenhagen Accord.* [online] Available at: https://unfccc.int/resourc e/docs/2009/cop15/eng/l07.pdf [Accessed 27 June 2022].

11. *Global carbon budget 2013.* [online] Available at: https://www.globalcarbonproject .org/carbonbudget/archive/2013/GCP_budget_2013.pd [Accessed 27 June 2022].

12. Aichele, R. and Felbermayr, G., 2013.

13. Sweet, W., 2016. p. 161.

14. Hoggan, J. and Littlemore, R., 2010.

15. Victor, D., Geels, F., and Sharpe, S., 2019.

16. Sabel, C. F. and Victor, D. G., 2022.

17. Victor, D., Geels, F., and Sharpe, S., 2019.

18. US Department of State, 2017. The *Montreal Protocol on Substances that Deplete the Ozone Layer.* [online] Available at: https://2009-2017.state.gov/e/oes/eqt/che micalpollution/83007.htm [Accessed 27 June 2022].

19. UNFCCC. *The Doha Climate Gateway.* [online] Available at: https://unfccc.int/ process/conferences/the-big-picture/milestones/the-doha-climate-gateway [Accessed 27 June 2022].

19. THE GREATEST PUBLIC RELATIONS GAMBLE IN HISTORY

1. *The Paris climate agreement: what's in the historic UN climate deal?* [online] Available at: https://eciu.net/analysis/briefings/international-perspectives/the-paris-climate-agreement [Accessed 27 June 2022].

2. *Guardian. Paris climate change agreement: the world's greatest diplomatic success.* [online] Available at: https://www.theguardian.com/environment/2015/dec/13/paris-climate-deal-cop-diplomacy-developing-united-nations [Accessed 27 June 2022].

3. Barrett, S., 2014.

4. MacKay, D., Cramton, P., Ockenfels, A., and Stoft, S., 2015.

5. Ad hoc working group on the Durban platform for enhanced action, ADP.2014.6. NonPaper. [online] p. 18. Available at: https://unfccc.int/sites/default/files/res ource/docs/2014/adp2/eng/6nonpap.pdf [Accessed 27 June 2022].

6. Wikipedia. *Kellogg–Briand pact.* [online] Available at: https://en.wikipedia.org /wiki/Kellogg%E2%80%93Briand_Pact [Accessed 27 June 2022].

7. *Global carbon budget 2020.* [online] Available at: https://www.globalcarbonproject .org/carbonbudget/20/files/GCP_CarbonBudget_2020.pdf [Accessed 27 June 2022].

8. *Progress Tracking – Net Zero Climate.* [online] Available at: https://netzeroclimate .org/innovation-for-net-zero/progress-tracking/ [Accessed 27 June 2022].

9. UNEP, 2020.

10. Climate Action Tracker, 2021.

11. UNEP, 2015; and UNEP, 2021.
12. UNEP, 2021.
13. IEA. *Tracking Clean Energy Progress.* [online] Available at: https://www.iea.org/topics/tracking-clean-energy-progress [Accessed 27 June 2022].
14. Beinhocker, E., Farmer, D., and Hepburn, C., 2018.
15. Page, S. E., 1999.
16. *China GDP Growth Rate 1961–2022.* [online] Available at: https://www.macrotrends.net/countries/CHN/china/gdp-growth-rate [Accessed 27 June 2022].
17. YieldReport. *IMF growth forecasts consistently wrong.* [online] Available at: https://www.yieldreport.com.au/news/imf-growth-forecasts-consistently-wrong/ [Accessed 27 June 2022].
18. Depledge, J., 2022.

20. SYSTEM CHANGE, NOT CLIMATE CHANGE

1. IRENA, 2019.
2. Beinhocker, E., Farmer, D., and Hepburn, C., 2018.
3. IPCC, 2018.
4. Geels, F. W., 2006a.
5. Roberts, C. and Geels, F. W., 2019.
6. Geels, F. W., 2005b.
7. Geels, F. W., 2006b.
8. Victor, D., Geels, F., and Sharpe, S., 2019.
9. Sabel, C. F. and Victor, D. G., 2022.
10. Way, R., Mealy, P., Farmer, D., and Ives, M., 2021.
11. Shearer, C., 2019.
12. CNN. *This is the world's busiest airport.* [online] Available at: https://edition.cnn.com/travel/article/worlds-busiest-airports-2018/index.html [Accessed 27 June 2022].

21. BETTER LATE THAN NEVER

1. Oberthür and Ott, 2011. pp. 119–124.
2. Ibid.

22. FROM COAL TO CLEAN POWER

1. COP26. *Green Grids Initiative – One Sun One World One Grid: One Sun Declaration.* [online] Available at: https://ukcop26.org/one-sun-declaration-green-grids-initiative-one-sun-one-world-one-grid/ [Accessed 28 June 2022].
2. *S. Korea's Moon vows to end new funding for overseas coal projects.* [online] Available at: https://www.reuters.com/article/global-climate-summit-southkorea-idUSL4N2MF3R2 [Accessed 28 June 2022].

3. Climate Home News. *G7 commits to end unabated coal finance in 2021 to 'keep 1.5C within reach'*. [online] Available at: https://www.climatechangenews.com/2021/05/21/g7-commits-end-unabated-coal-finance-2021-keep-1-5c-within-reach/ [Accessed 28 June 2022].

4. PPCA. *New PPCA members tip the scales towards 'consigning coal to history' at COP26*. [online] Available at: https://www.poweringpastcoal.org/news/press-release/new-ppca-members-tip-the-scales-towards-consigning-coal-to-history-at-cop26 [Accessed 28 June 2022].

5. Aleem, Z., 2021.

6. Carbon Brief. *Analysis: How power shortages might 'accelerate' China's climate action*. [online] Available at: https://www.carbonbrief.org/analysis-how-power-shortages-might-accelerate-chinas-climate-action [Accessed 28 June 2022].

7. Wikipedia. *Eskom*. [online] Available at: https://en.wikipedia.org/wiki/Eskom#Financials [Accessed 28 June 2022].

8. *Statement by H.E. President Cyril Ramaphosa of South Africa to the United Nations Secretary-General's Climate Summit, 23 September 2019*. [online] Available at: http://www.dirco.gov.za/docs/speeches/2019/cram0923.htm [Accessed 28 June 2022].

9. European Commission, 2021.

10. *South Africa $8.5bn finance package offers a model for ending reliance on coal*. [online] Climate Home News. Available at: https://www.climatechangenews.com/2021/11/04/south-africa-8-5bn-finance-package-offers-model-ending-reliance-coal/ [Accessed 28 June 2022].

11. Climate Investment Funds. *Accelerating Coal Transition*. [online] Available at: https://www.climateinvestmentfunds.org/topics/accelerating-coal-transition [Accessed 28 June 2022].

12. COP26. *Global Coal to Clean Power Transition Statement*. [online] Available at: https://ukcop26.org/global-coal-to-clean-power-transition-statement/ [Accessed 28 June 2022].

13. *Guardian. More than 40 countries agree to phase out coal-fired power*. [online] Available at: https://www.theguardian.com/environment/2021/nov/03/more-than-40-countries-agree-to-phase-out-coal-fired-power [Accessed 28 June 2022].

14. Carbon Brief. *Guest post: How world's coal-power pipeline has shrunk by three-quarters*. [online] Available at: https://www.carbonbrief.org/guest-post-how-worlds-coal-power-pipeline-has-shrunk-by-three-quarters [Accessed 28 June 2022].

23. FROM OIL TO ELECTRIC VEHICLES

1. *Los Angeles Times. GM, Chrysler and Toyota side with Trump in emissions fight with California*. [online] Available at: https://www.latimes.com/business/story/2019-10-28/automakers-trump-emissions-california-lawsuit [Accessed 28 June 2022].

2. Cui, H., Hall, D., Li, J., and Lutsey, N., 2021.

3. International Council for Clean Transportation, 2019.

4. BloombergNEF, 2019.
5. Using EV scenario data for a fast transition from the Exponential Roadmap, and for a slow transition from the International Energy Agency. Comparison not published.
6. *COP26 declaration on accelerating the transition to 100% zero emission cars and vans.* [online] Available at: https://www.gov.uk/government/publications/cop26-declaration-zero-emission-cars-and-vans/cop26-declaration-on-accelerating-the-transition-to-100-zero-emission-cars-and-vans [Accessed 28 June 2022].
7. BloombergNEF. *Electric vehicles to be 35% of global new car sales by 2040.* [online] Available at: https://about.bnef.com/blog/electric-vehicles-to-be-35-of-global-new-car-sales-by-2040/ [Accessed 28 June 2022].
8. BloombergNEF, 2021.
9. Knobloch, F., Hanssen, S., Lam, A., et al., 2020.
10. FT. *COP26: Deal to end car emissions by 2040 idles as motor giants refuse to sign.* [online] Available at: https://www.ft.com/content/8c4a1809-902f-4582-a29e-1c83a97b9dff [Accessed 28 June 2022].
11. *E-fuels won't save the internal combustion engine.* [Blog] Available at: https://theicct.org/e-fuels-wont-save-the-internal-combustion-engine/ [Accessed 28 June 2022].
12. Geels, F., 2005a.
13. *Zero Emission Vehicles Transition Council: 2022 action plan.* [online] Available at: https://www.gov.uk/government/publications/zero-emission-vehicles-transition-council-2022-action-plan [Accessed 28 June 2022].

24. FROM DEFORESTATION TO SUSTAINABLE DEVELOPMENT

1. Carbon Brief. *Corsia: the UN's plan to 'offset' growth in aviation emissions.* [online] Available at: https://www.carbonbrief.org/corsia-un-plan-to-offset-growth-in-aviation-emissions-after-2020 [Accessed 28 June 2022].
2. *These charts show what forest loss looks like across the globe.* [online] Available at: https://www.weforum.org/agenda/2020/06/rainforest-deforestation-global-charts-football-pitch/ [Accessed 28 June 2022].
3. Haupt, F., Streck, C., Schulte, I., and Chagas, T., 2017.
4. *New York Declaration on Forests*, 2014. Available at: https://forestdeclaration.org/wp-content/uploads/2021/10/EN-NYDF-Refresh.pdf [Accessed 23 June 2022].
5. Gibbs, H., Rausch, L., Munger, J., et al., 2015.
6. Overdevest, C. and Zeitlin, J., 2017.
7. *Joint statement on principles for collaboration under the Forest, Agriculture and Commodity Trade (FACT) Dialogue.* [online] Available at: https://www.gov.uk/government/news/joint-statement-on-principles-for-collaboration-under-the-forest-agriculture-and-commodity-trade-fact-dialogue [Accessed 28 June 2022].
8. FACT Dialogue, 2021.

9. COP26. *Glasgow Leaders' Declaration on Forests and Land Use.* [online] Available at: https://ukcop26.org/glasgow-leaders-declaration-on-forests-and-land-use/ [Accessed 28 June 2022].

10. *World Leaders Summit on 'Action on forests and land use'.* [online] Available at: https://www.gov.uk/government/publications/cop26-world-leaders-summit-on-action-on-forests-and-land-use-2-november-2021/world-leaders-summit-on-action-on-forests-and-land-use [Accessed 28 June 2022].

11. Aklin, M. and Mildenberger, M., 2018.

25. THE BREAKTHROUGH AGENDA

1. IEA, 2021.

2. Sharma, A., 2020.

3. IEA. *Seven Key Principles for Implementing Net Zero.* [online] Available at: https://www.iea.org/news/seven-key-principles-for-implementing-net-zero [Accessed 28 June 2022].

4. *G7 Climate and Environment: Ministers' Communiqué, London, 21 May 2021.* [online] Available at: https://www.gov.uk/government/publications/g7-climate-and-environment-ministers-meeting-may-2021-communique/g7-climate-and-environment-ministers-communique-london-21-may-2021 [Accessed 28 June 2022].

5. *World leaders join UK's Glasgow Breakthroughs to speed up affordable clean tech worldwide.* [online] Available at: https://www.gov.uk/government/news/world-leaders-join-uks-glasgow-breakthroughs-to-speed-up-affordable-clean-tech-worldwide [Accessed 28 June 2022].

6. COP26. *COP26 World Leaders Summit – Statement on the Breakthrough Agenda.* [online] Available at: https://ukcop26.org/cop26-world-leaders-summit-statement-on-the-breakthrough-agenda/ [Accessed 28 June 2022].

7. IEA. *UK government and IEA spearhead largest ever global initiative to make products more energy efficient.* [online] Available at: https://www.iea.org/news/uk-government-and-iea-spearhead-largest-ever-global-initiative-to-make-products-more-energy-efficient [Accessed 28 June 2022].

8. COP26. *Nations and businesses commit to create sustainable agriculture and land use.* [online] Available at: https://ukcop26.org/nations-and-businesses-commit-to-create-sustainable-agriculture-and-land-use/ [Accessed 28 June 2022].

9. UNIDO. *UNIDO at COP26: industrial development and climate change.* [online] Available at: https://www.unido.org/news/unido-cop26-industrial-development-and-climate-change [Accessed 28 June 2022].

10. Geels, F., 2002.

11. *COP26 Clydebank Declaration for green shipping corridors.* [online] Available at: https://www.gov.uk/government/publications/cop-26-clydebank-declaration-for-green-shipping-corridors [Accessed 28 June 2022].

12. *Guardian. Ratchets, phase-downs and a fragile agreement: how COP26 played out.* [online] Available at: https://www.theguardian.com/environment/2021/nov/15/ratchets-phase-downs-and-a-fragile-agreement-how-cop26-played-out [Accessed 28 June 2022].
13. Carbon Brief. *COP26: Key outcomes agreed at the UN climate talks in Glasgow.* [online] Available at: https://www.carbonbrief.org/cop26-key-outcomes-agreed-at-the-un-climate-talks-in-glasgow [Accessed 28 June 2022].
14. COP26. *Breakthrough Agenda – launching an annual global checkpoint process in 2022.* [online] Available at: https://ukcop26.org/breakthrough-agenda-launching-an-annual-global-checkpoint-process-in-2022/ [Accessed 28 June 2022].

26. TIPPING CASCADES

1. Sharpe, S. and Lenton, T., 2021.
2. Ripple, W. and Beschta, R., 2012.
3. Lenton, T., 2020.
4. Victor, D., Geels, F., and Sharpe, S., 2019.
5. Beinhocker, E., 2010. p. 143, citing the work of Stuart Kauffman.

Select Bibliography

Adger, W. N., Pulhin, J. M., Barnett, J., et al., 2014. Human security. In: *Climate Change 2014: Impacts, Adaptation, and Vulnerability. Part A: Global and Sectoral Aspects*. Contribution of Working Group II to the Fifth Assessment Report of the Intergovernmental Panel on Climate Change [Field, C. B., V. R. Barros, D. J. Dokken, et al. (eds.)]. Cambridge University Press, pp. 755–792.

Aichele, R. and Felbermayr, G., 2013. The effect of the Kyoto Protocol on carbon emissions. *Journal of Policy Analysis and Management*, 32(4), 731–757.

Aklin, M. and Mildenberger, M., 2020. Prisoners of the wrong dilemma: why distributive conflict, not collective action, characterizes the politics of climate change. *Global Environmental Politics*, 20(4), 4–27.

Aleem, Z., 2021. *Joe Manchin's coal ties are worse than we thought – yet legal.* [online] MSNBC.com. Available at: https://www.msnbc.com/opinion/joe-manchin-s-co al-ties-are-worse-we-thought-yet-n1285934 [Accessed 28 June 2022].

Ambec, S., Cohen, M. A., Elgie, S., and Lanoie, P., 2011. The Porter Hypothesis at 20: can environmental regulation enhance innovation and competitiveness? Resources for the Future Discussion Paper No. 11-01. *SSRN Electronic Journal*. [online] Available at: https://ssrn.com/abstract=1754674 or https://doi.org/10 .2139/ssrn.1754674 [Accessed 23 June 2022].

Anderson, P. W., 1972. More is different. *Science*, 177(4047), 393–396.

Andrews, O., Le Quéré, C., Kjellström, T., Lemke, B., and Haines, A., 2018. Implications for workability and survivability in populations exposed to extreme heat under climate change: a modelling study. *The Lancet Planetary Health*, 2(12), e540–e547.

Appleyard, D., 2014. *Comparing the costs of biomass conversion and offshore wind.* [online] Available at: https://www.renewableenergyworld.com/baseload/comparing-the -costs-of-biomass-conversion-and-offshore-wind/#gref [Accessed 24 June 2022].

Arthur, W. B., 2013. *Complexity economics: a different framework for economic thought.* [online] Available at: https://www.santafe.edu/research/results/working-papers /complexity-economics-a-different-framework-for-eco [Accessed 23 June 2022].

Australian Financial Review, 2015. *Climate change model environmental damage claims are just smoke.* [online] Available at: https://www.afr.com/opinion/climate-change-model-environmental-damage-claims-are-just-smoke-20150707-gi6ux0 [Accessed 23 June 2022].

Bank of England Prudential Regulation Authority, 2015. *The impact of climate change on the UK insurance sector.* [online] Available at: https://www.bankofengland.co.uk/-/media/boe/files/prudential-regulation/publication/impact-of-climate-change-on-the-uk-insurance-sector.pdf [Accessed 23 June 2022].

Barrett, S., 2008. Climate treaties and the imperative of enforcement. *Oxford Review of Economic Policy*, 24(2), 239–258.

Barrett, S., 2014. *Why have climate negotiations proved so disappointing?* [online] Available at: https://www.pas.va/content/dam/casinapioiv/pas/pdf-volumi/extra-series/es41pas-acta19pass.pdf [Accessed 27 June 2022].

Beinhocker, E., 2010. *The Origin of Wealth.* Harvard Business School Press.

Beinhocker, E., Farmer, D., and Hepburn, C., 2018. *The tipping point: how the G20 can lead the transition to a prosperous clean energy economy – G20 insights.* [online] Available at: https://www.g20-insights.org/policy_briefs/the-tipping-point-how-the-g20-can-lead-the-transition-to-a-prosperous-clean-energy-economy/ [Accessed 24 June 2022].

Bettis, O., 2014. *Risk management and climate change: risk of ruin.* [online] Available at: https://www.lse.ac.uk/GranthamInstitute/wp-content/uploads/2014/01/Oliver-Bettis-Risk-Management-and-Climate-Change-Risk-of-Ruin.pdf [Accessed 23 June 2022].

Betts, R., 2018. *Hothouse Earth: here's what the science actually does – and doesn't – say.* [online] Available at: https://helixclimate.eu/the-conversation-featured-article-hothouse-earth-heres-what-the-science-actually-does-and-doesnt-say/ [Accessed 23 June 2022].

Black, J., 2003. *A Dictionary of Economics.* Oxford University Press.

BloombergNEF, 2019. *EV Outlook 2019.* [Blog] Available at: https://about.bnef.com/blog/electric-transport-revolution-set-spread-rapidly-light-medium-commercial-vehicle-market/ [Accessed 28 June 2022].

BloombergNEF, 2021. *EV Outlook 2021.* [online] Available at: https://bnef.turtl.co/story/evo-2021/ [Accessed 23 June 2022].

Boers, N. and Rypdal, M., 2021. Critical slowing down suggests that the western Greenland ice sheet is close to a tipping point. *Proceedings of the National Academy of Sciences*, 118(21), https://www.pnas.org/doi/10.1073/pnas.2024192118

Boulton, C., Lenton, T., and Boers, N., 2022. Pronounced loss of Amazon rainforest resilience since the early 2000s. *Nature Climate Change*, 12(3), 271–278.

Brulle, R., 2013. Institutionalizing delay: foundation funding and the creation of U.S. climate change counter-movement organizations. *Climatic Change*, 122(4), 681–694.

Chappin, E., 2011. *Stimulating Energy Transitions.* PhD thesis, TU Delft, pp. 101–114. Available at: http://chappin.com/ChappinEJL-PhDthesis.pdf

Chatham House, 2021. *Climate change risk assessment 2021.* [online] Available at: https://www.chathamhouse.org/2021/09/climate-change-risk-assessment-2021 [Accessed 23 June 2022].

Church, J. A., Clark, P. U., Cazenave, A., et al., 2013. Sea level change. In: *Climate Change 2013: The Physical Science Basis*. Contribution of Working Group I to the Fifth Assessment Report of the Intergovernmental Panel on Climate Change [Stocker, T.F., D. Qin, G.-K. Plattner, et al. (eds.)]. Cambridge University Press, pp. 1137–1216.

Climate Action Tracker, 2015. *Climate pledges will bring 2.7°C of warming, potential for more action*. [online] Available at: https://climateactiontracker.org/publica tions/climate-pledges-will-bring-27c-of-warming-potential-for-more-action/ [Accessed 23 June 2022].

Climate Action Tracker, 2021. *Glasgow's one degree 2030 credibility gap: Net Zero's lip service to climate action*. [online] Available at: https://climateactiontracker.org/press/Gl asgows-one-degree-2030-credibility-gap-net-zeros-lip-service-to-climate-action/ [Accessed 27 June 2022].

CNA Military Advisory Board, 2014. *National security and the accelerating risks of climate change*. [online] Available at: https://www.cna.org/archive/CNA_Files/pdf/ma b_5-8-14.pdf [Accessed 23 June 2022].

Committee on Climate Change, 2017. *UK climate change risk assessment 2017*. [online] Available at: https://www.theccc.org.uk/uk-climate-change-risk-assessment-201 7/ [Accessed 23 June 2022].

Cui, H., Hall, D., Li, J., and Lutsey, N., 2021. *Update on the global transition to electric vehicles through 2020*. [online] Available at: https://theicct.org/sites/default/fil es/publications/global-update-evs-transition-oct21.pdf [Accessed 28 June 2022].

Cullen, J. and Allwood, J., 2010. The efficient use of energy: tracing the global flow of energy from fuel to service. *Energy Policy*, 38(1), 75–81.

De Meyer, K., Howarth, C., Jackson, A., et al., 2018. *Developing better climate mitigation policies: challenging current climate change risk assessment approaches*. UCL Policy Commission on Communicating Climate Science Report 2018–01.

Department for Business, Energy & Industrial Strategy, 2017. *Industrial Strategy: Building a Britain Fit for the Future*. HM Government, UK.

Depledge, J., 2022. The 'top-down' Kyoto Protocol? Exploring caricature and misrepresentation in literature on global climate change governance. *International Environmental Agreements: Politics, Law and Economics*, https://doi .org/10.1007/s10784-022-09580-9

Diamond, J., 2011. *Collapse*. Penguin, p. 436.

Dickens, G. and Forswall, C., n.d. Methane hydrates, carbon cycling, and environmental change. *Encyclopedia of Earth Sciences Series*, pp. 560–566.

Downey, E., 1910. The futility of marginal utility. *Journal of Political Economy*, 18(4), 253–268.

Drollette, D., 2016. Taking stock: Steven Chu, former secretary of the Energy Department, on fracking, renewables, nuclear weapons, and his work, post-Nobel Prize. *Bulletin of the Atomic Scientists*, 72(6), 351–358.

Earle, J., Moran, C., and Ward-Perkins, Z., 2017. *The Econocracy*. Manchester University Press.

Economists' Statement on Carbon Dividends Organized by the Climate Leadership Council, 2019. *Economists' Statement on Carbon Dividends Organized by the Climate Leadership Council*. [online] Available at: https://www.econstatement.org [Accessed 24 June 2022].

Environment Agency, 2012. *Thames Estuary 2100: managing risks through London and the Thames Estuary. TE2100 Plan; 2012.* [online] Available at: https://brand .environment-agency.gov.uk/mb/CtyxlR [Accessed 23 June 2022].

European Commission, 2021. *France, Germany, UK, US and EU launch ground-breaking International Just Energy Transition Partnership with South Africa.* [online] Available at: https://ec.europa.eu/commission/presscorner/detail/en/IP_21_5768 [Accessed 28 June 2022].

FACT Dialogue, 2021. *FACT Dialogue roadmap.* [online] Available at: https://www .factdialogue.org/fact-roadmap [Accessed 28 June 2022].

Farmer, J. D., Hepburn, C., Ives, M. C., et al., 2019. Sensitive intervention points in the post-carbon transition. *Science*, 364(6436), 132–134.

Femia, F. and Werrell, C., 2012. *Syria: climate change, drought and social unrest.* The Center for Climate and Security. [online] Available at: http://climateandsecurity .org/2012/02/29/syria-climate-change-drought-and-social-unrest/ [Accessed 23 June 2022].

Femia, F. and Werrell, C. (eds.), 2013. *The Arab Spring and climate change.* Center for American Progress, The Center for Climate and Security. [online] Available at: https://climateandsecurity.files.wordpress.com/2012/04/climatechangearab spring-ccs-cap-stimson.pdf [Accessed 23 June 2022].

Friedman, M., 1966. The methodology of positive economics. In: *Essays in Positive Economics.* University of Chicago Press, pp. 3–16, 30–43.

Funke, F. and Mattauch, L., 2018. *Why is carbon pricing in some countries more successful than in others?* [online] Our World in Data. Available at: https://ourworldindata .org/carbon-pricing-popular [Accessed 24 June 2022].

Funtowicz, S. and Ravetz, J., 1994. The worth of a songbird: ecological economics as a post-normal science. *Ecological Economics*, 10(3), 197–207.

Geels, F., 2002. Technological transitions as evolutionary reconfiguration processes: a multi-level perspective and a case-study. *Research Policy*, 31(8–9), 1257–1274.

Geels, F., 2005a. *Technological Transitions and System Innovations.* Edward Elgar.

Geels, F. W., 2005b. The dynamics of transitions in socio-technical systems: a multi-level analysis of the transition pathway from horse-drawn carriages to automobiles (1860–1930). *Technology Analysis & Strategic Management*, 17(4), 445–476.

Geels, F. W., 2006a. Co-evolutionary and multi-level dynamics in transitions: the transformation of aviation systems and the shift from propeller to turbojet (1930–1970). *Technovation*, 26(9), 999–1016.

Geels, F. W., 2006b. The hygienic transition from cesspools to sewer systems (1840–1930): the dynamics of regime transformation. *Research Policy*, 35(7), 1069–1082.

Geels, F., 2014. Regime resistance against low-carbon transitions: introducing politics and power into the multi-level perspective. *Theory, Culture & Society*, 31(5), 21–40.

Geels, F. and Schot, J., 2007. Typology of sociotechnical transition pathways. *Research Policy*, 36(3), 399–417.

Gibbs, H., Rausch, L., Munger, J., et al., 2015. Brazil's soy moratorium. *Science*, 347 (6220), 377–378.

Grubb, M., Drummond, P., Mercure, J. F., et al., 2021. *The new economics of innovation and transition: evaluating opportunities and risks.* [online] Available at: https://eeist .co.uk/eeist-reports/ [Accessed 27 June 2022].

Grubb, M., McDowall, W., and Drummond, P., 2017. On order and complexity in innovations systems: conceptual frameworks for policy mixes in sustainability transitions. *Energy Research & Social Science*, 33, 21–34.

Haldane, A. and Turrell, A., 2017. *An interdisciplinary model for macroeconomics.* Bank of England Staff Working Paper No. 696. [online] Available at: https://www .bankofengland.co.uk/-/media/boe/files/working-paper/2017/an-interdisciplinary-model-for-macroeconomics.pdf [Accessed 23 June 2022].

Hallegatte, S. and Rozenberg, J., 2019. *All hands on deck: mobilizing all available instruments to reduce emissions.* [online] Available at: https://blogs.worldbank.org/climate change/all-hands-deck-mobilizing-all-available-instruments-reduce-emissions [Accessed 24 June 2022].

Hansen, J., 2009. *Storms of My Grandchildren.* Bloomsbury.

Haupt, F., Streck, C., Schulte, I., and Chagas, T., 2017. *Progress on the New York Declaration on Forests: Finance for Forests – Goals 8 and 9 Assessment Report.* [online] Available at: https://www.climatefocus.com/publications/progress-new-york-declaration-forests -finance-forests-goals-8-and-9-assessment-report [Accessed 28 June 2022].

Henbest, S., 2020. *The first phase of the transition is about electricity, not primary energy.* [online] BloombergNEF. Available at: https://about.bnef.com/blog/the-first-phase-of-the-transition-is-about-electricity-not-primary-energy/ [Accessed 24 June 2022].

Henrich, J., 2015. *The Secret of Our Success.* Princeton University Press.

HM Treasury, 2020. *Final Report of the 2020 Green Book Review.* [online] Available at: https://www.gov.uk/government/publications/final-report-of-the-2020-green-book -review [Accessed 23 June 2022].

Hoegh-Guldberg, O., Cai, R., Poloczanska, E. S., et al., 2014. The ocean. In: *Climate Change 2014: Impacts, Adaptation, and Vulnerability. Part B: Regional Aspects.* Contribution of Working Group II to the Fifth Assessment Report of the Intergovernmental Panel on Climate Change [Barros, V. R. , C. B. Field, D. J. Dokken, et al. (eds.)]. Cambridge University Press, pp. 1655–1731.

Hoggan, J. and Littlemore, R., 2010. *Climate Cover-up.* Greystone Books.

Horton, B. P., Rahmstorf, S., Engelhardt, S.E., and Kemp, A. C., 2014. Expert assessment of sea-level rise by AD2100 and AD2300. *Quaternary Science Reviews*, http://www.sciencedirect.com/science/article/pii/S0277379113004381

Huerta de Soto, J., 2009. *Four Hundred Years of Dynamic Efficiency.* Available at: https://mises.org/library/four-hundred-years-dynamic-efficiency [Accessed 23 June 2022].

Huerta de Soto, J., 2014. *The Theory of Dynamic Efficiency*. Routledge/Taylor & Francis Group.

IEA, 2019. *Global EV outlook 2019*. [online] Available at: https://www.iea.org/reports/global-ev-outlook-2019

IEA, 2020. *Energy technology perspectives 2020*. [online] Available at: https://www.iea.org/reports/energy-technology-perspectives-2020 [Accessed 23 June 2022].

IEA, 2021. *Net Zero by 2050. A roadmap for the global energy sector*. [online] Available at: https://iea.blob.core.windows.net/assets/deebef5d-0c34-4539-9d0c-10b13d840027/NetZeroby2050-ARoadmapfortheGlobalEnergySector_CORR.pdf [Accessed 28 June 2022].

IMF, 2010. *Rethinking macroeconomic policy*. [online] Available at: https://www.imf.org/external/pubs/ft/spn/2010/spn1003.pdf [Accessed 24 June 2022].

IMF, 2019a. *How to mitigate climate change*. [online] Available at: https://www.imf.org/en/Publications/FM/Issues/2019/10/16/Fiscal-Monitor-October-2019-How-to-Mitigate-Climate-Change-47027 [Accessed 24 June 2022].

IMF, 2019b. *The economics of climate*. [online] Available at: https://www.imf.org/external/pubs/ft/fandd/2019/12/pdf/fd1219.pdf [Accessed 25 June 2022].

International Council for Clean Transportation, 2019. *Overview of global zero-emission vehicle mandate programs*. [online] Available at: https://theicct.org/wp-content/uploads/2021/06/Zero-Emission-Vehicle-Mandate-Briefing-v2.pdf [Accessed 25 June 2022].

IPCC, 2013. Summary for Policymakers. In:*Climate Change 2013: The Physical Science Basis*. Contribution of Working Group I to the Fifth Assessment Report of the Intergovernmental Panel on Climate Change [Stocker, T. F., D. Qin, G.-K. Plattner, et al. (eds.)]. Cambridge University Press.

IPCC, 2014a. *Climate Change 2014: Impacts, Adaptation, and Vulnerability*. Contribution of Working Group II to the Fifth Assessment Report of the Intergovernmental Panel on Climate Change [online]. Cambridge University Press. Available at: https://www.ipcc.ch/report/ar5/wg2/ [Accessed 23 June 2022].

IPCC, 2014b. Summary for Policymakers. In: *Climate Change 2014: Impacts, Adaptation, and Vulnerability. Part A: Global and Sectoral Aspects*. Contribution of Working Group II to the Fifth Assessment Report of the Intergovernmental Panel on Climate Change [Field, C. B., V. R. Barros, D. J. Dokken, et al. (eds.)]. Cambridge University Press.

IPCC, 2018. Summary for Policymakers. In: *Global Warming of 1.5°C*. An IPCC Special Report on the impacts of global warming of 1.5°C above pre-industrial levels and related global greenhouse gas emission pathways, in the context of strengthening the global response to the threat of climate change, sustainable development, and efforts to eradicate poverty [Masson-Delmotte, V., P. Zhai, H.-O. Pörtner, et al. (eds.)]. Cambridge University Press, pp. 3–24. https://doi.org/10.1017/9781009157940.001

IPCC, 2021. Summary for Policymakers. In: *Climate Change 2021: The Physical Science Basis*. Contribution of Working Group I to the Sixth Assessment Report of the

Intergovernmental Panel on Climate Change [Masson-Delmotte, V., P. Zhai, A. Pirani, et al. (eds.)]. Cambridge University Press, p. 11. https://doi.org/10.1017/9781009157896.001

IPCC, 2022. *Climate Change 2022: Impacts, Adaptation and Vulnerability.* Contribution of Working Group II to the Sixth Assessment Report of the Intergovernmental Panel on Climate Change [Pörtner, H.-O., D. C. Roberts, M. Tignor, et al. (eds.)]. Cambridge University Press.

IRENA, 2019. *Renewable capacity statistics 2019.* [online] Available at: https://www.irena.org/publications/2019/Mar/Renewable-Capacity-Statistics-2019 [Accessed 27 June 2022].

IRENA, 2021. *Renewable capacity highlights.* [online] Available at: https://www.irena.org/-/media/Files/IRENA/Agency/Publication/2021/Apr/IRENA_-RE_Capacity_Highlights_2021.pdf [Accessed 24 June 2022].

Jennings, T., Andrews Tipper, H., Daglish, J., Grubb, M., and Drummond, P., 2020. *Policy, innovation and cost reduction in UK offshore wind.* [online] Available at: https://www.carbontrust.com/resources/policy-innovation-and-cost-reduction-in-uk-offshore-wind [Accessed 24 June 2022].

Kattel, R., Mazzucato, M., Ryan-Collins, J., and Sharpe, S., 2018. *The economics of change: policy and appraisal for missions, market shaping and public purpose.* [online] Available at: https://www.ucl.ac.uk/bartlett/public-purpose/publications/2018/jul/economics-change-policy-and-appraisal-missions-market-shaping-and-public [Accessed 23 June 2022].

Kauffman, S., 2003. *Investigations.* Oxford University Press.

Kavlak, G., McNerney, J., and Trancik, J., 2016. *Evaluating the changing causes of photovoltaics cost reduction.* [online] Available at: https://papers.ssrn.com/sol3/papers.cfm?abstract_id=2891516 [Accessed 24 June 2022].

Kean, T. and Hamilton, L., 2004. *Public statement on the release of 9/11 Commission Report.* [online] Available at: https://govinfo.library.unt.edu/911/report/911Report_Statement.pdf [Accessed 23 June 2022].

Keen, S., 2017. *Why economists have to embrace complexity to avoid disaster.* [Blog] Evonomics. Available at: https://evonomics.com/why-economists-have-to-embrace-complexity-steve-keen/ [Accessed 24 June 2022].

Kelley, C. P., Mohtadi, S., Cane, M. A., Seager, R., and Kushnir, Y., 2015. Climate change in the Fertile Crescent and implications of the recent Syrian drought. *Proceedings of the National Academy of Sciences,* 11, 3241–3246.

King, D., Schrag, D., Zhou, D., Qi, Y., and Ghosh, A., 2015. *Climate change: a risk assessment.* [online] Available at: https://www.csap.cam.ac.uk/projects/climate-change-risk-assessment/ [Accessed 22 June 2022].

Knobloch, F., Hanssen, S., Lam, A., et al., 2020. Net emission reductions from electric cars and heat pumps in 59 world regions over time. *Nature Sustainability,* 3(6), 437–447.

Kriegler, E., Hall, J. W., Held, H., Dawson, R., and Schellnhuber, H. J., 2009. Imprecise probability assessment of tipping points in the climate system.

Proceedings of the National Academy of Sciences, 106, 5041–5046. https://doi.org/10 .1073/pnas.0809117106

Krugman, P., 2009. *Opinion | Fighting off depression*. [online] Nytimes.com. Available at: https://www.nytimes.com/2009/01/05/opinion/05krugman.html?_r=0 [Accessed 24 June 2022].

Kuhn, T., 1970. *The Structure of Scientific Revolutions*. University of Chicago Press.

Lenton, T., 2011. Early warning of climate tipping points. *Nature Climate Change*, 1, 201–209. https://doi.org/10.1038/nclimate1143

Lenton, T., 2020. Tipping positive change. *Philosophical Transactions of the Royal Society B: Biological Sciences*, 375(1794), 20190123.

Lovejoy, T. and Nobre, C., 2018. Amazon tipping point. *Science Advances*, 4(2), https:// doi.org/10.1126/sciadv.aat2340

Lowe, J. and Bernie, D., 2018. The impact of Earth system feedbacks on carbon budgets and climate response. *Philosophical Transactions of the Royal Society A: Mathematical, Physical and Engineering Sciences*, 376(2119), 20170263.

Lubchenco, J., 1998. Entering the century of the environment: a new social contract for science. *Science*, 279(5350), 491–497.

Lucas, R. E., 2004. Professional memoir. In: *Lives of the Laureates*, 4th ed. [Breit, W. and B. T. Hirsh. (eds.)]. MIT Press

MacKay, D., 2015. *Why 'good energy policy' is difficult*. [online] Available at: https://www .eprg.group.cam.ac.uk/presentation-why-good-energy-policy-is-difficult-reflections-on-5-years-in-the-decc-by-d-mackay/ [Accessed 23 June 2022].

MacKay, D., Cramton, P., Ockenfels, A., and Stoft, S., 2015. Price carbon – I will if you will. *Nature*, 526(7573), 315–316.

Mazzucato, M., 2018. Mission-oriented innovation policies: challenges and opportunities. *Industrial and Corporate Change*, 27(5), 803–815.

McGrath, A., 2018. *The clockwork god: Isaac Newton and the mechanical universe*. Available at: https://s3-eu-west-1.amazonaws.com/content.gresham.ac.uk/dat a/binary/2628/2018-01-23_AlisterMcGrath_TheClockworkGod.pdf [Accessed 23 June 2022].

Meadows, D., 2008. *Thinking in Systems: A Primer*. Chelsea Green.

Mercure, J., Pollitt, H., Bassi, A., Viñuales, J., and Edwards, N., 2016. Modelling complex systems of heterogeneous agents to better design sustainability transitions policy. *Global Environmental Change*, 37, 102–115.

Mercure, J., Sharpe, S., Vinuales, J., et al., 2021. Risk-opportunity analysis for transformative policy design and appraisal. *Global Environmental Change*, 70, 102359.

Mirowski, P. and Plehwe, D., 2009. *The Road from Mont Pèlerin*. Harvard University Press.

National Research Council, 2009. *Panel on Strategies and Methods for Climate-Related Decision Support*. National Academies Press.

Nelson, R. and Winter, S., 1982. *An Evolutionary Theory of Economic Change*. Belknap Press of Harvard University.

New Weather Institute, 2017. *The new reformation: 33 theses for an economics reformation.* [online] Available at: https://www.newweather.org/2017/12/12/the-new-reformation-33-theses-for-an-economics-reformation/ [Accessed 27 June 2022].

Nordhaus, W., 2018. *Climate change: the ultimate challenge for economics.* Available at: https://www.nobelprize.org/prizes/economic-sciences/2018/nordhaus/lec ture/ [Accessed 23 June 2022].

O'Neill, B., van Aalst, M., Zaiton Ibrahim, Z., et al., 2022. Key risks across sectors and regions. In: *Climate Change 2022: Impacts, Adaptation and Vulnerability.* Contribution of Working Group II to the Sixth Assessment Report of the Intergovernmental Panel on Climate Change [Pörtner, H.-O., D. C. Roberts, M. Tignor, et al. (eds.)]. Cambridge University Press, pp. 98–119.

Oberthür, S. and Ott, H., 2011. *The Kyoto Protocol: International Climate Policy for the 21st Century.* Springer.

OECD, 2012. *Environmental outlook to 2050: the consequences of inaction.* [online] Available at: https://www.oecd.org/env/indicators-modelling-outlooks/oecden vironmentaloutlookto2050theconsequencesofinaction-keyfactsandfigures.htm#: ~:text=modelling%20and%20outlooks-,OECD%20Environmental%20Outlook %20to%202050%3A%20The%20Consequences%20of%20Inaction%20%2D% 20Key,that%20supply%20energy%20and%20food [Accessed 23 June 2022].

OECD, 2016. *The economic consequences of Brexit: a taxing decision.* [online] Available at: https://www.oecd.org/unitedkingdom/The-economic-consequences-of-Brexit-27-april-2016.pdf [Accessed 23 June 2022].

Oppenheimer, M., Campos, M., Warren, R., et al., 2014. Emergent risks and key vulnerabilities. In: *Climate Change 2014: Impacts, Adaptation, and Vulnerability. Part A: Global and Sectoral Aspects.* Contribution of Working Group II to the Fifth Assessment Report of the Intergovernmental Panel on Climate Change [Field, C. B., V. R. Barros, D. J. Dokken, et al. (eds.)]. Cambridge University Press.

Otto, F. E. L., Massey, N., vanOldenborgh, G. J., Jones, R. G., and Allen, M. R., 2012. Reconciling two approaches to attribution of the 2010 Russian heat wave. *Geophysical Research Letters,* 39, L04702.

Overdevest, C. and Zeitlin, J., 2017. Experimentalism in transnational forest governance: implementing European Union Forest Law Enforcement, Governance and Trade (FLEGT) voluntary partnership agreements in Indonesia and Ghana. *Regulation & Governance,* 12(1), 64–87.

Page, S. E., 1999. Computational models from A to Z. *Complexity,* 5(1), 35–41.

Perez, C., 2014. *Technological Revolutions and Financial Capital.* Edward Elgar.

Pindyck, R., 2017. The use and misuse of models for climate policy. *Review of Environmental Economics and Policy,* 11(1), 100–114.

Porter, J. R., Xie, L., Challinor, A. J., et al., 2014. Food security and food production systems. In: *Climate Change 2014: Impacts, Adaptation, and Vulnerability. Part A: Global and Sectoral Aspects.* Contribution of Working Group II to the Fifth Assessment Report of the Intergovernmental Panel on Climate Change

[Field, C. B., V. R. Barros, D. J. Dokken, et al. (eds.)]. Cambridge University Press, pp. 485–534.

Prospect Magazine, 2017. *Dismal ignorance of the 'dismal science' – a response to Larry Elliot.* [online] Available at: https://www.prospectmagazine.co.uk/economics-and-finance/dismal-ignorance-of-the-dismal-science-a-response-to-larry-elliot [Accessed 23 June 2022].

Prospect Magazine, 2018. *In defence of the economists.* [online] Available at: https://www.prospectmagazine.co.uk/economics-and-finance/dianecoyle [Accessed 23 June 2022].

PwC, 2013. *International threats and opportunities of climate change for the UK.* [online] Available at: https://pwc.blogs.com/files/international-threats-and-opportunities-of-climate-change-to-the-uk.pdf [Accessed 23 June 2022].

Raworth, K., 2018. *Doughnut Economics.* Random House Business Books.

Reeder, T., Wicks, J., Lovell, L., and Tarrant, T., 2009. Protecting London from tidal flooding: limits to engineering adaptation. In: *Adapting to Climate Change: Thresholds, Values, Governance.* [Adger, N. W., I. Lorenzoni, and K. O'Brien (eds.)]. Cambridge University Press, pp. 54–63.

Ripple, W. and Beschta, R., 2012. Trophic cascades in Yellowstone: the first 15 years after wolf reintroduction. *Biological Conservation*, 145(1), 205–213.

Roberts, C. and Geels, F. W., 2019, Conditions for politically accelerated transitions: historical institutionalism, the multi-level perspective, and two historical case studies in transport and agriculture. *Technological Forecasting and Social Change*, 140, 221–240.

Rogelj, J., Shindell, D. Jiang, K., et al., 2018. Mitigation pathways compatible with 1.5°C in the context of sustainable development. In: *Global Warming of 1.5°C.* An IPCC Special Report on the impacts of global warming of 1.5°C above pre-industrial levels and related global greenhouse gas emission pathways, in the context of strengthening the global response to the threat of climate change, sustainable development, and efforts to eradicate poverty. [Masson-Delmotte, V., P. Zhai, H.-O. Pörtner, et al. (eds.)]. Cambridge University Press, p. 151.

Romer, P., 2016. *The trouble with macroeconomics.* Available at: https://paulromer.net/trouble-with-macroeconomics-update/WP-Trouble.pdf [Accessed 23 June 2022].

Ryan-Collins, J., Lloyd, T., and Macfarlane, L., 2017. *Rethinking the Economics of Land and Housing.* Zed Books.

Sabel, C. F. and Victor, D. G., 2022. *Fixing the Climate: Strategies for an Uncertain World.* Princeton University Press.

Schmidt, G., 2006. *Runaway tipping points of no return.* [Blog] RealClimate. Available at: https://www.realclimate.org/index.php/archives/2006/07/runaway-tipping-points-of-no-return/ [Accessed 23 June 2022].

Scientific Advisory Board of the United Nations Secretary-General, 2016. *Assessing the risks of climate change: Policy Brief.* [online] Available at: https://unesdoc.unesco.org/ark:/48223/pf0000246477 [Accessed 23 June 2022].

Sharma, A., 2020. *COP26 President's closing remarks at Climate Ambition Summit 2020.* Available at: https://www.gov.uk/government/speeches/cop26-presidents-closing-remarks-at-climate-ambition-summit-2020#:~:text=The%20progress%20on%20vaccines%20has,a%20step%20change%20in%20mitigation [Accessed 23 June 2022].

Sharpe, B., 2010. *Economies of Life.* Triarchy Press.

Sharpe, B., 2013. *Three Horizons.* Triarchy Press, p. 111.

Sharpe, S., 2019. Telling the boiling frog what he needs to know: why climate change risks should be plotted as probability over time. *Geoscience Communication,* 2(1), 95–100.

Sharpe, S. and Lenton, T., 2021. Upward-scaling tipping cascades to meet climate goals: plausible grounds for hope. *Climate Policy,* 21(4), 421–433.

Shearer, C., 2019. *Guest post: How plans for new coal are changing around the world.* [online] Carbon Brief. Available at: https://www.carbonbrief.org/guest-post-how-plans-for-new-coal-are-changing-around-the-world [Accessed 27 June 2022].

Sherwood, S. and Huber, M., 2010. An adaptability limit to climate change due to heat stress. *Proceedings of the National Academy of Sciences,* 107(21), 9552–9555.

Smith, J., 1976. What determines the rate of evolution? *The American Naturalist,* 110 (973), 331–338.

Smith, K. R., Woodward, A., Campbell-Lendrum, D., et al., 2014. Human health: impacts, adaptation, and co-benefits. In: *Climate Change 2014: Impacts, Adaptation, and Vulnerability. Part A: Global and Sectoral Aspects.* Contribution of Working Group II to the Fifth Assessment Report of the Intergovernmental Panel on Climate Change [Field, C. B., V. R. Barros, D. J. Dokken, et al. (eds.)]. Cambridge University Press.

Solow, R., 1994. Perspectives on growth theory. *Journal of Economic Perspectives,* 8(1), 45–54.

Staffell, I., Jansen, M., Chase, A., Cotton, E., and Lewis, C., 2018. *Energy revolution: a global outlook.* [online] Available at: https://www.drax.com/wp-content/uploads/2018/12/Energy-Revolution-Global-Outlook-Report-Final-Dec-2018-COP24.pdf p. 6. [Accessed 26 June 2022].

Stavins, R., 2020. The future of US carbon-pricing policy. *Environmental and Energy Policy and the Economy,* 1, 8–64.

Steffen, W., Rockström, J., Richardson, K., et al., 2018. Trajectories of the Earth System in the Anthropocene. *Proceedings of the National Academy of Sciences,* 115 (33), 8252–8259.

Stern, N., 2013. The structure of economic modeling of the potential impacts of climate change: grafting gross underestimation of risk onto already narrow science models. *Journal of Economic Literature,* 51(3), 838–859.

Stern, N., 2018. Public economics as if time matters: climate change and the dynamics of policy. *Journal of Public Economics,* 162, 4–17.

Sutton, R., 2019. Climate science needs to take risk assessment much more seriously. *Bulletin of the American Meteorological Society,* 100(9), 1637–1642.

Sweet, W., 2016. *Climate Diplomacy from Rio to Paris.* Yale University Press.

Systemiq, 2020. *The Paris effect.* [online] Available at: https://www.systemiq.earth/wp-content/uploads/2020/12/The-Paris-Effect_SYSTEMIQ_Full-Report_December-2020.pdf [Accessed 26 June 2022].

The Economist. 2014a. *Rueing the waves.* [online] Available at: https://www.economist.com/britain/2014/01/04/rueing-the-waves [Accessed 24 June 2022].

The Economist. 2014b. *Sun, wind and drain.* [online] Available at: https://www.economist.com/finance-and-economics/2014/07/29/sun-wind-and-drain [Accessed 24 June 2022].

Tremaine, S., 2011. *Is the Solar System stable?* [online] Institute for Advanced Study. Available at: https://www.ias.edu/ideas/2011/tremaine-solar-system [Accessed 24 June 2022].

UK Government Cabinet Office, 2017. *National Risk Register of Civil Emergencies.*

UNEP, 2015. *Emissions gap report 2015.* [online] Available at: https://wedocs.unep.org/bitstream/handle/20.500.11822/7450/_The_Emissions_Gap_Report_2015_1.pdf?sequence=4&isAllowed=y [Accessed 27 June 2022].

UNEP, 2020. *Emissions gap report 2020.* [online] Available at: https://wedocs.unep.org/bitstream/handle/20.500.11822/34438/EGR20ESE.pdf?sequence=25 [Accessed 27 June 2022].

UNEP, 2021. *Emissions gap report 2021.* [online] Available at: https://wedocs.unep.org/bitstream/handle/20.500.11822/36991/EGR21_ESEN.pdf [Accessed 27 June 2022].

US Department of State, 2017. *The Montreal Protocol on Substances that Deplete the Ozone Layer.* [online] Available at: https://2009-2017.state.gov/e/oes/eqt/chemicalpollution/83007.htm [Accessed 27 June 2022].

Van Buskirk, R., Kantner, C., Gerke, B., and Chu, S., 2014. A retrospective investigation of energy efficiency standards: policies may have accelerated long term declines in appliance costs. *Environmental Research Letters,* 9(11), 114010.

Victor, D., Geels, F., and Sharpe, S., 2019. *Accelerating the low carbon transition: the case for stronger, more targeted and coordinated international action.* [online] Available at: https://www.energy-transitions.org/publications/accelerating-the-low-carbon-transition/ [Accessed 27 June 2022].

Vogt-Schilb, A., Meunier, G., and Hallegatte, S., 2018. When starting with the most expensive option makes sense: optimal timing, cost and sectoral allocation of abatement investment. *Journal of Environmental Economics and Management,* 88, 210–233.

Watson, J., 2012. *Climate change policy and the transition to a low carbon economy.* [online] Available at: https://www.ippr.org/files/images/media/files/publication/2012/09/complex-new-world_Aug2012_web_9499.pdf [Accessed 25 June 2022].

Way, R., Mealy, P., Farmer, D., and Ives, M., 2021. *Empirically grounded technology forecasts and the energy transition.* [online] Available at: https://www.inet.ox.ac.uk/publications/no-2021-01-empirically-grounded-technology-forecasts-and-the-energy-transition/ [Accessed 27 June 2022].

Weitzman, M., 2011. Fat-tailed uncertainty in the economics of catastrophic climate change. *Review of Environmental Economics and Policy*, 5(2), 275–292.

Wolff, E., Shepherd, J., Shuckburgh, E., and Watson, A., 2015. Feedbacks on climate in the Earth system: introduction. *Philosophical Transactions of the Royal Society A: Mathematical, Physical and Engineering Sciences*, 373(2054), 20140428.

World Bank, 2014. *Turn down the heat: confronting the new climate normal*. [online] Available at: https://openknowledge.worldbank.org/handle/10986/20595 [Accessed 23 June 2022].

World Bank, 2020. *State and trends of carbon pricing 2020*. [online] Available at: http s://openknowledge.worldbank.org/bitstream/handle/10986/33809/9781464 815867.pdf [Accessed 25 June 2022].

Wright, T., 1936. Factors affecting the cost of airplanes. *Journal of the Aeronautical Sciences*, 3(4), 122–128.

Wunderling, N., Donges, J., Kurths, J., and Winkelmann, R., 2021. Interacting tipping elements increase risk of climate domino effects under global warming. *Earth System Dynamics*, 12(2), 601–619.

Young, O. and Steffen, W., 2009. The Earth System: sustaining planetary life-support systems. In: *Principles of Ecosystem Stewardship*. Springer Science + Business Media, pp. 295–315.

Index